PRIVATE LAW

The relationship between private and public law has long been the focus of critical attention, but recent years have seen the growing influence upon private law of statutory intervention, public regulation, corporate globalisation and constitutional and international human rights norms. Such developments increasingly call into question the capacity of private law reasoning to operate in isolation from public institutions and goals. Commencing with three contrasting visions of the nature and importance of distinctions between public and private in the modern day, this book traces a number of encounters between private law and 'public' values in key areas of private law doctrine, such as charity law, commercial law, tort law and class actions, across several jurisdictions. It examines the influence within these fields of public concepts and goals, such as behavioural modification, accountability and anti-discrimination norms, as well as the (reverse) influence that private law has upon ('public') human rights jurisprudence.

KIT BARKER is Professor of Law at TC Beirne School of Law, The University of Queensland.

DARRYN JENSEN is a Senior Lecturer at TC Beirne School of Law, The University of Queensland.

PRIVATE LAW

Key Encounters with Public Law

Edited by

KIT BARKER

and

DARRYN JENSEN

CAMBRIDGE
UNIVERSITY PRESS

CAMBRIDGE
UNIVERSITY PRESS

University Printing House, Cambridge CB2 8BS, United Kingdom

Published in the United States of America by Cambridge University Press, New York

Cambridge University Press is part of the University of Cambridge.

It furthers the University's mission by disseminating knowledge in the pursuit of education, learning and research at the highest international levels of excellence.

www.cambridge.org
Information on this title: www.cambridge.org/9781107039117

First published 2013

Printed in the United Kingdom by CPI Group Ltd, Croydon CR0 4YY

A catalogue record for this publication is available from the British Library

Library of Congress Cataloguing in Publication data
Private law : key encounters with public law / [edited by] Kit Barker, Darryn Jensen.
p. cm.
Includes bibliographical references and index.
ISBN 978-1-107-03911-7 (hardback)
1. Civil law. 2. Public law. I. Barker, Kit, editor of compilation. II. Jensen, Darryn, editor of compilation.
K623.P747 2013
346–dc23
2013019971

ISBN 978-1-107-03911-7 Hardback

CONTENTS

CONTRIBUTORS

KIT BARKER is Professor of Law at the TC Beirne School of Law, The University of Queensland, Brisbane, Australia.

JEFF BERRYMAN is Professor of Law at the Faculty of Law, University of Windsor, Ontario, Canada and of the Faculty of Law, University of Auckland, New Zealand (fractional chair).

ROBYN CARROLL is Professor of Law at the Faculty of Law, University of Western Australia, Western Australia.

MICHELLE FLAHERTY is Assistant Professor of Law at the Faculty of Law at the University of Ottawa, Canada.

MATTHEW HARDING is Associate Professor of Law at the Melbourne Law School, The University of Melbourne, Australia.

STEVE HEDLEY is Professor of Law at University College, Cork, Ireland.

ALASTAIR HUDSON is Professor of Equity and Finance Law in the Faculty of Law at the University of Southampton, UK.

DARRYN JENSEN is Senior Lecturer in Law at the TC Beirne School of Law, The University of Queensland, Brisbane, Australia.

ANITA K. KRUG is Assistant Professor at the University of Washington School of Law, USA.

WILLIAM LUCY is Professor of Law at Durham Law School, Durham University, UK.

ADAM PARACHIN is Associate Professor of Law in the Faculty of Law, the University of Western Ontario, Canada.

DAN PRIEL is Assistant Professor of Law at Osgoode Hall Law School, York University, Canada.

CHRISTIAN TURNER is Assistant Professor of Law at the School of Law, The University of Georgia, USA.

ALEXANDER WILLIAMS is Lecturer in Law at Durham Law School, Durham University, UK.

PREFACE

The relationship between private and public law has long been the focus of critical attention, but recent years have seen the intensification of a significant number of 'public' pressures on private law. These have taken the form of the growing influences of statutory intervention, public regulation, corporate globalisation, class actions and constitutional and international human rights norms. Such developments increasingly call into question the capacity of private law to operate in isolation from public law, public institutions and public goals. They invite a critical re-examination of the ways in which private and public law and the values and aims underpinning these fields relate to each other.

This collection makes a significant contribution to the current debate. It examines a number of key encounters between private law and public law and their respective value sets in the fields of charity law, property law, commercial law, tort law, human rights and the law of private law remedies (in particular remedies available in class actions). It also addresses important theoretical, definitional and taxonomic debates that influence the way in which these interactions may be understood and resolved. It includes essays from leading private law scholars and theorists drawn from several different jurisdictions in which these debates are increasingly prominent and important, including the United Kingdom, Canada, Australia and the United States of America.

ACKNOWLEDGEMENTS

This book emerged from an international conference entitled 'Public and Private Law: Intersections in Law, Value and Method' hosted by the TC Beirne School of Law, The University of Queensland in Brisbane on 21–22 July 2011.

We would like to express our gratitude to the School of Law for its generous support of the conference and to those who worked so very hard behind the scenes to make it a success, including Professor Ross Grantham and Beth Williams. We are also more than usually grateful to those who participated in the conference proceedings for their insightful and collegial contributions to the project. The chapters contained in this work are all the better for their questions and thoughts. We would like to say a special thank you to James McNicol for his assistance and painstaking attention to detail in preparing the manuscript for this volume; and to the Australian Centre for Private Law at the TC Beirne School of Law for its financial assistance in facilitating this process.

PART I

Introduction

1

Private law

Key encounters with public law

KIT BARKER

1 Introduction

The relationship of private and public law is an immense topic – too large to be exhausted by a single collection of essays. Statements of the relationship are also notoriously complicated by a lack of terminological clarity. What is it that one intends to contrast with what, when one distinguishes private law from public law, and what is one's purpose in doing so? Is one's objective simply an interpretive, classificatory one – a process of sorting and better understanding legal material so as to bring to it some greater rational order – or is the purpose instead a normative one – to change the legal order for the better in some way or illuminate its deficiencies from a particular point of view? Is defining the relationship between private and public law intended to make the practical task of legal actors easier – to make it simpler, for example, for a court to dispose of a particular case before it? Is the aim to promote consistency in decision-making? None of this is very clear. The truth is that the nature and purpose of inquiries into the relationship between private and public law depends entirely on the inquirer and that there is a great deal of variation on such matters.

Such complexities make a clear opening statement of our own assumptions and purposes particularly important. The objective of this collection of essays is to re-examine the relationship between private law, on the one hand, and public law, public institutions and public values, on the other, through the lens of a selected range of 'key encounters'. The term 'private law' in the last sentence is taken to refer to that body of positive law which governs relationships between private individuals (natural or otherwise), as opposed to the relationship between individuals and the

I would like to thank Darryn Jensen, Robert Burrell, Jason Neyers and Jenny Steele for helpful comments on an earlier draft of this chapter.

state[1] acting in its capacity as mediator of the public good. This is a very traditional conception and it is subject to the challenge of numerous alternative constructions, some of which are considered in this and the next chapter. Nonetheless, we must start somewhere and the definition I have just provided is at least relatively clear and well understood. It is also one that makes obvious sense in the context of contemporary Western society, where the contrast between the relationships of individual actors and the relationship between citizens and the state (qua state) is encountered every day.

The substantive fields of private law (as I have just defined it) upon which the book focuses comprise charity law, property law, corporate and commercial (finance) law, the law of torts and the law of private law remedies. The encounters between these fields and public law and public values are considered 'key', not in the sense that they are exhaustive or necessarily more important than any other examples, but simply in the sense that they help to unlock a fuller understanding of the relationship in question. Our purpose is to understand private law better, at a time when its normative foundations, capacities and limitations are increasingly contested. Nonetheless, we hope that by better understanding private law, we may also prompt a fuller appreciation of the nature, strengths and weaknesses of public law too. The lessons are not intended to proceed in just one direction. Indeed, many parts of this work point to strong mutual influences between the two spheres.

By way of contrast with its subject matter, the structure of the book is very simple. In this chapter (Part I), we set the project in its context, demonstrate its contemporary significance and provide a critical overview of the contributions that follow, drawing out a number of lessons from them. From this summative and contextual beginning, the work proceeds through general and theoretical issues to the more specific and substantive. Part II of the book hence addresses general definitional, theoretical and taxonomic questions about the relationship between 'private' and 'public'. Its central concerns are: (1) the nature and utility of the various distinction(s) between private and public that are made by lawyers and others (economists, philosophers, sociologists), (2) the truth of the idea that private law is really 'private' to relationships between particular individuals and normatively isolated from broader social purposes and (3) different ways in which our legal categories might usefully be structured, in the light of what we know about the respective

[1] Or between states, as in the case of public international law.

institutional capacities of public and private actors regarding law creation and enforcement. Part III then outlines key encounters between public and private in each of the substantive fields of law mentioned above, highlighting the importance of the encounter for particular doctrinal or theoretical questions within that particular legal field.

2 Public pressures on private law

Private law existed in one form or another long before the rise of the modern nation-state,[2] even if, in England, it finally disentangled itself from the formulary system and emerged as a distinct body of legal doctrine only during the latter half of the nineteenth century. Since that time, however, it has encountered increasingly persistent and well-documented pressures from the 'public' that have tended to undermine its institutional autonomy or 'privateness' in one way or another.[3] One such twentieth-century pressure is the rise of the welfare state,[4] which has brought with it an increased tendency towards political intervention in the substantive content of the law. In any such state, Mauro Zamboni has observed, law becomes the natural and first instrument of choice for instilling values into a community and the effect is inevitably to propel law closer to politics, even if the two remain institutionally distinct.[5] As law increasingly claims its legitimacy from democracy, so democracy sets law to work in the delivery of its political ends.

A second, associated pressure stems from the dramatic increase in the volume and influence of legislation in private law matters since the nineteenth century. Not only is more private law now *created* and *expressed* 'publicly' through the democratic process, but courts are ever more inclined to mould common law doctrines so as respectfully to avoid

[2] Charles Donahue, Jr, 'Private Law Without the State and During its Formation' (2008) 56 *American Journal of Comparative Law* 541 (citing as examples Roman, Talmudic and Islamic law). The birth of the modern nation-state is generally set in the sixteenth century.

[3] I should *not* be taken to suggest that, prior to the rise of the nation-state, private law had no 'political' aspect and was therefore somehow entirely isolated from the public. In so far as private law, as law, has links to public authority, power and force, it has always been susceptible to 'public' influence, even if that influence has not always been mediated through the devices of the modern state.

[4] Ralf Michaels and Nils Jansen, 'Private Law Beyond the State? Europeanization, Globalization, Privatization' (2006) 54 *American Journal of Comparative Law* 843, 856.

[5] Mauro Zamboni, *The Policy of Law: A Legal Theoretical Framework* (Oxford: Hart Publishing, 2007), pp. 2–3, 92–3.

'conflict', or so as to 'cohere' with legislative policy.[6] The full implications of legislative interventions in (and around) the modern law of tort are only now being considered in detail[7] and the conclusions of contemporary studies seem set to challenge our conceptions of that field in the twenty-first century as fundamentally as root conceptions of the law of contract(s) were shaken by writers such as Hugh Collins[8] in the twentieth century. More broadly, there is probably good reason to think that, where private law theory is concerned, legislation is still the proverbial elephant in the room – a matter of which writers are consciously and increasingly aware, but which they too regularly fail to address. It may even be that the reluctance of private law theorists to talk much about legislation is symptomatic of an entrenched suspicion that legislative interventions somehow adulterate the principled, long-term development of law with short-term political agendas.[9] It is certainly not difficult to find examples of fragile interventionist expediencies that bear this out on occasion,[10] but whatever we think of such cases, we cannot provide an accurate picture of private law in the modern day while leaving legislation off the map. The sheer volume of legislative activity, both primary and secondary, makes it impossible to ignore in the modern age.

To the extent that codification represents a more comprehensive, definitive and exhaustive manifestation of the legislative impulse, the plethora of recent proposals to codify significant parts of private law[11]

[6] E.g. *Caparo Industries Plc* v. *Dickman* [1990] 2 AC 605; *Marcic* v. *Thames Water Utilities* [2004] 2 AC 42; *Graham Barclay Oysters Pty Ltd* v. *Ryan* (2002) 211 CLR 540 at [80]; *Equuscorp Pty Ltd* v. *Haxton & Ors* [2012] HCA 7 at [34]; *Koubi v. Mazda Canada Inc.* [2012] BCCA 310.

[7] See T. T. Arvind and Jenny Steele (eds.), *Tort Law and the Legislature* (Oxford: Hart Publishing, 2012); Neil Foster, 'The Merits of the Civil Action for Breach of Statutory Duty' (2011) 33 *Sydney Law Review* 67. Looking more broadly across the law of obligations, see James Lee, *Legislation and Reform in the Law of Obligations* (Oxford: Hart Publishing, 2014, forthcoming).

[8] Hugh Collins, *The Law of Contract* (London: Weidenfeld and Nicolson, 1986); Hugh Collins, *Regulating Contracts* (Oxford University Press, 1999).

[9] This type of suspicion has strong historical roots and was probably at its keenest in the nineteenth century, when judges saw legislation in precisely this manner and did their best to limit its impact. See further Morton J. Horwitz, 'The History of the Public/Private Distinction' (1982) 130 *University of Pennsylvania Law Review* 1423.

[10] For a possible contemporary example in Australia of legislation born in part on the back of short-term pressures experienced by the insurance industry (and rushed through in quick time), see the various Civil Liability Acts in place in all States and Territories. For the background and process, see Peter Cane, 'Reforming Tort Law in Australia: A Personal Perspective' (2003) 27 *Melbourne University Law Review* 649.

[11] On the history of codification attempts, problems and recent developments in relation to the Draft Common Frame of Reference in respect of European Private Law (not in itself a

clearly add to existing pressures to *create* more and more private law publicly. Moreover, when the interpretation of legislative provisions is open to doubt, courts are nowadays entitled to have regard to an increased range of 'political' material (parliamentary debates in particular[12]), from which to draw guidance in deciding how to apply law. It is therefore not simply that more private law is now sourced publicly through the democratic process, but that instruments of legal interpretation have themselves become more permeable to arguments in the political arena.

A third pressure towards the public, identified by Steve Hedley, Anita Krug and Alastair Hudson later in this volume, is the rapid rise of the corporation since the latter part of the nineteenth century.[13] The fact that so many parties to private litigation are now publicly constituted (by which I mean that their recognition as persons is publicly regulated) and the fact that such unnatural persons represent the collective financial interests of sizeable investor communities both present challenges to the traditional paradigm of private law as a set of norms existing 'between individuals'. Analogous challenges to the same individualistic conception of the law have flowed from the abolition of Crown immunities (making the state itself the object of more and more private law actions), by the rise and rise of compulsory liability insurance (which clearly reallocates and spreads individual liabilities) and by extensions to the doctrine of vicarious liability, which in practice relocate significant remedial responsibilities to an individual wrongdoer's employer (normally corporate, sometimes the state), even (now) when the activity constituting the wrong furthers no interest of the employer itself.[14] It is therefore not just the case that many of the persons we identify as private legal actors tend these days to be corporate, but corporations are almost always in the

code, but potentially a draft of one), see Steve Hedley, 'Is Private Law Meaningless?' (2011) 64 *Current Legal Problems* 89, 106–10. In Australia, the most recent fixation is with contract codification: Commonwealth of Australia, *Improving Australia's Law and Justice Framework: A Discussion Paper to Explore the Scope for Reforming Australian Contract Law* (Canberra: Australian Government Attorney-General's Department, 2012). See further Andrew Stuart, 'What's Wrong with the Australian Law of Contract?' (2012) 29 *Journal of Contract Law* 74.

12 In the UK, see *Pepper* v. *Hart* [1993] AC 593.

13 Corporations were known to law (in particular Roman law) much earlier than this, but the emergence of the public corporation from the law of partnership is predominantly a late nineteenth-century and twentieth-century phenomenon. For an English history, see Laurence Gower, *Gower's Principles of Modern Company Law*, 4th edition (London: Stevens, 1979), Chapters 2 and 3.

14 *Bazley* v. *Curry* [1999] 2 SCR 534 (SCC); *Lister* v. *Hesley Hall Ltd* [2002] 1 AC 215 (HL); *New South Wales* v. *Lepore* (2003) 212 CLR 511 (HCA).

background in one way or another in private litigation, even where the particular legal interaction forming the focus of the litigation is between natural persons. Corporate entities either step directly into the shoes of natural parties via the subrogation process, or they provide a secondary mechanism for the socialisation of the latter's liabilities via market-pricing and insurance processes.

State interests in corporate entities (such as the interests taken by the state in failing banks in the wake of the recent global financial crisis) further widen (and democratise) these insurance effects. The way in which insurance systems as a whole interact with private law principles is itself a complex topic, of course, and it is no longer clear that insurance is an entirely passive party in the relationship.[15] Does insurance really only redistribute risks that the law has previously fixed, as traditional views would have us believe, or does the institution of insurance affect the way in which private law chooses to fix them in the first place?[16]

Finally, corporations (in particular financial institutions such as banks) are central to a shift in our understanding of 'private' and public in another way. Some international corporations are so powerful and so influential upon key aspects of our public economy these days that there may be good reasons for subjecting them (on some occasions and for some purposes) to similar levels of scrutiny and accountability as the state itself. As Alastair Hudson's work in Chapter 8 suggests, these 'public' aspects of private corporations may well invite into their private law responsibilities a range of stricter 'public' (regulatory) standards.

A fourth, very significant pressure is the rise of a 'public' jurisprudence of human rights, whether constitutionally embedded or not. The impacts of this jurisprudence upon private law rights (direct and/or indirect, depending on the jurisdiction in question) are well documented in recent

[15] For recent challenges to the passive characterisation of insurance's role, see Rob Merkin, 'Tort, Insurance and Ideology: Further Thoughts' (2012) 75 *Modern Law Review* 301; Jenny Steele and Rob Merkin, *Insurance and the Law of Obligations* (Oxford University Press, 2013). Contrast Ernest J. Weinrib, 'The Insurance Justification and Private Law' (1985) 14 *Journal of Legal Studies* 681; Jane Stapleton, 'Tort, Insurance and Ideology' (1995) 58 *Modern Law Review* 820.

[16] The uncertainty on this issue is neatly exemplified in Australia by a contrast between the approaches of McHugh J in *Perre* v. *Apand Pty Ltd* (1999) 198 CLR 180 at [130] (insurance 'generally' irrelevant to the duty of care issue in negligence law) and Gillard J in *Johnson Tiles Pty Ltd* v. *Esso Australia Pty Ltd* [2003] VSC 27 at [1093]–[1110] (fact that first-party insurance widely available and in fact held by plaintiff relevant to exclusion of any duty of care on part of the defendant in respect of pure economic harm). See also Tracey L. Carver, 'Insurance and the Law of Negligence: An Influential or Irrelevant Persuader?' (2011) 22 *Insurance Law Journal* 51.

works.[17] Michelle Flaherty alludes to some of them in Chapter 7. In the United Kingdom, the interactions between public law actions against the state under the Human Rights Act (HRA) 1998 and private law actions are particularly interesting and complex, not least because courts – as public authorities – are obliged by the terms of the Act to apply the norms of the European Convention in developing traditional private law doctrines.[18] In some instances, such as in the domain of privacy law, English private law has effectively imported the substance of these 'public' norms wholesale into individual civil law actions.[19] At the same time, many of the rights protected by the Act, although technically exigible by individuals only against state agencies, bear close resemblance in their substantive terms to the rights (property, physical liberty, rights to life) traditionally protected by private law doctrines of ancient pedigree. 'Human' rights, as they exist in the modern day, have a 'public' dimension in the sense that they circumscribe liberties and goods that democratically accountable public authorities have positive obligations to protect. At the same time, however, some of these are matters in respect of which private law has developed its own robust reasoning structures, remedies, checks and balances.

There is obvious potential for collision. In the recent *Rabone* case,[20] for example, an action under the HRA seems to have undermined the regime of bereavement damages laid down by a domestic private law statute, by according distressed parents compensation for the state's failure to protect their child's right to life. Although English parents have no action of their own in negligence against other private parties for bereavement flowing from the death of an adult child, they may now sue the state for precisely this emotional harm, where the latter fails in its positive obligations under the HRA to protect the child's life. Such developments seem likely to (further) increase the incentive for litigants to allocate blame wherever possible to public (state) parties. They also demonstrate the complexity of the public–private rights relations in issue in interactions of this sort. In *Rabone*, private law disclosed no individual (private) interest of the parent giving rise to a right to compensation. By contrast, the (public law)

[17] E.g. Daniel Friedmann and Daphne Barak-Erez (eds.), *Human Rights in Private Law* (Oxford University Press, 2001); David Hoffman (ed.), *The Impact of the UK Human Rights Act on Private Law* (Cambridge University Press, 2011).

[18] Human Rights Act (HRA) 1998 (UK), s. 6(3).

[19] *Campbell* v. *Mirror Group Newspapers Ltd* [2004] 2 AC 457; *McKennitt* v. *Ash* [2008] QB 73 at [11].

[20] *Rabone* v. *Pennine Care NHS Trust* [2012] 2 AC 72 ('*Rabone*').

action under the HRA seems to have given rise to damages for harm to *precisely that private interest*, on the hypothesis that it resulted from the infringement of a *public law* right belonging to a *distinct*, private party (the child).[21] Unpicking this Gordian knot of public and private rights is not easy, but it remains an important aim if we are to determine the respective functions and purposes of public and private law in respect of these important human interests in the twenty-first century. Such interests are now protected by both legal domains and the respective systems of public and private rights are only loosely coordinated and therefore capable of chafing uncomfortably against one another.[22]

A fifth 'public' pressure upon private law stems from the phenomenon of legal globalisation, which Zamboni defines as 'the circulation of legal models (i.e. legal categories and concepts) in a way that ... render[s] ... many different aspects of ... different legal systems homogenous'.[23] It has sometimes been said that globalisation renders private law *more private* (because it extends the operation of the law beyond the reach of nation-states and places it more in the hands of the market),[24] but there is also a sense in which globalisation makes the source of relevant private law norms more 'public', in so far as it sources them in a wider range of trans-jurisdictional legal materials. European human rights law provides a classic example of (geographically limited) globalisation as Zamboni defines it: the jurisprudence of the European Convention supplying the relevant norms for domestic courts to apply and the European Court of Human Rights (ECtHR) itself comprising judges drawn from a wide variety of different constitutional backgrounds. United Kingdom domestic private law still retains a degree of 'norm-sourcing' autonomy as a consequence of principles of state derogation from (some Articles of) the Convention and via generous margins of appreciation, but it is nonetheless obliged to

21 This was made possible by construing the parents as 'victims' of the right-violation. An alternative analysis, perhaps more compatible with the conventional view that the HRA creates no private rights per se, is that this is the 'private damage' suffered by the parents as a result of the state's violation of their *own public* right that the state properly implement the pattern of rights contained in the Convention. On this view, the HRA effectively creates a statutory 'public' tort specific to public authorities: Robert Stevens, *Torts and Rights* (Oxford University Press, 2007), p. 239. For trenchant criticism of *Rabone* for trivialising the human rights exercise and for blurring the line between human rights actions and tort law, see Andrew Tettenborn, 'Wrongful Death, Human Rights and the Fatal Accidents Act' (2012) 128 *Law Quarterly Review* 327.

22 Some might say, of course, that this is the whole point of human rights – to act as constant correctives to domestic law, both public and private.

23 Zamboni, *The Policy of Law*, p. 200.

24 Michaels and Jansen, 'Private Law Beyond the State?', 873.

look outward ('publicly' in another sense), not just inward, in developing key protections. Moreover, it is the jurisprudence of the ECtHR that has been regarded by English courts as ultimately binding even in relation to some matters – such as the quantification of damages – in respect of which domestic private law provides a wealth of useful historical precedents.[25] That has proven a marked source of domestic controversy, as one might imagine, because damages awards under the ECtHR jurisprudence are actually often *less* generous than those traditionally provided at common law. For those who are committed to advancing the protections accorded to particular human interests, the remedial deficiencies of more 'global', public human rights law in this regard constitute a rather bitter irony.

Another, perhaps more fragile, example of legal globalisation is to be found in commercial law – particularly in corporations law, although debates continue to rage here as to whether harmonisation is actually occurring, normatively desirable, or ever likely to be possible. The topic forms a significant focus of Anita Krug's important study of the public and private dimensions of corporations law in Chapter 9 (considered further below), where the author explores in detail the 'public' nature of the conversations that are necessary for the resolution of questions about trans-jurisdictional convergence. Part of the 'public' characterisation of the challenge of globalisation in corporations law lies not simply, she suggests, in the fact that norms are sourced and formulated across national boundaries, but also in the normative justifications that are given for this process, which are typically located in arguments about efficiency and the collective public good.

This last point discloses a sixth pressure towards 'public' understandings of private law that can be characterised crudely as theoretical and/or philosophical. It consists in the rise of instrumentalist understandings of the private law during the course of the twentieth century – commencing, arguably, with the American Legal Realist movement and culminating in the Law and Economics and Critical Legal Studies movements in their various manifestations.[26] So influential has this type of thinking proven

[25] See Jason Varuhas, 'Damages: Private Law and the HRA – Never the Twain Shall Meet?', Chapter 11 in David Hoffman (ed.), *The Impact of the UK Human Rights Act on Private Law* (Cambridge University Press, 2011).

[26] For a critical analysis of instrumentalism's rise, see Brian Tamanaha, *Law as Means to an End* (Cambridge University Press, 2006). In the common law itself, the author argues that the phenomenon really only appeared in the twentieth century (cf. contra Morton J. Horwitz, *The Transformation of American Law 1780–1860* (Cambridge, MA: Harvard University Press, 1977)). It was nonetheless rife in the legislation of the nineteenth century.

in North American law schools that 'distinct', 'internal' or 'doctrinal' studies of the field have all but disappeared. Private law is regarded as so embedded in public politics as to be normatively (if not institutionally) indistinct from it. Borrowing the apocalyptic words of John Langbein, it is almost as if a neutron bomb has gone off across the Atlantic – all the structures of the private law remain in place, but they are shrouded in a deathly silence and lack a working population.[27] All law has come to be regarded as 'public' (instrumental) law. The explanations for this theoretical turn are not wholly clear. James Gordley characterises it as an impoverishment of legal thought, attributing its origins to a crisis in Western legal thinking thrown up by the Cartesian, rationalist tradition.[28] The way in which law has come to be taught alongside – or sometimes as an instantiation of – the empirical sciences in American Universities has apparently further embedded the instrumentalist philosophy into generations of young graduates and has contributed to the decline of 'doctrinal' private law studies.[29]

This philosophical movement towards public understandings of private law has not, however, gone unopposed. It has triggered a powerful counter-reaction on the part of modern 'corrective justice' and 'rights' theorists, who have set out with vigour in the latter part of the twentieth century and the first part of the twenty-first century to reclaim significant autonomy for private law and legal doctrine in both institutional and substantive terms.[30] One very significant figure in this counter-movement

[27] John Langbein, 'The Later History of Restitution', in William R. Cornish, Richard Nolan, Janet O'Sullivan and Graham Virgo (eds.), *Restitution Past, Present and Future* (Oxford: Hart Publishing, 1998), p. 61 (talking specifically of the field of restitution, but the comment might be further generalised).

[28] James Gordley, 'The State's Private Law and Legal Academia' (2008) 56 *American Journal of Comparative Law* 639. The summary is necessarily oversimplified. Expanding slightly, Gordley's point is that the dissatisfaction of realists with the work of nineteenth-century jurists such as Blackstone stemmed from the latter's ill-fated attempts to combine deductive rationalism with positivism. The American reaction was to turn to the empirical sciences as a source of truth.

[29] On the challenge that the rise of 'interdisciplinary' education presents for private law, see Ernest J. Weinrib, *Corrective Justice* (Oxford University Press, 2012), Chapter 9.

[30] To mention but some: George P. Fletcher, 'Fairness and Utility in Tort Theory' (1972) 85 *Harvard Law Review* 537; Richard Epstein, 'A Theory of Strict Liability' (1973) 2 *Journal of Legal Studies* 151; Jules Coleman, *Risks and Wrongs* (Cambridge University Press, 1992), esp. Chapter 19; Ernest J. Weinrib, *The Idea of Private Law* (Cambridge, MA: Harvard University Press, 1995); Stephen Smith, *Contract Theory* (Oxford University Press, 2004); Stevens, *Torts and Rights*; Allan Beever, *Rediscovering the Law of Negligence* (Oxford: Hart Publishing, 2007). As may be expected, the precise claims made for the normative autonomy of private law in these works differ. Most recently, the revival of private

is Professor Ernest Weinrib, to whose views I refer in more detail in the next section. For Weinrib, the reconstruction of private law as a set of rules derived from (and therefore secondary to) public purposes disrespects and overlooks the bilateral ('correlative') normative structure of private law as an instantiation of individual purposiveness and corrective justice. Regarding private law as an instrument for achieving social goals such as wealth maximisation, social equality, happiness and the like fails to account, he argues, for the way in which rights and remedies are structured in private law as interactions between the doer and sufferer of a particular injustice. Only (Kantian) reasons that are truly private (in the sense that they reflect the bilateral normative relationship of the parties themselves) are consistent with the formal structure of private law and only they are able to present it in a fully intelligible and coherent light.

For Weinrib, it does not follow that private law is completely isolated from public law or public institutions. Public institutions such as courts are required for private rights to be determined, declared and coercively enforced as a system. The basic function of these institutions is, nonetheless, to systematise and make those rights omnilateral.[31] The rights are to be understood in abstraction from the institutions themselves[32] and express the freedom of individuals to determine their own ends. Private law and public law are thus conceptually distinct, private rights being logically prior to the public apparatus for the adjudication and enforcement of those rights. At the same time, private law adjudication involves 'not the achievement of a collective goal ... but a declaration of principles and standards that could be accepted by all as expressing their nature as free wills'.[33] This is not to say that private rights may not be modified or overridden in the pursuit of collective community goals, but if this is to occur it must be done explicitly through publicly enacted legislation, rather than by judicial moulding of the received principles and standards.

Even those who take a completely different philosophical starting point in legal realism and who reject Weinrib's formalist and Kantian premises now apparently concede his point that private law is a distinctively

law thinking in America is symbolised by the publication of a symposium optimistically entitled 'The New Private Law' in (2012) 125 *Harvard Law Review*.

[31] Ernest J. Weinrib, 'Private Law and Public Right' (2011) 61 *University of Toronto Law Journal* 191. Private rights are defined at 195 as 'moral capacities for putting others under correlative obligations'.

[32] *Ibid.*, 195.

[33] Ernest J. Weinrib, 'Law as a Kantian Idea of Reason' (1987) 87 *Columbia Law Review* 472, 497–8.

bilateral *form* of justice with significant attendant constraints.[34] The result is that today much of the current philosophical debate in private law is focused on identifying the types of judicial reasons and arguments that can be regarded as commensurate with these constraints. It concerns the nature of the constraints themselves – are they moral, constitutional, practical?[35] – and the question of which and how many of the reasons that animate private law's bilateral structure are really 'public' (instrumental) and how many 'private' (individual, deontological).

Although apparently abstract, the debate is important and increasingly necessary. It forms the background context of much of the discussion in the rest of this book. It is central to our understanding of what can be achieved through private law and to the proper division of the normative workload between public and private law domains. In just the last few years, it has given rise to several important studies dedicated to identifying the 'goals' and 'philosophical foundations' of private law and the respective roles of 'policy' and 'rights' in private law reasoning.[36] It has prompted a number of recent conferences on the 'Intersections between Private and Public Law, Values and Method',[37] 'Tort Law and Social Policy',[38] the

[34] See, e.g., Hanoch Dagan, 'The Limited Autonomy of Private Law' (2008) 56 *American Journal of Comparative Law* 809; Hanoch Dagan, 'The Public Dimension of Property' (2013) 24(2) *King's Law Journal*, 260.

[35] Moral constraints might reflect the view that private law can only reflect deontological relationships of right and duty between parties to a dispute. Constitutional constraints reflect the idea that judges have only limited authority to create law or engage in certain types of reasoning. Practical constraints relate, inter alia, to the limited amount of information available to a court, in turn limiting the types of decisions that can in practice be made, or made efficiently. For a paper focusing on constraints of the second and third type, see Darryn Jensen, 'Theories, Principles, Policies and Common Law Adjudication' (2011) 36 *Australian Journal of Legal Philosophy* 34, 52–4. See also James Penner, 'Legal Reasoning and the Authority of Law', in Lukas H. Meyer, Stanley L. Paulson and Thomas W. Pogge (eds.), *Rights, Culture, and the Law: Themes from the Legal and Political Philosophy of Joseph Raz* (Oxford University Press, 2003) p. 71, at pp. 93–4.

[36] E.g., Stevens, *Torts and Rights*; Beever, *Rediscovering the Law of Negligence*; Andrew Robertson and Tang Hang Wu (eds.), *The Goals of Private Law* (Oxford: Hart Publishing, 2009); Robert Chambers, Charles Mitchell and James Penner (eds.), *Philosophical Foundations of the Law of Unjust Enrichment* (Oxford University Press, 2009); A. Robertson, 'Justice, Community Welfare and the Duty of Care' (2011) 127 *Law Quarterly Review* 370; Donal Nolan and Andrew Robertson (eds.), *Rights and Private Law* (Oxford: Hart Publishing, 2012); Gregory Keating, 'The Priority of Respect over Repair' (2012) 18 *Legal Theory* 293. See also the various contributions in *Festschrift for Robert Rabin: Seventeenth Annual Clifford Symposium On Tort Law And Social Policy* (2012) 61 *De Paul Law Review*.

[37] TC Beirne School of Law, The University of Queensland, July 2011.

[38] Proceedings are published in *Festschrift for Robert Rabin*.

'Public Life of Private Law',[39] 'Contract as Public Law'[40] and 'The Interface of Public and Private Law Concepts of Property'.[41] It has also stimulated further reflection on the nature of the relationship between 'private' and 'public' rights in Kant's legal philosophy,[42] and the relationship between corrective and distributive justice.[43] It raises fundamental questions about the propriety of using private law as a mechanism of deterrence, retribution, regulation, social norm-creation, economic efficiency, social equality, autonomy or welfare. It also requires us to think again – and think more carefully – about whether judges who invoke 'policy' arguments in private law are really reasoning instrumentally, and about the way in which 'consequences', 'effects' and 'values' can legitimately be taken into account in the creation or restriction of private law rights without unduly sacrificing individual freedoms, or treating individuals as mere components of some cruel social calculus.

A significant number of writers now seek a difficult middle path between 'public' (instrumental) and 'private' (non-instrumental) conceptions of private law – by suggesting a 'limited' autonomy for the field, or a 'constrained' role for 'policy' argument within it.[44] They accept the importance of recognising private law as a system of interpersonal justice, whilst refusing to accept that the personal rights that lie at its heart can be – or are – formulated without regard to social values and consequences. It is worth noting that Kant himself would have regarded at least some of the reasons that modern writers and courts describe as 'policy' concerns as being relevant to the determination of private law rights. Izhak Englard

[39] Economic and Social Research Council seminar series, *The Public Life of Private Law*, 2013–2014.

[40] Emory University School of Law, Atlanta, Georgia, 1–2 March 2013 (the full title of the workshop was 'Contract as "Public Law" at the Intersection of Globalization and Privatization').

[41] Institute of Advanced Legal Studies, London, 13 June 2012.

[42] Arthur Ripstein, *Force and Freedom* (Cambridge, MA: Harvard University Press, 2009); Arthur Ripstein, 'Private Order and Public Justice: Kant and Rawls' (2006) 92 *Virginia Law Review* 1391; Weinrib, 'Private Law and Public Right'.

[43] E.g., Steven R. Perry, 'On the Relationship between Corrective and Distributive Justice', in Jeremy Horder (ed.), *Oxford Essays in Jurisprudence*, fourth series (Oxford University Press, 2000); Peter Benson, 'The Basis of Corrective Justice and its Relation to Distributive Justice' (1992) 77 *Iowa Law Review* 515; Izhak Englard, *Corrective and Distributive Justice* (Oxford University Press, 2009).

[44] See, e.g., Dagan, 'The Limited Autonomy of Private Law'; Andrew Robertson, 'Constraints on Policy-Based Reasoning in Private Law', Chapter 11 in Andrew Robertson and Tang Hang Wu (eds.), *The Goals of Private Law* (Oxford: Hart Publishing, 2009); Alan Calnan, 'The Instrumental Justice of Private Law' (2010) 78 *University of Missouri-Kansas City Law Review* 559.

makes the point that considerations of efficiency in the administration of justice were regarded by Kant as directly relevant to the substance of these rights – a fact he describes as 'remarkable'.[45] Weinrib has also suggested that on many of the occasions that courts refer to public policy, they are not really engaged in any exercise of social engineering at all, but simply referring to the importance of non-instrumental values in legal thinking, such as human dignity, or coherence in judicial decision-making.[46] It follows that we need to be very clear about what we mean by 'policy' arguments before we endorse or dismiss their use in determining private law disputes. Some 'policy' arguments will challenge conceptions of the constitutional limits of the judicial role, the practical informational capacities of judges, or deontological understandings of private law. By contrast, there are others relating to the operation of the *system* of private justice as a whole (such as 'certainty' or 'determinacy' in the delineation of the rights the system supports, respect for institutions of justice, respect for human dignity, the importance of maintaining coherence in the development of legal doctrines, and so on) that will not. Some policy is 'social' policy in the broadest sense and certainly belongs in the hands of the public (democratic) process, whereas some policy might better be described as 'legal' policy and is clearly less challenging to (and is indeed assumed by) deontological private law paradigms. Ultimately, which types of argumentation are regarded as acceptable and commensurate with the forms and procedures of private law depends on the way in which the constraints of the system are understood ideologically.

Almost every chapter in this book touches on these issues and there is little unanimity on the question as to how they are to be resolved, as one might expect. At one end of the spectrum, Steve Hedley strongly rejects explanations of private law that are entirely internal and that divorce it from its complex history and ever-changing context, and he characterises private law as not simply a relationship between private (individual) parties, but also as an important relationship between individuals and

[45] Englard, *Corrective and Distributive Justice*, p. 181 and fn. 776.

[46] Lorraine Weinrib and Ernest J. Weinrib, 'Constitutional Values and Private Law in Canada', Chapter 3 in Daniel Friedmann and Daphne Barak-Erez (eds.), *Human Rights in Private Law* (Oxford University Press, 2001), pp. 62–3; Ernest J. Weinrib, 'The Disintegration of Duty' (2006) 1 *Advocates Quarterly* 212, esp. 245–55. See also Neil MacCormick, *Rhetoric and the Rule of Law: A Theory of Legal Reasoning* (Oxford University Press, 2005), pp. 119–20. For an example of a case in which the 'policy' question whether to allow restitution of benefits provided under an illegal contrast was identified as being one of 'coherence', see *Equuscorp Pty Ltd* v. *Haxton & Ors* [2012] HCA 7 at [34] (French CJ, Crennan and Kiefel JJ).

government. This thinking echoes transatlantic theoretical developments depicting private law as a manifestation of the rights that private citizens have against the *state* to 'civil recourse'.[47] In Chapter 11, Jeff Berryman and Robyn Carroll describe an unashamedly instrumental role for private law class action remedies (in particular, the cy-près distribution remedy) as mechanisms for effecting behavioural change. In the same vein, in Chapter 10, Dan Priel reconsiders what it means for private law to 'vindicate' rights in tort law, ascribing a *public, instrumental* aim to the private law concept of vindication (exposure of the wrongs of the state and public accountability). This reinvigorates claims, popularised in the 1970s, that tort law plays a key role as a regulatory 'ombudsman',[48] reining in the force of the state and playing a key role in the investigation and exposure of matters bearing upon the public good. It also, in a cheeky twist, characterises as 'public' an idea that is most often claimed as paradigmatic of deontological understandings of private law. The views of Matthew Harding and Adam Parachin, writing on charity law in Chapters 5 and 6, display an intermediate approach. For Harding, the 'point' of charity law is both to advance the liberal value of individual freedom (personal choice) by conferring power on individuals to set their own ends *and* to provide incentives for those individuals to further autonomy-enhancing goods such as human nourishment, education and health care. Considerations of efficiency and social justice may sometimes play a part in the design, but should be regarded with some suspicion to the extent that they significantly set back personal autonomy. Similarly, Adam Parachin starts from the proposition that the legal concept of charity as it is defined in private law is not as inconsistent with the (public law) concept of unlawful discrimination as is often assumed. An overall theme emanating from these contributions is that different parts of the private law give effect to different blends of private and public reasons. The precise relationship of priority between these reasons nonetheless remains highly contested.

Let me summarise. In setting the context of the current work, I have observed that private law has come under ever-increasing pressures from the 'public' in one way or another. These pressures derive from: (1) the rise of the welfare state, (2) burgeoning legislation, (3) corporatisation,

[47] Benjamin Zipursky, 'Rights, Wrongs and Recourse in the Law of Torts' (1998) 51 *Vanderbilt Law Review* 1; Benjamin Zipursky, 'Civil Recourse, not Corrective Justice' (2003) 91 *Georgia Law Journal* 695; John Goldberg and Benjamin Zipursky, 'Accidents of the Great Society' (2005) 64 *Maryland Law Review* 364.

[48] Allen M. Linden, 'Tort Law as Ombudsman' (1973) 51 *Canadian Bar Review* 157; John W. Wade, 'Tort Law as Ombudsman' (1986) 65 *Oregon Law Review* 309.

(4) human rights, (5) globalisation and (6) instrumentalism. We should add to this list (7) a shift towards greater 'collectivism' in private litigation through class actions (the explicit focus of Jeff Berryman and Robyn Carroll's work in Chapter 11), and (8) the 'marketisation' of significant sectors of state welfare activity through the creation of 'internal markets' in major areas of provision, such as public health.[49]

These developments place their own strains on traditional private law concepts, requiring (in the latter case) a revised understanding of 'contract'[50] and (in the former) a revised approach to standing. It is not the case that the dynamics of public and private are all one way. There is, Zamboni points out, a sense in which private law has become more 'discrete' from politics as a result of its increased disciplinary specialisation,[51] and it has rightly been observed that less and less private law is 'made public' these days, because parties are subject to very strong procedural incentives to arbitrate, mediate and settle out of court.[52] So powerful have these incentives proven in the USA, it seems, that civil cases have all but vanished from the courts.[53] Civil justice has in practice become a set of individually negotiated outcomes between parties taking place behind closed doors. It is no longer justice 'held up' for the world to see. Ultimately, this could become a significant problem in its own right, if it prevents important points of principle being litigated to an institutionally adjudicated solution.[54] The common law relies upon precedent, but what is it to do if no precedent is set? Will (common law) private law wither on the vine as a public institution? The same phenomenon also has significant implications for private law's capacity to express and affirm social

[49] On the early UK experience, see Robert Flynn and George Williams (eds.), *Contracting for Health: Quasi-Markets and the NHS* (Oxford University Press, 1997).

[50] David Hughes, 'The Reorganisation of the National Health Service: the Rhetoric and Reality of the Internal Market' (1991) 54 *Modern Law Review* 88; Kit Barker, 'NHS Contracts, Restitution and the Internal Market' (1993) 56 *Modern Law Review* 832; Pauline Allen, 'Contracts in the National Health Service Internal Market' (1995) 58 *Modern Law Review* 321; Peter Vincent-Jones, *The New Public Contracting* (Oxford: Clarendon Press, 2006).

[51] Zamboni, *The Policy of Law*, p. 3.

[52] For one such, powerful incentive to settlement, see *Calderbank* v. *Calderbank* [1975] 3 All ER 333.

[53] John Langbein, 'The Disappearance of Civil Trial in the United States' (2012) 122 *Yale Law Journal* 522. The pattern is not unique to the USA, being replicated in both Canada and the UK.

[54] See Beverley McLachlin, 'Developing the Private Law in the Face of the "Vanishing Trial"', speech delivered at *Obligations VI* Conference, London, Ontario, 18 July 2012, available at: http://vimeo.com/46694021 (last accessed 17 May 2013).

norms publicly – if no institutional announcements of right and wrong are made, how is the law to signal anything to anyone? Will this now be left to the public law alone, or to publicly made law (statute)? Nonetheless, even if there are (which there clearly are, from one perspective or another) some 'privatising' tendencies detectable in the modern law, our argument is that the principal and most important dynamic in recent years has been from 'the public' into private law. The function of everything that follows in this book is to test the nature, extent and fertility of this dynamic.

3 Definitions, theory and taxonomy: what is at stake in the public–private distinction?

Part II of this volume (Chapters 2 to 4) is dedicated to general definitional, theoretical and taxonomic debates about private and public. That is, it primarily concerns what it means (if anything) to distinguish between private and public, why one might wish to do so and, to some extent, what our law will end up looking like if one does, depending on the type of distinction that we choose to deploy.

Classifications and distinctions exist (and persist) largely because of their utility in conveying important information about the phenomena that are being classified and differentiated. The classifications of the law are particularly vulnerable to instability and suspicion – compared to, for example, botanical or zoological taxonomy – because the things being classified – and, thereby, assimilated and differentiated – are concepts of 'right' and have no empirical existence outside of the minds of the classifiers.[55] Notwithstanding the protracted historical dispute about whether the giant panda was a type of bear or a type of raccoon,[56] there continued to be furry, bamboo-eating creatures in southern China that were what they were. The extent to which private law and public law persist as distinct legal phenomena, on the other hand, depends entirely upon how legislators, adjudicators, legal scholars and other participants in legal systems think about these categories and, in particular, upon whether or not they regard the distinction in question as useful in illuminating the system's practices.

[55] See Geoffrey Samuel, 'English Private Law: Old and New Thinking in the Taxonomy Debate' (2004) 24 *Oxford Journal of Legal Studies* 335, 341.

[56] Ernst Mayr, 'Uncertainty in Science: is the Giant Panda a Bear or a Raccoon?' (1986) 323 *Nature* 769, 769.

The need for classifications to be practically significant in this way is emphasised by William Lucy and Alexander Williams in Chapter 2. The authors remark upon how there is no single version of the distinction between 'private' and 'public' and that the diversity 'accommodate[s] many apparently contradictory intuitions' about 'the' distinction. Some of the distinctions are made by lawyers, some by philosophers, some by economists, some by historians and some by sociologists – and the purposes of the various observers in making their own type of distinction differ markedly. Not only are there many (not one) private/public distinctions at stake, but no particular version of the distinction (even a legal version) is likely to be conclusively dispositive of any particular hard case. This is, in part, because the question 'is this public or private?' does not always invite a bivalent 'yes or no' answer. A phenomenon may be 'more or less' public or private (on a scale), depending on the point one is trying to make. It is also because some of the ideas placed in opposition to one another in formulating the distinction are themselves inherently *malleable*, so that the distinction lacks a clean edge. Hard cases are simply too hard to be disposed of so conveniently. Lucy and Williams stop short of saying that public/private distinctions are never of use – some of these may carry 'some weight' in judicial decisions – but they maintain that there is a tendency to overestimate the extent to which such distinctions are decisive.

It is certainly true to say that the divide between public and private can be mapped in a very wide variety of ways. In attributing to law some 'public' character, one could be making any one of a number of very different propositions. Some of these were identified in a useful comparative analysis conducted by Michaels and Jansen in 2006.[57] One might be saying (the following list is non-exhaustive) that parts of the law:

(1) protect collective, as opposed to individual interests;
(2) instantiate principles of distributive, as opposed to corrective justice;

[57] Michaels and Jansen, 'Private Law Beyond the State?' The authors note at 846 that different definitions of 'state' and 'private law' in the USA and Germany have resulted in the distinction between public and private playing different roles in German and US legal discourses. On the protean nature of such distinctions see also Randy E. Barnett, 'Four Senses of the Public Law–Private Law Distinction' (1986) 9 *Harvard Journal of Law and Technology* 267; Peter Cane, 'Public Law and Private Law: A Study of the Analysis and Use of a Legal Concept', in John Eekelaar (ed.), *Oxford Essays in Jurisprudence*, third series (Oxford: Clarendon Press, 1987), p. 57.

(3) govern relations between the citizen and the state, as opposed to relations between private individuals (the distinction I myself started with);
(4) govern 'vertical' relationships between unequal parties, as opposed to 'horizontal' relationships between equal ones;[58]
(5) order the distribution of goods, services and property through a mandatory process, rather than through the voluntary processes of the market;
(6) are *made* by the state, as opposed to private parties or private bodies;
(7) are *enforced* by and at the initiative of the state;[59]
(8) are administered by special, not ordinary courts;[60]
(9) are domestic (internal to one state's jurisdiction) as opposed to trans- or inter- national (governing relations between states or between parties resident in different states);
(10) govern individuals' 'formal' (external) as opposed to 'informal' (intimate – personal – family) relationships;
(11) are informed by regulatory standards; or
(12) give effect to instrumental, as opposed to deontological values.

The varied nature of these distinctions explains why it is that a legal doctrine can be described, without contradiction, as having both public and private dimensions at one and the same time. It undermines the idea that there is any single or unique point to be made.

Despite their inconclusive nature, public/private classifications of the law persist. At a practical level, legal practitioners still need to know how, where and via which procedure to lodge a claim. Beyond this, many of the distinctions (particularly (3) above) are simply too obvious, too well embedded and arguably too important to be ignored.[61] Even if they lack the power to be *dispositive*, they can still be *representative* of important

[58] According to Michaels and Jansen, this definition subsumes the previous one, construing as 'public' the law governing relations between individuals and *anyone* (not just the state) exercising monopoly power.

[59] As in cases of public nuisance, or charitable trust.

[60] This distinction has special relevance in civilian jurisdictions, such as Germany and France, but is also relevant in the UK since the recognition of a separate administrative law court. For criticism, see Carol Harlow, '"Public" and "Private" Law: Definition Without Distinction' (1980) 43 *Modern Law Review* 241, 250–8.

[61] The distinction between the realm of the state and the realm outside the state is especially robust. For an excellent account of the historical reasons for this, see Horwitz, 'The History of the Public/Private Distinction'.

concerns and *informative* of judicial and legislative decisions in a more general way. In this respect, whilst those who famously proclaimed the 'public/private distinction' to be 'dead' no doubt had important points to make, the proposition must surely be regarded as more rhetorical than realistic.[62] Once one appreciates the diversity of the propositions that are being made when commentators refer to 'the' public–private distinction and once it is understood that not all of these distinctions are intended to be legally conclusive, merely informative, they become a lot easier to live with. In fact, they become a fertile source of critical argumentation.

In Chapter 3, Steve Hedley moves us away from these difficult definitional questions into substantive private law theory. He takes issue with the claim – that is at least implicit in the work of Weinrib – that private law is conceptually prior to public law and that public law is simply an apparatus for assuring private justice. Hedley notes that Weinrib's account appeals to those who are suspicious of the claims of the state to improve upon the order of actions underpinned by private rights, but he also suggests that the real aim of Weinrib's project is 'to insulate private law from politics altogether' and that it is untenable for that reason. His central objection to Weinrib's account is that it fails to explain the extent to which private law is the product of the efforts of public officials (legislators and judges) to improve the legal system. In Hedley's view, private law is the result of the outworking of public goals that are perceived by authorised public officials as worth pursuing. The one-way relationship contemplated by Weinrib, in which the public exists for the sake of the private, becomes a two-way relationship in which private law becomes the means or instrument by which *politically approved* public goals are carried into effect. According to this view, the argument that goal-driven reforms might imperil traditional private law categories (unsurprisingly) carries no weight. Accordingly, the law of contract and the law of trusts are not to be understood solely in terms of the internal logic of the parties' relationship, but are susceptible to reconfiguration in the light of collective policy choices about whether to pursue certain types of outcomes or goals – for example, public policies to eliminate discrimination against persons on the grounds of sex, race and religion.[63] In this context, at least, the public does *not* exist solely for the sake of the private. Instead, the private realm is enlisted for the pursuit of public goals as to the distribution of benefits and burdens. In other words, restrictions are placed upon

[62] Cane, 'Public Law and Private Law', p. 78.

[63] On which see further Chapter 6.

individual persons' freedom in the disposal of the resources that would otherwise be under their control *in order to* facilitate the achievement of public goals.

In considering these arguments, it seems unlikely that Weinrib would regard Hedley's objection as undermining his thesis about the distinctiveness of private law. Indeed, Weinrib has denied that he was ever suggesting that the state lacks the power to override or interfere with private law's categories. In particular, he has denied that, in insisting that the immanent rationality of tort law finds its expression in the corrective justice idea, he is also insisting that tort law should be preferred to other accident compensation schemes, such as universal social insurance schemes.[64] Accordingly, when considering Hedley's criticisms, it is helpful to recognise that Weinrib's position is not that private law is to be understood as *completely* isolated from public goals. Choices must simply be made about which system (the civil justice system, social insurance and so on) should be used to which end. Furthermore, he does not deny that private law (as I have defined it) has socially beneficial *effects*. His position is that, in the absence of direct legislative interventions that implement discernible public goals, private law is *intelligible* without any reference to public goals and, moreover, is better understood in terms of its characteristic forms than in terms of goals. Accordingly, a case that turns upon a point of contract, tort or property law that has not been the subject of legislative modification is 'private' in the sense that it is to be understood purely in terms of certain received categories rather than in terms of a social purpose that those categories are supposed to advance. This is not an argument that those categories may never be modified (by legislation) in order to advance contemporary social purposes. Indeed, to the extent that Weinrib thinks of private law as being goal-free, he appears to be referring to that part of the law governing the rights of individuals *inter se* that is pronounced by judges rather than legislated[65] and his definition of private law therefore differs markedly from the one I myself deployed at the outset. The existence of statutory caps on damages awards (or even comprehensive no-fault accident compensation schemes) that are motivated by public policy concerns would do nothing to change his view about the

[64] Ernest J. Weinrib, 'Legal Formalism: On the Immanent Rationality of Law' (1988) 97 *Yale Law Journal* 949, 973. See also Allan Beever, 'Corrective Justice and Personal Responsibility in Tort Law' (2008) 28 *Oxford Journal of Legal Studies* 475, 498–9.

[65] A possible exception is where statutory law shares the same formal structure as the common law, as for example under a civil code such as the Code Napoleon. I am grateful to Jason Neyers for this point.

independence of private law from social ends. These points, important though they are, do not fully answer Hedley's criticisms and to the extent that they do not, we reach something of an impasse.

Weinrib's thesis represents merely one attempt to rationalise the distinction between private and public law. In Chapter 4 of this book, Christian Turner uses the public–private distinction in a very different way, with dramatic taxonomic consequences. Turner's vision is inspired in part by the very same law and economics movement that Weinrib's work criticises[66] and his concern is therefore certainly not to isolate 'law' from 'politics'. He nonetheless regards a separation of public from private as inevitable in *any* legal system.[67] Whereas Weinrib starts with the idea of private right and adopts its demands as the basis for a public system of coercion, Turner begins with a public enterprise (described as the 'management of a set of coercive resources') and works out what the conditions of coercion must be in such an enterprise. In this context, the public/private distinction 'makes transparent [the fact] that many questions … are in fact questions of the competence of institutions'. In actual fact, the distinction relied upon by Turner is less concerned with public and private *institutions* than with 'specific institutional *decisions* [that] are made publicly and privately'. Turner calls these decisions 'lawmaking' and 'prosecution' – so, for example, contract law can be understood as the law where both law-making and prosecution are private decisions while tort law involves public (that is collective) law-making and private prosecution. The assignment of a decision to public or private actors is to be determined by the relative competency of those actors to make decisions that accord with the preferences of those who will be bound by the decisions. A key aspect of actors' competency in this regard relates to their capacity to make, receive and process information.

Two comments may be made about Turner's use of the public/private distinction. First, as I intimated above, it is not an example of the phenomenon identified by Horwitz whereby jurists 'create a legal science that would sharply separate law from politics'.[68] Turner acknowledges that any system of private law will have distributive consequences and that these are subject to political revision. Second, Turner's use of the public/

[66] In particular, by Guido Calabresi and A. Douglas Melamed, 'Property Rules, Liability Rules, and Inalienability: One View of the Cathedral' (1972) 85 *Harvard Law Review* 1089.

[67] Turner, p. 119 this volume: 'The public–private distinction is inseparable from law itself'.

[68] Horwitz, 'The History of the Public/Private Distinction', 1425.

private distinction, apart from offering a justification for the basic structure of Anglo-American private law (including the distinction between contract and tort and their distinction from criminal law) enables one to adopt a critical aspect in relation to that legal system. This critical aspect involves posing questions about whether the actors to which questions of law-making and prosecution have been assigned are, in fact, competent to make those decisions. This critical aspect operates both *ex ante* – that is, 'that an institution be composed and empowered in a way likely to render it institutionally competent' – and *ex post* – that is, by 'invalidation of a decision that manifests the incompetence of the institution that reached it'. The various doctrines assembled under the label of 'unconscionability' are examples of such *ex post* critique, in so far as they operate upon 'contracts manifesting unusually poor private calculations'.[69] The critical intuitions that Turner's analysis excites form the basis of a number of practical suggestions he has regarding doctrinal aspects of the law, including the availability of *qui tam* actions and the calculation of punitive damages in tort.

The multiplicity of public/private distinctions and reasons for distinguishing between public and private preclude any hard and fast conclusion that the distinction is always significant or never significant. If the conclusion that there is a private law domain that is never touched by collective (that is public) goals is untenable, the conclusion that the distinction is never informative as to the types of considerations that ought to inform legal reasoning seems equally untenable. Of course, different ideological starting points produce different prescriptions as to what types of considerations ought to be relevant in public and private law. The contributions to Part II of this work all make this point patently clear.

4 Charity law, property law and human rights

The law governing charitable dispositions is a particularly vivid illustration of the encounter between the 'public' and the 'private' in private law. On the one hand, charitable activity is a product of individual (or non-government at least) initiative to allocate resources – by establishing a trust or augmenting the trust assets of a pre-existing foundation – for the assistance of others. It involves a 'private' project to assist others but, since the recipients of that assistance are not a finite class of individuals who

[69] Christian Turner, 'Law's Public/Private Structure' (2012) 39 *Florida State University Law Review* 1003, 1042.

may be identified at the time of the allocation of resources, the enforcement of the trust cannot be achieved 'privately' (that is, on the initiative of the supposed 'beneficiaries') for it is impossible to identify with certainty anyone in whose favour a court can order performance of the trust.[70] Such trusts are enforced by public officials – such as Charity Commissioners (in England) or the relevant state Attorney-General by way of a *relator* action (in Australia). In Turner's scheme (discussed in the previous section), charitable trusts belong to the category *Parens Patriae*, in which obligations are privately created but publicly prosecuted.[71] The involvement of public officials is not merely in the adjudication of a dispute but in prosecution of the proceedings for enforcement of the trust.

Matthew Harding (Chapter 5), writing from within a 'perfectionist' liberal perspective,[72] presents charity law as having facilitative, promotive and creative functions. The encounter between a private project and public enforcement is central to the first function. The facilitative function refers to the state's role in enabling the benefactor's private project as a legally enforceable transaction – charity law, Harding says, maximises the choices that are available to a person to confer benefits upon others. At the same time, Harding concedes that the value of freedom to choose one's projects (so facilitated) is not absolute. The state may, in particular, choose to pursue public goals of efficiency or social justice but the cost to autonomy 'should not be viewed with indifference'.

A logical consequence of the involvement of public officials in the enforcement of private projects is that there are limitations upon the types of private projects that may be pursued by way of charitable dispositions. In other words, the public reasons that motivate the involvement of the state in enforcement do not justify the involvement of the state in every case. Moreover, there may be public reasons that demand that the state refrain from involving itself in the enforcement of some private projects. The limitation has become manifest in at least two ways:

(1) in the requirement that the benefactor's purpose benefits the 'public' (or a significant section of the public);

[70] The 'classic' authority is *Morice* v. *Bishop of Durham* (1804) 9 Ves 399; 32 ER 656 at 658 (Sir William Grant MR).

[71] Turner, p. 138, this volume.

[72] 'Perfectionist' liberalism is concerned with 'the freedom that comes of living a life that is the product of self-directed choices across time among a range of genuine, plausible and valuable options': Harding, p. 151, this volume.

(2) since the advent of 'public' law (statutory) anti-discrimination norms, in a question about the enforceability of trust terms that discriminate between persons on the grounds of race, religion or other unlawful grounds.

The demand for private projects to conform to these public norms gains further impetus from the existence of numerous tax concessions and exemptions for entities engaged in charitable activity.

Adam Parachin (Chapter 6) remarks upon how the cases concerning the public benefit requirement for charitable trusts and anti-discrimination norms are neither precisely aligned, nor wholly at odds with each other. In so far as one can identify a consistent theme in the case law on the public benefit requirement, it is that there must be a rational connection between the class of potential beneficiaries and the benefactor's stated charitable purpose. As Parachin points out, the endowment of a church that chooses to perform marriage ceremonies for heterosexual couples only is likely to survive the public benefit requirement, whereas a scholarship fund for the benefit of persons in heterosexual marriages would be unlikely to do so. Both are prima facie discriminatory but, in so far as the church has a theology of marriage that contemplates marriage as heterosexual in character, the basis of discrimination adopted by its benefactor has a rational connection with the advancement of religion. Similarly, trusts that are said to be for the relief of poverty *must* – not merely may – discriminate against people who are too wealthy to require assistance.[73] Parachin's ultimate point is that although charitable trusts may sometimes be unenforceable because of the way that they exclude certain groups of people from the class of potential beneficiaries, the idea of a discriminatory charity is nonetheless not a contradictory or nonsensical one, as some have suggested. Charity law's own doctrines may, coincidentally, prevent the enforcement of *some* trusts the terms of which happen to violate public law (statutory) anti-discrimination norms, but when they do so, it is not *because* the trust violates these public norms. This does not rule out striking down the trust on public grounds, but if this occurs, it is not to be misunderstood as a consequence of private law's own internal logic.

Michelle Flaherty (Chapter 7) also considers the encounter between private law and public law equality jurisprudence as part of a broader investigation of the relationship between private law and human rights.

[73] For an example of a trust that failed on this basis, see *Re Gwyon* [1930] 1 Ch 255.

Her central point is that the interaction between private law and human rights is a 'cross-pollination', rather than an unidirectional flow of human rights jurisprudence into private law. There is both 'common ground' and 'tension' between the two. Flaherty uses the Canadian case law on testamentary clauses that are conditional upon the testator's widow remaining unmarried to illustrate her point. Differences between the Canadian common law jurisdictions and Quebec in relation to this issue represent different ways of resolving the tension between private law concepts and human rights concepts. In the common law jurisdictions, the question as to whether such a condition is enforceable is typically resolved within a private law paradigm. The dominant formal concern is with the nature of the testator's intentions in imposing the condition.[74] The private law analysis nonetheless remains sensitive to considerations of the public (collective) interest, such as the importance of upholding the institution of marriage. In Quebec, by way of contrast, the condition is subject to the scrutiny of the Quebec Charter and its enforceability is therefore a 'public' human rights question. Within this paradigm, the testator's intentions are formally irrelevant, the key issue being simply whether or not the condition's *effect* is unlawfully to discriminate against the widow on grounds of marital status. Although this approach might appear to be radically different, some account of the intention of the testator nonetheless features in the analysis, by indirectly influencing courts' assessment as to whether a condition's effect is to discriminate on the basis of the widow's marital status.[75] Courts in both the common law jurisdictions and Quebec therefore arrive at similar outcomes but by different paths of reasoning. The analysis of the Quebec courts illustrates the influence of private law concepts on the interpretation of public law human rights concepts. The common law approach does not depend upon public law human rights concepts as such, but incorporates consideration of public (collective) values into its analysis. The point this rather neatly serves to make is that *both* private and public law are engaged in their own ways in balancing individual and collective interests and that the respective positions they take regarding this balance can prove mutually informative.

[74] If the intention is to prevent the widow from remarrying, the condition is invalid, but if it is to protect the widow from being exploited by 'opportunists', it will usually be upheld.

[75] So, for example, a condition that is based upon the impecunious status of the widow's new husband – and that, so it might be inferred, expresses an intention on the part of the testator to protect the widow – has been found not to be a distinction based on the marital status of the widow.

5 Commercial law – corporate and finance law

Commercial law is a meta-category that extends beyond 'private law' as I have defined it, but which encapsulates parts of private law within it. Like charity law, it provides a topical showcase for current debates about private and public. It yields cross-overs and contrasts between the interests of individuals and groups, domestic and transnational norms, the realms of the state and the market, between party autonomy and social regulation and between privately created and democratically created law.

In Chapter 8, Alastair Hudson describes a breakdown of the boundaries between public and private in the field of finance law, a sphere that he describes as a synthesis of substantive concepts drawn from contract, tort, property law, criminal law, equity, private international law and legislative regulation. In his description, he points to some important differences between regulation and the 'substantive' private law, which include not simply the former's overtly coercive orientation, but also its consultative nature, its susceptibility to rapid policy change, its unpredictability and the patchiness of its enforcement practices. At the same time, he argues that it is crucial to recognise a number of ways in which 'private' financial institutions, such as banks, are now in reality 'quasi-public': the recent 'credit-crunch' has forced many banks into state ownership, their services are as vital to the collective interests of citizens as many public services, their capacity to dictate public policy in light of the impoverishment of nations following the global financial crisis is enormous and, even after the ripples of the UK swaps scandals have finally begun to subside, they continue to fund vast tracts of state activity. The implication is that banks are nowadays effectively engaging in (or indirectly controlling) quasi-governmental activity without the attendant restraint of democratic accountability. This, Hudson suggests, has repercussions for the way in which private law should set its standards when adjudicating their behaviour – the more 'public' private financial institutions become, the more appropriate it is to use regulatory standards to inform the content of the duties that private law applies to them in their dealings with other persons and institutions.

Hudson's main call is therefore for greater permeability between the standards applied to financial institutions under traditional common law doctrines and those (often stricter) regulatory standards applied to them by the Financial Services Authority (FSA). Permeation can work usefully in both directions – FSA regulatory standards ought to be used by courts to fill out and bolster the private law obligations of banks and sellers of financial products, and private law concepts (such as equitable notions of 'inequality of bargaining power', 'undue influence' and 'good conscience') can in turn be utilised to help interpret and re-energise regulatory standards where these are lacking, or lack detailed content. The premise of this argument for synthesis between regulation and the substantive private law is that the two serve common functional ends ('protecting customers' and 'keeping the economic world turning'). One of its most immediate and important implications is that courts currently place too much weight on traditional 'private law' values such as party autonomy and freedom of contract when determining the standards expected of financial actors. This has allowed the accountability of such actors in private law to slip well below that which exists in public law.

Whilst some courts are receptive to the idea of transposing public law standards into private law, others are hesitant, as Hudson admits. It is not clear whether this is because judges regard the forms of accountability that exist in public (regulatory) and private law as generically different, or simply because they are ignorant of public law standards when adjudicating private law disputes. That the former may be the case is suggested by the way in which courts deal with similar invitations to 'synthesise' public and private standards when called upon to fix the tort liabilities of public authorities for maladministration. Here, courts reject the idea that 'public' failings are necessarily also 'private' failings – if they were, all administrative error adversely affecting a person's private interests (including perhaps even procedural errors) would resound in private law damages. We must therefore be sure, when engaging in any project of synthesis, that the entities being synthesised share a common purpose. The point that our maladministration example makes is that administrative law and tort law are probably not engaged in the same sort of exercise – one addresses the *validity* of public action, the other addresses responsibility of a different sort for its harmful consequences. Similarly, the synthesis of private law and public regulation proposed by Hudson is only likely to be sustainable, I suggest, to the extent that the two share the same deterrent and standard-setting goals and this is clearly a question on which judges currently take different views. This does not so much undermine Hudson's normative thesis, perhaps, as highlight the urgency of resolving some of the fundamental theoretical issues referred to in the previous section regarding the basic aims of public and private law.

The thrust of Anita Krug's chapter on corporate law (Chapter 9) is akin to Hudson's, in the sense that she also invites us to think of that field as importantly 'public', even though it is often conceived of as describing a private contractarian relationship between individuals (directors, managers and shareholders).[76] Her case for regarding (US) corporate law as 'public' is not, however, built simply on the fact that corporations are regulated. Rather, it is built on intuitions derived from the debate about corporate globalisation and the associated movement towards cross-jurisdictional corporate law 'convergence'. Whether such convergence is ever likely to occur is debatable, but in the context of Krug's argument, that is beside the point. Her argument is that, whatever the answer to this question, the very terms of the globalisation debate disclose the fact that decisions about the proper shape of corporate governance laws entail judgments about a wide range of social issues, including economic efficiency, environmental protection, respect for human rights, freedom, deterrence and social equality. In contrast to the sort of 'bottom-up' thinking that is characteristic of conventional private law reasoning, this type of 'public interest' thinking is 'top-down' and conducted from a 'highly elevated position', which makes it much more akin to social policy analysis than traditional private law reasoning. Decisions about corporate law, being decisions about these fundamental values, are 'constitutive' of a society in the same way as are a society's criminal laws – they say something crucial about the community, its standards and expectations.

A good reason for understanding corporate law in this 'public' way is that it might encourage those framing corporate laws 'to think more critically … about broader social and economic effects' of their decisions than they otherwise would. In an age crying out for greater corporate social responsibility (and still angry about the market failures that led to the global financial crisis), this clearly touches a nerve. Attempting to craft the levers for 'responsible' corporate action from traditional private law, market-moulded tools such as share-pricing, voluntarism and contract is beset with difficulties and it seems probable that only a more 'public' (non-market-oriented, non-voluntary) paradigm of thinking will yield the sort of responsibility practices that the public desires and the world collectively needs.[77] Krug's important critique makes that fact patent and

[76] For another account challenging the private paradigm of corporate law, see Marc T. Moore, 'Is Corporate Law "Private" (and Why Does it Matter)?' (20 December 2012), available at: http://ssrn.com/abstract=2192163 (last accessed 17 May 2013); Marc T. Moore, *Corporate Governance in the Shadow of the State* (Oxford: Hart Publishing, 2013). The mixed political economy of the company is explored from a variety of perspectives in John Parkinson, Andrew Gamble and Gavin Kelly (eds.), *The Political Economy of the Company* (Oxford: Hart Publishing, 2000).

[77] For a recent approach that lies half way between market and regulatory approaches to the problems of social cost (and premised on the view that neither regulation nor voluntarism

helps to recharacterise the types of conversations that are needed when thinking about the future of corporate law.

6 Torts, class actions and remedies

The intersection between public and private in the law of torts is equally fertile. The origins of tort and the criminal law are so historically wedded that functional overlaps between the two spheres tend to persist, even where they are no longer logically demanded.[78] The rise of welfarism gave rise in the latter part of the twentieth century to acute debates about tort's compensatory 'function' and to the sense that tort law was itself 'just another system' for doing the work that public social insurance schemes might (more efficiently) do in redressing the effects of illness and injury.[79] Similarly, the more overt use of 'policy-based reasoning' in common law courts – particularly in relation to negligence liabilities[80] – acted as an intense irritant to those conservative 'private' models of tort law that aim to push law and politics into entirely discrete domains. As a sphere of private law protecting some of our most basic human interests such as life, limb and liberty, the law of torts has also proven particularly open to the influence of 'public law' human rights arguments, as I intimated above. The abolition of Crown immunities and the proliferation of public powers (with associated increased social expectations of protection) have made the state a relatively new and especially attractive (solvent) defendant in contemporary tort litigation. Finally, the advent of class action litigation for 'mass torts' has allowed individual tort claims to be procedurally

work), see A. Johnson, 'Facing up to Social Cost: The Real Meaning of Corporate Social Responsibility' (2011) 20 *Griffith Law Review* 221. The idea is to use procedural regulation to require corporations to identify their social costs, so that these may then be dealt with voluntarily.

78 As, for example, in the case of punitive damages, where a retributive aim arguably persists in the civil law that might be confined to the criminal law.

79 P. S. Atiyah, *Accidents, Compensation and the Law* (London: Weidenfeld and Nicolson, 1970); Terence G. Ison, *Accident Compensation: A Commentary on the New Zealand Scheme* (London: Croom Helm, 1980). Atiyah is well known for a later shift from welfarism to the market in P. S. Atiyah, *The Damages Lottery* (Oxford: Hart Publishing, 1997).

80 For an influential analysis, see Jane Stapleton, 'Duty of Care and Economic Loss: A Wider Agenda' (1991) 107 *Law Quarterly Review* 249; Jane Stapleton, 'Duty of Care Factors: A Selection from the Judicial Menus', in Peter Cane and Jane Stapleton (eds.), *The Law of Obligations: Essays in Honour of John Fleming* (Oxford University Press, 1998), p. 59.

'grouped' in unprecedented ways.[81] The way in which the class action system is set up and funded in many jurisdictions now effectively places the decision to initiate private law actions in respect of widespread harms in the hands of commercial litigators (the market), rather than in the hands of individual tort victims. In substance, the inception of actions in such cases lies beyond the remit of the tort victim and in private calculations about the potential costs and benefits to litigators, even where the action's purpose is to protect the victim's interests. At one and the same time, class actions are often conceived of as complementing, challenging or rivalling the state's authority to act in the public good.[82] This is especially so in the United States, where private law is viewed as a critically important mechanism for the enforcement of public standards and for the implementation of regulatory aims such as consumer and environmental protection, on the basis that the state is simply not up to – or cannot be trusted with – the task.[83]

In his contribution to this work (Chapter 10), Dan Priel notes these and other historical causes of tort becoming 'public'. He observes that much of the public characterisation of tort has hitherto taken place in the context of the tort of negligence, with the 'intentional' torts tending to be thought of as bastions of traditional, deontological, rights-based thinking. His chapter seeks to turn that assumption on its head. Whilst it is indeed the case that courts often regard the intentional torts as 'vindicating' individual rights, he argues that there is at least one important sense of 'vindication' in such cases that has nothing to do with constituting relationships of right *between individuals*, but which is demonstrably public. According to this conception, vindicating a person's rights entails 'providing a public forum in which claims of infringement ... are ... both examined and, where a violation has been found, protected *by the state*'. Vindication consists in a '*finding* [in the wake of *investigation*] [in a "public and impartial forum"] that a particular individual's rights have been violated and the recognition that on certain occasions such a finding is of general public significance'. According to Priel, therefore, the machinery of private law is sometimes legitimately used to serve public, not private ends. This

[81] At least twenty-one countries now support class actions: Deborah R. Hensler, 'The Future of Mass Litigation: Global Class Actions and Third-Party Litigation Funding' (2011) 79 *George Washington Law Review* 306, 307.

[82] Samuel Issacharoff, 'Class Actions and State Authority' (2012) 44 *Loyola University Chicago Law Journal* 369.

[83] For an account of the phenomenon and its social explanations, see Paul D. Carrington, 'The American Tradition of Private Law Enforcement' (2004) 12 *German Law Journal* 1413.

explains why a court may legitimately, as in *Ashley* v. *Chief Constable of Sussex Police*,[84] allow a battery claim to proceed against the police, even when the latter has accepted liability in negligence for all the harm that resulted from it. Tort law in this instance provides an exceptional, court-ordered public inquiry, investigating government behaviour in the collective interest of all members of society and potentially strengthening *constitutional* values.

It is important to recognise, as Priel does, that the extent to which these public functions can be achieved systematically by tort law is necessarily constrained by its form. The irony is that if tort really does have a 'public interest' function as investigatory ombudsman, this is a function that is ultimately controllable by the very party who stands to be investigated – all inquiries can be stopped in an instant by a simple admission of liability and an appropriate payout by the defendant. Whether the case is one of a battered citizen, misfeasance in public office resulting in economic harm[85] or a case of a foreign national being falsely imprisoned,[86] the capacity for tort to act as forensic investigator in respect of events is limited by the state's effective capacity to buy the right to silence. In such cases, there seem to be real risks in 'privatising' the process of public inquiry.

The difficulties that this point poses for an instrumental understanding of *Ashley* are noted elsewhere[87] and invite speculation as to whether the result might equally be explained by non-functional approaches. If it is a requirement of a *system* of private rights that there be a process in place for their declaration and adjudication, as Weinrib suggests, it is surely also necessary for individuals to have a (public law) right against the state to bring actions before courts to have infringements of their private rights adjudicated. This does not explain, of course, why private litigants should have to bear the costs of this operation. This coerces litigants into funding state adjudication functions that probably ought to be funded collectively by the taxpayer. It must also be acknowledged that there is strong support for a Priel-style 'public' conception of 'rights vindication' in a range of recent 'public law' cases involving 'constitutional'

[84] [2008] 1 AC 962 (*Ashley*).

[85] *Northern Territory* v. *Mengel* (1995) 185 CLR 307; *Three Rivers District Council* v. *Bank of England (No 3)* [2003] 2 AC 1.

[86] *Walumba Lumba* v. *Secretary of State for the Home Department* [2011] UKSC 12.

[87] See Kit Barker, 'Private and Public: The Mixed Concept of Vindication in Torts and Private Law', in Stephen G. A. Pitel, Jason W. Neyers and Erika Chamberlain (eds.), *Tort Law: Challenging Orthodoxy* (Oxford: Hart Publishing, 2013).

torts.[88] In a number of these cases, Commonwealth courts have awarded symbolic sums of 'vindicatory' damages to individuals in actions against the state, even where the individual has suffered no harm, simply in order to 'mark' the infringement of his or her right. This adds an interesting and controversial 'public messaging' function to damages awards – one that is distinct from compensation of losses, restitution of gains, or punishment. The idea of what it means to vindicate rights in such cases is a little different to Priel's own conception (the idea is to *declare* important rights rather than to forensically investigate matters in the public interest), but they share his 'public' characterisation of the idea. They ascribe to the very idea of vindication purposes that extend beyond the parties to the dispute in question.

The functional approach to tort law taken by Priel is pursued more broadly by Jeff Berryman and Robyn Carroll in the final chapter of the book, which focuses on an increasingly important phenomenon in tort litigation – the class action. The authors consider one remedy in particular that can be deployed in the context of such actions, namely cy-près distribution by a court of class damages funds.[89] The remedy is available in Canada (though not yet in Australia) in instances in which it is impossible to identify all individual tort victims in the victim class, or where individual distributions of the damages fund to these victims would be uneconomic because the cost of the distribution would exceed their losses. Whilst the authors acknowledge that a main purpose of cy-près distribution in such cases is to provide a form of 'indirect' compensation to tort victims, they argue that such distributions also serve a secondary purpose in deterring wrongs and providing wrongdoers with efficient incentives to modify their behaviour. From this point of view, it does not really matter whether a cy-près distribution remedy benefits only the victims themselves – a judge could equally order that the damages fund be used to any end (for example, funding a public education conference) that is likely to achieve behavioural modification. The key priority is that the wrongdoer be forced to fully internalise the social costs of its actions, by ensuring that it does not retain any part of the damages fund. Not only can cy-près distribution deter wrongdoing in this way, but it can align

[88] E.g., *Attorney General of Trinidad and Tobago* v. *Ramanoop* [2006] 1 AC 328 (PC); *Vancouver* v. *Ward* [2010] 2 SCR 28. For discussion, see Barker, 'Private and Public'.

[89] These funds can in principle comprise the court's assessment of the overall damage done by a defendant; or, it now seems, the gains that the defendant has made by doing the wrong.

closely with victims' remedial preferences, since one of the things victims appear to want (perhaps as much, or even more, than monetary compensation) is an acknowledgement by a wrongdoer that wrong has been done, education and a change in the wrongdoer's future behaviour. Cy-près distribution orders hence join a number of other private law remedies including disgorgement, punitive damages and injunctive relief in seeking directly to prospectively change behaviour. Equally, tort law itself has to be understood as a pluralistic collaboration between corrective justice and deterrent goals.

This functional approach to private law remedies could not, on its face at least, be further removed from Weinribian understandings of private law. In the Kantian conception, private law remedies are simply the mirror reflection of primary rights – they are not to be picked and mixed with a view to achieving behavioural ends. This does not mean that all forms of 'deterrence' are inconsistent with Weinrib's vision. Arthur Ripstein has made the point that some forms of deterrence brought about by private law remedies are entirely consistent with it – the prospect of enforcing bilateral private rights is a perfectly acceptable means of protecting them.[90] What is impermissible in the Weinribian/Kantian scheme is *determining or justifying the content* of private law rights or remedies by reference to their likely behavioural effects – private law remedies cannot be *constructed* by social purposes.[91] Although Berryman and Carroll hence depict interpersonal justice and deterrence as plural aims that can collaborate effectively within the same private adjudication system, this is not a view that Weinrib shares. For him, the idea is impossibly incoherent, unless all we mean by 'deterrence' is encouraging people to respect rights that are determined non-instrumentally.[92]

We therefore come to the end of the book confronted by the question of which comes first – justice or its behavioural effects? For Weinrib, the justice 'chicken' precedes the behavioural 'egg' and any incentive effects

[90] Ripstein, *Force and Freedom*, p. 84: 'Because wrongdoing grounds redress, coercive enforcement of private remedies can also operate to deter wrongdoing, for deterrence is just the public manifestation of the prophylactic sense of coercion … if … I keep my hands off your goods … because I fear that I will be made to disgorge my gains or repair your losses, your rights operate on my capacity for choice indirectly … That is just to say that the prospect of enforcing rights may be used to protect right.' See also Ernest J. Weinrib, 'Deterrence and Corrective Justice' (2002) 50 *University of California Los Angeles Law Review* 621. Weinrib distinguishes at 624 between deterrence as a 'component in the justification of particular tort norms' and deterrence going to the 'operation of the ensemble of norms as a system of positive law'.

[91] *Ibid.* [92] *Ibid.*

simply reflect the existence of an effective system of rights. In the more pragmatic, instrumental world of Berryman and Carroll, behavioural incentives can actually drive the way remedies are modelled and the egg therefore, in a sense, hatches into the chicken. The paradox of the chicken and the egg is perhaps a good place to close our discussion, if only because it demonstrates the impossibility of deriving an answer to the question posed through the application of abstract logic. It can only be resolved through an honest appraisal of our ideological priorities.

7 Conclusions

It is not apposite in an essay collection of this sort to dictate the conclusions that readers should draw from the various interactions between public and private that it describes. Nonetheless, I offer three basic conclusions that I think can be drawn from this exercise, whilst allowing readers to reach many more of their own.

The first and perhaps most obvious conclusion is that, despite rumours to the contrary spread by realists in the twentieth century, the private/public 'distinction' is far from dead. No doubt Heracles thought the game was over when first he struck the Hydra's head, but he swiftly suffered a sobering surprise when several more grew in its place. In the myth, the process of division was ultimately stemmed with the help of Heracles' nephew Iolaus, but that seems to be an unlikely conclusion to this particular story, which, if anything, is only now really heating up. Whilst it is true to say that no single distinction between public and private exists in the law and that the various different distinctions referred to throughout this work are unlikely to prove 'dispositive' for legal purposes for the reasons Lucy and Williams provide, there is nevertheless very good reason to think that these distinctions will continue to prove informative and, in some measure, influential upon judges and policy-makers alike. Peter Cane once astutely remarked that the public/private distinction only really begins to be useful when its multifaceted nature is properly appreciated.[93] I would add that it is important to bear in mind that the many distinctions adverted to serve different purposes, being the product of questions asked by inquirers from different disciplines and in different contexts. Since all distinctions begin with a question, we must ascertain the purpose and context of the question before passing judgment on the answer it prompts. There is, of course, always some risk involved in multiplying distinctions,

[93] Cane, 'Public Law and Private Law', p. 78.

at least if one's purpose is to achieve clarity or systemic stability in the law. But there is also no doubt that the more distinctions we make, the more we understand. Law is no exception to this rule.

A second conclusion is that, despite the pressures from the 'public' that I have identified, there remain key aspects of private law's 'privateness' (in one sense or another of that term) that are persistently important and that explain its resistance to being swallowed up in all that is 'public'. These features include:

(1) the facilitative nature of many of its rules (particularly those regarding agreement and donation – whether charitable or not – but also regarding the division and enjoyment of property in sophisticated ways);
(2) the respect private law traditionally accords to personal freedom, consent, dignity and trust;
(3) the relative stability and predictability that is associated with its common law (judicial) origins and precedential wealth;[94]
(4) the right of initiative (and control) it presumptively places in the hands of those who have suffered wrong; and
(5) the strong levels of protection it has accorded (and continues to accord) to some of our most basic individual interests and liberties.

The strength of private law's protections – in particular its 'in principle' commitment of private law to the idea of *full* restoration for individual victims of injustice (corrective justice) – is enduringly morally attractive, so much so that it can usefully inform public debate and public policy responses to these same types of event. Is it good enough, for example, for the Australian government to pay stolen generation victims A$5,000 *ex gratia* and make an apology for historic public policy failings in removing aboriginal children from their parents?[95] Public policy currently appears to approve of this approach, but private law rightly questions it and this questioning may be morally important not just in precipitating private actions (perhaps that path will prove fruitless, or too expensive), but also in leading to a reappraisal in the *public* sphere of the way in which administrative reparation schemes currently operate. If private law

[94] Much 'public law' in the sense in which I have defined it has judicial origins too, of course. The word 'privateness' here is being used to refer to the non-legislative origins of the law. Public law can also be 'private' in this sense.

[95] On which, see Andrea Durbach, 'The Cost of a Wounded Society: Reparations and the Illusion of Reconciliation' (2008) 12 *Australian Indigenous Law Review* 22, 28.

suggests a more generous, more thorough commitment to making victims good, should this not at least be *taken into account* in formulating public policy? It hardly seems right that the norms private law expresses should simply be disregarded, given that they represent centuries of institutionally approved 'right thinking' about the question. Equally, it is sometimes pointed out that some of the key personal values traditionally associated with private law (personal consent, facilitation and trust in particular) are so important that they undergird (and are assumed by) frameworks of public democracy.[96] None of this is meant to suggest that private law or 'private values' necessarily trump or are prior to 'public' law or 'public' values historically or normatively. In so far as private law existed even prior to the nation-state, it was still subject to the influence of public authority in one sense or another. We know (and this is illustrated in several chapters in this book) that private law has always balanced public (collective) and individual interests; and the capacities and effectiveness of private law rules clearly depend in practical (if not deontological) terms on public institutions being available to adjudicate upon and enforce them. The capacities of private law also nowadays seem to depend increasingly on a type of procedural 'collectivism' that is more traditionally associated with *relator* actions and public prosecutions in the criminal law. The question of normative 'priority' between public and private lies well beyond the scope of this chapter. All I suggest is that there are very good explanations for the persistence of 'private' ideology(ies) in modern thinking; and that these ideologies also extend (and could usefully now be further extended in some cases – particularly when reviewing the adequacy of public 'reparation' regimes) to the 'public' sphere.

A third and final conclusion takes the form of a characterisation. It is that the challenges presented for private law by its encounters with 'the public' raise a series of complex coordination problems. That is to say, rational decisions about the future shape of private law doctrines require further thinking about:

(1) the coordination of the interests of ('private') individuals with those of groups and society as a whole;
(2) the relative use of legislative ('public') and judicial techniques within private law itself and the impacts of any particular balance upon the

[96] Allan Beever, 'Our Most Fundamental Rights', Chapter 3 in Donal Nolan and Andrew Robertson (eds.), *Rights and Private Law* (Oxford: Hart Publishing, 2012).

system's stability from both a constitutional and practical point of view;[97]

(3) the coordination of public (state) and private (market) resources in the initiation, funding and settlement of private law claims (who brings and sponsors private law actions and why?);
(4) the coordination of the private laws of one state with those of others in the context of globalised markets;
(5) the coordination of systems of private law rules with 'public' (state-run) welfare systems, such as social security, 'compensation' and 'reparation' schemes, as well as with 'market' mechanisms for dealing with risk and harm, such as first- and third-party insurance systems; and
(6) the coordination of private law rules with public law rules, such as human rights provisions, administrative law rules and criminal provisions.

There are, no doubt, many other types of coordination that are needed. For coordination to be complete, of course, we would need a single stable control point from which decisions can be made about the appropriate strategy to adopt in the exercise. Public and private systems have several different control points: judges, legislatures (both primary and secondary) and public policy-makers, the composition of which varies greatly. Perhaps the best we can hope for in the end is a praxis – a system in which those developing the common law part of private law, on the one hand, and those legislating (within it) and formulating public policy (around it), on the other, will look in some measure to each other's actions and reasons in determining the wisdom or appropriateness of their own – what one might call a model of voluntary coordination, that operates reflexively and horizontally between the various actors and systems.[98] Thinking about these challenges as coordination problems nonetheless alerts us to the fact that what is required in decisions about the reach and shape of private law in the twenty-first century is not *simply* an ideological matter (though it is certainly this), but a practical one too. Whatever are the ends

[97] For one, recent construction of this relationship, see Peter Cane, 'Taking Disagreement Seriously: Courts, Legislatures and the Reform of Tort Law' (2005) 25 *Oxford Journal of Legal Studies* 393.

[98] Such a model cannot offer *perfect* coherence but still promises *some* level of coherence – a greater level, at least, than one in which all actors and systems simply ignore what each other are doing. In practical terms, also, the idea of a set of systems coordinated from a singular, higher point is likely to run into epistemological difficulties. How could any single, centralised actor ever know all that needs to be known to make perfect coordination possible?

of private law, or the moral principles it serves, we must be certain that it is indeed the best way of meeting those ends or instantiating those principles, given all options. Moreover, the fact that achieving those ends or instantiating those principles requires the participation of public institutions (and public funds) cannot be left out of account in determining its proper contours.

PART II

Private and public: definitions, theory and taxonomy

2

Public and private

Neither deep nor meaningful?

WILLIAM LUCY AND ALEXANDER WILLIAMS

... to some faint meaning make pretence ...
John Dryden, *Mac Flecknoe* (1682), I.1

Visionaries and philosophers are often prone to grandiose statements. Friedrich Nietzsche's declarations that God was both dead and our longest lie are among the most grandiose.[1] While such claims have almost no equivalents in the pragmatic discipline and practice of law, this certainly does not guarantee that we lawyers work and think free from questionable, mystifying and outmoded beliefs. One such belief is the idea that there is a single and deeply significant distinction between 'public' and 'private' that lawyers have struggled – and are currently struggling – to unearth. Being lawyers, we are almost occupationally unable to make any grandiose claim, not least the one that this belief in the significance of 'the' public/private distinction is one of our longest lies. Our argument is instead that this belief requires substantial amendment. This is because there are many distinctions between public and private, not only one; and because the various versions of that distinction operative in law are almost never doctrinally dispositive. We unpack these claims in the three sections that follow. It should, however, be noted at the outset that in denying that 'the' public/private distinction is deeply significant we are not affirming that it is *in*significant. Our claim is that lawyers are prone to exaggerate its importance, to regard it as more fundamental and determinative than it really is. It is no more significant than the legion of complex and

[1] See Friedrich Wilhelm Nietzsche, *The Gay Science*, Bernard Williams (ed.), Josefine Nauckhoff (trans.) (Cambridge University Press, 2001), paras. 108, 125, 343, 344.

multiform concepts – such as reasonableness, intention, causation and so on – that lawyers interpret, apply and contest every day.

1 Not one but many

The claim that there are not one but many versions of the public/private distinction can be disaggregated into two principal components.[2] The first holds that there is no single version of the public/private distinction operative in law and life but a number of them; the second insists that some legal versions of the distinction operate either practically (in particular cases) or juristically (in legal thought, teaching and commentary). We attempt to unpack and substantiate both components in this section and the next. In this section, we elucidate five versions of the public/private distinction, each of which is worth separating because, when taken together, they accommodate many apparently contradictory intuitions about 'the' public/private distinction. These intuitions inform the sense many lawyers have, when grappling with questions of public and private, of hitting an impasse or falling into a quagmire. This sense reduces once we appreciate that our apparently conflicting intuitions embody some or many of the following different distinctions between public and private. It is further alleviated by noting two other related points. First, there is a degree of permeability between the versions of the public/private distinction such that attempts to delineate one version can be affected, both positively and negatively, by delineations of other versions of the distinction.

[2] That this claim is something of a platitude in the social sciences and humanities is evident from S. Benn and G. Gaus (eds.), *Public and Private in Social Life* (London: Croom Helm, 1983); B. Moore, Jr, *Privacy* (New York: M. Sharp, 1984); J. Habermas, *The Structural Transformation of the Public Sphere* (Cambridge: Polity, 1989); J. Weintaub and K. Kumar (eds.), *Public and Private in Thought and Practice* (University of Chicago Press, 1997); M. P. d'Entreves and U. Vogel (eds.), *Public and Private: Legal, Political and Philosophical Perspectives* (London: Routledge, 2000); R. Geuss, *Public Goods, Private Goods* (Princeton University Press, 2001). Peter Cane is one of the few jurists to grasp this feature of 'the' public/private distinction in the legal context: see Peter Cane, 'Public and Private Law: A Study in the Analysis and Use of a Legal Concept', in J. Eekelaar and J. Bell (eds.), *Oxford Essays in Jurisprudence: Third Series* (Oxford: Clarendon Press, 1987); Peter Cane, 'Accountability and the Public/Private Distinction', in N. Bamforth and P. Leyland (eds.), *Public Law in a Multi-layered Constitution* (Oxford: Hart Publishing, 2003). On the propriety of extending the claim to the juristic realm, see William Lucy, 'Private and Public: Some Banalities about a Platitude', in C. Mac Amhlaigh, C. Michelon and N. Walker (eds.), *After Public Law* (Oxford: Clarendon Press, 2013), Chapter 2, s. II. Section III of that chapter overlaps with section 1 of this chapter and we are grateful to the editors and publisher of that volume for permission to use that material here.

Second, different versions of the public/private distinction can play different roles within our thought and practice. This issue – dubbed, for want of a better term, 'methodological' – and the permeability of the boundaries between the various versions of the distinction are the fulcrum of section 2. That different versions of the distinction can function in three quite different ways – within legal discourse, externally to it and simultaneously internally and externally to it – adds to the complexity of our thought about public and private. But it does not show that that distinction is either deeply meaningful or completely dispositive in legal disputes. Section 3 addresses the latter point by examining the role one version of the public/private distinction played in some relatively recent cases. We argue that in these cases the role played by the distinction was not dispositive and that this point should not be regarded as news. It is, rather, a banality with which we lawyers are completely familiar, although sometimes prone to forget.

The order of treatment begins with the broadest versions of the distinction (those that apply to all or many social domains) and concludes with a fairly narrow version (which operates in only one social domain).[3] This expository strategy is adopted in part as a cue for the issues explored in sections 2 and 3.

1. The first way of distinguishing public and private is by contrasting matters of general concern with matters of individual concern. The idea that issues of general, communal concern exist independently of those matters of concern to individuals qua individuals had a vivid life in the Roman republic. Matters of general communal concern and ownership were originally marked by the term *res publica*, which, in one sense, was used to highlight the property and interests of the Roman army. That term came to be used in a more general sense, to include matters of concern to the community of Roman citizens in general, including their interest in various public spaces (the Forum and so on).[4] Yet the term is seemingly always contrasted with those matters of concern only to individuals as individuals rather than individuals qua members of subgroups within

[3] By 'social domains' we have in mind nothing more precise than the discernibly different sets of institutions, practices, rules and expectations that constitute social reality.

[4] For an admirably clear and brief discussion of these issues, see Geuss, *Public Goods, Private Goods*, Chapter 3. The Greeks, it seems, did not view these matters in the same way: for an interesting discussion of fourth-century Athenian thought, see Moore, *Privacy*, Chapter 2. A. Saxonhouse, 'The Classical Greek Conceptions of Public and Private', Chapter 15 in S. Benn and G. Gaus (eds.), *Public and Private in Social Life* (London: Croom Helm, 1983) provides a broader but no less interesting survey.

the community. The latter restriction is in need of justification, since the assumption that, when defining the realm of the private, 'individual concern' must mean 'single individual concern' (and not the concern of a collection of individuals) is just that: an assumption.

This assumption makes it impossible for groups of individuals (incorporated or unincorporated, but smaller than everyone or the vast majority) to join together in their concern over some matter and remain private.[5] But there is no obvious and strong reason why we should not regard the interest a group of individuals has in some matter as private, provided this group is a subgroup of some larger group. The contrast between public and private in this context is therefore one between all, on the one hand, and many, some or few on the other. Where the group of individuals with some or other interest is identical with all the members of the only grouping in play, then it seems proper to characterise their interest not as private but as 'the' public interest. The absence of hard and fast rules of usage here also allows another twist: we might, quite properly, regard the interests of a group larger than a mere handful of people as representing the public interest in some circumstances. So, for example, it is not crazy to say that the public interest in a particular community would be served by the construction of a bridge across a river or a busy road, even when that community is small and when far fewer than all members will use the bridge. This scenario could also be justifiably characterised as an instance of private interest – where that means something more than 'single individual concern' but less than 'the concern of each and every member of the group'.

Bearing in mind these leeways of usage, a plausible interpretation of this version of the distinction between public and private can take alternate forms. The two terms could be used to contrast matters of relevance and interest to the whole or the vast majority of a community, on the one hand, with matters that are of relevance and interest to either individuals taken singly or to subgroups of individuals (parents, occupants of a particular locale and so on) on the other. The contrast here is between almost all (public) and some (private), rather than between many and

[5] This seems to have been James Harrington's view: 'the people, taken apart, are but so many private interests, but if you take them together they are the public interest': J. Harrington and J. Toland, *The Oceana and Other Works of James Harrington* (London: A. Millar, 1656, 1700), pp. 154–5. For Quentin Skinner, this is an expression of the neo-Roman view that the will of the people is nothing more than 'the sum of the wills of each individual citizen': Quentin Skinner, *Liberty Before Liberalism* (Cambridge University Press, 1998), pp. 28–9.

one. Alternatively, the terms public and private could be used to characterise either the interests of all, or the interests of any but the very smallest group, on one hand, and the interests of individuals qua individuals on the other. The contrast here is between the related many (public) and the unrelated few (private).[6] Since usage licenses both characterisations, a case should be made for preferring one over the other. No such case made is made here, however, since our argument requires only that these different uses be brought to light.

This variability of usage, and the way in which it permits lines to be drawn slightly differently in one and the same context, is evident in the deliberations of the English courts when determining the charitable status of a trust. One test that any trust must satisfy in order to be regarded as charitable in English law is that it be of public benefit.[7] The courts distinguish between sufficiently and insufficiently public groups for this purpose in ways that make use of each alternative formulation of this version of the public/private distinction. Thus it has been held that a trust can be of public benefit even if it benefits only a small number of people in a particular locality. The 'public' here is therefore envisaged as a very small, small or medium-sized group of individuals with an interest in common; it must, however, be more than just 'private individuals' or 'a fluctuating body of private individuals'.[8] Furthermore, even a very large number of individuals, such as 110,000 employees of a large multinational company, may not be enough to constitute the public.[9] What marks the line between a sufficiently and insufficiently 'public' group is thus not immediately obvious. It is something the courts struggle with and, viewed generously, is clearly a matter of judgment.

In the exercise of this judgment, the courts have concluded that trusts for the benefit of numerically very small groups, such as elderly Presbyterians or the occupants of a particular old persons' home, benefit a sufficiently public group.[10] By contrast, it seems that a trust for the building and

[6] We do not claim that the quantifiers ('almost all', 'many', 'some', 'few') in these two formulations are ultimately logically robust; we hold only that they have some intuitive and serviceable 'everyday sense'.

[7] Charities Act 2006, s. 2(1)(b) and s. 3. The case law on public benefit prior to the Act is still valid by virtue of s. 3(3) of the Act. The Charity Commission's guidance on the nature of public benefit has recently been found wanting: *The Independent Schools Council* v. *The Charity Commission* [2011] UKUT 421.

[8] *Verge* v. *Summerville* [1924] AC 496 (PC) at 499 (Lord Wrenbury).

[9] See *Oppenheim* v. *Tobacco Securities Trust Co. Ltd.* [1951] AC 297 (HL) (*Oppenheim*).

[10] See *Joseph Rowntree Memorial Trust Housing Association* v. *Attorney General* [1983] Ch 159 (Ch); *Re Neal* (1966) 110 SJ 549 (Ch).

maintenance of a bridge open only to impecunious Methodists would not be of public benefit.[11] The former small groups are a segment of the public while the latter group, which could be numerically identical, is not: the distinction the courts are drawing here is therefore not one between the very many (public) and the very few (private). The courts have also accepted that trusts for the giving of public masses in a particular church and for the benefit of a specific synagogue are of public benefit, one reason being that both the church and synagogue in question were open to the public at large.[12] A trust for the benefit of a Carmelite order was held to be non-charitable on the grounds that, inter alia, the order's life had no public aspect, but was given over entirely to 'private' religious worship and meditation.[13] It seems that the only sure-fire blocks to charitable status, when the public benefit requirement is in play, is the fact that the group that stands to benefit is either much too small ('numerically negligible'[14]) or consists of members all or many of whom have a personal nexus with the benefactor(s).[15] While the courts will sometimes regard a numerically negligible group as private on grounds of its size, they will also usually regard a numerically very significant group as private if there is a personal nexus.[16]

The current version of the distinction, understood as marking a line either between almost all and some, on the one hand, or between related many and unrelated few, on the other, is not only significant because it is instantiated in this area of law. It is also significant because it presents a particularly vivid contrast with the second version of the distinction, examined below. This contrast concerns the state. While to the forefront of the second version of the distinction, the state is almost completely absent in the current version: it is not even a necessary condition of 'publicness' in the latter, while in the former it assuredly is. However, since the state is an almost unavoidable part of contemporary societies, a version of the public/private distinction that does not register its presence risks

[11] *Inland Revenue Commissioners* v. *Baddeley* [1955] AC 527 (HL) at 592 (Lord Simonds) (*Baddeley*).

[12] See *Re Hetherington (Deceased)* [1990] Ch 1(Ch); *Neville Estates* v. *Madden* [1962] Ch 832 (Ch).

[13] *Gilmour* v. *Coats* [1949] AC 426 (HL).

[14] *Oppenheim* [1951] AC 297 at 306 (Lord Simonds).

[15] The personal nexus limit was thoroughly explored by the House of Lords in *Oppenheim, ibid.*

[16] See *Baddeley* [1955] AC 527 (Methodists in West Ham and Leyton too small a group to be 'public').

being thought eccentric.[17] That risk is nevertheless worth taking because the current version of the distinction provides both a salutary reminder about the state itself and warns of an egregious elision.

The reminder is that the state was not always with us. Which is to say, humankind has not always lived with an agency of power and ostensibly legitimate authority separate from a collective body of people, on the one hand, and a powerful and presumably charismatic individual or collection of individuals, on the other. The state as we know it, and as it was 'invented' in modernity, is something different, in terms of its life-span, deployment of power and ostensible authority, from both kings and the multitude.[18] How this difference is to be conceived has been a staple of some strands of political philosophy since Thomas Hobbes posed the question and offered a distinctive and tremendously influential answer to it. One important point, for present purposes, is that we need a vocabulary to capture matters of public concern in those contexts, as in the classical (not just Roman) world, in which the state as we know it seems not to have existed.

The temptation is to read our modern notion of the state back into the historical record. Because we are familiar with this locus of power, distinct from personal and people power, we tend to assume that everyone, during every epoch, was familiar with it. Once we start doing this, we are no distance at all from the egregious elision. It consists of blurring – or simply assuming out of existence – the distinction between public concerns and interests that are conceptually independent of the state and those public concerns and interests that unavoidably involve the state. The elision usually involves assuming that the latter must subsume the former, that is that anything of public or collective interest must *ipso facto* involve the state or be of state interest. This assumption must be converted into an argument and that, surely, is unlikely to be general. It is simply very difficult to imagine that *every* instance of the public interest, as conceived here, is also an instance of state interest or should involve the state.

[17] On which, see N. Bamforth, 'The Public Law–Private Law Distinction: A Comparative and Philosophical Approach', in P. Leyland and T. Woods (eds.), *Administrative Law Facing the Future: Old Constraints and New Horizons* (London: Blackstone Press, 1997), p. 136. For a recent attempt to conceptualise the state, see N. Barber, *The Constitutional State* (Oxford: Clarendon Press, 2010).

[18] The argument belongs to Quentin Skinner: a lucid and magisterial presentation is Chapter 14 of his *Visions of Politics*, volume II (Cambridge University Press, 2002). A shorter version is 'The State', in T. Ball, J. Farr and R. Hanson (eds.), *Political Innovation and Conceptual Change* (Cambridge University Press, 1989).

If the state is not crucial to this version of the distinction, one might well wonder what relevance, if any, the distinction has for law. A rearrangement of legal doctrine around the two poles of this distinction can be attempted. The areas of law currently regarded as constituting private law might be conceived as involving matters of individual concern. The law of contract, torts, trusts, personal and real property certainly allow individuals qua individuals, or as members of corporate or unincorporated bodies, to give legal effect to their decisions. Private law not only provides protection for a number of interests that individuals have (in their persons and holdings, for example), but also allows future planning through contracts and trusts. Public law might be regarded as entailing only matters of collective concern, being of relevance to all or the vast majority of the community. The community's constitution and rules for the deployment of force, for example, could be regarded in this light.

There might be a problem, however, with this attempt to inscribe this distinction in law. The distinction might not actually work as a general structuring principle for legal systems because it defines one of its poles out of existence. This worry arises once the examples mentioned in the previous paragraph are scrutinised. Think, again, of contract and tort, equity and trusts, personal and real property. While these areas of law surely protect various 'private' interests that individuals have, and allow individuals to achieve various goals, is it not equally true that all members of the community have an interest in these areas of law functioning in those ways? If so, then private law, no less than public law, is a matter of public concern, an interest of, and of relevance to, each and every member of the community in which it exists. If all of a community's law is of interest and relevance to all members of that community, then all law is in one sense public (law).

The claim that a community's law is of interest and relevance to all members of that community is only plausible if understood as something other than an empirical truth. The claim normally contains an implicit 'ought' as well as another restriction, for it usually means: all *engaged* members of the group *ought* to interest themselves in their community's law. This 'ought' need not be a moral ought or in any sense other-directed; it can be purely prudential or self-interested. The weight carried by 'engaged' in this claim is considerable and it requires the support, at the very least, of an account of what group membership entails. In the context of the modern state this usually becomes a discussion of citizenship and its limits, although we should not forget that the notion of citizenship predates that of the state.

Is it the case, then, that when deployed in the legal context this distinction actually defines one of its poles away? No. For although the distinction generates a plausible and informative sense in which all law – public and private – is public, it also allows us to say in conjunction that some areas of law are more private than others. Some areas of law appear designed so as to facilitate and protect individuals in their pursuit of their own personal projects. This might seem like keeping one's cake and eating it, but only if we assume that a distinction between public and private must be unique, comprehensive and dispositive. But this version of the distinction is clearly neither comprehensive nor dispositive, since it does not generate bivalent answers in every instance. It allows us, instead, to say that one and the same area of law is in some respects public and in other respects private. Some might regard that kind of judgment as sophisticated and informative, but it seems unlikely that all lawyers will agree.

Of all versions of the public/private distinction, the current one exercises strong gravitational force over the second, at least as that distinction is sometimes drawn by lawyers in the context of administrative law. Almost all lawyers are uneasy about accepting the distinction as drawn in administrative law as a comprehensive and deeply significant version of the public/private distinction. As drawn therein, the distinction misses too much about public and private. This sense is plausibly explained by the hold that the current version of the distinction has on us. All lawyers know (or feel they know) that all law is significantly public. The current version of the distinction accommodates and nurtures this view.

2. The second version of the distinction between public and private is often to the forefront of contemporary minds. It is a distinction between the public conceived as the realm of the state, on the one hand, and the private understood as the realm beyond or free from the state on the other.[19] This version of the public/private distinction has different applications, including a role in relation to the provision of goods and services, where public (state) provision is contrasted with private (non-state) provision, and in relation to economic regulation, where public (state) regulation of the economy is compared with private (non-state) regulation. The 'public' pole of this version of the distinction can overlap with the public pole of the first version of the distinction, particularly when we move (too)

[19] S. Benn and G. Gaus, 'The Liberal Conception of the Public and the Private', in S. Benn and G. Gaus (eds.), *Public and Private in Social Life* (London: Croom Helm, 1983), pp. 50–2, provide a brief survey of instances in which this version of the distinction – or something very like it – has been invoked by social and political theorists.

quickly from 'matter of interest to all or the vast majority' to 'matter of state interest'.

The principal difficulty with this version of the distinction is that it cannot always yield a bivalent answer to the question 'is this activity or conduct, practice or institution either public or private?' This is primarily because the domain of the state and that of the non-state are both malleable, subject to extension, contraction and hybrid blurring. As to the latter, take the traditional state provision of some standard 'public' services, such as public transport, refuse collection, education and health care as examples. It is not only in the UK that these services have relatively recently been provided by private companies through a web of genuine and sometimes mock contracts with a local or central government authority.[20] Indeed, this process of semi-privatisation and 'contractualisation' of public services is now a fairly common feature of many nation-states. It is a process that, while undoubtedly public, is also significantly private.[21] There are two quite different senses in which this process is public. First, it is public because the services provided are of interest and benefit to almost all members of the community; and, second, it is public in the sense that those services are funded, via various forms of taxation, by undeniable instruments of the 'state' (local and central government). It is also meaningfully private, this being most evident from the fact that the services in question are delivered by companies under a web of contracts that often link not only the funders and providers of services, but also the providers and consumers of services. These contracts include not just provisions relating to cost and quality but also related requirements attempting to ensure responsiveness to consumers.

Is this type of service provision either public or private? Posing the question in this form shows its foolishness. It is clearly a hybrid that does not sit entirely comfortably under either description but can be accommodated by both. The most natural answer to the question, given the way in which the service provision process has just been sketched, is surely: both. There are, as we have seen, useful and intelligible senses in which that process can be described as both public and private. Once we

[20] There are many treatments of this process. One of the most interesting discussions of English developments is P. Vincent-Jones, *The New Public Contracting* (Oxford: Clarendon Press, 2006).

[21] Indeed, the practice of contracting out has caused the courts a great deal of classificatory difficulty in the administrative and human rights law contexts: see, notably, *R* v. *Servite Houses; ex parte Goldsmith* (2001) 33 HLR 35 (QB); *YL* v. *Birmingham City Council* [2007] UKHL 27 (*YL*).

understand that the question 'is X public or private?' can be answered in a more-or-less, matter-of-degree way, then our understanding of 'the' public/private distinction might improve. For if some activity or conduct, practice or institution might sensibly be both private and public in a number of ways, then it becomes plausible not just to chart those various ways, but also to consider the point of mapping the distinction in each of those various ways. We might then be able to offer judgments like this: for the purpose of constitutional oversight and accountability, activity A is public but, for the purpose of applying the rules of contract law, it is private. The temptation to view such judgments as contradictory bespeaks simple-mindedness.

If this picture is accurate, then it in part explains why the two principal legal versions of this distinction between public and private (or between public and non-public) are far from dispositive.[22] In England, these two versions have been developed by public lawyers in an effort to distinguish between the state, conceived as the government, and the proper realm of its activities, on the one hand, and civic society (or the non-state realm), on the other. It seems that both efforts to distinguish public from non-public are intended to do dispositive legal-doctrinal work, although as a matter of fact they rarely succeed in doing so. The two ostensibly different ways of formulating the public/private distinction are best labelled 'institutional' and 'functional'.[23] Elements of each appear when the courts are deciding whether or not some conduct or decision is subject to judicial review and/or covered by the Human Rights Act 1998 and/or falls within the ambit of EC law.[24] What, then, do these two approaches tell us?

The institutional approach to determining 'publicness', conceived as the domain of the state, is reducible to a disarmingly simple question: 'is the body or agent in question part of government?' The approach is most evident in Strasbourg, where the European Court of Human Rights must determine under Article 34 of the European Convention on Human Rights (ECHR)[25] whether a particular body is a 'governmental

[22] As will be seen in section 3, our view is that there are indeed more than two versions of the distinction in play in this context.

[23] We are following Cane, 'Accountability and the Public/Private Distinction', p. 249.

[24] For a helpful overview of the principal cases under each head, see C. Campbell, 'The Nature of Power as Public in English Judicial Review' (2009) 68 *Cambridge Law Journal* 90.

[25] Council of Europe, Convention for the Protection of Human Rights and Fundamental Freedoms, opened for signature 4 November 1950, entered into force 3 September 1953 (ECHR).

organisation' precluded from filing Convention claims of its own,[26] but it also looms large in domestic law.[27] The functional approach is also reducible to a single, albeit slightly more complex question: 'is the process, conduct or decision in question one that is typically public or discharged by government?' The first approach is a matter of determining where, in the social-cum-political structure, the decision-making body or agent is located; the second involves determining what the decision-making body or agent actually does. Each approach has been refined to include additional subsidiary questions and tests, but, even in their most refined form, each is discernibly distinct in that they can generate quite different answers in one and the same case. Hence the Advertising Standards Authority and the Panel on Takeovers and Mergers could both quite comfortably be regarded as public bodies on the functional approach, whereas neither could be so regarded on the institutional approach.[28]

That each approach can yield different answers in the same case could be regarded as showing that both do dispositive doctrinal work in such cases. We do not believe that this is always or even often so, which is not to say that these approaches, and the various subsidiary tests they have spawned, do no work at all. They undoubtedly carry some weight in the judicial decision-making process. But why have these two approaches in particular taken root? As a matter of chronology, the institutional approach predated the functional approach, but the latter arose and has assumed prominence because of the weaknesses of the former. One particularly glaring weakness is that, when viewed from the perspective of the institutional approach, the processes of contracting out and privatisation serve to remove many state activities from the purview of judicial review. The functionalist approach is more obviously interested in the locus rather than the form of public power. Contemporary administrative practices and institutional forms are therefore as much grist to its mill as were more traditional organisational forms of state power. For

[26] Art. 34 provides that Strasbourg 'may receive applications from any person, non-governmental organisation or group of individuals claiming to be the victim of a [Convention] violation'.

[27] See, e.g., *Holy Monasteries* v. *Greece* (1995) 20 EHRR 1; and for analysis of the law in this area, A. Williams, 'A Fresh Perspective on Hybrid Public Authorities under the Human Rights Act 1998: Private Contractors, Rights-Stripping and "Chameleonic" Horizontal Effect' [2011] *Public Law* 139, 145–54.

[28] *R* v. *Datafin; ex parte Panel on Takeovers and Mergers* [1987] QB 815 (CA) (*Datafin*); *R* v. *Advertising Standards Authority Limited, ex parte The Insurance Service Plc.* [1990] 2 Admin LR 77 (QB).

current purposes, the crucial point is that even in this relatively limited segment of law – the component of administrative law concerned with judicial review – there is more than one version of the public/private distinction simply by virtue of there being available at least two different, non-dispositive approaches to drawing that distinction. Although the two different, approaches might generate the same answers in some cases, they can also generate different answers in one and the same case.

Finally, a point that has been lurking in the shadows of the discussion in this subsection should be brought to light. It is that the contrast yielded by the institutional and functional approaches to determining 'publicness' is probably not well understood as one between the public on the one hand, and the private on the other. Rather, the distinction generated seems to be between the public and the non-public, and the latter, of course, can include much more than just the realm of the private (however understood). Remember that public, in terms of this distinction, is a surrogate for 'state' and the realm of the non-state can surely include not just aspects of the paradigmatically private realm (what one chooses for breakfast and what one does with one's earnings), but also the public realm as understood in terms of the second distinction (*res publica* and so on). This is important because it can explain the disquiet often felt with institutional and functional approaches when taken as a means of distinguishing public and private. For we suspect that not all that is meaningfully public is covered by these two approaches and that not all they relegate to the non-public realm is meaningfully private. This is the point of claiming, as we did above, that the first version of the distinction exerts a gravitational pull over other versions, such as to create a slight but insistent disquiet with them.

3. The third version of the distinction, like the first, warrants the judgment that there is an interesting and informative sense in which all law is public. The senses that 'public' and 'private' bear here are not, however, the same as the senses they have in either of the previous two versions of the distinction. The distinction between public and private as drawn here is altogether more technical and, while not as obvious in either law or the general culture as the first and second versions, it nevertheless captures and conveys an important insight. The distinction has been drawn principally by economists and consists of distinguishing between public and private goods. Pure public goods, on this view, are non-excludable and non-rivalrous. A good is non-excludable if, once available, beneficiaries cannot be prevented from using it. The light from lighthouses has this property since, once lighthouses are functional, seafarers cannot be

prevented from benefiting from their light: it is available for all to see. The light from lighthouses is also non-rivalrous, which means that its use by some does nothing to reduce its availability to others. This is clearly not true of many other goods, such as cake and apples, which are excludable and rivalrous. Such goods are quintessential private goods.

One key property of pure public goods – non-excludability – shows the difficulty in providing such goods. How might lighthouses and their attendant light be provided and maintained? An obvious path would be to seek contributions from all who will and do benefit from them. A consensual levy upon seafarers is a natural consequence, but purely self-interested seafarers have reason to avoid such a levy and to free-ride. Once light is provided, its non-excludability means that it is provided to all who stand to benefit from it whether or not they have contributed to its provision. An allegedly rational but purely self-interested individual seafarer will therefore conclude that it is better for them to benefit from the good without paying for it, rather than benefit from the good and pay for it. So, too, will all other allegedly rational but purely self-interested seafarers. Yet if this is so, the free-rider problem not only arises after provision of the good, as in our hypothetical; it will also prevent any pure public good being provided in the first place, if a sufficient number of potential beneficiaries asked for a contribution are rational and purely self-interested. They will conclude that it is better not to contribute and take the benefit if and when the good is provided by contributions from the rest. *All* economists and rational choice theorists accept that coercion is a standard solution to free-rider problems, particularly in the form of power to compel the beneficiaries of public goods to contribute towards their provision and upkeep. *Many* economists and rational choice theorists therefore conclude that the state, in the form of an organised monopoly of legitimate force, is the best or perhaps even the only way of ensuring the provision of public goods.[29]

While the argument just sketched takes as its example the light from lighthouses, the view of some influential economists is that it works equally well with regard to law.[30] They think this despite the fact that law,

[29] For an introduction to the alleged necessity of the state (and law) as a means of providing public goods, see D. Osterfeld, 'Anarchism and the Public Goods Issue: Law, Courts, and the Police' (1989) 9 *Journal of Libertarian Studies* 47; T. Cowen, 'Law as a Public Good' (1992) 8 *Economics and Philosophy* 249; D. Friedman, Comment (1994) 10 *Economics and Philosophy* 319; T. Cowen, Rejoinder (1994) 10 *Economics and Philosophy* 329.

[30] See J. Buchanan, *The Limits of Liberty* (University of Chicago Press, 1975), Chapters 1–4 and 7.

unlike the light from lighthouses, is an impure public good at best and that much is often subsumed under the rubric 'law'. Nevertheless, if their claim is that all law is a public good, that provokes a number of questions. First and foremost is this: '*all* law?' This question arises because 'law', when used in the claim that all law is a public good, includes not just the substantive law structured by traditional juristic divisions but also (1) the idea of the rule of law and its components; (2) the fundamental constitutional compact that is the basis of any polity; and (3) the notion of security (or lawfulness or stability) that supposedly flows from the presence of (1) and (2).

One obvious worry is that these different aspects of law are not truly the same and might not therefore all be public goods. Some notions in play under the rubric 'law' seem more like 'indivisible lumps' than others: the idea of security appears, when conceived as characterising a measurable property of community life, to be one from which some members cannot be excluded without wrongdoing.[31] So, for example, if a community has the institutions, practices and personnel to ensure that its life is relatively free from crime and disorder, then it is hard to remove that benefit from some without subjecting them to victimisation. Similarly, the benefits of the original constitutional compact, once entered into, appear difficult to ration in anything like a legitimate way. That the benefits and burdens of such a compact affect all who live under it is a fundamental component of its legitimacy. Any subsequent attempt to redistribute those benefits and burdens seems unavoidably to undermine the power of the original compact.

While security and the original constitutional compact both look a great deal like indivisible lumps, and thus like public goods, private law does not. Not, at least, at first glance. Consider this hypothetical, originary possibility about the private law (or laws) of contract. The merchants and consumers of one geographical area use different standards to those in other areas, with merchants and consumers in different areas of economic activity doing likewise. While these different customary laws of contract could well be public goods for the various subgroups in question, they are certainly not public goods for those outside these groups. The system of contract law used by bakers for bakers cannot be a public good for the candlestick-makers excluded from it. This point – that it is

[31] The term belongs to Osterfeld, 'Anarchism and the Public Goods Issue'; his principal argument is that security is not such an 'indivisible lump'.

conceivable that different laws of contract can emerge in different areas of one and the same polity – could be generalised across all aspects of private law. Thus, just as various groups might rely upon different rules for the creation or interpretation of contracts, so they might also use different rules to protect (inter alia) bodily integrity and physical holdings, or to distribute holdings on death.

The possibility of a plurality of systems of private law speaks against private law being a public good, at least at some originary hypothetical moment. Yet the existence of a plurality of such systems within a single polity gives rise to externalities, the principal one being the costs involved to those participants who have to operate within more than one system.[32] A single private law system for all would reduce this particular cost and others besides. Therefore, such a system might qualify as a public good for, once it is provided, its use is hard to limit on legitimate grounds. The doubt expressed by 'might' is appropriate, however, because even if it can be shown that the good that a general system of private law would provide is non-excludable, there remains a question as to whether that good is indeed non-rivalrous. For, insofar as a court system and adjudication are adopted as the means of resolving private law and other legal disputes, the use of that system by some can in some circumstances prevent its use by others. One such circumstance is that in which the justice system is operating at or beyond the limits of its capacity.

This worry and the non-excludability problem highlight the same general difficulty: 'is private law a pure public good?' But the answer to that question, although interesting as a general matter, is not crucial in this context. Even if the argument in play here does not show that private law is a pure public good, it certainly shows that it has some features similar to such goods. And that is all that needs to be shown to make the point that all law – private and public – is public, in the sense of being either a pure or impure public good.

4. The fourth version of the distinction between public and private is claimed to be implicit within many legal systems, operating as an insufficiently noticed structuring principle underpinning legal doctrine. The distinction is that between the public realm of politics, law and the market on the one hand, and the private realm of family, the household and intimacy on the other. It is often invoked as a critical tool, a means of

[32] The term 'externality' is almost as vague and mystifying as its close bedfellow 'transaction costs'. For guidance on both, a good starting point is C. Dahlman, 'The Problem of Externality' (1979) 22 *Journal of Law and Economics* 141.

illustrating the gender inequality embedded within the formal equality of modern legal systems in particular and of liberal thought more generally.[33] On this critique, these legal systems have provided less protection for women who are subject to violence by men in domestic contexts, have valued the labour of women in the home less than the labour of men outside the home, and have been loath to enforce allegedly 'domestic' agreements between men and women in relationships. The rationale for the law's hesitancy to intervene in these and other areas is, in part, the thought that these realms are quintessentially private and therefore beyond the law's reach.

Few or no proponents of this gender critique of the law deny that there are some areas of social and individual life that should be beyond the law's reach. The difficulty critics highlight with this thought, as currently or recently embodied in contemporary legal systems, is that it serves to systematically devalue women, their work and their interests. The question of where the limits upon the law's reach lie is one that should be posed and answered in a genuinely open way and not just on the basis of embedded social practices, assumptions and stereotypes, particularly where these embody morally and politically questionable judgments. It might be thought that contemporary liberal polities already have an answer to this question and there is some truth in that. Most such polities do indeed have a conception of the limits of state power and influence that coexists with a commitment to equality under and before the law. A problem can, however, arise with the way in which such conceptions and their limits are instantiated within legal doctrine, as well as with the way in which they inform policing and prosecutorial practice.

As to legal doctrine, consider Article 8 of the ECHR, which holds, inter alia, that everyone has a right to respect for their private life. Such a right would be recognised by almost all liberal accounts of the limits of the state, yet the qualified guarantee it offers is by no means certain to accord the same value to the interests of men and women. If we set aside the actual case law on this Article and consider how provisions *might* be interpreted, an obvious and apparently innocuous starting point is to construe them in light of the language, cultural context and everyday common sense of

[33] A classic treatment of English law is K. O'Donovan, *Sexual Divisions in Law* (London: Weidenfeld and Nicolson, 1985); a classic from political philosophy is C. Pateman, 'Feminist Critiques of the Public/Private Dichotomy', Chapter 12 in S. Benn and G. Gaus (eds.), *Public and Private in Social Life* (London: Croom Helm, 1983).

the society in which they figure.[34] The hope is that recourse to these factors will resolve any alleged ambiguity or guide interpreters as to the limits of the proposition or concept in play.

This interpretative strategy is certainly not the only one the courts use. They must, for example, apply propositions of law and their constitutive concepts in light of existing law and that, almost always, necessitates consideration of other similar cases. But the contextual interpretative strategy is significant because it can constitute a Trojan horse by which common but morally and politically dubious judgments and assumptions enter into the law. This could happen with regard to Article 8 in this way. When provoked to deliberate upon the nature and range of 'private life', the courts could simply replicate the notion of private embodied in this version of the public/private distinction. The view that private life – the domain of family life and intimate relationships – is the realm of women is not particularly uncommon in most societies with which we are familiar. If the courts follow this relatively widespread view of gender roles and the division of domestic labour, then they entrench it in the law and, in so doing, immunise it against legal and political change. For if the division of domestic labour is unequal, and if women's work in and contribution towards family life is placed beyond the reach of law, then legal redress of that inequality is difficult. The difficulty, then, is not one of straightforward and explicit gender bias in either Article 8 itself or in the courts' decisions. It is, rather, a problem of 'subtle distortions of prejudice and bias'[35] that enter into adjudication via some of the common assumptions and understandings of ordinary language. Therefore, as our hypothetical tale about Article 8 suggests, and as some studies of private law have shown, these distortions of prejudice and bias can 'effectively discriminate against certain groups in the judicial process'.[36]

Exactly the same distortions of prejudice and bias can inform decision-making in policing and prosecution. The view that the domestic realm of the private is and should be beyond the law certainly seems to explain the hesitancy that police forces and prosecutors have traditionally displayed

[34] For the actual case law, a good starting point is D. Harris, M. O'Boyle, E. Bates and C. Buckley, *Harris, O'Boyle and Warbrick: The Law of the European Convention on Human Rights*, 2nd edition (Oxford: Clarendon Press, 2009), Chapter 9.

[35] John Rawls, *A Theory of Justice* (Cambridge, MA: Harvard University Press, 1971), p. 235.

[36] *Ibid.* The study of private law we have in mind is M. Moran, *Rethinking the Reasonable Person* (Oxford: Clarendon Press, 2003). Moran reminds us of the significance of Rawls' observation at p. 10 and in Chapter 5.

when dealing with domestic violence. Nowhere is this more obvious than in the once common view among police officers that violence in the home is 'just a domestic'.[37] This view automatically downgrades the alleged crime in question, suggesting it is not worthy of a proper police response. The consequence is simply to attach less weight to the interests of alleged victims of this kind of crime than to those who suffer exactly the same type and level of violence but in other contexts. Nor need this set of attitudes and assumptions be confined to the policing of domestic violence. There is evidence to suggest that they also inform – or have informed – the exercise of prosecutorial discretion.[38]

It is important to realise that propositions of law need not, as a matter of necessity, be informed by common understandings and assumptions that are morally and politically dubious and that often serve to subvert the law's commitment to formal equality. While it is true that the law must be interpreted in the light of the language, concepts and understandings of the community of which it is part, not all aspects of that language and those concepts and understandings will be morally and politically dubious. Propositions of law must, first and foremost, be interpreted in such a way as to either embody or be consistent with the legal system's fundamental values and commitments. Only when that constraint is met should the law aim for broad consistency with ordinary language and common sense.

This version of the public/private distinction calls contemporary legal systems to account for various aspects of their practice in light of their fundamental values. There is no claim that either all law is public or all law is private or that all law is neither. Rather, the fundamental claim that proponents of this version of the distinction make is usually a warning and it counsels, at its broadest, something like this: that words, concepts, ideas and distinctions have power in the world when embodied in conduct, practices and institutions and this power is not always benign. Taken more narrowly, the warning is that 'the' public/private distinction has just this kind of non-benign power and we must be aware of this and resist it. In practical terms, it warns us that the realm of the private should not automatically be thought of as a law-free zone and, when it is, that the valuation such a judgment entails should always be made explicit.

[37] See L. Richards, S. Letchford and S. Stratton, *Policing Domestic Violence* (Oxford University Press, 2008), p. 10.

[38] S. Edwards' now dated *Policing Domestic Violence: Women, Law and State* (London: Sage, 1989) was a pioneering study.

5. The final way of distinguishing public and private is a means of distinguishing only public and private *law*. It is a purely legal-doctrinal version of the public/private distinction and, in English law at least, it seems both undeniable and unproblematic. The distinction consists of highlighting the various doctrinal and procedural differences between private and public law. For much of the common law's history in England the remedies for public law wrongs, the rules of standing, as well as the doctrinal requirements for establishing such wrongs and obtaining remedies, have been for the most part different from the wrongs, remedies and doctrinal requirements embodied in private law.[39] There is now an administrative court in England, thus reinforcing a public law/private law divide. This set of doctrinal, remedial and procedural differences between public and private law is not, of course, the only possible set. Other jurisdictions draw the distinction in rather different ways,[40] but there can be no doubt that they add up to a significant distinction between the two domains.

The puzzle here is that some jurists find this way of distinguishing public and private law unsatisfying, without being perfectly clear as to why. They are content to note this legal-doctrinal distinction, yet then proceed as if it is in need of further explanation and justification.[41] What, then, is their worry? Perhaps that the legal-doctrinal distinction is insufficiently 'deep' or, what likely amounts to the same thing, is altogether too contingent. Thus, the distinction as currently embodied in English law might simply be a historical accident rather than a well-founded and valuable means of distinguishing private and public law. Espousing this view does not require great scepticism of the jurist or lawyer, but simply awareness that the law, either in the hands of judges, legislators, or both, can take wrong turnings. These turnings can be wrong in legal, moral or political terms. A statute, judicial decision or line of decisions can inhibit desirable doctrinal development, or impact adversely on some aspect of commercial, social or cultural life, as well as embodying morally and politically

[39] For an overview of administrative law remedies and related issues, see P. Craig, *Administrative Law*, 6th edition (London: Thomson, 2008), Part 3; H. Wade and C. Forsyth, *Administrative Law*, 10th edition (Oxford: Clarendon Press, 2009), Part VII.

[40] For a warning that the distinction as currently embodied in English law is a worrisome legal transplant, see J. Allison, *A Continental Distinction in the Common Law* (Oxford: Clarendon Press, 1996). A contemporary overview of the distinction in French and English law is provided by the essays in Mark Freedland and Jean-Bernard Auby (eds.), *The Public Law/Private Law Divide: Une Entente assez Cordiale?* (Oxford: Hart Publishing, 2006).

[41] See Cane, 'Accountability and the Public/Private Distinction', pp. 248–9 for some interesting observations on this issue.

objectionable distinctions or suppositions.[42] This awareness inhibits the tendency to regard all legal-doctrinal development as always prima facie desirable and justified; it is part of the process of 'demystifying the law'.[43]

But there are at least two quite different responses to this aspect of law's fallibility. One response combines a perfectly proper critical awareness of law's normative (moral and political) fallibility with an equally proper awareness of law's normative (moral and political) contingency. The latter entails little more than a realisation that some areas of law – taken to include not just chunks of substantive legal doctrine and their constitutive standards, but also procedural rules and broader aspects of institutional design such as the organisation of the trial process – are morally and politically either over-, under- or undetermined. The last possibility exists when some legal rule has no moral or political content, resonance or analogue, the first when quite different substantive moral or political values actually determine the content of the same area of law. The second possibility is realised when various different substantive moral or political values are consistent with the same area of law.

Awareness of law's moral and political contingency and fallibility provides a fertile soil for this legal-doctrinal distinction between public and private. This version of the distinction is malleable, context-dependent and unlikely to be dispositive in every legal dispute. Its contours have undeniably changed over time and, equally clearly, it has not been and is not now drawn in the same way as its legal-doctrinal equivalent in, for example, French law. Moreover, while the distinction is expected to bear some weight in particular cases, it seems rarely in and of itself dispositive. Judges and jurists usually provide a panoply of reasons to support their decisions in cases in which a public/private question arises and this version of the distinction is almost never itself conclusive. In his dissenting judgment in *R (Weaver)* v. *London and Quadrant Housing Trust*, for example, Rix LJ cited no less than ten different factors to justify his conclusion that a registered social landlord was not performing a public function when managing and allocating housing stock.[44]

The other response to the mutability and context- (or jurisdictional) dependence of the legal-doctrinal version of the public/private distinction

[42] A common law list of shame usually includes *Lochner* v. *New York* 198 US 45 (1905) and *Bartonshill Coal Co.* v. *Reid* (1858) 3 Macq 266.

[43] Possibly initiated or at least made prominent, in the anglophone world, by Jeremy Bentham. See H. L. A. Hart, *Essays on Bentham* (Oxford: Clarendon Press, 1982), Chapter I.

[44] [2009] EWCA Civ 587 (*Weaver*) at [148]–[159].

is quite different to that just noted. For some, this very mutability and context-dependence are sources of worry, since the distinction might well be drawn in a morally or politically mistaken way. This view implies some or other normative blueprint against which various ways of drawing the public/private distinction are measured; the current legal-doctrinal version of the distinction is or becomes objectionable if and when it departs from the ukases of the blueprint. Needless to say, this response fits badly with the tenor of this chapter and some of its difficulties have been explored elsewhere.[45]

2 Functions, labels, permeability

There is an obvious objection to the discussion in the previous section: it has passed too glibly over legal and non-legal versions of the public/private distinction and, in doing so, has failed to note that different versions of the distinction might operate in quite different ways and with reference to very different criteria of success and failure. It is hard for us to deny the force of this objection, since its substance is the crux of the point we made earlier, namely, that different versions of the public/private distinction might differ quite markedly in their 'methodological' standing. Once it is accepted that some versions of the distinction are constructed within different intellectual, pragmatic and cultural contexts, that they might therefore utilise different criteria of success and failure, and that they can perform quite different functions, it becomes deeply tempting to place all five versions within one or other of two allegedly mutually exclusive categories. The temptation must, however, be resisted.

The first category includes *general* versions of the distinction. These are so named because they have a life in the wider culture of particular societies, being part of ordinary discourse, yet are often given more precise expression, and certainly more sustained attention, by historians, sociologists and other social scientists. It might be the case that versions of the public/private distinction at large in the culture of particular societies cannot be given more precise expression by social scientists because they are already as precise as they can be. But it is almost always true that social scientists, rather than minting new versions of the public/private distinction, purport to articulate and discover already existing but not sufficiently appreciated versions of the distinction. Already existing but insufficiently noticed versions have life not just within scholarly social

[45] For further discussion, see Lucy, 'Private and Public', s. II A 1.

scientific work but also beyond it, in some particular social and cultural context.

The other category includes *specific* versions of the public/private distinction, which, in contrast with general versions, are coined only by lawyers about the law. This contrast must be extended a little, for specific versions of the public/private distinction are additionally *internal* to the law. This says more than that they are made only by lawyers and jurists, for the lawyers and jurists who espouse specific versions of the public/private distinction do so from the viewpoint of participants in, rather than external observers of, the legal system. This might be because some lawyers and jurists are indeed participants in the legal system in a limited sense: they are practitioners, such as judges, advocates and legal advisers. Yet it is also because the participants' point of view is the default mode of all doctrinal and much jurisprudential scholarship.[46] Moreover, specific versions of the public/private distinction are usually intended by their proponents to operate *within* particular areas of legal doctrine (such as, for example, administrative law). These versions of the distinction therefore cannot often – if at all – be used as a means of organising or structuring legal systems as a whole. Some general versions of the distinction can be used to do just that, being invoked as organising principles under which many or all substantive legal doctrines are allegedly subsumable. General versions of the public/private distinction are also (1) rarely formulated from within the perspective of participants in the legal system; and (2) almost never expected by their proponents to do legal-doctrinal work. This is mainly because the methodological commitments of academic proponents of general versions of the distinction – they are, inter alia, historians, economists and sociologists – entail that the participant's perspective is either suspect or not easily available.

All but one of the five versions of the distinction sketched above can take general form. The first version, henceforth labelled 'the public/private interest' version, is general because it is neither developed by lawyers nor used exclusively by them. It operates as a general structuring principle for whole legal systems and has so significant a gravitational pull over many

[46] Some effort has been made to substantiate this claim elsewhere: see William Lucy, *Philosophy of Private Law* (Oxford: Clarendon Press, 2007) pp. 26–44; William Lucy, 'Method and Fit: Two Problems for Contemporary Philosophies of Tort Law' (2007) 52 *McGill Law Journal* 605; William Lucy, 'The Crises of Private Law', in T. Wilhelmsson and S. Hurri (eds.), *From Dissonance to Sense: Welfare State Expectations, Privatization and Private Law* (London: Dartmouth, 1998), p. 177; William Lucy, *Understanding and Explaining Adjudication* (Oxford: Clarendon Press, 1999), Chapters 2–3.

specific versions of the distinction as to cause dissatisfaction with them. However, we also noted that something like this general version of the public/private interest distinction is frequently articulated and refined by the courts in one particular legal context and its dual resonance – sounding in both legal and non-legal contexts – is significant. First, it serves as a reminder that, while neither the Charity Commission nor the lawyers and judges who grapple with the question of public benefit see themselves as striving to articulate non-legal common sense – they look almost exclusively to the previous cases and the body of doctrinal writing on the topic in order to reach decisions in particular cases[47] – they are nevertheless grappling with exactly those issues that animate any effort to utilise a general form of the public/private interest distinction. Second, it is clear from these cases that while general versions of this distinction resonate within the law, the specific legal articulations of this distinction have no equivalent resonance at the general level. There is thus an undoubtedly asymmetric relation of influence between general and specific in this context that might be replicated elsewhere. Third, the dual resonance of the public/private interest distinction shows that the categories of 'general' and 'specific' really cannot be mutually exclusive. Just two versions of the public/private distinction can be appropriately assigned only to one or other category, while the public/private interest version and the other two clearly resonate or have analogues in both.

The second version of the distinction – hereinafter 'the state/non-state' distinction – is one of these, having both a general and a specific form. In both forms the distinction is intended to function as a means of drawing and policing the parameters of the state. And while that aim is indeed important, the intention can be thwarted by the very malleability of the 'state'. Like all social products, this complex of institutions, practices, norms and expectations can be remade, sometimes intentionally and deliberately – as we see in the privatisation of some state functions that has been portrayed in some jurisdictions as a 'rolling back' of the powers of state and government – and sometimes as the unintentional consequence of other intentional actions (as when temporary economic imperatives trigger state intervention in a particular domain which then becomes permanent and extended to other similar domains). The very plasticity of the social world thus ensures that efforts to map it are always

[47] See *The Independent Schools Council* v. *The Charity Commission* [2011] UKUT 421 at [14].

at risk of redundancy and supersession.[48] Changes in the role and extent of the state are therefore almost guaranteed to cause difficulty for this version of the public/private distinction, insofar as it is rooted in a particular social and historical context, for changes in that context will likely affect the efficacy and accuracy of the distinction. Some might take this risk as a reminder of the futility of offering historically specific versions of the state/non-state distinction, turning instead to the task of developing a respectable normative blueprint for the role of the state wherever and whenever found. While there can be no general intellectual objection to that process, its utility as a means of mapping and understanding our present condition can rightly be questioned.

Although it is important to realise that the courts in many common law jurisdictions are articulating specific legal analogues of the state/non-state distinction when deciding judicial review or some human rights cases, it is equally important to appreciate what they are not doing when doing this. One thing the courts clearly do not do is enter into an open-ended analysis of the role of the contemporary state. They almost never inform themselves of contemporary social-scientific accounts of the modern state, nor do they catalogue, except insofar as it is crucial to the dispute in hand, the changing tidemarks of state activity over time. Nor is it the case that many social scientists engaged in exactly this kind of study of the state/non-state spheres inform themselves of the efforts of the courts in marking these boundaries. But this is not to say that the delineation and interrogation of both general and specific versions of the state/non-state distinction go on completely independently. For it seems to be the case that the asymmetry noted in the discussion of the public/private interest distinction operates here, in the sense that while general versions of the state/non-state distinction pay no heed to specific versions, specific versions can in two senses be conditioned by the discourse about general versions.

One sense is this: lawyers can make use of and recommend distinctions, ideas and theories formulated outside the methodological perspective of their discipline. Legal academics might do this in order to throw light on some aspects of the law, either at the level of specific doctrinal issues or at the level of broad structuring principles for the legal system as a whole. And legal practitioners might do this insofar as it promises a

[48] For a bold and ambitious statement about the made and thus 'remake-able' nature of social reality, see R. M. Unger, *Social Theory: Its Situation and Its Task* (Cambridge University Press, 1987), Chapters 1–6 and pp. 210–15.

solution to a particular legal dispute acceptable to a court. In these two ways, then, general versions of the state/non-state distinction can penetrate the legal domain, the domain of specific versions of the distinction. Furthermore, there is a second sense in which general versions of the state/non-state distinction might well affect the specific versions of the distinction lawyers articulate. The effect here is less direct than that just noted, but no less significant, and has already been hinted at in our discussion of the public/private interest distinction. All general versions of the public/private distinction, current in the wider culture, can serve to destabilise and breed dissatisfaction with most specific versions. That, we think, is evident when lawyers struggle with the notions of public interest and public benefit in equity, and is also in play when lawyers endeavour to pin down the sources or function of the 'state' in administrative law. The specific distinctions drawn are almost always regarded as tentative and in some sense ultimately unsatisfying. The latter sense, we suggest, flows either from what we (lawyers) know of the general version of the distinction we are articulating and deploying in a specific legal context, or by what we know of different general versions of the distinction. Knowing, for example, of both the first and third versions of the public/private distinction means we are aware of the plausible senses in which all law is public; distinctions drawn between public and private legal power, as are sometimes required in the administrative law context, come to seem unsatisfactory in this light.

The fourth version of the public/private distinction, which we will christen the 'public/private life' version, is the remaining distinction of the five that has dual resonance. In its general form, the public/private life distinction is portrayed by social scientists, philosophers and jurists as a morally and politically questionable organising principle of many existing legal systems. Yet efforts to map a boundary between public and private life also exist within the law, as we saw from the discussion above: insofar as most legal systems incorporate a provision or doctrine akin to Article 8 of the ECHR, then they will need to draw this boundary. As well as this dual resonance, the asymmetry noted in the discussion of the public/private interest and state/non-state distinctions probably exists here also. Even a superficial familiarity with the courts' efforts to draw a boundary between private and public life, and an equally superficial grasp of the various general versions of this distinction, shows that the former make almost no impact on the latter, save that they sometimes function as grist for a critical mill. For on the rare occasions that proponents of general versions of the public/private life distinction do indeed engage with specific versions, the latter are almost invariably regarded as unsatisfactory.[49]

Given their obvious dissimilarities, it seems odd to hold that the third and fifth versions of the public/private distinction have something in common. The similarity is methodological: both versions are similar among the five sketched here because their status is univocal, resonating within only one domain. The third version, hereinafter the 'public/private goods' version, is interesting in that it lacks any specific analogue, while the fifth version – the 'legal-doctrinal' version – is interesting for the exact opposite reason: it lacks any general analogue.[50] The public/private goods distinction lacks any specific analogue or resonance possibly because of its genesis at the hands of economists and game theorists. Their concerns seem to have no specific legal equivalents, except in the sense that the existence of law itself, or particular branches thereof, is or might be a public good. The legal-doctrinal distinction lacks any general analogue for a substantively similar reason – it is the product only of lawyers' hands and is responsive (or was thought to be responsive) only to uniquely legal concerns.

The fact that three of the five versions of the public/private distinction have a dual resonance is quite compatible with the claim that specific and general versions of these distinctions have different functions. Some specific versions are intended to answer a precise legal question, usually within the realm of some specific statutory provisions and body of case law, whereas some general versions are efforts to understand and explain aspects of the social world at a fairly abstract level. But these different functions do not prevent accounts of one or other version of the distinction at the general level influencing accounts of the same distinction at the specific level; nor do they prevent different general versions of the distinction affecting – positively or negatively – one another. What seems unlikely, though, is that different specific versions of the distinction will or can affect one another, for the simple reason that these occupy quite different legal-doctrinal domains. That the two former claims (general versions of the distinction can and do affect specific versions, and that different general versions can affect one another) do indeed characterise

[49] See, e.g., O'Donovan, *Sexual Divisions in Law*, Chapter 5.

[50] Unless this version of the distinction is regarded as a misguided surrogate for the second, in which case it must have a general analogue. We, however, do not see any strong connection between the second and the fifth distinction.

much contemporary thought about 'the' public/private distinction cannot be shown in any detail here, since that would require a broad and detailed survey of the various idioms used, along with an elucidation of their many intersections and disjunctions. In lieu of such a survey, we proffer those two claims, henceforth combined into one and labelled 'the permeability thesis', as a putative explanation of the sense of quagmire, impasse and dissatisfaction lawyers often experience when articulating 'the' public/private distinction. It is therefore especially troubling that the permeability thesis is likely to be received with some scepticism by lawyers.

Two considerations animate this scepticism. One is that all lawyers are familiar with what we might call the law's stipulative sovereignty – its power to define words and concepts in its own way and for its own purposes.[51] From the surely undeniable point that the law can to some extent coin its own technical vocabulary, it is tempting to move to the claim that the law's store of language and concepts stands independently of the language and concepts of non-legal life. This claim becomes radically implausible in so far as it holds that all the law's concepts and words can have a technical meaning bearing no relation at all to the meaning those same words and concepts have in non-legal life. For even if that were possible, it would be profoundly undesirable, since it thwarts the very point of law and legal systems, namely, to act as a means of subjecting human conduct to the governance of rules.[52] That point is, of course, one that embraces many other more specific and far less abstract goals and purposes, none of which could be achieved if the directives that make up a legal system are utterly unintelligible to its addressees. So, while some legal concepts and words can and do bear a technical meaning for some specific purposes, not all can if law is to fulfil its principal function. Lawyers long familiar with the law's technicality must neither exaggerate its range nor forget the significance of law's many and myriad overlaps with ordinary meaning, language and concepts. The point may seem abstract, but it is also viscerally practical for any judge who must direct a jury or make him/herself plain to non-lawyers. Practical

[51] Transport Act 1968, s. 159(1)(b) ('"land" includes land covered by water'); Roads (Scotland) Act 1984, s. 151(1) ('"days" means clear days').

[52] This, of course, is Lon Fuller's characterisation of law's ultimate function: L. L. Fuller, *The Morality of Law*, revised edition (New Haven: Yale University Press, 1969) at, e.g., pp. 46 and 96.

concerns such as these surely also animate the doctrine of judicial notice in the common law world.[53]

It is, then, a mistake to think that law's stipulative sovereignty undermines the permeability thesis. For while it is clearly not impossible for most legal systems with which we are familiar to contain provisions defining 'public' and 'private' in a technical way for some specific purpose, this possibility cannot of itself rule out the 'interference' from other, broader legal and non-legal conceptions of public and private that the permeability thesis posits. Furthermore such interference, albeit across a broad range of legal concepts and words rather than just the notions of public and private, is to be expected. If law is indeed a means of subjecting human conduct to the governance of rules, then its rules must be intelligible to their addressees. And that presupposes that the content of some of those rules overlap, in terms of meaning, with the language, words and concepts of those to whom they apply.

There is, however, a second and related reason why lawyers might be sceptical about the permeability thesis. All lawyers and many non-lawyers know that legal analysis, either in chambers, the court room or the seminar room, is not an argumentative free-for-all. The kind of considerations that lawyers can invoke in this process form a relatively limited class, but they go slightly beyond the bare letter of the law, as found in statutes and cases. For cases and statutes are read by lawyers in light of more general legal considerations, which include not just broader principles of law under which particular cases and statutory provisions can be subsumed, but also 'internal' legal considerations of fairness and efficiency, as well as general extra-legal considerations of justice and common sense. While the latter might present a door through which the permeability thesis can enter, lawyers are likely to resist this prospect because they know well that the number and type of both legal and extra-legal factors to which they and other lawyers can properly refer are rigorously policed. How? Simply by the existing expectations and standards of their professional group. Socialisation into that group, through both non-vocational and vocational legal training, informs would-be lawyers of the type of considerations, in addition to the bare letter of the law, that carry weight in legal analysis. Those considerations also often provide a particular 'reading' of specific cases and legal issues, for the mere fact that a case has been decided by a senior appellate court does not determine how, exactly, lawyers subsequently understand or interpret the case. Indeed, it is quite possible for

[53] On which, see E. M. Morgan, 'Judicial Notice' (1944) 57 *Harvard Law Review* 269.

the reading of a case to change quite radically among lawyers, and not just as a result of a later appellate court decision.[54] How might that come about?

The best answer also seems to be the least informative: the professional group changes 'its' mind on some matter. But is the group really so cohesive that it can be personified in this way? Some have thought so. Consider Brian Simpson's account of cohesion in a customary legal order, of which common law systems are obvious instances:

> A customary system of law can function only if it can preserve a considerable measure of continuity and cohesion, and it can do this only if mechanisms exist for the transmission of traditional ideas and the encouragement of orthodoxy. There must exist within the group – particularly amongst its most powerful members – strong pressures against innovation; young members of the group must be thoroughly indoctrinated before they achieve any position of influence, and anything more than the most modest originality of thought treated as heresy.[55]

Were this account true of the contemporary legal profession, then it might indeed seem like a potential block to the permeability thesis. But this is only a matter of appearance: this account does not purport to characterise contemporary common law legal systems, nor does it. Rather, it is an account of conditions that 'were almost ideally satisfied' in 'past centuries'.[56] That those conditions are not currently 'ideally satisfied', nor are particularly likely to be so in the near future, is evident, in many areas of the common law world, from both the nature of contemporary legal education and the practices of appellate courts and senior judges. Legal education is now much more a matter of exploring the insights other disciplines offer about law than it once was,[57] while appellate courts, in the UK at least, are ostensibly much broader in their reading and citations than they were. The latter is plain not only from the fact that judgments in, for example, the Supreme Court and former House of Lords are often dotted with references to the law and legal commentary of other jurisdictions;[58]

[54] The fate of the dissenting judgment in *Candler* v. *Crane and Christmas & Co.* [1951] 2 KB 164 (CA) is a vivid instance of an appellate court rereading or reinventing a precedent.

[55] A. W. B. Simpson, 'The Common Law and Legal Theory', in A. W. B. Simpson (ed.), *Oxford Essays on Jurisprudence, 2nd Series* (Oxford: Clarendon Press, 1973), Chapter IV at p. 95.

[56] *Ibid.*

[57] Data over and beyond the anecdotal evidence of those who have taught for a number of years is hard to come by, but see H. Barnett, 'The Province of Jurisprudence Determined – Again!' (1995) 15 *Legal Studies* 88.

[58] For interesting discussion, see M. Siems, 'Citation Patterns of the German Federal Supreme Court and of the Court of Appeal of England and Wales' (2010) 21 *Kings Law Journal* 152; T. H. Bingham, *Widening Horizons: The Influence of Comparative Law and*

they also frequently cite and discuss academic and related legal commentary. Of course, these changes are assuredly a matter of degree but, when combined with the apparently increasingly common propensity of our judges to engage in extra-judicial speaking and writing,[59] they suggest that the legal profession is nowhere near as inward-looking and insular as it might have been. Indeed, it is not a great exaggeration to claim that these are signs of an unprecedented general intellectual openness and engagement across all aspects of the legal profession. Such openness and engagement provides a fecund environment for the permeability thesis and a barren one for the conditions Simpson identifies.

Lawyers' scepticism about the permeability thesis seems, then, to be misplaced. But even if the thesis is immune to these lawyerly concerns, its status must not be exaggerated. It is forwarded here only as an empirical claim and, as such, it is ripe for testing and either confirmation or rejection. It is certainly not a conceptual truth. The thesis might therefore at some point fail to characterise our thinking about public and private. If and when it does, then our thinking about 'the' public/private distinction will assuredly have changed.

3 Indeterminacy

We now turn to our second principal claim, that the versions of the public/private distinction operative in law are almost never doctrinally dispositive. By the latter we mean simply that, when in play in the kind of cases with which we are familiar, 'the' public/private distinction is rarely utterly conclusive to the resolution of those cases.[60] In part this is a result of the properties of that kind of case and in part a result of properties 'the' distinction itself has, most of which we have already noted. That is the argument offered here, but, before unpacking it, two preliminary points

International Law on Domestic Law (Cambridge University Press, 2010); B. Markesinis and J. Fedtke (eds.), *Judicial Recourse to Foreign Law: A New Source of Inspiration?* (London: Routledge, 2006); B. S. Markesinis, *Comparative Law in the Courtroom and Classroom: The Story of the Last Thirty-Five Years* (Oxford: Hart Publishing, 2000).

59 Which brings with it some hazards: see Susan Bartie and John Gava, 'Some Problems with Extrajudicial Writing' (2012) 34 *Sydney Law Review* 637; David Dyzenhaus, *The Constitution of Law* (Cambridge University Press, 2006), pp. 27–32.

60 See the cases referred to in relation to the first and second versions of the public/private distinction in subsection 1 above; a typically sure-footed treatment of some of the principal public law cases is provided by Cane, 'Accountability and the Public/Private Distinction', pp. 249–61.

must be made. The first highlights an obvious limitation: the argument we actually provide shows only that *one* version of the distinction, invoked in only *one* area of law, is almost never doctrinally dispositive. The version of the distinction in play is the second – the state/non-state distinction – and, as we will see, our brief characterisation of the way in which it operates in the case law in section 2 was far too bluntly drawn. Considerations of space and time dictate this narrowness of focus, but so, too, do considerations of argumentative clarity and weight. A powerful case in relation to one instance of the distinction can ground a presumption that such a case could be made in other instances, although it is an obvious mistake to move too quickly from *one* to *all*. The second point is a calming notice. Some might regard our effort to show that 'the' public/private distinction is almost never dispositive in the case law as a pointlessly sustained restatement of the blindingly obvious, for whoever thought the contrary? Who, that is, ever thought that 'the' public/private distinction should or ought to do dispositive doctrinal work? Our answer to that question is this: many influential legal scholars in the common law world.[61]

The cases in which the state/non-state version of the distinction is in play are, like the cases where other versions are in play, hard appellate court cases. Hard cases are complex and require judgment. They cannot be solved by judges in anything like an automatic way by, for instance, a 'logarithmic' invocation of the state/non-state distinction or of any other proposition of law. This, it has been said, is because hard cases are those 'in which reasonable lawyers disagree' and 'where no settled rule dictates

[61] Some instances: D. Kennedy, 'The Stages of the Decline of the Public/Private Distinction' (1982) 130 *University of Pennsylvania Law Review* 1349, 1350–4 (the distinction is problematic in particular cases and thus does not do the work it should); Henry J. Friendly, 'The Public–Private Penumbra. Fourteen Years Later' (1982) 130 *University of Pennsylvania Law Review* 1289; Karl E. Klare, 'Public/Private Distinction in Labor Law' (1982) 130 *University of Pennsylvania Law Review* 1358 (holding that the distinction 'is devoid of significant, determinate analytical content' (at 1360) when invoked in the cases, this being taken as an indictment); M. Hunt, 'Constitutionalism and the Contractualisation of Government in the United Kingdom', in M. Taggart (ed.), *The Province of Administrative Law* (Oxford: Hart Publishing, 1997), p. 38 (the courts' reluctance to expand judicial review to contracted-out power presumptively threatens the law's ability to ensure that 'constitutional values are observed by private actors performing public functions', the implication being that the public/private distinction is the sole means of determining whether such power can be regulated by the law); C. Harlow, '"Public" and "Private" Law: Definition without Distinction' (1980) 43 *Modern Law Review* 241, 242–50 (purported demonstration that the distinction does not do any substantive work in the English cases, this being regarded as baleful). It is senseless to complain that the distinction does little or no work in the cases if one thinks, as this chapter argues, that it can do little or no work in the cases.

a decision either way'.[62] A more expansive and helpful, but still abstract statement of the hallmarks of hard cases was offered by Neil MacCormick, who maintained that such cases usually present one or more of three possible doctrinal snags. First, they might raise a question as to which interpretation, from a range of two or more available interpretations of an agreed proposition of law, applies to the case at bar. Second, they arise from doubt as to which proposition of law, from a range of two or more incompatible propositions of law, applies to the case at bar. Finally, they might raise the question of whether or not any proposition of law applies to the case at bar.[63] These cases thus require not just a statement of the correct applicable proposition of law, but also argument justifying that precise statement of the law. MacCormick shows that in the UK judges typically seek to justify their doctrinal choices in hard cases by three different kinds of argument. Two of the three kinds of argument are intra-systemic, involving considerations internal to the legal system. Of these two, one kind – arguments from consistency – embody 'a fundamental judicial commandment: Thou shalt not controvert established and binding rules of law'.[64] Arguments from consistency are narrow in the sense that they focus solely on propositions of law in the immediate vicinity of the dispute in question, holding that no argument will be acceptable if it: (1) is clearly incompatible with a closely contiguous proposition of law; and (2) is unsupported by one of the remaining two kinds of argument.

The focus of the second kind of argument – from coherence – is still upon considerations internal to the legal system, but is nevertheless wider than the focus of arguments from consistency. This is because considerations of coherence test, reject or commend an argument in a hard case by reference to its resonance (or lack of it) with principles and values of the legal system as a whole, rather than just the area of doctrine within which the case has arisen. Such arguments, says MacCormick, rest on the assumption 'that the multitudinous rules of a developed legal system should "make sense" when taken together'.[65] The focus of consequentialist arguments – the third type of argument invoked by judges to justify their

[62] Ronald Dworkin, *Taking Rights Seriously* (London: Duckworth, 1978), pp. xiv and 83 respectively.

[63] Neil MacCormick, *Legal Reasoning and Legal Theory*, revised edition (Oxford: Clarendon Press, 1978, 1993), Chapters V–VIII. For a more recent elaboration of this position, see Neil MacCormick, *Rhetoric and the Rule of Law* (Oxford: Clarendon Press, 2005), Chapters 3–10. MacCormick's hard case typology is only in some respects compatible with Dworkin's (on which, see Dworkin, *Taking Rights Seriously*, Chapters 4–5).

[64] MacCormick, *Legal Reasoning and Legal Theory*, p. 195.

[65] *Ibid.*, p. 152.

decisions in hard cases – is extra-systemic, looking to the effects of a hard case ruling one way or another on society as a whole. Rather than being concerned with what makes sense within the legal system, they are concerned with 'what makes sense in the world'.[66] What, then, is the criterion of sense here? It consists of evaluating the consequences of a decision one way or another. It is a matter of 'choosing between rival possible rulings in a case [and] involves choosing between what are to be conceived of as rival models for, rival patterns of, human conduct in society'.[67] It seems to be the case that consequentialist arguments are often the strongest kind of argument in this trio.[68]

This account of how judges do and should decide hard cases can be contested, but, for non-sceptics at least, the space for dispute is limited. Just about all non-sceptical jurists accept a picture of what hard cases look like that is very similar to that offered by MacCormick; the same jurists also agree that the arguments MacCormick finds judges actually using when deciding cases are indeed appropriate considerations for judges to use.[69] Disagreement arises, however, as to which of these kinds of consideration should dominate: Ronald Dworkin, for instance, has little truck with MacCormick's claim that consequentialist arguments do and should dominate other arguments. Consequentialist arguments are, of course, far too similar to arguments of policy in the Dworkinian schema and, as we all now know, arguments of principle trump arguments of policy.[70] However interesting they might be, the details of this internecine jurisprudential dispute are not germane here. Our point, remember, is the claim that most reported cases in which the (or 'a') public/private distinction features are hard cases. Being such, they raise the three broad doctrinal issues, and are resolved by any combination of the three distinct kinds of argument, just noted.

What, then, is the moral of this story? That expecting any version of the distinction between public and private law to be *of use* in judicial decision-making is a mistake, if 'of use' is taken to mean 'conclusively dispositive

[66] *Ibid.*, p. 103. [67] *Ibid.*, p. 104. [68] *Ibid.*, pp. 127–8.

[69] A smattering of relatively recent studies (all, curiously, published in English within four years of one another) illustrates the point: R. Alexy, *A Theory of Legal Argumentation* (Oxford: Clarendon Press, 1978, 1989); S. Burton, *Judging in Good Faith* (Cambridge University Press, 1992); K. Gunther, *The Sense of Appropriateness* (Albany: State University of New York Press, 1988, 1993); J. Levin, *How Judges Reason* (New York: Peter Lang, 1992).

[70] Ronald Dworkin, *Law's Empire* (London: Fontana, 1986), p. 244. See also Dworkin, *Taking Rights Seriously*, Chapter 4.

of any particular hard case'. Hard cases are not, and can never be, so easily resolved. Even a cursory glance at the Human Rights Act 1998 and judicial review case law illustrates this. Furthermore, these cases are not merely hard cases: they are hard cases that manifest a relatively high level of indeterminacy as a result in part, at least, of the existence of multiple sub-versions of the state/non-state, public/private distinction. We therefore supplement the principal argumentative claim of this chapter – that there are many versions of the public/private distinction – with a related but subsidiary claim, that there are numerous versions of this particular public/private distinction.

Consider section 6 of the Human Rights Act 1998, which provides that '[i]t is unlawful for a public authority to act in a way which is incompatible with a [European] Convention right'. The term 'public authority' is undefined but includes what are known as 'hybrid' public authorities: that is, 'any person[s] certain of whose functions are functions of a public nature'.[71] But s. 6 also implicitly includes 'core' or 'obvious' public authorities, which are unlike hybrids because they must comply with the Convention in everything they do, whether public or private activity. This is due to s. 6(5), which relieves hybrids, but not core public authorities, of the obligation to obey the Convention when 'the nature of the act is private'. Section 6 is therefore something of a matryoshka doll, containing a nest of different sub-versions of the public/private distinction, all supposedly ultimately geared to distinguishing 'state' from 'non-state'. The first, between core public authorities and private persons, is institutional in nature. It looks to who the body in question is, focusing on the distinction between bodies constitutionally bound to act for others and those, on the other hand, permitted to act for their own ends within the confines of the law.[72] The second sub-distinction, between public and private *functions*, focuses instead on what the body *does* in the circumstances in question: it is the function that gives rise to its classification as either public or private.[73] The third, generated by s. 6(5), is between public and private *acts*. Even if a body is presumptively a hybrid public authority by virtue of

[71] Human Rights Act 1998, s. 6(3)(b).

[72] See *Aston Cantlow* v. *Wallbank* [2003] UKHL 37 at [7], [14] (Lord Nicholls), [62] (Lord Hope), [86] (Lord Hobhouse), [156] (Lord Rodger).

[73] This was made clear in *YL* [2007] UKHL 27 at [61] (Baroness Hale), [105] (Lord Mance), in the wake of a heavily institutional focus in earlier cases such as *Poplar Housing and Regeneration Community Association* v. *Donoghue* [2001] EWCA Civ 595 (*Poplar Housing*) and *R (Heather)* v. *Leonard Cheshire Foundation* [2002] EWCA Civ 366. Whether *YL* actually marked a substantive shift away from the institutional approach is

performing a public function, the Convention will still not apply if the act in question is public rather than private. The distinction between functions under s. 6(3)(b) and acts under s. 6(5) is tricky and underdeveloped, leaving this third sub-distinction somewhat stunted and malformed compared to the first two.

Section 6(5) was overlooked altogether in early cases concerning the meaning of public authority under s. 6,[74] and even when, as in more recent cases, courts do recognise its significance, they apply it so as to denude it of any real purpose. In *Weaver*, Elias LJ and Lord Collins MR believed that the act in question would be of the same nature as the function to which it pertained if the former was 'part and parcel' of or 'inextricably linked' with the latter.[75] The idea was applied broadly, too, with the termination of a tenancy by a registered social landlord being regarded as part and parcel of its function of managing and allocating housing stock. Whilst a broad application is understandable given the obvious need to prevent s. 6(5) from unduly undermining the scope for rights protection set by s. 6(3)(b), it has the side-effect of suggesting that s. 6(5) will make little difference in practice. This is principally because the courts are yet to rule that a given act is not part and parcel of the public function to which it is said to pertain by the applicant. On a conceptual level, the distinction between functions and acts was restated and affirmed by Lord Neuberger in *YL*:

> The former has a more conceptual, and perhaps less specific, meaning than the latter. A number of different acts can be involved in the performance of a single function.[76]

Yet the crucial point is that, if viewed as a conclusively dispositive touchstone, this statutory version of the public/private distinction is a complete failure. If the courts are satisfied that the body is not an institutionally public person, they must still go on to ask whether it is performing a public function and then, if it is, a particular public act. They can only resolve the public/private issue *itself* by considering three different iterations of the state/non-state (public/private) divide. Even having found that the

another matter, however: see J. Landau, 'Functional Public Authorities after *YL*' [2007] *Public Law* 630, 636.

74 In *Poplar Housing* [2001] EWCA Civ 595 at [69]–[70], for instance, Lord Woolf CJ simply gave a list of factors to support his conclusion that the body was a hybrid public authority, giving no indication as to whether they bore on the nature of its function or of its act.

75 *Weaver* [2009] EWCA Civ 587 at [76] (Elias LJ), [102] (Lord Collins MR).

76 [2008] 1 AC 95 at [130].

body *is* a public authority, the courts will still have a number of other issues to tackle.

The House of Lords' decision in *Aston Cantlow* v. *Wallbank*[77] provides a good illustration of the range of issues that can be in play. This case did indeed raise a question about the nature of public and private functions, since one of the issues the court had to address was whether or not a parochial church council of the Church of England was a public authority under s. 6. It might thus be regarded as an instance of 'the' public/private distinction being invoked to determine conclusively the decision in the case. But the public/private issue was only one of a number of pertinent issues in the case, the remaining ones including: (1) the state of the law on chancel repairs; (2) the retrospective applicability of the Human Rights Act 1998; and (3) the question of whether or not the parochial church council's order to lay rectors was compatible with the lay rectors' rights under Article 1 of the First Protocol of the ECHR. At least three of the four issues in this case – the law on chancel repairs being relatively unambiguous – are easily subsumable under one or more of the abstract hallmarks of hard cases. So, for example, the issue of the applicability of the Human Rights Act 1998 raises the question of which interpretation of an agreed proposition of law applies (the interpretative choice being between (1) the Human Rights Act 1998 does apply retrospectively and (2) the Human Rights Act 1998 does not apply retrospectively). Determining the compatibility issue (was the parochial church council's order compatible with Article 1?) was a matter of choosing between either different propositions of law or different interpretations of an agreed proposition of law.

It is undeniable that two of the issues in *Aston Cantlow* v. *Wallbank*[78] were closely related: the question of incompatibility with Article 1 becomes live only if the parochial church council is a public authority under s. 6. Yet it is simply wrong to regard the public/private issue as the only or even the most significant matter in the case. Furthermore, it is no surprise to find the judges resolving the question of the public or private status of a parochial church council via arguments of coherence and consistency. The judgments of Lords Hope, Hobhouse and Rodger include not just arguments of consistency, in which they address the English cases on the legal standing of the Church of England, but also arguments of coherence, in which they consider Strasbourg's decisions on, inter alia, the status of

[77] [2003] UKHL 37. [78] *Ibid.*

Greek monasteries and the Swedish church.[79] These strands of legal doctrine were less significant in Lord Scott's judgment, perhaps because his view, unlike that held by Lords Nicholls, Hope, Hobhouse and Rodger, was that the parochial parish council was a hybrid public authority, exercising a public function.[80] The nature of public authorities under legislation such as the Scotland Act 1998 was also discussed by Lord Hope.[81] Interestingly, consequentialist arguments featured in the judgments only fleetingly. They took the form of discontent about the potential harshness of the law on chancel repairs and played a role in bolstering the view that parochial church councils should not be regarded as public bodies.[82]

Cases in the judicial review context also rarely revolve around one single disputed interpretation of the public/private (state/non-state) distinction. The issues in play in such cases are just as diverse as those animating the Human Rights Act cases. Thus, even if a body is found to be performing a public function under the Civil Procedure Rules (CPR), so the decision in question is amenable to judicial review, this will not of itself determine the outcome of a hard case. A court will still have to satisfy itself that the body has acted unlawfully according to the principles of good administration (the duty to act fairly, rationally and the like), that there is no reason to make use of the judicial discretion to withhold the remedy the claimant seeks, and so on. One particularly well-known case illustrates the point. In *Datafin*[83] the Court of Appeal held that the Panel was amenable to judicial review in its capacity as de facto regulator of City takeovers, but nevertheless held that it had not acted unlawfully by dismissing the applicant's complaint that a bidding rival had breached the Panel's City Code.[84] This raised three quite separate issues: whether the Panel was amenable, whether it had acted unlawfully according to the relevant substantive principles and whether, if the answer to the two previous questions was affirmative, the court should issue the remedy sought.

Although Sir John Donaldson MR believed that the answers to the second and third questions were relatively clear,[85] the resolution of all three undoubtedly called for judgment and consequentialist arguments

[79] *Ibid.*, at [42], [48]–[53], [59]–[64] (Lord Hope), [86]–[88] (Lord Hobhouse), [153]–[157], [159]–[164] (Lord Rodger).

[80] *Ibid.*, at [130]–[132]. [81] *Ibid.*, at [42].

[82] *Ibid.*, at [15], [17] (Lord Nicholls).

[83] [1987] QB 815 (CA).

[84] The Panel's regulatory activities have now been placed on a statutory footing: see Companies Act 2006, s. 942(2).

[85] See *Datafin* [1987] QB 815 at 844.

featured at each stage. Donaldson MR was particularly vocal in his view that the Panel should in principle be amenable to judicial review – for the reason that it wielded wide-ranging de facto powers that would otherwise lie beyond the law's reach: 'Suppose, perish the thought, that it were to use its powers in a way which was manifestly unfair? … Parliament could and would intervene … but how long would that take and who in the meantime could or would come to the assistance of those who were being oppressed by such conduct?'[86] Arguments from consistency featured in the amenability analysis, too, as is evident from the lengths to which Their Lordships went to emphasise the compatibility of their conclusion with the existing case law in this area. Donaldson MR remarked that 'given its novelty, the panel fits surprisingly well into the format which this court had in mind in [*R* v. *Criminal Injuries Compensation Board; ex parte Lain*]'.[87] Lloyd LJ was more emphatic: 'I do not accept … that we are here extending the law.'[88]

Consequentialist arguments feature in the Court's analysis of the second and third issues, which analysis centred around the Panel's curious position as a de facto regulator responsible both for devising and policing the City Code. Donaldson MR believed there was 'little scope for a complaint that the panel has promulgated rules which are ultra vires, provided that they do not clearly violate the principle proclaimed by the panel of being based upon the concept of doing equity between one shareholder and another'.[89] As for remedies, he held that the 'only circumstances in which I would anticipate the use of … certiorari and mandamus would be in the event, which I hope is unthinkable, of the panel acting in breach of the rules of natural justice'.[90] Declaratory orders, he believed, were generally more appropriate:

> in the light of the special nature of the panel, its functions, the market in which it is operating, the time scales which are inherent in that market and the need to safeguard the position of third parties … I should expect the court to allow contemporary decisions to take their course, considering the complaint and intervening, if at all, later and in retrospect by declaratory orders which would enable the panel not to repeat any error and would relieve the individuals of the disciplinary consequences of any erroneous finding of breach of the rules. This would provide a workable

[86] *Ibid.*, at 827. See also at 845–846 (Lloyd LJ).

[87] *Ibid.*, at 838. *R* v. *Criminal Injuries Compensation Board, ex parte Lain* is reported at [1967] 2 QB 864 (QB).

[88] *Datafin* [1987] QB 815 at 849.

[89] *Ibid.*, at 841. [90] *Ibid.*, at 842.

> and valuable partnership between the courts and the panel in the public interest.[91]

More interestingly still, in certain judicial review cases – a domain in which the various sub-versions of the state/non-state distinction are most obviously in play – the courts also have recourse to a quite different version of public/private distinction. It is the fifth, legal-doctrinal version of the distinction and it is invoked in the effort to ensure that an applicant is not abusing the process of the court by pursuing the wrong procedure. This is the 'procedural exclusivity' rule. Whereas the amenability issue relates to the function the defendant performs, this rule implicates a different version of the public/private distinction because it seeks to distinguish between public and private *claims*.[92] It operates to prevent applicants taking undue advantage of any choice they might have as to whether to follow public law or private law procedure by channelling them into the appropriate procedure given the nature of their claim. Public law claims should reside in judicial review; private law claims in private law causes of action such as contract, tort and so on.

The rule derives from *O'Reilly* v. *Mackman*,[93] in which the claimants were prisoners who sought to contest their conviction of disciplinary offences under the Prison Rules by proceeding through writ in the Queen's Bench and Chancery Divisions of the High Court. The House of Lords unanimously held that this was an abuse of process. Although the claimants proceeded in private law, the decision-maker (the board of prison visitors) was fairly obviously a public body, the claimants were arguing their claim on the basis of a breach of the rules of natural justice

[91] *Ibid.*

[92] The courts keep the two issues quite separate in the sense that amenability cases determine the amenability issue and procedural exclusivity cases determine the procedural exclusivity issue. Even though the courts will often need to address the amenability issue before deciding whether there has been an abuse of process in the circumstances (they cannot be sure, for instance, that a claimant should have pursued a judicial review rather than a private law claim without being sure that the defendant was amenable to judicial review in the first place), the *issues* are distinct: there is almost no cross-referencing and no cross-fertilisation between the two. However, a notable trend-bucking judgment is *R* v. *East Berkshire Health Authority; ex parte Walsh* [1985] QB 152 (CA), in which the Court of Appeal held that it was an abuse of process for the applicant, a nurse, to seek judicial review against the defendant health authority, his employer, when dismissed for misconduct. Although the judgment was couched in procedural exclusivity terms, the real issue should have been amenability: it is clear that the applicant would never have had a viable judicial review claim because of the courts' well-established rule that judicial review will not lie against the use of contractual power.

[93] [1983] 2 AC 237 (HL).

and they sought a declaration that the board's decisions were void. To all intents and purposes, their claim, if successful, would have had the same effect as the award of a quashing order in judicial review. As Lord Diplock explained, this was because the Secretary of State was empowered to remit a disciplinary award and would presumably have done so following a declaration by the High Court that the award was a nullity.[94] The claimants also seemed to have no arguable cause of action in private law, their choice of procedure merely camouflaging an altogether different type of claim.[95] All things considered, Their Lordships thought that the claimants' choice of private law procedure served only to circumvent the various procedural protections designed to safeguard the decision-maker (shorter time limits, and so on) in judicial review.

The procedural exclusivity rule has proved difficult to apply in circumstances where applicants have arguable claims in both public and private law on the same set of facts. This might be the case, for example, if 'private' rights that would usually be enforceable against a public body in contract or tort can be enhanced or diminished by the exercise by that body of a statutory discretion. If the applicant wishes to challenge the use of that discretion, it is by no means self-evidently clear which procedure they should pursue. Fiddly and unconvincing distinctions arise as a result.[96] In recent years the courts seem to have taken a more relaxed stance than they did immediately post-*O'Reilly*, tolerating a greater degree of flexibility and allowing choice to claimants whose claims straddle both public and private law. As Sedley LJ remarked in *Clark* v. *University of Lincolnshire and Humberside*, 'the ground has shifted considerably since 1982 when *O'Reilly* v. *Mackman* was decided'.[97] In *Clark* itself, which concerned a contractual challenge to a university's decision to fail the claimant's undergraduate dissertation for plagiarism, the Court of Appeal held, in Lord Woolf MR's words, that 'the court will not strike out a claim which could more appropriately be made [in judicial review] … solely because of the procedure which has been adopted'.[98] But the *O'Reilly* rule still remains, as Lord Woolf was at pains to stress: the court may strike out a claim 'if it comes to the conclusion that in all the circumstances, including the delay

[94] *Ibid.*, at 274.

[95] As Lord Scarman recognised in *Gillick* v. *West Norfolk and Wisbech Area Health Authority* [1986] AC 112 (HL) at 178.

[96] Contrast, e.g., *Cocks* v. *Thanet District Council* [1983] 2 AC 286 (HL) and *Roy* v. *Kensington and Chelsea and Westminster Family Practitioner Committee* [1992] 1 AC 624 (HL).

[97] [2000] 1 WLR 1988 (CA) (*Clark*) at [16].

[98] *Ibid.*, at [38].

in initiating the proceedings, there has been an abuse of the process of the court'.[99] Thus, for some applicants at least, the public/private nature of their claim will continue to *matter.* The procedural exclusivity rule is therefore a further issue that may stand in the way of the courts' disposal of a hard case and yet another example of our central claim, that there are many public/private distinctions rather than just one.

That these particular cases – all of which concern various iterations of the state/non-state version of the public/private distinction and some of which concern the legal-doctrinal version of that distinction – are hard cases seems certain. If we are right in this, then they constitute the first step of a more general claim unsubstantiated here, namely, that almost all cases that concern any version of the public/private distinction are hard cases. And if that is so, then it is surely a mistake to expect the distinction to perform anything like a doctrinally dispositive role in those cases. Furthermore, we have offered additional reasons why no version of the distinction should be expected to do doctrinally dispositive work: first, because it is rare for there to be only one single version in play; and second, even if there is only one single version in play in a hard case, that single version is assuredly no less malleable than any other version of the distinction nor less subject to 'interference' from other versions of the distinction. That is the force of the permeability thesis outlined in section 2. Yet there is one further and quite different reason that suggests it is implausible to think that any version of the public/private distinction can do doctrinally dispositive work. It is most economically expressed by this question: 'how many other equally broad or even much narrower legal distinctions are ever dispositive in particular hard cases?'

The distinction between *mens rea* and *actus reus* in the criminal law is often just as contested and as unhelpful – as in need of mediation and elaboration – as that between public and private law. The distinction, which all common lawyers take for granted, between contract and tort is equally tricky and hardly ever dispositive; nor is the fact that it rarely resolves particular hard (or perhaps even easy) cases ever regarded as a reason for rejecting the distinction. Rather, this fact is taken to indicate something meaningful about the nature of the distinction itself. Lawyers' expectations about the pragmatic power of these distinctions are apparently nowhere near as high as the expectations held of the public/private distinction. There are, of course, two quite different inferences that can be drawn from this observation. One is that we are wrong to expect so little

[99] *Ibid.*

of these other distinctions. The other is that low expectations are justified, because distinctions of this kind are of limited use when faced with the fine detail and broad range of issues presented by hard cases. Obviously, the arguments already advanced in this chapter give reason to favour the latter, rather than the former, inference. And this has important implications for the ongoing debate about 'the' public/private distinction in the contexts we have just considered.

Since 'the' distinction is indeterminate and rarely if ever dispositive, lawyers are issued with the stark reminder that it just cannot be an 'algorithmic' solution to any interesting or complex legal question. It is, rather, but one piece in a broader jigsaw that seeks to dispose of hard cases justly. Awkward terms such as 'public function' and 'public authority' – which, as our analysis suggests, are unavoidably open to reinterpretation and contestation – are therefore unlikely to be defined in such a way as to generate unanimous assent. Nor is much lost if this is so. For even if the courts' definition of these terms happens to exclude the activities of some bodies that wield considerable power from the scope of judicial review or the Human Rights Act – the Jockey Club, for example[100] – it does not follow that the definition is flawed and must be rethought. There may be other useful ways in which the common law can regulate such bodies, as the courts themselves have recognised,[101] and legislation surely remains a viable option in the event that the common law as a whole proves inadequate. Parliament should, after all, retain some role in regulating society's myriad power imbalances.

Conversely, over-inclusiveness is not necessarily a problem. In the event that the definition of a public function is extended by the courts to encompass, say, the activities of private and charitable organisations providing services on behalf of central and local government – an inclusion that may be unpalatable to some[102] – it should be borne in mind that a number of mechanisms will remain open to the courts to mitigate any resulting harshness to the would-be public authority. In the Human Rights Act context, for instance, nothing stops private organisations pleading their

[100] See, notably, *R* v. *Disciplinary Committee of the Jockey Club; ex parte Aga Khan* [1993] 1 WLR 909 (CA) (on judicial review) and *R (Mullins)* v. *Jockey Club Appeal Board (No. 1)* [2005] EWHC 2197 (Admin) (on judicial review and the Human Rights Act 1998).

[101] As demonstrated by, e.g., *Nagle* v. *Feilden* [1966] 2 QB 633 (CA); *Bradley* v. *Jockey Club* [2005] EWCA Civ 1056.

[102] Dawn Oliver would be against such a move in the Human Rights Act context at least: Dawn Oliver, 'Functions of a Public Nature under the Human Rights Act' [2004] *Public Law* 329.

own Convention rights as a defence to Convention-based claims against them – even when they are performing public functions under s. 6(3)(b).[103] In the judicial review context, too, the substantive principles of good administration should be malleable enough to adjust to the particular situation. *Datafin*[104] provides a good example of this, through its cautious application of those substantive principles to the City Panel.[105] In short, public authority status is not the only factor that determines a body's legal liability. Given the malleability of terms such as 'public authority' and 'public function', and the resulting disagreement that can ensue over how to interpret them, lawyers would do well to remember that algorithmic determinacy here is a chimera.

The arguments of this chapter must not be misunderstood. By showing that there are many versions of 'the' public/private distinction rather than only one, and that various versions of the distinction should not be expected to do dispositive doctrinal work, we are not aiming to close down the conversation about public and private, either among lawyers or any other group. Rather, our aim is to engender more and better conversation. If there are indeed many salient distinctions between public and private, some of which have analogues within the law while others extend far beyond it, then attending to and interrogating these various distinctions is surely worthwhile. Only that will allow us to see the true complexity of our situation. Our thinking about public and private manifests a range of sometimes related and intersecting, sometimes divergent and discontinuous issues and we ought not to be surprised when this complexity is inscribed in various practices and social-institutional forms. This messy reality is not, however, immediately visible. It becomes clear only when we reject the urge to regard all that we see and think about public and private as manifestations of a single, ostensibly simple, issue.

[103] See Williams, 'A Fresh Perspective on Hybrid Public Authorities'.

[104] [1987] QB 815.

[105] Malleability is also particularly evident in the procedural fairness context, which is notoriously fact-sensitive. Lord Reid made this clear, for instance, in *Ridge* v. *Baldwin* [1964] AC 40 (HL) at 64: 'What a minister ought to do in considering objections to a scheme may be very different from what a watch committee ought to do in considering whether to dismiss a chief constable.'

3

Courts as public authorities, private law as instrument of government

STEVE HEDLEY

> One more word about giving instruction as to what the world ought to be. Philosophy in any case always comes on the scene too late to give it. As the thought of the world, it appears only when actuality has completed its process of formation and attained its finished state ... When philosophy paints its grey in grey, then has a shape of life grown old. By philosophy's grey in grey it cannot be rejuvenated but only understood. The owl of Minerva begins its flight only with the falling of dusk.
>
> G. W. F. Hegel, *Outlines of the Philosophy of Right*, T. M. Knox and S. Houlgate (trans.) (2008), p. 16

1 Public and private

The title of this collection presupposes a good deal: that there are such things as private law and public law; that these two are at least in some ways distinct from one another; but equally that each has something to do with the other – that on some occasions at least they *encounter* one another, and that some description of those encounters might interest this collection's readership. It is obvious enough, perhaps, why they might be thought distinct – public law is (roughly) about how government agencies interact with private people, whereas private law is (roughly) about how those private people interact with one another. So it is clear enough why we might think of those two bodies of law as separate, even though they occasionally rub shoulders with each other.

I would like to complicate that picture a little. You can think of private law as just being between private individuals, if you like. But when private law gets serious, a court is involved, and courts are most definitely not private individuals. Courts are public authorities, they are part of the machinery of government – they are usually reckoned as the third branch of government, after the Parliament and the Executive Government. Can we say that the law itself is private, that it is just between the parties? In a limited sense, it is. It settles what is mine and what is yours, it says how certain disputes between us should be resolved and it keeps each of us to our side of the line. But who drew that line, why did they draw it there and not elsewhere, and what are the assigned legal consequences of crossing it? Those are public questions, as they necessarily bring in public officials such as judges and legislatures.

So this is my starting point: we can talk of private law, and much of the time we are clear what we mean when we do, but the public is never *not there*. Courts, whatever else they are, are public authorities, and private law, whatever else it is, is a technique or instrument used by those authorities. That is not to say that the 'publicness' or 'privateness' of some issues does not shout louder in some cases than others. To say that courts are public authorities does not begin to exhaust what there is to say about them. And to say that private law is an instrument is not to endorse all the uses that are made of it – on the contrary, recognising how it is being used, and who is responsible for that use, can often be the start of demanding that it be put to better uses. My purpose is to lay down a marker in relation to private law issues generally. *Courts are public authorities; they have been very much involved in putting private law in the state it is now in; and where there are problems with private law, the courts have to be part of the solution.* We should have no Nimbyism, by which courts, and the lawyers and academics who help them, say that they are not involved, on the grounds that any solution would amount to 'making law' or 'usurping the place of the legislature', or something of that sort. They are always involved. *Whatever* they do involves 'making law' at some level – and the proper place of the legislature is always a matter of negotiation.

A On academic motivation

As another introductory matter, it is interesting to note the reactive nature of much legal scholarship in this area, as in others. I was particularly struck by Charles Fried's description of how his (justly famous) *Contract as Promise*[1] was written against the background of views of which he disapproved, particularly those of Patrick Atiyah and Duncan Kennedy, both of whom sought to assign Contract a very different place

[1] Charles Fried, *Contract as Promise, A Theory of Contractual Obligation* (Cambridge, MA: Harvard University Press, 1981).

in the scheme of things.[2] All of these writings were, of course, excellent contributions to the scholarship of the time, and none from any point of view disproves the argument of the others, though, obviously enough, they are somewhat opposed in their approaches. Various things struck me on reading Fried's account. (I should perhaps add that I am familiar with the views criticised, and have rather more sympathy with them than Fried has.) One thing is that this sort of irritation, while no doubt in some respects a mere passing phase, nonetheless is more profound than that. It is the culmination of a more involved process, of feeling that something is very wrong with the opposing approach, and that somebody ought to say so. Another is that the chain of irritation is substantially lengthened when we look at *all* of those involved. Atiyah, with others who wrote and still write in the area, was no doubt in his turn irritated by the lack of substance in much of the writing that had based contract on promise. No doubt Fried's book, too, irritated others in turn. Each generation of scholars irritates the next into denouncing their core views, and from the resulting hubbub new legal theory emerges. This sort of reaction can, in its way, be a spur to great academic productivity.[3]

Perhaps the main conclusion I reached was about how this sort of irritation can make academic writers overshoot the mark. The wish to prove the other guy wrong and to show up nonsense for what it is, is often a useful spur. Unfortunately, it can also freeze the terms of the argument in unproductive ways – you are *so* determined to prove the other guy wrong that you lose track of the good there may be in the argument you are attacking, or of why anyone else might think it a useful approach. That is not good – or not usually good, anyway.

B Weinrib's The Idea of Private Law

All of which leads fairly directly to Ernest Weinrib's *The Idea of Private Law*.[4] I do not think that my annoyance is with Professor Weinrib as such, a man I do not know, and have no reason to doubt I would find perfectly pleasant if I did – as well as a renowned scholar in his field. Rather, perhaps, my annoyance is with the place his book occupies in the current

[2] Charles Fried, '*Contract as Promise* Thirty Years On' (2012) 45 *Suffolk University Law Review* 961, 961–2.

[3] For another psychological factor possibly at work here, see Patrick O'Callaghan, 'Monologism and Dialogism in Private Law' (2010) 7 *Journal Jurisprudence* 405.

[4] Ernest Weinrib, *The Idea of Private Law* (Cambridge, MA: Harvard University Press, 1995).

scholarship. Anyone who asks why private law is as it is, why it approaches matters the way it does and not in some other way, is almost bound to be referred to Weinrib's book sooner or later. Yet what answer does he give to the question of what private law is for, why it is there, why the universe is a better place for its being here (if it is)? His answer is a Zen-like insistence that private law has no purpose, no goal. It is not *for* anything. It just *is*.

> Private law, I will claim, is to be grasped only from within and not as the juridical manifestation of a set of extrinsic purposes. If we *must* express this intelligibility in terms of purpose, the only thing to be said is that the purpose of private law is to be private law.[5]

From my own perspective – which includes a fair amount of study in nineteenth- and twentieth-century legal history – the idea that private law has *no purpose at all* goes beyond absurdity. Private law reached the state it is in because of the efforts of a great many people – judges, lawyers, reformers, politicians, academics – over a considerable period of time. Of course, not all the results can be said to be intentional – compromises had to be made between competing goals, mistakes were made, circumstances changed, and the behaviour of complex legal systems is hard to predict – but private law is a human product, and much of it is intelligible in terms of human purposes. To abstract away all of those purposes, to ignore what the law is for and to consider it as a purposeless intellectual exercise, seems a bizarre thing to do, and is the more bizarre for Weinrib's insistence that it is an exercise in *understanding* private law, as distinct from a deliberate attempt to remove any hope of understanding.

In trying, in my turn, to make coherent sense of *The Idea of Private Law*, the only way I have is to treat it as a thought-experiment, asking: if we had never encountered private law before, and set aside all other concerns in the attempt to render it intelligible, what would we make of it? This seems to me the best way to avoid a total rejection of Weinrib's work, to see what is good in it – and there clearly are some good things in it. Weinrib's description of the internal intelligibility of private law undoubtedly resonates at some level – lawyers do indeed try to make sense of private law as a closed system, which runs best when we forget that private law was made, by human beings, for reasons that seemed good to them and that to some

[5] Weinrib, *The Idea of Private Law*, p. 5. For other critiques of Weinrib's key ideas, see, e.g., George Brencher IV, 'Formalism, Positivism and Natural Law in Ernest Weinrib's Tort Theory' (1992) 42 *University of Toronto Law Journal* 318; Joanna Perkins, Book Review (1997) 17 *Legal Studies* 204; John Gardner, 'What is Tort Law For? Part 1: The Place of Corrective Justice' (2010) 1 *Oxford Legal Studies Research Paper Series*.

extent we still share. Where Weinrib goes wrong is in over-egging the pudding – in saying that private law 'is to be grasped only from within'.[6] Weinrib is setting up false alternatives – that we either try to understand private law from within or we try to understand it from without – when in fact we need to do both, each perspective having something valuable to say. We need to understand it from both within and without if we are to understand it at all. For each of us, to assert that which we consider important should not entail the further step of denying importance to what other people think. We are all in this together.

C *Argument of this chapter*

In short, then, the aim of this chapter is to establish the public nature of much of what goes on in so-called 'private law'. Private law is the product of public officials working as part of the Commonwealth's legal system, and like other public officials, they should be improving what they do as part of the ordinary process of doing it. Some will say that while this is true, it is only one part of what there is to say about private law – I entirely agree. If I seem unduly insistent or monomaniacal on the 'publicness' of private law, it is because some prominent scholars have denied it, and have been treated as making a serious point when they have done so. Some – Weinrib is a prime example – have denied it because they seek to make private law a closed system, administered in such a way as to be internally coherent, but without wider social responsibilities. Others – academics, lawyers, judges – have denied it on the rather different grounds that tackling the problems of private law constitutes 'making law', which they take to be fundamentally different from what they are engaged in. They do not deny that reform in the public interest might be needed; their argument is that it is not their problem. I will refer to both points of view in the body of the chapter.

D *The bogey of 'pure instrumentalism'*

My final introductory point is about what this chapter is *not* arguing for. In reviewing the literature for this chapter, I noticed an odd thing. There were a number of writers arguing in a vein similar to mine, but they seemed curiously diffident about it. We do not believe that private law makes any sense as a closed system, they say, but we do not believe in a 'pure instrumentalism' either. By this they seem to mean that they

[6] Weinrib, *The Idea of Private Law*, p. 5.

do not want to get to the stage where *everything* in private law is clearly labelled with a public purpose divorced from what serves the cause of justice between the parties. Seeing private law as all about justice between the parties will not do – it is about other things as well – but it is not all about serving the public interest either.[7]

I agree. If that is really the choice, then I also agree that the middle course, between the extremes, is best. Yet I am puzzled. I know a number of people on the first extreme – the Weinrib extreme. That is a real point of view, held by real people. Yet who, precisely, has argued for a 'pure instrumentalism'? This seems to me a bogeyman – a made-up point of view to terrify intellectual innocents into paying more respect to legal doctrine – 'Read your law reports, or the bogeyman will get you!' Who are these people, who entirely neglect fairness, or refuse to discuss law using its own vocabulary? Weinrib's own account of instrumentalism stresses preferring the collective good over any considerations of fairness between individual parties, and substituting its own vocabulary for the more traditional talk of 'reasonableness, fault, cause, duty, and so on'.[8] He refers to various other writers as pure instrumentalists, but none of those mentioned seem to hold this extreme view. They refer to the collective good rather more than Weinrib cares for, but I see no hint that they would reduce the law to this question alone.[9] There is a long history of legal thinkers worrying that instrumentalists will make them obsolete – most famously Oliver Wendell Holmes in 1897, saying that while the lawyer is 'the man of the present', 'the man of the future is the man of statistics and the master of economics'.[10] Well, this is the future – Holmes' future, anyway – and it has not happened. So much for prediction.

While there may be someone, somewhere, who believes in 'pure instrumentalism', they are keeping their view to themselves. You will not find such a person in a law school, since such a pure instrumentalism would have no place for law; indeed, this supposed point of view seems to

[7] For example, Hanoch Dagan, 'The Limited Autonomy of Private Law' (2008) 56 *American Journal of Comparative Law* 809 (criticising both 'autonomist theory' and 'unlimited instrumentalism'); Alan Calnan, 'The Instrumental Justice of Private Law' (2010) 78 *University of Missouri-Kansas City Law Review* 559 (criticising both 'instrumentalists' and 'deontologists'). Dagan's recent writings seem more assertive – see especially Hanoch Dagan, 'Pluralism and Perfectionism in Private Law' (20 June 2011), available at: http://ssrn.com/abstract=1868198 (last accessed 21 May 2013).

[8] Weinrib, *The Idea of Private Law*, p. 49.

[9] Weinrib's antagonists (from *The Idea of Private Law*, pp. 4–6) seem to include Robert Bush, Guido Calabresi, Richard Epstein, Owen Fiss and Richard Posner.

[10] Oliver Wendell Holmes, Jr, 'The Path of the Law' (1897) 10 *Harvard Law Review* 457, 469.

harbour a huge naivety as to how easy it is to define the public interest, and how ready people would be to accept it without argument, especially if it conflicted with their private interest. I rather suspect that you will not find a 'pure instrumentalist' anywhere, because anyone who has thought through the problems of the legal system will see that the system *has* to give weight to fairness between the parties, at some level. No political system can survive long if it deliberately and ostentatiously ignores what those involved in it think is fair; and differing views on fairness is the very stuff of politics. To put it another way, 'pure instrumentalists' who are also practical politicians would have *no option* but to concern themselves with fairness; and even someone seeking to tear down the entire legal system is unlikely to be able to free themselves from its vocabulary. Maintaining the legitimacy of the system in the eyes of those involved with it is always a concern, which can only be addressed by appeals to what is fair.

The academic dispute, then, is *not* between those who want to achieve fairness between private parties and those who do not care for fairness, with people like me weaving a delicate course between. It is not even a dispute between those who think there are instrumentalist or functional elements in the legal system and those who do not, because I am sure that (with sufficient attention to definitions) all would admit that there are. The issue is over whether the two can usefully be separated. To this I now turn.

2 The past

In one way, the argument here is over the distinction between public law and private law – but it is not really an argument about whether that distinction exists, or even (particularly) about where you draw it. Of course we *can* distinguish private from public, and while we would not always agree on where the line should be drawn, that incoherence does not make the distinction meaningless. The argument is over what significance the distinction has. In a sentence, Weinrib takes this distinction – and other logically related ones – much more seriously than I do. Some aspects of this are obvious, but I think the full extent of it needs a bit more emphasis, because the difference is as much one of method as anything else. Lawyers do not always reason in the same way as philosophers, even when they (think they) are discussing the same topic.

The primary argument Weinrib makes is asserted directly in the text – private law is distinct from other areas with which it might be confused. It is a sore point, because Weinrib is a bit careless about what those other areas are. They obviously include public law but also politics (which he takes to be lawless), and some backs have been put up by casual references that seem to equate the two, suggesting that public law is not law at all. It is kinder, and probably more accurate, to assume that he is praying in aid the traditional set of distinctions here: that law is different from non-law; that substantive law is different from procedure; and that public law is different from private law. These distinctions together give him a sort of map of what the world of law is like. He focuses on his one discrete and, to his mind, tightly defined region, within which he thinks the barriers are less important – yes, it may be traditional or convenient to distinguish property from contract from tort, but it is all private law, governed by the same fundamental concerns.

Seeing all of this with a lawyer's eyes, I would say: certainly, it is always possible to draw maps, and they are sometimes useful. In every generation there are some accepted ideas about what a good map of the system would look like, and some people who work hard to make the map more detailed – or (as they think) to perfect it. But what are the rest of us up to? We are mostly working on projects with the potential to sabotage the map, to give arguments why particular lines should be drawn in a slightly different place, or even a *very* different place, or perhaps erased entirely. These things are always the product of particular circumstances. A barrister in court may well put up a stout defence of traditional doctrine – if traditional doctrine favours their client and there is no better argument at hand. Their opponent may well deride traditional doctrine and insist on modern law for the modern age, or they might say that traditional doctrine really favours *their* client once it is properly understood, or they might change the subject and say that the real issue is quite different – and I would hazard a guess that the identity of the judge they are trying to convince might be a factor here. The point is that these maps are used as *arguments*, as *rhetoric*, as *attempts to persuade*. Since there are many forums and many opportunities for persuasion, the argument is perpetually modified to meet new circumstances.

Any one 'map' or system for viewing the law, then, is a continually shifting body of arguments and rhetorical resources. And much of the more traditional sort of legal history is concerned with tracing the fortunes of these bodies of thought, watching the activities of courts and parliaments as they continually stretch or compress existing notions to get the results that they want. In the course of that history, you often come across people who seem genuinely interested in the map for itself – people whose main motivation is simply to clarify existing notions, and who seek no further reward. You meet all sorts. But legal historians have no business giving such clarifiers any special place, or taking them any more seriously than their contemporaries did. The changes in attitude between succeeding generations are often profound – what seems at one point a promising idea for making the law clearer may seem like old hat within a short time indeed. When I say that ideas shift, I do not mean that they would always be small shifts. Sometimes whole systems of thought, really big ideas for organising the law, sink so thoroughly out of favour that they might seem to have died.

A *How we got here – medieval*

To give some kind of perspective on this, it is worth pointing out that Weinrib's attempt to give order to common law – distinguishing public from private, substance from procedure, and so on – is ancient, and was not the first such attempt but the second. In its early days – and, measured by the calendar, for most of its history – the common law was ordered on a quite different principle, usually called the system of the forms of action.

That system was logical enough in its essentials. If you had a grievance that you thought the royal courts ought to be interested in, you applied to the relevant government officer – a Chancery clerk, as he was known – and bought a writ. The writ would spell out your story in a stereotyped way, and ordered that if what you were saying was proved to be true, then you should have the remedy you were asking for. The 64-groat question was, of course, what sort of accusations this could be applied to; what sort of facts were the ones that, if proved, should lead to a remedy? There was an early, seat-of-the-pantaloons phase where the clerks could just answer this one as they thought best, but in 1258 it was settled that new writs usually had to be based on an existing established writ, so that novel forms of action could not spring into life merely at the whim of an inventive Chancery clerk.[11] The rules governing each form were usually clear, and were applied with some rigour. All legal complaints either had to be on a pattern already recognised as giving rise to legal

[11] Provisions of Oxford 42 Hen. 3 (1258). For the forms of action, see, e.g., John Baker, *An Introduction to English Legal History*, 4th edition (Oxford University Press, 2002), Chapter 4.

consequences, or some very good reason had to be given why the system should be extended to cover it – by either a novel form being recognised, or an existing one stretched a little to accommodate the new claim, or establishing a new tribunal to deal with problems the existing ones could not solve.

That was the system, and it proved quite durable – in the order of six centuries from the establishment of the Register of Writs to the final abolition of the system.[12] Was it a good system? It is rather late to be asking that question, of course, but most of the modern objections to it would have made little sense in the system's heyday. A more intellectually robust system would have been hideously wasteful in an age where most people were illiterate. To modern eyes, the old system seems to put all the emphasis on procedure, not substance, but that is not accurate. The apparent lack of substance is an artefact of the record-keeping – the place to argue substance was usually before a jury, whose reasons would never have been written down, if indeed they were ever articulated orally. And if it sometimes seemed to critics that there were too many tribunals with overlapping remits, or that cases were won or lost on outrageous technicalities, or that the system made too many concessions to the convenience of the officials and practitioners who profited from it – well, they say the same today.

My point is not whether the system of forms of action was a good system, but merely that it was a system. It let lawyers know where they stood, it told them how to frame their claims and what sort of arguments they might have to meet in reply. Of course, the legal history of that period is precisely concerned with the fate of particular forms: the ways in which forms were stretched, bent or compressed to achieve useful results. Anyone who has studied this will remember the slow growth of new forms of action, and the outrageous legal fictions that were often employed to achieve this – one generation of judges would pretend that A was B (because B was within the form of action but A was not), and it would take a later generation to admit that the two were different but that A was just as worthy of a legal remedy as B, and so deserved recognition in its own right. Legal fictions are perennial – we often pretend that *earlier* generations used fictions whereas we do not – a view that perhaps deserves recognition as a legal fiction in itself.

[12] What counts as 'final abolition' may be a matter of opinion – by some criteria, the forms are not dead even now – but the key legislative move is usually regarded as the Common Law Procedure Act 1852 (England and Wales).

In time, the forms of action lost most of their attraction as a system: the legal system had become so large and so varied in its operations that the list of possible actions seemed endless; the number of distinct tribunals seemed inconveniently large; and the piling of legal fiction on legal fiction compromised the system's intelligibility. So the newer idea of doctrinal law, of separating substance from procedure and dividing substance into ordered categories, came to seem preferable: and this second wave of common law systematisation achieved great things over the nineteenth and twentieth centuries. But consider briefly the end of the medieval system, bearing in mind that we may now be coming to the end of the second, doctrinal, wave too. Three morals from the medieval story, if you like.

First, systemisation only goes so far, and substance will not be denied. Working within a system is one thing; deciding how much importance you are going to attach to it is another. As lawyers, we put up mental walls to make life easier for ourselves by dividing up the law – but those walls are always porous to some degree, something always seeps through them, and sometimes what seeps through is more important than what does not. Lawyers of earlier centuries would argue furiously over whether the right action in certain circumstances was trespass or an action on the case. Perhaps our modern arguments over whether a particular decision was a bold use of doctrine or an illegitimate exercise in judicial activism are not so different.

Second, while we can talk of the 'life' and 'death' of the forms of action, we must not allow our metaphors to confuse us. The medieval system never died entirely. The various distinct torts are, for the most part, simply relabelled common law forms of action: trespass in all its forms is still a vital part of tort. And of course the great counterweight within the medieval system – that common law courts were supplemented by a Court of Equity, to rub the harsher edges off the rigid forms of action – is still a force to be reckoned with. I well remember the 2004 conference in Sydney at the University of New South Wales, focusing on the (relatively recent) fusion of law and equity in that jurisdiction. A wake, it most definitely was not.[13] The old reason for separating out equity has long gone. There is no longer a Court of Equity – but both professionally and intellectually it is still a distinct system in rude health. Was everyone at the conference happy with that state of affairs? Of course not. Leading the charge

[13] The conference proceedings volume is Simone Degeling and James Edelman (eds.), *Equity in Commercial Law* (Sydney: Lawbook, 2005).

against equity were exactly the people you would expect – those who are still fighting the nineteenth-century battle, trying to assert their doctrinal version of order against the medieval version. How many people did they convince? I do not know, though I certainly do not recall the conference ending on any great note of unanimity. The struggle continues. No legal idea ever truly dies, although, at any one time, some look fitter than others.

My third conclusion – which again I suggest is relevant not simply to the fate of the forms of action but also to the likely fate of doctrinal law – is that the rise and fall of such intellectual systems is never *just* about internal technical arguments. Political arguments also play a role. No doubt a purely technical case could have been made for abandoning the forms of action, but it would not have been a very strong one. Those in the best position to argue about it would have been the more skilled common law practitioners, who knew the existing system very well indeed, and would have been very hard to convince either that it was incoherent, or that some other system, not yet invented, would be better. *We* know that good doctrinal writing would quickly take off given the chance – that up-and-coming lawyers would find it a useful way of occupying quiet periods and advertising their expertise, and that law teachers in the newly established or newly invigorated law faculties would also see personal and career benefits in writing clear and logical doctrine. But it is hard to see how a typical nineteenth-century observer could have foreseen that. And, of course, overhanging that whole period would have been the issue of whether to codify the law – would-be codifiers were employing their usual double-bind argument, that either the common law is chaotic (in which case it should be swept away and replaced with a code), or it is well ordered under the apparent chaos (in which case we should extract the ordered rules and put them in a code). This was never just a technical argument – for every code there is a codifier, and for most common lawyers codes were pretty much tied up with that nineteenth-century hate figure, Napoleon Bonaparte. Over the nineteenth century there always were excellent technical arguments for codifying the law, but none powerful enough to counter the revulsion at being seen to copy the *Code Napoléon*.

Replacing one system with another is a *process*, which only happens slowly; and often it is not obvious to those going through the process where it will end. We do not know how long the traditional doctrinal category of 'private law' will last. It is a fair bet, however, that one major factor that will determine this is the strength of the arguments either way aired in collections like this.

B How we got here – nineteenth and twentieth centuries

In retrospect, and given what a vast change it was in the common law mindset, the shift to thinking about law primarily in terms of doctrine happened rather quickly, over the latter part of the nineteenth century. Private law was no longer something that emerged as a by-product when considering a wild array of different possible legal procedures, but was considered as a rather limited set of doctrines in their own right – often wild and disorderly doctrines, but doctrines nonetheless. Much of this relied on putting up stout intellectual barriers against confusing inroads by the rest of the legal system. It became axiomatic that procedure was separate from law – not simply that it was not the same, but that it was possible to write whole books, or even spend whole university careers, discussing law without mentioning procedure once – and, similarly, that cases involving public or state interests were utterly separate from cases involving private parties. In short, a significant intellectual space was made in which (say) torts could be discussed as self-standing entities, almost as if they were laboratory specimens, without referring to the processes by which they came to public attention or the reasons why they were thought to merit that attention. The world of private law had come into its own.[14]

The change was, as I say, rather sudden. Key points of the process would appear to be:

- *The creation of a relatively rigid and internally controlling hierarchy of courts*. Old, rival jurisdictions were merged into unitary courts. Even law and equity were made to share a court, with the proviso (on which various views were held) that equity was to prevail in any conflict between them. The doctrine of precedent transmuted from the old idea that a general climate of opinion in the courts is part of the law, to a new view that a single authoritative judgment binds all judges, perhaps for all time. Judgments became more careful, more focused on domestic precedents to the exclusion of all else, and longer. Jury trial slowly declined – private law became more and more the field of the legal specialist.[15]

[14] Of course, these developments affected much else in the law in addition to the matters here under consideration. See, e.g., Simon Stern, 'The Analytical Turn in Nineteenth-Century Legal Thought' (31 May 2011), available at: http://ssrn.com/abstract=1856146 (last accessed 21 May 2013).

[15] See generally Steve Hedley, 'Words, Words, Words: Making Sense of Legal Judgments 1875–1940', in Chantal Stebbings (ed.), *Law Reporting in England* (London: Hambledon Press, 1995), p. 169. Which of the matters mentioned in this paragraph are Cause and which Effect is not the subject of this chapter.

- *The establishment of university law schools as serious intellectual forces.* Old universities were secularised, new universities established, and Law managed to establish at least a toe-hold in most of them. It is always a tough fight for a new field of knowledge to win a place as a respectable academic discipline, and Law in the late nineteenth century had at least as much trouble as Media Studies was to have in the late twentieth century. But it made it, and at least part of the reason was the intellectual clarity of the brave new private law, illustrated by (for example) Anson on *Contract*[16] or Pollock on *Torts*[17] – both bold attempts to state aspects of private law without undue reference to procedure, policy or regulation.
- *A sweep-out of obsolete medieval regulation.* For a rather brief period, it seemed progressive and responsible to argue for most parts of the economy to be unregulated. A pure laissez-faire attitude was in fashion. As Atiyah notes, this was a *very* brief period, barely a single human lifetime.[18] The mid-Victorian faith in laissez-faire, with its apparently naive faith that economic actors could be on the whole trusted to do the right thing even when their economic interests plainly clashed with everyone else's, did not last long. It was right to abolish the remnants of medieval regulatory systems that had long since ceased to do anything useful, but inevitably it was merely a precursor to more modern forms of regulation with which we are all familiar. The age of laissez-faire was also the age in which private law doctrine was established in its current form, and the absence of regulation from it is an important constituent element.

It is only too clear, then, why the great Victorian doctrinalists wrote as they did. Of course, they would ignore procedure as much as possible. To do otherwise would have seemed an unhealthy reversion to their past. Of course, they plagiarised their major doctrinal ideas from Continental European sources. Those ideas were the most systematic on offer – but of course, as patriotic common lawyers, they placed very little emphasis

[16] William Anson, *Principles of the English Law of Contract* (Oxford University Press, 1879).

[17] Frederick Pollock, *The Law of Torts* (London: Stevens and Sons, 1887).

[18] When George Bramwell (b.1808) was a young man, his support for laissez-faire would have marked him out as a progressive, even a radical; by the time he was a judge (1856), his was an established if rather old-school view; by the time he died (1892) such views were only held by the deepest of conservatives. See generally Patrick Atiyah, *The Rise and Fall of Freedom of Contract* (Oxford University Press, 1979), pp. 329ff.

on the point. Of course they would be wary of any idea that common law doctrine might act as regulation. They would have known that medieval common law often did precisely that, but would have regarded those ancient practices as a failed experiment in government that should not be repeated. That government would try again, that regulation would grow and that the common law would be part of it was not an idea they sought to encourage.

We should not overestimate how much was done in that formative period, especially as many of our current problems represent unfinished intellectual work left over from it. Different jurisdictions were fused into unitary entities, but very often the differences lived on as distinct professional specialisms – equity being a leading example. Many local or extraordinary courts were abolished, but those who regretted that abolition quietly renamed their judges as 'arbitrators', allowing the old institution to continue under a new banner.[19] The old forms of action did not go quietly – in 1909 Maitland was still protesting that '[t]he forms of action we have buried, but they still rule us from their graves'.[20] While the form of the doctrinal law of contract – with its offer-and-acceptance and consideration as key doctrines – took form very early in the process, tort evaded any consensus on its structure well into the twentieth century.

So, while the essentials of the doctrinalist mode of thought were well established in many minds significantly before 1900, the implementation of those ideas necessarily took rather longer. Over the twentieth century much of what we see in the law journals and the law reports can be read as attempts to expound the law within the confines of that vision. But the world outside did not cease to turn, and many of the elements that the doctrinal writers of the twentieth century had to deal with would have been alien to those in the previous century. There was more and more litigation, and thus more and more case law to fit into the doctrinal structure. Juries became less and less common, meaning that judges and doctrinal writers had to concern themselves more and more with factual complications. Filling out the doctrinal structure of the law was perhaps an even bigger task than the most pessimistic Victorian might have guessed.

Another confounding thing happened as well: nineteenth-century doctrinal writers concerned themselves with the legal rights and

[19] See Harry Arthurs, *Without the Law: Administrative Justice and Legal Pluralism in 19th Century England* (University of Toronto Press, 1985), Chapter 3.

[20] Frederic Maitland, *The Forms of Action at Common Law* (Cambridge University Press, 1909, 1936), Lecture 1, p. 1.

responsibilities of individuals. (What else, indeed, could they do?) When they talked of what 'reasonable people' were obliged to do or could reasonably be expected to do, they meant just that. What happened from the late nineteenth century on, however, was the quiet growth of the body corporate, the organisation masquerading for legal purposes as an individual. This occurred both on the public side and the private side. The private business corporation rapidly became the main legal form of business organisation, largely supplanting more individualistic forms such as the trust business, the partnership or the sole trader. The idea that the business of government was done by discrete corporations or agencies was a rather older one, but making those corporations responsible for their actions took a little longer – legislation was necessary to subject them to the law. Well before the close of the twentieth century, of course, this process was complete. Yet private law doctrine continued as if nothing much had happened. It is very hard to imagine many modern negligence actions that do not have a corporation as the *real* defendant (by which I mean, the entity that stands to lose if the action is won) – though that corporation is sometimes an insurer, sometimes another sort of business or non-profit organisation, sometimes a public body. The public world has become a world of organisations, while private law still talks of individuals – a modern legal fiction.

3 Where we are

While the world of the nineteenth-century doctrinalist is long gone, it is another question whether it is convenient to sweep away the nineteenth-century doctrine. In some cases the legislature has indeed disposed of it. In others, the legislature has chosen to work with it, often in the process transforming it into something quite different. A doctrine devised for a world without proper regulation, workable business structures or adequate liability insurance is made to work in a world with all three – but, of course, its significance is now entirely different.

Let us take the example of the liability of a road driver to pedestrians injured by his or her bad driving. This makes good nineteenth-century doctrinal sense. The misbehaving driver is made to compensate those injured by the misbehaviour. It would seem that justice is being done. From a twentieth-century governmental point of view, by contrast, this initially seems to have no attraction at all, and indeed to present a failure of proper government. Is the fate of the injured pedestrians to turn on the sheer chance of whether the driver's fault can be established, and whether the driver has sufficient assets to compensate? That would indeed make a lottery of the law. The preferred solution to the problem was not to sweep away the common law, but to tweak it a little, by insisting that all drivers carry liability insurance. The solution is not perfect – the administration of this system is not cheap – but it turns out that rival solutions are not all that easy to administer either. The requirement of fault on the part of the driver begins to look odd, but removing it would cost more than voters are prepared to pay, so it remains. So the form of the nineteenth-century solution is retained and has survived into the twenty-first century. Of course, the heart is ripped from the original nineteenth-century idea. The bad driver is not the one who pays the cost of the accident, and his/her theoretical liability to compensate is an embarrassment rather than (as it would originally have been) the whole point of the law – but we pass over all that.

Accordingly, attempting to make sense of, or to justify, the common law rules *in their own terms* misses much of their point. No responsible legislator or administrator would seek to justify them in those terms. Such common law rules as we still have were developed and modified at the same time as modern regulation was being developed and modified. Common law and statute are not in different worlds but in constant dialogue, as each seeks to accommodate the other.

A Contract

Contract Law was the most prominent early product of the late nineteenth-century doctrinal movement, and that law, with its insistence on agreement, has remained relatively stable since then. Yet the apparent commitment to freedom of contract was never quite what it seemed, because while the insistence on agreement *to contracts* was genuine enough, the insistence on agreement *to contract terms* was a more sketchy or surface affair, with much of the contents of contracts bearing only a passing resemblance to what the parties may have agreed. The (largely instrumental) convenience of lawyers and courts strongly inclined them to oust orally agreed terms in favour of any document drawn up purporting to contain the terms. It was soon established that written terms would form part of the parties' contract, regardless of whether they were in any normal sense agreed, so long as their author had given notice of them to the other – 'notice' usually meaning no more than that they had afforded the other party a (purely theoretical) opportunity to read them. This lawyerly loophole, when added to the material interest of business corporations in reducing their legal liabilities whenever possible, led by the 1930s to a situation where any business corporation could be free of any contractual liability it did not wish to assume, at least when dealing with parties weaker or less legally sophisticated than themselves.

In the period that followed there was a fight-back by both legal and regulatory authorities – through consumer protection legislation, prohibitions on certain specific terms and competition law, and by a general judicial tightening-up on contractual rules that inconvenience the weaker party. This has culminated (for now) in general legislation on standard forms in consumer contracts, which attempts to outlaw contract terms that are unbalanced to the detriment of consumers. The techniques used enlist both the judiciary and regulatory agencies: unfair terms may be tackled either by the relevant regulatory body, or they may be struck down as encountered by judges in ordinary litigation. The law of contract has therefore, in one major area at least, embraced the doctrine that contracts will be upheld only when they are fair. Yet the formal common law doctrine in the books still repeats the nineteenth-century dogma, that contracts will be upheld whether fair or not. Someone who looks at the common law alone cannot be made to admit that a fundamental change has taken place; but then, someone who looks at the common law alone has ceased to describe the legal system as it actually is.

B Tort

Tort Law was not so precisely defined by the nineteenth-century doctrinalists. Indeed, well into the twentieth century a reasonable observer might well have doubted that it formed a doctrinal subject in its own right – and it has never attained the apparent unity and clarity that contract has reached. Given the distinctness and rigidity of each of the individual torts – a legacy of the forms of action – it would not have been surprising if it had remained as a mere archipelago of isolated liabilities, with obvious family resemblances to one another but without much potential for more general theorising. What saved it from this fate was the very substantial impetus given by overall regulatory policy, which encouraged potential plaintiffs to look to the tortfeasor for compensation, and encouraged potential defendants to insure against such claims. In employment, in road traffic and in medical care contexts the same solution was adopted. From a regulatory perspective, a measure of compensation was provided for the victims of accidents, and an incentive of sorts was provided to deter future accidents. From a doctrinal perspective, the relevance and significance of torts were assured, though at the price of blowing the doctrinal project onto a different course, one in which 'negligence' gradually ceased to be a mode of committing torts and became a tort in its own right – increasingly, *the* tort, as it began to absorb the more ancient torts into its increasingly unruly theory.

Again, we see the stark contrast between the individualistic, almost Victorian language of doctrinal theory, and the regulatory reality of the doctrine in action. Negligence liability directs defendants to act as a reasonable person does, doing no less than the ordinary decent woman or man would do – though no more either – and they must compensate their victims if they turn out to have fallen below that standard. In reality, tort defendants are not people but corporations, under a number of legal obligations, the reasonableness of which they do not have the luxury of assessing, but which must be borne as unavoidable business risks. As for paying compensation, they will (long before the accident) have decided whether to insure against such claims, influenced both by the size of likely claims and any relevant legal obligation to insure.

As to the personal liabilities involved, which doctrinal theory treats as central, they are, in most contexts, irrelevant. In road traffic cases the nominal plaintiff and defendant play as little a part in any legal claim as they can manage, leaving the way clear for the real issue, namely, which insurer should pay the costs of the accident. In cases involving vicarious liability, the actual wrongdoer may not be sued at all – after all, no one imagines that he or she is in a position to pay the claim – and their theoretical liability is allowed to remain in the realm of theory. Sometimes, rarely, the employer's insurer plays the doctrinalist card, claiming to enforce the wrongdoer's personal liability via the doctrine of subrogation – but this is poor industrial relations, as few employees are in a position to pay such damages, and they make their employers aware of this in no uncertain terms. As a result, some jurisdictions have actually outlawed such subrogation.[21] Does this mean that personal liability in negligence is irrelevant today? That is not my argument, and there are some types of claim where it is still significant. In the health care context, for example, the personal liability of a careless nurse, midwife or doctor is a force to be reckoned with (though, of course, arguments focus on the level of insurance premiums, it being taken for granted that no one would

[21] This embarrassing personal liability, which cannot be abolished but cannot be enforced either, is accommodated in different ways by different legal systems. For an international survey, see Paula Giliker, *Vicarious Liability in Tort – A Comparative Perspective* (Cambridge University Press, 2011), Chapter 2.

assume such a personal liability without cover). My argument is rather that the true significance of the doctrinal rules cannot be understood merely by looking at those rules – we must also look to the regulatory context that determines how such claims are made, how they are paid for and what alternatives are afforded to those who might be considering an action. An 'understanding' of the law that leaves out that context does not give us much insight.

4 Private law

In summary, therefore, the idea of private law can be seen as an intellectual project, stretching over decades or even centuries. The aim of the project is to state or restate the law as a coherent set of liabilities between individuals. Doctrinal achievements of this project are all around us when we look at the law. But at no point was it the only societal project of importance within the legal system. Even though it is often treated as a 'traditional' approach, it is not particularly ancient; and when we confine ourselves to aspects of it that we recognise (such as 'the law of contract' and 'tort'), it is no older than the overtly regulatory projects with which it might be regarded as competing. Our modern doctrine has always had to develop itself in a world that includes regulation, and has had to accommodate itself to that reality.

It seems clear to me that this doctrinal private law project is in serious decline. Analytically, nearly all of the juice has been squeezed out of this particular mango, and while there may be a little more to come, the academic community seems at the end of what good is there. We know its good features and its bad features, and are anxious to look elsewhere for new inspiration. Politically, the public/private distinction has no traction at all – the argument that new reforms might imperil traditional private law categories carries no weight. Government might be held back by the charge that the reforms threaten *fundamental freedoms* or *human rights*, but those new categories only partially overlap with the traditional domain of private law. The appeal to private liberties remains a powerful one, but the conception of those liberties has changed substantially. It also seems to me that the clarity with which so many writers can discern it may well presage its end: Minerva's owl begins its flight only at dusk, and the lack of certainty about what will replace it in the legal consciousness is not likely to save it. It may take a long time in fading away – we have, after all, not *wholly* disposed of the forms of action, so it would be premature to suspect that their successors will disappear soon.

A 'Private law'

Reassertions of the value of the 'private law' approach, while late in the day, cannot be dismissed out of hand. Nonetheless, I am entirely unpersuaded by such reassertions as I have seen, and of which Weinrib's *The Idea of Private Law* may serve as the leading example.

Do we, indeed, even know what 'private law' is any more, or what subunits such as 'tort' are meant to mean? In an eighteenth- or nineteenth-century legal system, it would have been unambiguously clear what was meant. In a modern system, where minute regulation is commonplace and the legislature is both entitled and willing to amend any aspect of the system, it is far from clear which areas of law are properly to be regarded as 'private'. For those who care to define them at all, there are multiple definitions available. For example, which of the various legal mechanisms for raising an issue of product safety are 'private' ones, and which 'public'? I will not pursue this further here, not least because it would intrude on William Lucy and Alexander Williams' chapter preceding this.[22] Suffice it to say that confident assertions of the importance, rigour and distinct nature of 'private law' are unlikely to convince when their area of application is left up to the imagination of individual readers.

However private law is to be defined, does it make sense to justify it in isolation from the remainder of the legal system? This would need some solid argument, which Weinrib has not provided. Private law did not evolve in isolation from the rest of the system, and the continuing pressures to change are equally part of the wider system. This is not, of course, to argue that *all* the forces for change can be labelled as external to private law. To what extent private law evolves under its own dynamic and to what extent change is externally driven is an interesting question. But it is hard to pursue such questions if the efficacy of external forces is denied in principle, or if admitting that some changes are externally driven is seen as somehow denying that there really is such a thing as private law. As it is, an 'explanation' of private law that leaves out the main thing about it – that it is part of the legal system – cannot explain very much.

A difficulty is sometimes suggested, that it is very hard to list all purposes that private law serves, so much so that the very idea of its

22 See also William Lucy, *Philosophy of Private Law* (Oxford University Press, 2007), esp. Chapter 1.

'purposes' lapses into incoherence. But pointing out that a problem is a hard one does not show that it has no coherent answer; and pointing out that not *all* of the purposes can be achieved in full does not show that it is wrong to pursue them all. Humans are needy creatures, and listing all the purposes they seek to achieve does indeed lead to a rather unruly list. Indeed, such lists are for most purposes *too* long. When law reform is contemplated, it usually looks at much smaller units – and even then the list of purposes implicated can be unmanageable. For present purposes, it is sufficient to point out that the purposes embodied in private law are many and various. Private law is not an artwork or a symphony – while it is certainly possible (particularly from within a law school) to contemplate it simply for itself, and to admire or criticise it 'in itself', that cannot be the main criterion of its worth. We may judge a cathedral by its ability to inspire awe or to invoke the deeper emotions in those who enter it, but if we judge a railway station by the same criteria, dismissing all others as irrelevant, we have lost the plot. Law is a practical science. That does not exclude aesthetic considerations, but they cannot be centre stage.[23]

As a coda, and to hint at what might be in issue if the 'purposes' of private law are pursued further, I throw in a recent statement of what private law is for. This is purely as a talking point. I have little sympathy with the project from which it emanates – the ongoing attempt to state a European private law, over and above the diverse private laws of the individual member states – but whether or not the work should be done, its execution is of high quality, and so can be given as an example of what one team of academic private lawyers think its purposes are. This version lists four principal purposes – freedom, security, justice and efficiency – and with subdivisions within those.[24] Naturally, different groups would have produced different lists; there has been some discussion of how this list differs from earlier drafts, and the influence of different national ideologies on that question.[25] I do not propose this list as a definitive answer to

[23] Compare Allan Beever, 'Formalism in Music and Law' (2011) 61 *University of Toronto Law Journal* 213.

[24] See the appendix to this chapter, where the heads are reproduced.

[25] Martijn W. Hesselink, '"If You Don't Like our Principles We Have Others"; On Core Values and Underlying Principles in European Private Law: A Critical Discussion of the New "Principles" Section in the Draft CFR', in Roger Brownsword, Hans W. Micklitz, Leone Niglia and Stephen Weatherill (eds.), *The Foundations of European Private Law* (Oxford: Hart Publishing, 2011), p. 59.

the question of what private law is for – but it is a clue as to which answers are currently plausible.

B Less ambitious arguments?

Lawyers are literal creatures. Faced with a particular argument, they tend to take it in its own terms and either accept it or reject it. Even when it is made very obvious that the argument is deliberately exaggerated, there is rarely any effort to read it in that spirit – after all, it is for the person making the argument to explain why it is plausible, and making your audience pare the argument down to reasonableness seems like passing the buck. In Weinrib's case, however, I suspect this is a mistake, as much of its plausibility is more properly aimed at lesser propositions. Some of them are considered here.

Some would be making the simple plea that the most basic of private law issues – whether a contract debt is owing, whether the victim of a wrong can recover from the wrongdoer and so on – still exist and should receive adequate attention from the legal system. It should not be forgotten, in all the attention to the role of the state, that in many respects the economy operates on capitalist lines, and cannot work at all unless the essentials are respected. On some particular, discrete issues of law, this may be right. The argument cannot, however, be scaled up very far. The broader the look we take at economic law, the clearer state intervention becomes – and the more obvious it is that any traditional common law left alone has been so left *because* it does not impede modern economic purposes, rather than out of any respect for old law. If it is the health of the economy we are considering, then a minute concentration on law would constitute looking at the issue through the wrong end of the telescope. The need for an efficient economy strikes at a more basic level, and if it could not be achieved through law then it would be achieved by other means. As a way of separating legal concerns from wider societal concerns, it seems inept.

Others would favour Weinrib's approach because, on a quick reading, it seems to favour what we might call *private law values*, embodying respect for promise-keeping and other values of self-responsibility, coupled with suspicion of the state when it claims to have a better solution to such essentially private matters. It must be stressed that, whatever Weinrib thinks about 'private law values', this is *not* his argument in *The Idea of Private Law*. He is not seeking to win the political battle of ideas between private and public values, but to insulate private law from politics altogether.[26] Nonetheless, I suspect that many who find Weinrib's views persuasive are really motivated by concerns of that sort – and while it is absolutely true that Weinrib's argument is not an argument from values, many would subscribe to both arguments. From my perspective, all this seems confused. Private law values are perennial, and to emphasise the link to common law doctrine actually weakens the case for them. Policy discourse allows for private law values along with others, and disdain for policy means a failure to use a whole battery of arguments that might favour those values. It labels supporters of those values as looking backwards rather than forwards. The argument will not be won by disdain for policy. It can only be won by advocating a policy viewpoint superior to all others on offer.

Finally, some lawyers might support at least a limited version of Weinrib's view for reasons of self-image. Excessive concentration on policy makes many lawyers uncomfortable, not necessarily because they think policy argument misguided, but because they know it is not the exclusive property of the law – they wonder whether they have ceased to be lawyers and have become something else entirely. Either they are ceasing to be lawyers, they fear, or law is ceasing to be law.[27] This is certainly a genuine concern; but it has never been convincing to regard law as immutable. No doubt law is evolving into something new,[28] but it seems premature to conclude that that something will not equally be a form of law. If lawyers wish to counter trends that might make law less relevant to modern society, they will not achieve this by ignoring those very trends. If there is a danger here, it should be identified and countered head-on.

5 Conclusion

The first great system for organising the common law – the forms of action – lasted for over six centuries, and to the last it had its defenders.

[26] On this point, see Allan Beever, 'Corrective Justice and Personal Responsibility in Tort Law' (2008) 28 *Oxford Journal of Legal Studies* 475, esp. 498–9.

[27] See especially Nigel Simmonds, *The Decline of Juridical Reason* (Manchester University Press, 1984), esp. Chapters 2 and 9; Allan Beever, *Rediscovering the Law of Negligence* (Oxford: Hart Publishing, 2007), pp. 1–19.

[28] See esp. Richard A. Posner, 'The Decline of Law as an Autonomous Discipline: 1962–1987' (1987) 100 *Harvard Law Review* 761.

We are now living through the decline of its successor, the doctrinal system, which we now think of as 'traditional'. Whether that decline is to accelerate or even become terminal, or whether it will outlive us all, is in large measure down to whether it satisfies the needs of all relevant parties in their attempts to pin down the detail of the law and to make it fulfil the functions that we mean it to satisfy.

Appendix 3.1
What is private law for?

'Private law', however defined, is today an entity of considerable breadth, and seeking a definitive answer to the question 'what is it for?' is quixotic at best. Nonetheless, it is interesting to see how one group of European academics have answered that question. The following text is the statement of the principles underlying the multi-volume Draft Common Frame of Reference (DCFR), which is a recent product of attempts to harmonise (and possibly, eventually codify) European private law.

While the production of the DCFR involved wide consultation, it is nonetheless overwhelmingly academic in its inspiration and writing. The status of the DCFR – what it is, what authority it has, what it might lead to – is in itself a matter of lively debate. For those interested in a general introduction to the issues, I recommend Christian Twigg-Flesner (ed.), *The Cambridge Companion to European Union Private Law* (Cambridge University Press, 2010); Reinhard Zimmermann, 'The Present State of European Private Law' (2009) 57 *American Journal of Comparative Law* 479.

Reproduced here are the heads of the principles (in effect, a contents page for the 'principles' section of the DCFR). The 'principles' section is an interesting text in its own right. The DCFR is a largely descriptive work, though of course it does not conceal its normative premise of the desirability of a Europe-wide private law, in place of the twenty-seven national systems that already exist. To give context, it must be borne in mind that the rationale for any harmonisation – to what extent it is economic, to what extent it is designed to implement particular policies – has important procedural implications for debates over implementation. In the crazy-quilt of treaties defining whether, when and how individual nations can object to proposed EU action, the public aim of that action is often key. The game of saying what the DCFR is 'for' is therefore played for very high stakes indeed, and we can assume that every word of the 'principles' section was chosen with care. The entire section (forty-three pages in all) carries the signatures of four noted professors: Christian von Bar, Hugh Beale, Eric Clive and Hans Schulte-Nölke.[29]

The underlying principles of freedom, security, justice and efficiency[30]
1. The four principles

Freedom
2. General remarks

Contractual freedom
3. Freedom of contract the starting point
4. Limitations with regard to third parties
5. Contracts harmful to third persons and society in general
6. Interventions when consent defective
7. Restrictions on freedom to choose contracting party
8. Restrictions on freedom to withhold information at pre-contractual stage
9. Information as to the terms of the contract
10. Correcting inequality of bargaining power
11. Minimum intervention

Non-contractual obligations
12. Emphasis on obligations rather than freedom
13. Freedom respected so far as consistent with policy objectives

Property
14. Limited scope for party autonomy
15. Recognition and enhancement of freedom in some respects

[29] For discussion of the 'principles', see Nils Jansen, 'The Authority of an Academic "Draft Common Frame of Reference"', in Hans W. Micklitz and Fabrizio Cafaggi (eds.), *European Private Law After the Common Frame of Reference* (Cheltenham: Edward Elgar Publishing, 2010); Henning Grosse Ruse-Khan, 'The European Draft Common Frame of Reference – A Source of Comparative Law: A New Option for Choosing the Applicable Law – Or a Template for a European Civil Code?', International Seminar on Comparative Law, Conference Proceedings, Kuala Lumpur, November 2008, available at: http://ssrn.com/abstract=1319247 (last accessed 21 May 2013); Hesselink, 'If You Don't Like our Principles'; Antoni Vaquer, 'Farewell to Windscheid? Legal Concepts Present and Absent from the Draft CFR' (2 April 2009), available at: http://ssrn.com/abstract=1372139 (last accessed 21 May 2013); Horst Eidenmueller, 'Party Autonomy, Distributive Justice and the Conclusion of Contracts in the DCFR' (29 January 2009), available at: http://ssrn.com/abstract=1334648 (last accessed 21 May 2013); Filomena Chirico, Eric E. C. Van Damme and Pierre Larouche, *A Giant with Feet of Clay: A First Law and Economics Analysis of the Draft Common Frame of Reference (DCFR)*, Tilburg Law and Economics Center Discussion Paper No. 2010–025, available at: http://ssrn.com/abstract=1628558 (last accessed 21 May 2013).

[30] From Christian von Bar *et al.* (eds.), *Principles, Definitions and Model Rules of European Private Law – Draft Common Frame of Reference (DCFR)*, Outline Edition (Munich: Sellier, 2009), pp. 57–9.

Security

16. General remarks

Contractual security

17. The main ingredients
18. Third party respect and reliance
19. Protection of reasonable reliance and expectations
20. The principle of binding force
21. Exceptional change of circumstances
22. Certainty or flexibility
23. Good faith and fair dealing
24. Co-operation
25. Inconsistent behaviour
26. Enforcement of performance
27. Other remedies
28. Maintaining the contractual relationship
29. Other rules promoting security

Non-contractual obligations

30. Security a core aim and value in the law on non-contractual obligations
31. Protection of the status quo: non-contractual liability arising out of damage caused to another
32. Protection of the person
33. Protection of human rights
34. Protection of other rights and interests
35. Protection of security by the law on unjustified enrichment

Property

36. Security a core aim
37. Protection of reasonable reliance and expectations
38. The provision of effective remedies
39. Protection of the status quo

Justice

40. General remarks

Contract

41. Treating like alike
42. Not allowing people to rely on their own unlawful, dishonest or unreasonable conduct
43. No taking of undue advantage
44. No grossly excessive demands
45. Responsibility for consequences
46. Protecting the vulnerable

Non-contractual obligations

47. General
48. Not allowing people to gain an advantage from their own unlawful, dishonest or unreasonable conduct

4

Origins of the public/private theory of legal systems

CHRISTIAN TURNER

Wherever people are present and acting together, we can find in the social glue between them the process we call law. It is not a written list of rules, the collected judgments of courts or the decrees of a monarch. These things are the tools of law and the evidence of its practice, not law itself. Law is a process, the human-willed system of cause and effect that governs the evolution of the togetherness of those who choose to act together. It is a kind of inevitable source code on which a society runs, its output read and acted upon to yield one physical moment and then the next.[1] Always being rewritten and contested, this intellectual wraith that is the law, this thing that exists only in our minds and is given form only by our actions and communications, this is the object of our study.

Is the process of law as unpredictable and varied as the distinct and random neuronal firings of peoples separated by oceans and millennia? Are there, instead, basic principles or a logic of law that is invariant among its instances? The word 'law' suggests its practice may be thought to have at least some kinship with the natural laws of our universe. Those 'laws' are also abstract understandings of the connections between causes and effects. Indeed, various legal philosophies have taken this similarity nearly to the point of identity.[2] While most naturally associated with formalists,[3] even the archetypal legal realist Arthur Corbin noted that both 'rules of physics and rules of law … enable us to predict physical consequences and to regulate our actions accordingly'.[4] Taken to the extreme, the laws of the

[1] 'Law is the projection of an imagined future upon reality.' Robert M. Cover, 'Violence and the Word' (1986) 95 *Yale Law Journal* 1601, 1604.

[2] See, e.g., Thomas C. Grey, 'Langdell's Orthodoxy' (1983) 45 *University of Pittsburgh Law Review* 1, 16–32 (describing Langdellian legal science as analogous to the study of Euclidean geometry but with axioms capable of slow evolution).

[3] See, e.g., Guido Calabresi, 'An Introduction to Legal Thought: Four Approaches to Law and to the Allocation of Body Parts' (2002) 55 *Stanford Law Review* 2113, 2114–5.

[4] Arthur L. Corbin, 'Jural Relations and their Classification' (1921) 30 *Yale Law Journal* 226, 227. Corbin continued: 'When the physical event that we are predicting is the conduct of a

legal world just involve distinctive kinds of physical events and objects, in the same way that chemistry, biology and ecology are all, ultimately, physics but have developed special methods, conclusions and approximations concerning the complex physical processes within their domains.

We need not go that far. The law of a place is purely the product of human will. It can be contested, changed, incomplete, disastrous, ignored or followed.[5] Scientists attempt to induce and deduce the universal connections between cause and effect that exist independent of our own desires. Lawyers create and sever such connections, the causes of legal action and a society's responses to those causes, as it suits us. My goal in this chapter is not to deduce what law essentially is, a fruitless enterprise that misunderstands the possibilities of theoretical inquiry. Rather, I aim to explore the consequences of a few simple observations about human cooperation that can help us better understand what we are doing when we do law. I look not for axioms to which law must conform but to foundational decisions that those who maintain legal systems inevitably must make, the structure those decisions necessarily impose and the types of considerations that will bear on them.

My specific theory is that the practice of law in a society involves an unavoidable and fundamental division of authority over law-making and prosecution among various institutional types, characterised most basically by their public or private nature.[6] Legal systems divide other kinds of questions among institutions, and both public and private institutions can come in far more specific flavours. Yet this very simple

state agent, executive or judicial, acting for society, the rule that we are applying is called a rule of law; and with respect to the expected action of societal agents, our relations to our fellow men are commonly called legal (or jural) relations.' Corbin's suggestion could be taken as materialistic, that law is ultimately physics, and so as with the other sciences, our goal is to understand the principles that govern the evolution of such physical systems. This frees the legal thinker to bend conclusions to observations, liberating him or her from unexamined maxims, a key goal of realism. It also reclaims the mantle of science by cleverly reframing the objects responsive to scientific principles as human beings rather than legal data. At least as of his retirement, Corbin believed that while the sciences were, with respect to law, 'underlying disciplines', law itself could not reach scientific conclusions. See Calabresi, 'An Introduction to Legal Thought', 2121.

[5] See, e.g., H. L. A. Hart, *The Concept of Law*, 2nd edition (Oxford: Clarendon Press, 1994), p. 187 ('[P]rescriptive laws may be broken and yet remain laws, because that merely means that human beings do not do what they are told to do; but it is meaningless to say of the laws of nature, discovered by science, either that they can or cannot be broken').

[6] I first advanced this theory in Christian Turner, 'Law's Public/Private Structure' (2012) 39 *Florida State University Law Review* 1003, and applied it again in Christian Turner, 'State Action Problems' (2013) 65 *Florida Law Review* 281. The former contains a far more detailed treatment of the theory and its applications than appears here. This chapter is

understanding yields a striking picture of legal systems, one that has a great deal of explanatory power and points us in fruitful directions when faced with more specific questions concerning a society's law. It vividly divides and clarifies law's traditional fields of study. It clearly identifies the distinctions between primary and secondary rules and helps to reveal the essential similarities and differences among the secondary rules of the various fields. Most importantly, it shows us just how much of legal discourse is constructed from very basic institutional competency arguments. By way of preview, the picture of law that the theory reveals is the following:

		Constitutional Law	
		Privately Created	Publicly Created
Procedure	Privately Prosecuted	Contract Law	Tort Law
	Publicly Prosecuted	Parens Patriae	Criminal Law

To appreciate better what this picture is and why it is helpful, I will frame the summary of the public/private theory from the ground up. I will begin with a very elementary understanding of a public, showing its identification with the management of coercion, which I call law. Next, I will explore how a public must conduct the management of its coercive resources. Following Hart, this consists in using both primary and secondary rules but in a system that is itself a union of information and institutions. Finally, I will discuss the basic public–private distinctions (plural) that naturally define the intuitive, institutional taxonomy of legal systems summarised in the chart above.

Because it is impossible to imagine law without a public, one would reasonably expect the distinction between a public and its lexical opposite, the private, to loom large in legal theory. Curiously, though, the distinction has been textually derided at the same time as it has been subtextually and perhaps even subconsciously developed. No matter how frustrating these concepts are to identify and use, no matter how critical we might wish to be, the public–private distinction is inseparable from law itself.

intended both to summarise the theory, to motivate it philosophically and to show its continuity with diverse jurisprudential approaches.

In the course of arriving at the public–private theory of legal systems, I will attempt to show how the germs of the theory have been laid by movements ordinarily thought hostile to the distinction.

The goal of developing a model from simple and uncontroversial assumptions is not only to produce a clarifying description. From the model's structural features, it is often possible to surmise particular principles of law deductively after the addition of context. For example, a rule concerning the unconscionability of private contracts might be derived from a more general principle of institutional competency applied to the particular institution of private contracting parties. Where deduction does not fully settle the matter, that is, where more than one rule would seem to follow from a general, trans-substantive principle, we still gain from seeing the continuity of the unresolved problem with problems in other fields of law and, more practically, from the particular contextual difficulties that are creating an ambiguous application of principle.

The social practice of cooperation is as multifaceted as the human beings conducting it. An attempt to describe law's one true nature is doomed to fail. Nevertheless, I aim to provide a simplifying but rich model of its practice. The model is itself neither purely descriptive nor normative in the narrow doctrinal sense. It is instead an attempt to illuminate the largely inevitable basic plan of our social source code. How can we most easily understand this complex set of human interactions? Yes, law has no singular essence, but there is at least this simple way of seeing its patterns: as repeated divisions of authority among public and private institutions.

1 A public and its legal system

This volume generally concerns the most fundamental elements of the abstract process that is the law: the public and the private. From the mere assumption of cooperation, we can find the former, the public, and that is where I begin. People transcend the mere plural of person and become a public only when they desire to do at least some minimal set of things together and only with respect to those things. It is possible to imagine multiple solitary individuals acting separately upon the landscape, never cooperating. They may even act in ways that are mutually advantageous. Yet there still would be no public there, as there is only individual volition not coordination among the collection of human beings.

Modern societies are composed of layer upon superimposed layer of publics and, as we will see, legal systems. Corporations are publics. Families are publics, as are churches, law faculties, school districts and criminal gangs. Even two cooperating individuals engaged in traditional contracting are a public.[7] All are self-consciously groups, and all have different processes that maintain the cooperative ties that define them, effectuating the purposes that draw their constituents together.

In contrast to the non-interactive, individual wills that characterise mere parallel collections of human beings, or non-publics, law is the name we give to the process (and there is always a process, however changeable) by which a public realises its shared purposes through the management of a set of coercive resources. Such resources always exist where cooperation is present, because coercion is implicit in cooperation itself. If two humans cooperate, there is always the risk that cooperation will be discontinued. That minimal inducement is all we need to observe that cooperation is implicitly laden with conditions. Even so, the cooperative enterprise may be, and usually is, more complex, with additional means beyond defection to ensure continued participation. For example, if the reason collaborators continue their cooperation is that one has threatened the other with violence, then the coercion is plain.[8] A public, by definition, engages in processes to effectuate joint purposes, and these processes necessarily include among them management of coercive resources.

Every public, therefore, has a legal system, and every legal system belongs to a public.[9] The concept of law and the concept of a public are inseparable, one yielding the other. Groups of humans, again, may belong

[7] Contracting parties in a public that will enforce the contract may also form what I will define as a 'private institution'. But the definition of 'private', in the sense of the public/private theory, is dependent on the existence of a public. Without a public, there is no private entity, only an isolated one. Whether or not cooperating parties are recognised as a private institution within a larger public, they *also* form their own public.

[8] I do not assume that the form coercion takes is a specific consequence expressed in advance in a written law. It may not be specified in advance. It may not be written. And even if coercive acts are specified – a fine or imprisonment, say – the coercive effect may extend to unspecified stigma accompanying the specification or even to the personal disappointment a violator may feel. The so-called internal point of view of an actor who takes at least some laws as reasons in themselves to conform his or her conduct can thus be taken into account. The public's social glue is maintained, in such instances and such individuals, simply by announcing a rule, which announcement is a threat, as breaking the rule would be personally undesirable to the actor.

[9] We might reserve the term 'legal system' for law that has been organised into a predictable and manageable set of principles and procedures developed before disputes arise. That is, a legal system might only exist when law, the process, is purposefully managed. The existence of a system, though, does not imply self-conscious management of a process. I would call the process that is the law of a public a legal system even if one can only appreciate its existence from the external point of view – even when there is no internal point of view that understands there are standards of conduct.

to multiple interacting publics and therefore be governed by multiple interacting legal systems. This is intuitively obvious, as we find ourselves governed by family rules, local laws, state and national laws, rules of the workplace and the like.

This identification of law with the management of a public's coercive resources, the threats a public can make in order to foster cooperation, is so natural that it has been central, at least implicitly, to a diverse array of theoretical approaches to the concept of law. The simplest positivist model, conceptually, is probably Austin's, which characterises law as comprising the commands of a sovereign backed by threats.[10] The same type of approach is implicit in Blackstone's great work, which described law as 'rule[s] of civil conduct prescribed by the supreme power in a State, commanding what is right, and prohibiting what is wrong'.[11]

For Oliver Wendell Holmes, legal duties were 'nothing but a prediction that if a man does or omits certain things he will be made to suffer in this or that way by judgment of the court'.[12] Even as Holmes wrote against the idea that the acts of legislatures or the writings of judges established and reflected a separate, formal system of rules, he acknowledged as a premise that a public's legal system is efficacious on account of its ability to gain cooperation through the threat of unpleasant consequences.

Holmes' account is a significant refinement of Blackstone's model, which assumes a 'supreme power' and so fails to capture the complexity of law in real societies. Focusing on the predictions of law's subjects rather than the supremacy of law's makers permits us to understand legal systems that feature even rampant non-compliance and those that operate within and among societies that have pluralistic and competing sources of rules. A public pursuing cooperation may take the form of a violent dictator demanding and obtaining absolute obedience, but it may only be a weak social aggregation among much stronger ones, providing only slight disincentives to defection.

This, too, is the view of Robert Cover: 'Legal interpretation is (1) a practical activity, (2) designed to generate credible threats and actual deeds of violence, (3) in an effective way.'[13] Cover was writing about formal legal

[10] John Austin, *Lectures on Jurisprudence or the Philosophy of Positive Law*, Robert Campbell (ed.), 3rd edition (London: J. Murray, 1869), pp. 88–106. Austin's model is in part a restatement of ancient theory.

[11] William Blackstone, *Commentaries on the Laws of England*, vol. I (Oxford: Clarendon Press, 1765), p. 44.

[12] Oliver Wendell Holmes, 'The Path of the Law' (1997) 110 *Harvard Law Review* 991, 992.

[13] Cover, 'Violence and the Word', 1610.

systems like those of modern nation-states, but his insight is broader: that law is the name for the public's practical working out of the use of its coercive capacities, whatever they are, most often for maximum effect given all the public's competing values.[14] Among law and economists, it is a given that 'the fundamental thing that law does is to decide which of the conflicting parties will be entitled to prevail'.[15]

Even H. L. A. Hart, writing against the command theory, did not deny coercion's omnipresence in legal systems. In the Postscript to his *Concept of Law*, he stated: 'Legal rights and duties are the point at which the law with its coercive resources respectively protects individual freedom and restricts it or confers on individuals or denies to them the power to avail themselves of the law's coercive machinery.'[16] Coercion, Hart agrees, is law's ultimate action, even if not its purpose. The purpose of law, of course, is cooperation, and coercion and the threat of coercion are means a public has to achieve it. Law is the process for managing such threats, even if they will, one hopes, usually provide guidance for right conduct rather than signals about the expected cost of non-compliance.[17]

[14] I will not here detail in depth the possible distinctions between 'legal interpretation' as Cover uses the term and 'the law' or 'legal systems' as I have used the terms. Cover refers to more than the judicial extraction of the semantic meaning intended by the authors of some text. He instead uses the term, like Ronald Dworkin, to describe the *creation* of meaning using texts, among other sources, as data, with the intention that these culturally constructed meanings yield definitive action. Such activity has a central place in the more general enterprise of law, which Cover says is 'the attempt to build future worlds'. *Ibid.*, 1602 n. 2. See also *ibid.*, 1611 n. 24 ('[T]he dominant form of legal thought ought to be interpretive in the extended sense of the term').

[15] Guido Calabresi and A. Douglas Melamed, 'Property Rules, Liability Rules, and Inalienability: One View of the Cathedral' (1972) 85 *Harvard Law Review* 1089, 1090.

[16] Hart, *The Concept of Law*, p. 269.

[17] As Hart puts it: 'Since the occasions for legal coercion are mainly cases where the primary function of the law in guiding the conduct of its subjects has broken down, legal coercion, though of course an important matter, is a secondary function. Its justification cannot be sensibly taken to be the point or purpose of the law as such.' *Ibid.*, p. 249. I believe Hart's insight – that law's function is to signal expected conduct to people who will take the law's existence as a reason to conform their conduct – is correct in many applications. But the carrier signal for this information is coercive threat, the if–then formulation of a standard of conduct and consequence of defection. To understand the practice of law and a society's use of the law it makes, it is of course necessary to appreciate the internal points of view of the participants, many of whom take law as a signal, not a threat. The way the if–then language of law, to the extent the legal system under consideration even operates by *ex ante* rules, is taken up by members of the public will be relevant to the crafting of laws and remedies. But we need not assume anything about this in order to arrive at the public/private institutional model I will develop. The *application* of that model, though, certainly does depend on more specific information about the culture in which the legal system is embedded.

All of these observations reduce, in their weakest forms, to an unremarkable assertion about human cooperation. When we engage in cooperation, we do so against a set of information about the consequences of defection. The ability to impose consequences inheres in the idea of a public as a set of cooperating people. It is the management of these coercive resources that is a legal system.

Thus far we have an understanding of what it is we aim to study, but very little to help us understand it. In fact, in graphical form our model of legal systems looks like this:

Conditions of coercion

Yes, there is really nothing there other than the identification of a public with the management of coercive resources. To progress towards the institutional model, we need first a better, more realistic model of rules.

2 Primary and secondary rules

The analytical fulcrum across which Hart's *The Concept of Law* shifted the meaning of positivism is the distinction between so-called primary and secondary rules. Hart taught that law cannot be conceived entirely as a set of commands backed by threats. A legal system cannot be accurately understood as a list of rules of behaviour paired with unpleasant consequences, providing coercion to comply. There are, inevitably, rules about such rules. Even a list of rules chiselled into a stone tablet is not, in itself, a complete legal system. To understand the system in which the tablet plays a part, we must understand the, perhaps unwritten, rules about the tablet's rules. For example, if the tablet's rules are truly authoritative, it is only because there is an additional rule that they are authoritative. This is an example of a secondary rule, a rule about a primary rule governing conduct. All systems possess such rules, and Hart established the impossibility of understanding a legal system without taking account of them. The law, he says, is the union of primary rules of behaviour and secondary rules of recognition, change and adjudication.[18]

But the pathway to this simple and elegant conception of law had already been blazed by Wesley Newcomb Hohfeld.[19] Hohfeld is almost always cited for having established a framework of basic jural opposites

[18] Hart, *The Concept of Law*, pp. 94–9.

[19] Wesley Newcomb Hohfeld, 'Some Fundamental Legal Conceptions as Applied in Legal Reasoning' (1913) 23 *Yale Law Journal* 16.

and correlatives, the citation usually only making the general point that all law is relational in the sense that affecting A's rights necessarily affects someone else's duties. Hohfeld composed an eight-element periodic table of legal relations and two forms of relations (opposition and correlation) among them. His elaboration is more ornate than necessary and his discussion unfocused by modern standards. But the Hohfeldian framework is ingenious, powerful and ultimately very easy to understand.

There are two basic concepts:

(1) law's action is always relational, that is, between one entity within the public and another (often one individual against another); and
(2) legal rules are of two types: primary (duties) and secondary (powers). Primary rules concern the conditions for the application of public coercion. Secondary rules concern the authority to make (and thus change and repeal) primary rules.

First, Hohfeld teaches that whatever its system for recording rules and explicating them, law's action occurs when a public actually deploys the coercive powers it possesses. He does not say this directly, but it is implicit in his scheme. A duty has no meaning apart from a correlative right.[20] That is, to have a duty means that there is another member of the public with the authority to ask the public to coerce its performance. In this way, an understanding of a public's law is built from the ground up as the larger story of the pair-wise results of contested, if mostly hypothetical, calls for public coercion, or cases in the usual manner of speaking.

Although described by Hohfeld as fundamental, the first four legal relations – rights, duties, privileges and no-rights – are all derivative of the primitive concept of a duty imposed by a public. If one has a duty with respect to some other entity, then that entity has a right, in the sense that the entity can compel the public to coerce the duty holder into compliance. If one does not have a duty with respect to some conduct, then one is privileged and no person has a right to stop the conduct. To have a no-right is to have no ability to enforce a duty that would proscribe the conduct.[21] Thus, from the basic concepts of public and duty, the other relations can be deduced. There is duty and its absence. There is the ability to call for the enforcement of a duty and the absence of such an ability.

This first part of Hohfeld's analysis could be read as a comfortable amendment to the command theory. Law is indeed a set of rules backed by threats, but the rules are necessarily relational, meaning they are

[20] *Ibid.*, 30–2. [21] *Ibid.*, 32–44.

always either enforceable, or not, by some entity. What I characterise as the second part of Hohfeld's analysis is less amendment and more remaking of that theory. Here, Hohfeld established a legal concept distinct from duty: 'power'. One who has a power in a public has the authority to create an enforceable duty on another member of the public.[22]

As with duty, power alone generates the other three legal relations. Definitionally, power has an object – some entity or entities on whom the empowered entity can place a duty. One who is subject to such a power has a liability, and one who is not is immune. The absence of power is disability.[23]

Hohfeld has thus identified not eight fundamental relations but two fundamental concepts: duty and power. To put it in other terms, Hohfeld defined a legal system as the union of primary rules (the contents of duties) and secondary rules (the contents of powers) governing the public's coercive resources. Corbin's defence of Hohfeld fits even more nicely with the model under development. Hohfeld's central question, for Corbin, is whether 'the cumulative strength' of 'the multitude of ... citizens who constitute ... "the state"', which Corbin personifies as a giant, can or cannot be called upon to aid an individual.[24] All of Hohfeld's relations, Corbin explains, are derived from the question whether an individual can call upon the giant's help – enforcing a right – and the question whether an individual can influence the giant's actions – wielding a power. The entire frame assumes that at least the hypothetical coercion of a public is the very thing that law concerns.

What I wish to emphasise here is not that Hohfeld is the original author of some of the major ideas in *The Concept of Law*, which contains a much richer explanation of the virtue and nature of both secondary rules and rules in general, but that the very idea of human beings cooperating and thus forming a public necessarily includes the concepts of duty and power. To find a collective of human beings operating in a concerted way, rather than in parallel, is to find them operating conditionally. All cooperative enterprises have terms. Perhaps these terms are only the conditions of further cooperation. Perhaps they are conditions under which violence by one or more members will be withheld. Perhaps they are written. Perhaps

[22] *Ibid.*, 44. In Hohfeld's language, if a 'change in legal relations' may occur because of 'some superadded fact or group of facts which are under the volitional control of one or more human beings', then those who have such volitional control have a 'power'. *Ibid.*

[23] *Ibid.*, 44–58.

[24] Corbin, 'Jural Relations', 228.

they are unwritten. But wherever there is cooperation, there is not only coercion, but also a union of primary and secondary rules governing that coercion.

Hohfeld also helps us to appreciate that the management of coercion concerns the resolution of pair-wise conflicts (so long as one element of the pair is understood sometimes to be a representative of larger segments or perhaps all of the public). If the society is cooperating, rather than acting individually, we should be able to detect that fact in at least the hypothetical resolutions of such conflicts. If no conflicts are even hypothetically possible, then there is no interaction, and we have human beings acting in parallel on the landscape, not as a public.

When the public resolves a conflict, it takes up a claim that some entity has made against another. (Again, if no one makes a claim that the public should use coercion, then there is no conflict.) The public then decides whether to apply some of its coercive resources by consulting its laws. We need assume no particular structure here. This adjudication could involve the reading of ancient tomes, a Herculean exercise of fit and justification, or even a coin toss. The public must determine how it will decide who wins, how it will decide whether to coerce an unwilling party. Thus, from Hohfeld we see a distinction between the power to demand a public determination whether to coerce (the possession of a right) and the power to make the rules that will determine whether coercion will be ordered.

Hohfeld thus gives us this picture of a legal system:

	Rules concerning the exercise of powers
Rules concerning the enforcement of duties	Duties (conditions of coercion)

I call these sets of questions ones of prosecution (enforcement of duties) and law-making (exercise of powers, or the creation of duties). The next step towards a general understanding of legal structure is to observe the way in which a public must inevitably decide how to answer such questions. Here we find a world of information-generating institutions.

3 Institutions and information

Publics are groups of people, and to the extent a public ‘acts’, it does so through the actions of the people that compose it. Of course, humans undertake all sorts of actions. Only some of these actions refer to a public in which the actor is embedded. I may ride my bike to work, have a cappuccino at my local coffee house and read to my children. Which of these is a 'public act' depends on the processes governing the various publics of which I am a member.

An institution is a group within a public that generates information recognised as legally relevant by the public's secondary rules. A given group of people may at times and with respect to some actions be an institution in a public and at other times not. When my colleagues and I vote on faculty matters, we are an institution within the university. When we share food and drink afterwards, we are not that institution. This is a function of the secondary rules within the university that recognise the former but not the latter as the producers of information salient, ultimately, to the management of the university's coercive resources.

Because a public is not a group of people acting in parallel, but a cooperating group of people, it must communicate, in the form of information, intentions among its members. This is why the practice of law consists of a union of institutions and information.[25] It is a process by which a public evolves, its members exchanging publicly salient information and acting on the basis of that information.

H. L. A. Hart's definition of law, the union of primary and secondary rules, is not wrong or even so much incomplete, as such.[26] But without emphasising more explicitly the nature of law's practice, as an exchange of information among institutions, we have too static a picture of law as an abstract set of rules, like the instructions that accompany a board game (even if they are supplemented by social practices that modify or amend the instructions). The practice of law is a dynamic, bustling zoo of institutions generating and consuming information. All of a public's law is contained in a self-referential and continuously altered set of information, whether one takes that information to be the diverse array of data that permits Holmesian predictions of judicial action or the Hart-like sources of signals that provide grounds for criticism of rule-breakers.

[25] A complete description of this theory would require grappling with the institutional and informational context of ultimate rules of recognition and, in general, greater analytical rigour. I leave this project for another day.

[26] The recognition of institutions and their resulting information economy are, after all, consequences of Hart's secondary rules.

Consider a statute, an opinion or an executive order. While coercion – which would include the acts of handcuffing, jailing and seizing – is law's effect, the law itself is the information that officials use to decide what to do. A police officer who puts me in a squad car is not 'doing the law'; she is hopefully acting in accordance with the law, meaning consistently with the information the collective has generated regarding what actions its representatives will take in response to various events. Even the fact that the individual putting me in the car is a police officer, who bears some special status within the collective, is not a fact bound to the world. Rather, that individual has clothed herself in the official garb, has acted as if the universe of legal information justifies her actions, and has been treated by others as if she is doing what the collective wishes. If she is wrong about this, knowingly or not, the law will not approve her actions and may well provide information that others will rely on to punish her, by physically restraining her or forcing her to convey assets.

As Robert Cover puts it in his remarkable article, 'Violence and the Word':

> The context of a judicial utterance is institutional behavior in which others, occupying preexisting roles, can be expected to act, to implement, or otherwise to respond in a specified way to the judge's interpretation. Thus, the institutional context ties the language act of practical understanding to the physical acts of others in a predictable, though not logically necessary, way.[27]

Cover teaches us that the institutional understanding of a legal system, if the system aims to be effective, leads naturally to normative criteria. 'The practice of interpretation requires an understanding of what others will do with such a judicial utterance and, in many instances, an adjustment to that understanding, regardless of how misguided one may think the likely institutional response will be.'[28] That is the power of an institution and information approach to understanding legal systems: the fact that information has both an author and one or more audiences provides criteria of effectiveness that refer only to the processing capacities of the institutions involved.

I believe this to be the most important benefit of the public/private theory of legal systems. While I am attracted to the aesthetic qualities of its

[27] Cover, 'Violence and the Word', 1611.

[28] *Ibid.*

description (and the intuitions that seem to spring from it), its most critical feature is that it makes transparent that many questions that seem substantive and substance-area-specific are in fact questions of the competence of institutions to make and receive particular kinds of legal information. Before we deal with specifics, however, it is worth considering a bit more closely what sort of normative calculus we might derive from the institutional understanding of a legal system and Cover's insight concerning author and audience.

I suggest two guiding principles should and will very likely lurk behind a legal system's secondary rules governing institutions.[29] What I call the first principle, or *ex ante* principle, requires that an institution's decision-makers be selected and empowered in a way that is likely to render them institutionally competent. By competent I mean that they act consistently with an optimisation of a social welfare function. The second principle, or *ex post* principle, mandates invalidation of legal information (usually laws) when that information manifests the incompetence of the institution that generated it. The claim of the institutional theory is that a great many specific rules of law can be deduced from these broad principles when applied to a specific institutional setting.

Further, I have advanced a set of discrete indicators, or types of competency, against which an institution's selection mechanisms, scope of authority and informational output can be checked for compliance with the first and second principles. I derived them from a decomposition of a generic social welfare function.[30] They are as follows:[31]

- Private calculation competency reflects the ability of an institution to estimate the preferences of others with respect to the decision at hand.
- Public calculation competency refers to the ability to assess that portion, if any, of the collective good not reflected in individual preferences.
- Aggregation competency is the ability of a decision-making entity to combine these preference inputs, weighing and ordering them, according to the collective will.
- A particular kind of aggregation competency is the ability to weigh the preferences of another as heavily as one's own. This capacity to decide unselfishly I call distributive competency.

[29] See Turner, 'Law's Public/Private Structure', 1033–4.

[30] *Ibid.*, 1018–21. The basic idea is that any decision requires gathering inputs and computing an output. These inputs and the computation of the output can be broken down in the manner expressed here.

[31] The description of the competencies is adapted from my article applying the public/private theory to the problem of state action. Turner, 'State Action Problems', 298.

- And finally, resource competency is the possession of the means actually to effect a decision.

Armed with these tools, it is possible to reflect on the decisions an institution will be asked to make and to design secondary rules to govern the institution so as to encourage competent decision-making and to review for incompetency *ex post*. It is also possible to compare institutions to determine their relative advantages at addressing a legal problem. But to do any of that we obviously need more information about the decisions at issue and the institutional possibilities.

While adding this institutional method has not altered the taxonomy of legal systems we derived from Hart and Hohfeld, some modifications to the chart make clearer how legal institutions relate to the primary rules that govern behaviour. I will call the set of secondary rules governing the making of primary rules 'Constitutional Law' and the set of secondary rules governing the prosecution of the violation of primary rules 'Procedure'. Using these new terms and adding spaces for the institutions regulated by these secondary rules, we have the following chart:

		Constitutional Law
		Law-making Institutions
Procedure	Prosecuting Institutions	Primary rules (duties)

There is, however, still more that we can say before delving into the specifics of a particular working legal system. There is yet another inherent dynamic arising in any public that allows us better to see the structure of all legal systems and the basic templates of secondary rules. We now turn to the public/private distinction.

4 The public/private theory of legal systems

Primary rules are as variable as the societies that create them. We can examine the rules of a collective and the culture of a collective to attempt to discover what the consequences of its rules might be. Does a rule prohibiting murder and imposing a given punishment effectively serve a goal of reducing the incidence of murder? How fast will people in a society drive automobiles if the law limits their speeds and provides a given array of penalties? The answers will depend on social context and any number of particulars concerning culture, funding, enforcement effort and the like.

For the theorist, there is perhaps more immediate interest in wondering whether we can say more about the set of secondary rules in a society. How does a public make new primary rules or, for that matter, secondary rules? Are there limits to the kinds of rules it can or should make? Why? Are these rules as contingent on culture and as manifold as the myriad of possible primary rules, or do they inevitably deal with certain questions?

So far we have posited only a cooperating group of humans. From this assumption of cooperation, we have defined a public. That public necessarily realises cooperation through primary rules backed by threats of coercion. But to make, adjudicate and carry out this law, the public defines institutions that consume and generate the information that composes the system of primary and secondary rules, which ultimately manage the public's coercive resources. A legal system is, therefore, the name we give to the union of institutions and information created by a public, resulting in a set of primary and secondary rules. From Hohfeld and Hart, we know a little more about these secondary rules – that they govern both the creation of duties and the enforcement of duties.

The public/private theory of legal systems, initially, adds a single detail to the model we have derived from this bare assumption of cooperation. With this addition, the familiar structure and constraints of modern legal systems emerge. The detail that gives legal systems their familiar shape is indeed the often-maligned public/private distinction – but not the distinction in the general, vague sense that has left it so vulnerable to lawyerly attack. Rather, the specific use of these antithetical terms to describe the most basic character of the institutions that compose a legal system is what will make so much legal structure apparent as a mere consequence of our simple assumption of cooperation.

A What does it mean to say that an institution is public or private?

We have proceeded from the position that a public and a legal system are inseparable, a public being any cooperating group. All institutions within a public are in some sense 'public institutions' as they, by the definition above, are recognised by the legal system's secondary rules as informational participants. The public/private theory uses a finer institutional gradation than that between recognised institutions and unrecognised groups.[32] We will therefore distinguish among a public's institutions, labelling some institutions as public and others as private.

[32] Unrecognised groups are not part of the theory at all. Of course, such a group may form its own public, with its own legal system. That it is unrecognised means that none of its

The goal, following from the last section, is to develop a model of legal systems that is conducive to application of the two institutional principles developed in the last section. So, I ask whether there are, in all legal systems, fundamentally different types of institutions with respect to that institutional calculus. In short, yes. There are those institutions controlled by the public and those the public recognises but that are controlled by its members as individuals. It is to these types that I give the labels 'public' and 'private' respectively.

The terms public and private are, in general, obviously ambiguous. They possess a great many senses. Private can mean, among many other things, secluded from the view of others, relating to the affairs of the family rather than the community, or concerning voluntary markets rather than government. As Jeff Weintraub writes, '[t]he public/private distinction, in short, is not unitary, but protean. It comprises, not a single paired opposition, but a complex family of them, neither mutually reducible nor wholly unrelated.'[33]

My goal is not to delve deeply into the full range of activities we call private or public and the distinct but related reasons for which we use those terms.[34] Rather, I distinguish legal choices made by or on behalf of a group from those the group leaves for its members.[35] The distinction is between public and private agency, 'between an agent acting privately, i.e. on his own account, or publicly, i.e. as an officer of the city, community, commonwealth, state etc'.[36] To cabin the analysis further, I will not even ask whether an institution is public or private. Rather, I will ask whether

information-producing activities have legal significance in the public within which it is embedded. Its members are, of course, still regulated by the primary rules of that public.

[33] Jeff Weintraub, 'The Theory and Politics of the Public/Private Distinction', in Jeff Weintraub and Krishan Kumar (eds.), *Public and Private in Thought and Practice: Perspectives on a Grand Dichotomy* (University Of Chicago Press, 1997), p. 2.

[34] While 'public' and 'private' are words each bearing many senses, they are more than symbols gathering under themselves homonyms for unrelated concepts. Each sense bears relations to the others, all stemming from what Stanley Benn and Gerald Gaus call a 'complex-structured concept': Stanley I. Benn and Gerald F. Gaus, 'The Public and the Private: Concepts and Action', in Stanley I. Benn and Gerald F. Gaus (eds.), *Public and Private in Social Life* (London: Croom Helm, 1983), pp. 4–5. Though they would perhaps not simplify it in this way, I would argue that the shared kernel from which the different senses emerge is the distinction between 'togetherness' and 'separateness'.

[35] The restriction to 'legal' choices here is intended to reflect that a private institution is one that generates information recognised by secondary rules. Groups that do not have this property are not institutions within the public's legal system.

[36] Benn and Gaus, 'The Public and the Private', p. 9. Other than agency, Benn and Gaus identify 'access' and 'interest' as domains described by the concepts of public and private.

specific institutional decisions – law-making and prosecution – are made publicly or privately.[37] Publicly made decisions are those directed by the collective's will as expressed in secondary rules establishing agency. Privately made decisions may well be influenced by collective norms, but they do not entail collective control.

I choose to compare these two types of institutions for a couple of important reasons. First, this coarse choice of institution – private versus any number of public ones – is the predominant, high-level categorisation that appears in our legal system and in many others. Second, it is a basic choice, in that a collective's very definition depends, essentially, on what powers it takes for itself. An essential question every collective must answer is under what circumstances it will stand behind the will of its individuals rather than assert a will of its own.

This coarse taxonomy of institutions has several theoretical virtues, even beyond its demonstrable utility. It mostly avoids a number of criticisms of the public/private distinction made by the legal realists and the critical legal theorists. And it elaborates on and advances the uses of the distinction by some of the very same scholars.

First, the taxonomy avoids any conclusion that what is left private in a society must be non-political.[38] The distinction used here between private and public concerns only individual or collective control over a question. Private action, and not just in the aggregate, can surely have broad social impacts, to the point that such action can affect what it means to be a member of the collective. Choices influencing such meanings are public in effect, even if they are not publicly made.

The distinction I intend here does not divide law that ought to be policy-laden from that which is purely formal, as Morton Horwitz has argued was the goal of the relentless pursuit of a clean separation between private and public law in the nineteenth century.[39] This would be simply impossible to achieve. For the reasons already mentioned, any system of private law will have distributive consequences. The famous scholars and

[37] Another choice, concerning remedy valuation, yields a possible third dimension of the model that unifies the theory with the theory of property rules and liability rules.

[38] Weintraub, 'The Theory and Politics of the Public/Private Distinction', p. 36.

[39] Morton J. Horwitz, 'The History of the Public/Private Distinction' (1982) 130 *University of Pennsylvania Law Review* 1423, 1425–6 ('What were the concerns that created a virtual obsession with separating public and private law, both conceptually and practically, during the nineteenth century? Above all was the effort of orthodox judges and jurists to create a legal science that would sharply separate law from politics').

scholar-judges of the early twentieth century attacked the public/private distinction for its attempt to hide this fact.[40] What anti-progressive judges called private, these scholars argued, often carried enormous public consequences, and thus should conform to broader public policies.[41]

That, however, is not my battle here. How a state decides the conditions for enforcement and the methods for enforcement of private law is a different and more complex question than the simple one I initially ask: what law of a group is primarily defined by individuals and what is primarily defined by the group? The focus here is only, for the moment, on identification of a category, not on how laws within each category should be drafted or regulated. That legislators have a tendency to favour incumbents when crafting election laws, for example, may be a reason for creating special rules to pass, to review and to interpret such laws, but it does not make us doubt that public legislation exists. The category exists even if the laws within it are corrupt or unwise. Indeed, the distinction between public and private power to make publicly backed law looms larger when private coercive power is thought to be considerable. In any event, the sculpting of secondary rules through which private parties may make agreements that result in public coercion should surely be sensitive to the

[40] *Ibid.*, 1426; Robert L. Hale, 'Coercion and Distribution in a Supposedly Non-coercive State' (1923) 38 *Political Science Quarterly* 470, 470–9. Soviet theorists attacked the public/private distinction for the same reason. E. B. Pashukanis argued that private law, as opposed to public administration, creates a Republic of the Market, which serves only to hide The Despotism of the Factory. The judicialising of modern society was the work of the bourgeoisie and could not be carried out coherently: the bourgeoisie tended to privatise all law while yet needing public law to safeguard its position as a ruling class. The distinction between public and private was one of the (ideological) contradictions of capitalism: 'For us [the Soviets] there cannot even be a discussion of the limitation of state intervention in any sphere of economic activity – but this is the very first thing that follows from the division of law into two spheres.' Alice Erh-Soon Tay and Eugene Kamenka, 'Public Law – Private Law', in Stanley I. Benn and Gerald F. Gaus (eds.), *Public and Private in Social Life* (London: Croom Helm, 1983), pp. 84–5 (citing E. B. Pashukanis, *General Theory of Law and Marxism* (Moscow: Sotsiahsticheskoi Akademii, 1924) and quoting E. B. Pashukanis and L. la Gintsburg, *A Course on Soviet Economic Law* (1935), p. 330, available at: www.law.illinois.edu/p-maggs/pch8.htm (last accessed 22 May 2013) (brackets in original).

[41] Horwitz, 'The History of the Public/Private Distinction', 1426. Horwitz also describes (at 1427) how the horrors of the totalitarian regimes of the mid twentieth century sowed the seeds of retrenchment. Greater scepticism of regulating private affairs in order to achieve 'public' goals led to general acceptance of the idea that the state's role was to find accommodation between conflicting private interests, not to substitute a (potentially autocratic) public preference for those of the regulated individuals.

political reality of private power.[42] But that is an observation that relies on the distinction, not one that denies it.

The second critique of the distinction on which the model relies was most famously articulated by Duncan Kennedy. He raises the possibility that what is public and what is private are thoroughly and hopelessly indeterminate, that legal reality cannot be sensibly sorted by the criterion I propose.[43] Using the public/private distinction as a mere example, he argued that any legal dichotomy worth fighting over will (a) eventually spawn intermediate categories, (b) collapse as each case comes to be seen as a hybrid, (c) devolve into balancing tests that weigh in each case the relative influence of the omnipresent poles, and (d) finally descend into brain-dead litigation postures caricaturing the generic factors typical of every case in which the distinction is raised.[44]

The moral of this story, for it is not a legal history per se, is that the world is complex and efforts to paint it only in black and white will fail. Eventually reasonable people will point out all the grey staring them in their faces, and litigation will descend into intellectually insubstantial legal theatre in which grey is described, using standardised rhetoric, as black by one side and white by the other, but where everyone knows the game. Thus, Kennedy calls into question the sense of basing any serious analysis on the difference between the public and the private.[45]

While this critique correctly describes the descent into a formal game that befalls many bright-line rules, the primary source of confusion in distinguishing public from private stems from the indeterminacy of the question asked, not any inherent defect in the terms themselves. For example, in a society in which publicly raised taxes are often combined

[42] See, e.g., Hale, 'Coercion and Distribution', 493.

[43] Duncan Kennedy, 'The Stages of the Decline of the Public/Private Distinction' (1982) 130 *University of Pennsylvania Law Review* 1349.

[44] *Ibid.*, 1350–4.

[45] A similar argument is made by Tay and Kamenka: '[T]he significance of distinctions between public and private law is not well brought out by semantic analysis or by a classificatory approach. Both of these, in the case of law, tend to smack of circularity or to run into considerable conflict between the theoretical interest in consistency and the enormous impact of historical accident and peculiarity on the actual development of legal systems. Classificatory approaches are forced to recognise the existence of mixed forms and though they can do so without overt contradiction, such recognition does not help to illuminate the reasons for the mixture, the nature of the conflict or the character of legal trends. A far better approach is to think of private and public law in terms of conflicting paradigms or ideal types, representing internally coherent and externally conflicting logical trends or "moments" within the law.' Tay and Kamenka, 'Public Law – Private Law', p. 83.

with private funds to carry out projects, asking whether such a project is 'public or private' is an imprecise question, inevitably yielding an indeterminate answer. Even if one asks whether the project is 'publicly or privately funded', the answer can do no better than to reflect the problematic fit of the question to the social reality.

A model based on the distinction should pose better questions. The questions of institutional control that I pose – who creates law and who can force its adjudication – are derived from the way I believe legal systems in fact do and inevitably must structure themselves and, in any event, are designed to produce answers of minimal ambiguity. 'If we are careful to avoid the trap of describing law or some practice as public or private *in general* and instead focus on whether a public or a private entity is the source of a *particular* decision, much of the perceived incoherency of the distinction falls away.'[46]

The taxonomic concern of this chapter is only with how individuals representing themselves and institutions representing the collective make certain, discrete types of determinations. The distinction between such institutions is real, meaning that the public and the private really are different modes of decision-making. Coercion based on law devised by an individual for his or her own purposes invariably raises different issues than does coercion based on law created by the group at large for the public's purposes. The effort now is to discover the import of this fundamental difference.

B The public/private model of legal systems

It is now possible to refine the model of legal systems by distinguishing public from private institutions. Primary legal rules may either be publicly or privately made. And the decision whether to adjudicate an alleged violation of a primary legal rule (the power to force the collective to apply primary rules to determine whether to apply its coercive resources) may either be publicly or privately made. This observation refines the chart at which we had arrived after introducing the institutional theory, as now we have two basic types of institutions, public and private, that may make law-making and prosecution decisions and that are governed by Constitutional Law and Procedure, respectively.

Those primary rules that are privately made and privately prosecuted I call Contract Law. Those that are publicly made and privately prosecuted

[46] Turner, 'State Action Problems', 304 (emphasis in original).

I call Tort Law. Publicly prosecuted and publicly created rules are called Criminal Law. A rather odd category also appears in the model: privately made but publicly prosecuted rules. I call this last category *Parens Patriae* (the name often given to such suits as, for example, the public enforcement of the terms of a private charitable trust). The public/private model of legal systems is now complete:

		Constitutional Law	
		Privately Created	Publicly Created
Procedure	Privately Prosecuted	Contract Law	Tort Law
	Publicly Prosecuted	Parens Patriae	Criminal Law

An exploration of some of the consequences of conceiving legal systems this way reveals the simplifying power of the model.

> By creating a substantive map of legal systems in terms of institutional control over basic decisions, we can (1) understand apparently substantive problems in institutional terms and (2) translate problems and results from one substantive area of law to another by noting and adjusting for the different institutional environments.[47]

For example, both public and private Constitutional Law contain rules for law-maker selection, law passage and rights protection. The model gives us a unified way to think about these problems – how, for example, the rules governing contract formation and enforcement arise from the same principles as the rules for the creation and enforcement of torts, but refracted through a different institutional environment. As Hart wrote, 'many of the features which puzzle us in the institutions of contract or property are clarified by thinking of the operations of making a contract or transferring property as the exercise of limited legislative powers by individuals'.[48]

C *The institutional calculus and the public/private theory of legal systems*

The first (*ex ante*) and second (*ex post*) principles of institutions in combination with the core competencies (private preference calculation, public

[47] *Ibid.*, p. 295. [48] Hart, *The Concept of Law*, p. 96.

preference calculation, aggregation, distributive and resource) provide a way to analyse and to compare institutions tasked with various types of decisions. They can be applied here to analyse the relative capacities of and needed regulations on public and private law-makers and prosecutors. Put differently, the first and second principles generate many of the more specific rules of Constitutional Law and Procedure.

Recall that the first principle requires that an institution be composed and empowered in a way likely to render it institutionally competent, in the sense that it exhibits all of the core competencies. This principle will, for example, provide constraints on rules of law-maker selection and limitations on a law-making body's scope of authority. The second principle requires invalidation of a decision that manifests the incompetence of the institution that reached it. For example, a law may be invalidated when a first-principle-compliant law-making body passes a law that is, say, so harmful to the interests of others that it manifests the unequal weighing of their interests in the decision (a failure of the distributive competency).

I have elsewhere analysed the core competencies as they apply to public and private institutions in greater detail,[49] but a sketch and some examples can illustrate the possibilities of the theory. Consider the conditions under which private parties should be permitted to enact laws binding on others.

It is typically assumed that individuals know their own preferences better than others. That is, they maintain a private calculation advantage over others, including public agents. But aside from circumstances in which we expect self-interest to be muted,[50] individuals are not typically distributively competent, meaning that they are likely in reaching a decision to weigh their own preferences more heavily than others' even if they properly calculate them. This incompetency provides a general ground, under the first principle, not to recognise privately made rules as binding on others. If there are to be privately made laws, they must be made under circumstances in which the private law-makers are not likely to be distributively incompetent.

The solution is to insist on unanimity among those who will be bound by the privately created duties that result. A private group that can signal

[49] Turner, 'Law's Public/Private Structure', 1016–32.

[50] For example, the public is highly deferential to the rules parents make for their children. See, e.g., *Prince* v. *Massachusetts*, 321 US 158, 166 (1944) ('It is cardinal with us that the custody, care and nurture of the child reside first in the parents, whose primary function and freedom include preparation for obligations the state can neither supply nor hinder').

that it is, *collectively*, distributively competent and well calculating may satisfy the first principle. If the group manifests through agreement that it will be better off with a law that imposes duties only on its consenting members, many societies will enforce the law, on the grounds that individuals are superior to others at knowing their own preferences and that a law that makes some people better off and no one else worse off is desirable (meaning that the group is aggregatively competent as to such laws). Thus, a consenting group of private law-makers proposing to bind only itself has all the core competencies and satisfies the first principle.[51]

Public institutions, in contrast, make laws that are binding on those who do not necessarily consent to be bound. A welfare-oriented society, one concerned with the private preferences of its members, will maintain Constitutional Law that selects members of a public law-making body in a manner that maximises the body's potential to take account of the preferences of the individuals it will bind (private calculation competency) and minimises the possibility of self-dealing or favouritism at odds with public norms (distributive and aggregative competency). Such secondary rules, which we might gather under an umbrella term such as procedural due process, are often rule-like and can be individually tied to securing the core competencies.[52]

The important observation is that law-maker selection rules have the same goals in both the Constitutional Law of Contract (in which standards of consent, usually in the form of offer and acceptance, are the key paradigm) and in public Constitutional Law (in which agency-policing

[51] The theory also explains why different types of private laws often require different levels of evidence of consent. In 'Law's Public/Private Structure', I discussed the greater evidentiary requirements for wills, the very loose requirements for gifts and the requirement that covenants 'touch and concern' the land before their obligations will be found to 'run' to non-party successors-in-interest: Turner, 'Law's Public/Private Structure', 1036–8. See also Turner, 'State Action Problems', 310: '[W]hile a current landowner is not particularly likely to be a good calculator of the preferences his successor will have generally, he may be better when it comes to preferences concerning the use of the land, as to which he and the successor will be more similarly situated. In addition, it provides some comfort that when it comes to enacting land-specific obligations, the current owner will be more likely actually to *satisfy* the preferences of successors when he must shoulder the same obligations and personally suffer any diminished property value in exchange for the benefits the covenant regime provides. As to these preferences, he is reasonably likely to be a good agent, whereas we would assume no such competence in binding successors to arbitrary contractual arrangements that do not primarily concern the important asset the covenanting parties and his successors have in common.'

[52] Turner, 'Law's Public/Private Structure', 1039–40 (citing and discussing Adrian Vermeule, 'The Constitutional Law of Congressional Procedure' (2004) 71 *University of Chicago Law Review* 361).

rules are the paradigm). The consent-related doctrines of private Constitutional Law are twins of the procedural due process doctrines of public Constitutional Law.

The structural rules that flow from the first principle are mirrored by the rights-protecting provisions generated by the second, or *ex post*, principle. The second principle demands that we scrutinise law-making output for institutional failure. For example, 'contracts manifesting unusually poor private calculations or tort or criminal laws demonstrating peculiarly poor public calculations or unusually bad distributive consequences will, at some point along the spectrum, be deemed to go too far and will not be enforced'.[53] Here we again find twin doctrines, unconscionability and related doctrines within private Constitutional Law and substantive due process and related doctrines (including more specific provisions such as equal protection and speech rights) within public Constitutional Law.[54]

D *Applications*

I have only begun to explore the possibilities of the public/private theory. In 'Law's Public/Private Structure', for example, I analysed the application of the first principle to the procedural dimension of the model to understand the appropriate substantive line between Tort Law and Criminal Law.[55] The resulting analysis demonstrates the justifications for *qui tam* actions,[56] for restricting punitive damages in Tort claims to low-multipliers of compensatory damages,[57] and for permitting a private party to pursue criminal-like sanctions against a spouse for the violation of a protective order intended solely for her benefit.[58] Each of these substance-specific questions can be understood as an institution-specific application of the general principles of the model.

In another work, I used the theory to construct a principled state action doctrine, the doctrine in US law that evaluates whether a formally private actor should be treated as the state and put to constitutional scrutiny.[59] The famous case of *Shelley* v. *Kraemer*,[60] in which the only state involvement was the judicial enforcement of racially restrictive private covenants that purported to run with the land, has proved exceedingly difficult to justify.

[53] Turner, 'Law's Public/Private Structure', 1042.

[54] *Ibid.*, 1042–4. [55] *Ibid.*, 1045–64.

[56] *Ibid.*, 1056–7. [57] *Ibid.*, 1058–60. [58] *Ibid.*, 1060–4.

[59] Turner, 'State Action Problems'.

[60] 334 US 1 (1948) (*Shelley*).

The public/private theory reveals that the problem facing a court in such situations is not whether to apply Constitutional Law but *which body* of Constitutional Law to apply – the private Constitutional Law of contracts and covenants that insists mainly on consent or the public Constitutional Law of equal protection and due process that insists on good agency.

> [T]he legal constraints on contracting parties are tuned to the problems private lawmakers typically encounter. Some acts of private lawmaking are, however, far more like public lawmaking, for which there are different types of constraints addressed to the stereotypical problems that attend making laws that bind non-consenting others. Private actors engaged in the equivalent of public legislation therefore present a state action problem, meaning that they are poorly governed by the usual private secondary rules.[61]

The public/private theory, and the institutional perspective more broadly, led naturally to a two-step state action test that explains why the US Supreme Court was correct to strike down the racist covenants in *Shelley*. The key to the theory is the observation that the problem concerns the *selection* of alternative bodies of Constitutional Law tuned to the basic institutional types: public and private. And when a private actor gains the equivalent of law-making power over others, as in *Shelley* where the cabal of private owners was able to use the doctrine of running with the land to enact the equivalent of racist zoning laws, it is up to the other public institutions, preferably legislatures but perhaps ultimately courts, either to restrain the actor altogether or to import agency-policing provisions of public Constitutional Law into the system of secondary rules governing the powerful private actor.

There is much more to do. The theory has applications for international regimes, in which the public is a community of nations and the members of the public are self-interested nation-states. Contract Law within such a regime would be represented by treaties and Tort Law by public international law enforceable by individual states. Viewing international law in this way reveals that supposed analogies to domestic law are in fact much more than that. The similarities of the regimes owe to their both being undergirded by the same public/private template, subject to the same institutional competency principles. And so consent, standing, due process: all these should have roles in communities of nations similar to their roles in municipal legal systems. Moreover, the public/private theory provides a framework for evaluating how the systems might differ,

[61] *Ibid.*, at 285.

perhaps, on account of the more sophisticated and corporate nature of the individuals who compose the public of nation-states, but also might be surprisingly similar owing to the inherent self-interestedness of both nations and individuals.

5 Conclusion

Legal theorists' efforts of the last hundred and fifty years to paint a more realistic picture of law's practice have at times embraced, at times rejected, and at times simultaneously embraced and rejected the notions of public and private. From diverse approaches, however, a straight line emerges from the pre-Austinian world of law as lists of commands issued by an authoritative sovereign to the generic public/private atlas and institutional calculus that can provide routes to understanding even the loosest of legal regimes. Our society is a multi-tiered mosaic of publics, each with its own legal system, embedded in complex ways among one another. The coercive order emanating from the Tort Law of a private workplace is sometimes enforceable under the Contract Law of a state. A nation itself can be under a Contract obligation (a treaty within the public of a community of nations) not to enact a Criminal Law (within its municipal legal system governing the public of individuals who compose the nation). That so many levels of government and society can be understood as operating under the same template presents a potent opportunity better to understand the pluralistic world we all inhabit.

PART III

Private and public: key encounters

5

What is the point of charity law?

MATTHEW HARDING

1 Introduction

Charity law – the legal rules, doctrines, principles and practices that apply to 'charity' as such – remains remarkably underexamined from philosophical perspectives despite its great age.[1] While there is a vast and rich literature on not-for-profit activity from a variety of disciplinary perspectives, scholars who have turned their attention to that part of not-for-profit regulation that is made up of charity law have typically taken either historical or doctrinal approaches to the subject,[2] or recommended the abandonment of charity law for a broader regulatory framework built upon foundations that the legal concept of charity cannot provide.[3] Rarer are approaches to charity law that seek to explain it, and to consider the extent to which it is justified, on terms that are both philosophical and

My thanks to Natalie Burgess for her assistance, excellent as always, in helping me to prepare this chapter for publication, to Myles McGregor-Lowndes and Matthew Turnour for extensive comments on an early draft, and to Darryn Jensen for his insightful and challenging editing.

[1] The best account of the history of charity law, but only up to the nineteenth century, remains Gareth Jones, *History of the Law of Charity 1532–1827* (Cambridge University Press, 1969).

[2] See, e.g., Peter Luxton, *The Law of Charities* (Oxford University Press, 2001); Jean Warburton, Debra Morris and N. F. Riddle, *Tudor on Charities*, 9th edition (London: Sweet and Maxwell, 2003); Hubert Picarda QC, *The Law and Practice Relating to Charities*, 4th edition (London: Bloomsbury, 2010); Gino Dal Pont, *Law of Charity*, 2nd edition (Chatswood: LexisNexis Butterworths, 2010).

[3] See, e.g., Jonathan Garton, *The Regulation of Organised Civil Society* (Oxford: Hart Publishing, 2009). But note also Matthew Turnour, 'Beyond Charity: Outlines of a Jurisprudence for Civil Society', PhD thesis, Queensland University of Technology (2009), which recommends a regulatory framework for civil society that builds on, even though it goes beyond, the legal conception of charity.

specific to it.[4] The lack of philosophical interest in charity law is a matter of more than academic concern; at a time when charity law across the English-speaking world is being subjected to scrutiny and change, perhaps as never before,[5] it is especially important that we understand it better in light of at least the major schools of political and social philosophy that in many ways constitute the bedrock of intellectual endeavour on topics relating to state action and public discourse. What can we say about charity law in light of the social functions of law? What can we say about it in light of the role and limits of the state? And, perhaps most fundamentally, what is the point of having charity law in the first place? Only in the light of answers to questions like these may we evaluate proposals for the reform of charity law with a clear view of what charity law is and of what it could and should become.

In this chapter, I want to set out some preliminary thoughts in response to the third question I have just posed: what is the point of charity law? In other words, what can be said about the reasons why the state might enact, maintain and support the legal rules, doctrines, principles and practices that, taken together, make up charity law? The details of these rules, doctrines, principles and practices are notoriously tricky, and Lord Simonds' statement that '[n]o-one who has been versed … in this difficult and very artificial branch of the law can be unaware of its illogicalities' remains as true today as it was in 1951 when it was uttered.[6] However, when reflecting on the point of charity law, it is not necessary to descend to that level of detail. Instead, the inquiry can begin by concentrating on features that charity law displays when it is viewed at a greater level of generality, features in light of which the state's project for charity law is revealed. For the purposes of this chapter, it will be sufficient to present in outline two such general features.

First, through charity law the state extends legal privileges to those whose purposes are regarded as charitable in law.[7] With limited exceptions,

[4] Two exceptions are Francis Gladstone, *Charity, Law and Social Justice* (London: Bedford Square Press, 1982) and Michael Chesterman, *Charities, Trusts and Social Welfare* (London: Weidenfeld and Nicholson, 1979).

[5] A good indicator of this is the fact that statutory reform of charity law has taken place in recent years in Australia (Charities Act 2013), New Zealand (Charities Act 2005), Scotland (Charities and Trustee Investments (Scotland) Act 2005), England and Wales (Charities Act 2006 and Charities Act 2011), Northern Ireland (Charities Act 2008) and the Republic of Ireland (Charities Act 2009) and is now on the agenda in Hong Kong.

[6] *Oppenheim* v. *Tobacco Securities Trust Co. Ltd* [1951] AC 29 at 307.

[7] It is worth noting that the opposite was once the case: see the discussion of the Mortmain Act 1736 in Jones, *History of the Law of Charity*, Chapters VII and IX.

gifts and trusts for purposes are valid and enforceable in law only if they are for charitable purposes.[8] The state also puts at the disposal of those who must administer a gift or trust for charitable purposes resources that enable the terms of the gift or trust to be varied if this is appropriate.[9] Moreover, through those rules of the tax and transfer system that are also part of charity law, an organisation with a charitable purpose may be exempt from paying certain taxes that it would otherwise have had to pay or may qualify for certain transfers that it would otherwise not have qualified for.[10] And gifts to organisations with charitable purposes may attract state subsidies by being counted as deductions for the purposes of calculating taxable income or in other ways.[11] Finally, an entity with charitable purposes may thereby come within the purview of a regulatory authority established to oversee the 'charitable sector', and may benefit from this. For example, an authority may be empowered by government to register charitable trusts, entities and associations for regulatory and other purposes, and it may be that when raising funds or awareness of purposes in the community there are reputational benefits to be gained by being a registered charity.[12]

The second general feature of charity law that I want to introduce is that charity law is organised around what is usually called the 'legal definition of charity'. The legal definition of charity is a set of criteria that must be satisfied if a purpose is to be regarded as charitable according to law, and only a gift, trust, entity or association whose primary purpose is charitable according to law is itself regarded in law as charitable. The function of the legal definition of charity might therefore be thought of as controlling the conferral or withholding of a certain status in law, a status that is described using the word 'charity'. The criteria by which this charitable status is conferred or withheld in law vary in detail from jurisdiction to jurisdiction, but in all jurisdictions they are broadly similar. To begin with, the purpose under scrutiny must fall within one of a set of descriptions of prima facie charitable purpose, such as 'relief of poverty',

[8] *Morice* v. *Bishop of Durham* (1804) 9 Ves Jun 399; 32 ER 656 (Sir William Grant MR); (1805) 10 Ves Jun 522; 32 ER 947 (Lord Eldon LC); *Re Endacott* [1960] Ch 232.

[9] For the Australian rules, see Dal Pont, *Law of Charity*, Chapters 13, 15, 16.

[10] See, e.g., Income Tax Assessment Act 1997 (Cth) s. 50.

[11] See, e.g., Internal Revenue Code (US) § 170 (deductions); Finance Act 1990 (UK) s. 25, as amended by Finance Act 2000 (UK) s. 39 (Gift Aid).

[12] 'Charitable status brings with it valuable … reputational benefits': *Charity Commission for England and Wales* v. *Her Majesty's Attorney-General* [2012] UKUT B19 (TCC) at [17].

'advancement of education' and 'advancement of religion'.[13] The set is invariably open-ended in that it includes a 'catch-all' description capturing purposes that do not fall within any of the other descriptions but are analogous to purposes that have, in the past, been found by state officials to be charitable.[14] And, in addition, with the exception of purposes answering the description 'relief of poverty', it must be proved as a matter of fact – on the evidence, or by way of a presumption, depending on the purpose and on the jurisdiction – that carrying out the purpose under scrutiny will benefit the public in some way. This criterion is known as the 'public benefit test' of charity law.

These general features of charity law suggest that the state's project for that body of law is to mark out certain purposes as charitable in the legal sense and to extend legal privileges to those who pursue such purposes. In what follows, I consider the question of the point of charity law with the general features of charity law, and the associated state project for that body of law, in view. I describe three functions that charity law performs: a function of facilitating charitable purposes; a function of promoting charitable purposes; and a function of creating public meaning for charity in the legal sense. I consider the point of each of these functions in light of liberal philosophical commitments, presenting some arguments about the general features of charity law that I have just introduced, in particular the 'public' and the 'benefit' components of the public benefit test, as I go. The gist of the analysis is that, in the performance of all three functions, charity law reveals the state acting and reasoning in ways that are arguably defensible from a liberal perspective: in other words, from a liberal perspective, there may be a point to charity law in light of distinctly liberal values.

[13] In this way, the legal definition of charity is broader than the non-legal understanding of that concept as confined to poor relief: see *Commissioners for Special Purposes of Income Tax* v. *Pemsel* [1891] AC 531.

[14] In England and Wales, the 'catch-all' description is set out in s. 3(1)(m) of the Charities Act 2011. In Australia, until recently, it took the form of the so-called fourth 'head' of charity referred to by Lord Macnaghten in the *Pemsel* case. For a purpose to fall within the 'fourth head' of charity under Australian law, it not only had to be analogous to an existing charitable purpose, it also had to be within the 'spirit and intendment' of the preamble to the Statute of Charitable Uses 1601: see *Royal National Agricultural and Industrial Association* v. *Chester* (1974) 48 ALJR 304. The requirement that a purpose be within the 'spirit and intendment' of the preamble was criticised frequently and was abandoned once a statutory definition of charity was introduced in Australia.

2 The facilitative function of charity law

Charity law makes possible, to those whose purposes are charitable, what would not otherwise be possible. Through charity law, citizens are enabled to generate the rights, powers and obligations that characterise a charitable trust, to make legally enforceable claims to tax exemptions and other privileges, and to assert other rights against the state, for example the right to be registered as a charity. Many of the rules by which charity law makes possible what would not otherwise be possible are what H. L. A. Hart famously called 'power-conferring' rules: rules that empower citizens to bring about changes in the legal position both of themselves and of others.[15] Thus, the point of charity law may well become clearer in light of reflection on the point of power-conferring rules. According to Hart, the 'social function' of power-conferring rules is to 'provide individuals with *facilities* for realizing their wishes';[16] for Hart, this is 'one of the great contributions of law to social life'.[17] Thus, to the extent that charity law is made up of power-conferring and analogous rules, we may attribute to it a facilitative function. And the performance of this function is part – though as we will see, not the whole – of the point of charity law.

What is the point of the facilitative function of charity law? The answer to this deeper question demands some political philosophy. I want to begin with the liberal value of individual freedom, a value whose goodness I will not defend but rather assume for present purposes. How can the facilitative function of charity law be understood in light of that value? Here it is necessary to introduce the distinction, familiar to all philosophers in the liberal tradition, and accepted by many of them, between negative freedom and positive freedom. This is the distinction between the freedom that comes of being able to live one's life in the absence of the depredations or interference of others, and the freedom that comes of living a life that is the product of self-directed choices across time among a range of genuine, plausible and valuable options.[18] In what is often referred to as 'perfectionist' liberalism, the latter type of freedom – positive freedom – constitutes

[15] H. L. A. Hart, *The Concept of Law*, 3rd edition (Oxford: Clarendon Press, 2012), pp. 27–8.

[16] *Ibid.*, p. 27. [17] *Ibid.*, p. 28.

[18] See Isaiah Berlin, 'Two Concepts of Liberty', in his *Liberty* (Oxford University Press, 2002), p. 166. See also Charles Taylor, 'What's Wrong with Negative Liberty?', in his *Philosophy and the Human Sciences: Philosophical Papers 2* (Cambridge University Press, 1985), pp. 211, 213, discussing liberty as an 'opportunity-concept' and as an 'exercise-concept'.

the central value in a distinctly liberal conception of the good life, with implications for both personal ethics and political morality. It is to perfectionist liberalism that I will appeal in what follows.

The point of the facilitative function of charity law is revealed in light of the value of positive freedom, which I will call the value of autonomy, following a perfectionist liberal philosopher who has done as much as anyone to illuminate that value: Joseph Raz.[19] To some extent, engaging with the value of autonomy is a matter for each individual and depends on a willingness to cultivate and realise virtues, skills and capacities as well as a preparedness to make choices and commitments. However, as Raz explains, the value of autonomy also grounds principles of political action, including principles specifying what the state needs to do to bring about the conditions that make it possible for individuals to live autonomous lives. Among the conditions of autonomy is the presence of an adequate range of options to choose from; because autonomous lives are, among other things, lives characterised by choices among options, autonomous lives are possible only to the extent that an adequate range of options exists for those whose lives they are.

By performing its facilitative function, charity law makes a contribution to the conditions of autonomy. It enlarges the number of options available to individuals whose purposes fall within its purview. For example, it is because of charity law that I have the option of creating a trust for the purpose of relieving poverty; in the absence of charity law, I would lack that option and would be confined to relieving poverty in other ways. If I choose to relieve poverty through a corporate entity, charity law gives me the option of applying all of the income of that entity to its purposes, rather than paying some to the state in the form of income tax. In a jurisdiction where a regulator registers charities, it is through charity law that I gain the option of pursuing my purpose of relieving poverty through a registered charity, gaining access to reputational and other benefits that flow from receiving this form of endorsement from the state. The provision of these options is more than just an incidental consequence of charity law performing a facilitative function; to the extent that charity law consists of power-conferring and analogous rules, the provision of these options is the very point of that function. The contribution that such

[19] Joseph Raz, *The Morality of Freedom* (Oxford: Clarendon Press, 1986); Joseph Raz, 'Autonomy, Toleration and the Harm Principle', in Ruth Gavison (ed.), *Issues in Contemporary Legal Philosophy: The Influence of HLA Hart* (Oxford: Clarendon Press, 1987), p. 313; Joseph Raz, 'Facing Up: A Reply' (1989) 62 *Southern California Law Review* 1153.

options make to the full range of options available to those whose purposes fall within the purview of charity law is a contribution to the conditions of autonomy.

We might say, then, that insofar as it has a facilitative function, charity law reflects and expresses the commitment of a liberal state to the value of individual freedom, understood in its positive sense as the value of autonomy. Not that this is the only value to which even the liberal state should respond through its law. Notwithstanding that autonomy may be served by a facilitative charity law, the state might determine that the socially beneficial consequences of carrying out charitable purposes could be achieved more efficiently, or even more justly, if it repealed charity law altogether and pursued charitable purposes itself. Moreover, it is not inconceivable that such a determination might be justified as a matter of political morality.[20] However, while we cannot say that the only value to which the state must be sensitive in a charity law setting is autonomy, we can say that where the state chooses to pursue goals like efficiency or social justice by narrowing the scope of the power-conferring and analogous rules of charity law, this is likely to come at a cost in terms of autonomy. In a liberal state, this possibility should not be viewed with indifference. This point is worth bearing in mind when thinking about certain recent developments in charity law. For example, consider the 'contract culture' that now characterises relations between government and the charitable sector,[21] or recent suggestions that, in the interests of efficiency, those who would do charity be confined to carrying out their purposes via a single type of entity rather than the wide range of organisations that currently they may choose from.[22] When thinking about what the state might achieve by controlling the activities of charities through contracts, or by channelling the pursuit of charitable purposes through a single entity type, the possible cost to autonomy should not be forgotten.

[20] See Rob Atkinson, 'Keeping Republics Republican' (2011) 88 *Texas Law Review* 235.

[21] Jean Warburton and Debra Morris, 'Charities and the Contract Culture' [1991] *The Conveyancer* 419; Jane Lewis, 'Reviewing the Relationship between the Voluntary Sector and the State in Britain in the 1990s' (1999) 10 *Voluntas* 255; Alison Dunn, 'Demanding Service or Servicing Demand? Charities, Regulation and the Policy Process' (2008) 71 *Modern Law Review* 247; Matthew Harding, 'Distinguishing Government from Charity in Australian Law' (2009) 31 *Sydney Law Review* 559.

[22] Senate Standing Committee on Economics, *Disclosure Regimes for Charities and Not-for-Profit Organisations* (Commonwealth of Australia, 2008), Chapter 7, especially [7.59].

3 The promotive function of charity law

Looking across the part of charity law that extends legal privileges to those with charitable purposes, it is clear that this part of charity law does more than just facilitate the pursuit of such purposes. It also provides incentives – typically in the form of tax privileges – to people to pursue charitable purposes. Moreover, while the primary function of the legal definition of charity is to establish criteria by which it is determined whether or not purposes are charitable in law, a further function of those criteria is to express the state's endorsement of purposes of certain types. These incentive and expressive dimensions of charity law cannot be wholly explained in terms of the state facilitating autonomous choice. They reveal another, associated, function of charity law: the state-sponsored promotion of charitable purposes by giving citizens reasons to pursue charitable purposes that those citizens would otherwise lack.

A The point of the promotive function

What is the point of the promotive function of charity law? Let us again turn to the value of individual freedom, understood in its positive sense as autonomy, in order to get a handle on this question. If it can be said that charitable purposes contribute to the conditions of autonomy, and especially to the constitution of options that may be the subject of autonomous choice by citizens, then in light of the value of autonomy there would seem to be a point to the state's promotion of charitable purposes. In working out the extent to which charitable purposes contribute to the conditions of autonomy, it is necessary to look to the consequences of charitable purposes. This demands consideration of the goods that flow from the pursuit of such purposes. If the goods that flow from the pursuit of charitable purposes can be said to contribute to the conditions of autonomy, then the promotive function of charity law, just like its facilitative function, can be said to reflect and express liberal commitments. So in seeking the point of the promotive function of charity law from a liberal perspective, we should be looking for connections between charitable purposes and autonomy-promoting goods.

In this regard, the first point to note is that connections between charitable purposes and autonomy-promoting goods are more easily established in relation to some types of purpose than they are in relation to other types of purpose. For example, there can be little doubt that purposes within the description 'relief of poverty' tend to generate substantial goods, and that these goods contribute to the conditions of autonomy in substantial ways, say, by ensuring that people can maintain the physical and mental capacities that are among the fundamental conditions of autonomy, or by enabling people to be free from want and fear and thus situated so as to choose among options. Equally, purposes within the description 'advancement of education' tend to generate goods associated with the acquisition of knowledge and skills that are necessary in order both to access and to respond to options, and also help to constitute some options such as being a student or a teacher. These are all substantial contributions to the conditions of autonomy.

On the other hand, the connections between purposes within the description 'advancement of religion' and autonomy-promoting goods are less clear. There can be no doubt that on occasion conflicts may arise between religion and autonomy, such as where religious parents seek to withdraw their children from the sort of education that will both equip them to live autonomously and give them access to a wide range of options to choose from in life.[23] Some scholars even argue that religion and autonomy are generally inconsistent because the claims of religion are not experienced as options to be chosen.[24] These sorts of arguments tend to downplay the extent to which religion accommodates autonomy in matters of belief and practice, and may also misunderstand the nature of autonomy. Moreover, they are not necessarily arguments against the proposition that the various goods associated with religion – from private goods in the form of the spiritual, intellectual and emotional resources that various religions make available to their adherents, to private goods entailed in belonging to religious communities, to the public good of religious diversity – make a contribution to the conditions of autonomy. Nonetheless, the case for extending the promotive function of charity law to religious purposes is a case that, from a liberal perspective, must be carefully made, especially in respect of circumstances where religion and autonomy may conflict.

[23] Good examples, drawn from US constitutional law, are *Wisconsin* v. *Yoder*, 406 US 205 (1972) and *Mozert* v. *Hawkins County Board of Education*, 827 F 2d 1058 (6th Cir. 1987).

[24] See, e.g., Michael J. Sandel, 'Religious Liberty – Freedom of Conscience or Freedom of Choice?' [1989] *Utah Law Review* 597; Michael J. Sandel, *Democracy's Discontent: America in Search of a Public Philosophy* (Cambridge, MA: Belknap Press, 1996), pp. 65–71; Rex Ahdar and Ian Leigh, *Religious Freedom in the Liberal State* (Oxford University Press, 2005), pp. 60–1; Sonu Bedi, 'Debate: What Is So Special About Religion?' (2007) 15 *The Journal of Political Philosophy* 235.

The difficult case of 'advancement of religion' simply highlights that if a proper understanding of the point of the promotive function of charity law depends on establishing connections between particular types of charitable purpose and autonomy-promoting goods, then what is required is reflection on the likely consequences of each of the particular types of purpose that are promoted via charity law. That said, we might attempt one observation of a general nature about connections between charitable purposes and autonomy-promoting goods. As we have seen, the conditions of autonomy include an adequate range of options to choose from. The goods that help to constitute such options are in part excludable private goods such as education, employment, health care, books, holidays abroad, fine wines and so on. However, non-excludable public goods also make an important contribution to constituting an adequate range of options to choose from in realising an autonomous life. Many options are simply inconceivable except against a rich backdrop of cultural institutions, practices, understandings and arrangements, many of which entail public goods that relate to what Raz calls the 'general character of ... society'.[25] These public goods of a cultural character are numerous; they range from goods associated with living in a social setting that includes institutions and arrangements such as the family, friendship and marriage, to goods associated with a culture of progress and achievement in science, the humanities and the arts, to goods associated with the existence of various professions, occupations, forms of association and leisure activities, to goods as elevated as a tolerant, respectful or educated society. Such public goods generate social meaning, help to condition and define more specific instances of value,[26] and make available ways in which to engage with particular goods.[27] The importance of public goods of a cultural character to the provision of an adequate range of options, and therefore to the conditions of autonomy, cannot be overstated. Indeed, Raz's thinking on the importance of these goods takes him to the very limits of liberalism: he goes so far as to elevate 'common culture' alongside 'individual action' in the 'shaping of the moral world'.[28]

[25] Raz, *The Morality of Freedom*, pp. 198–9, 205–7, 308–13 (the quotation is at 198–9). See also Joseph Chan, 'Legitimacy, Unanimity and Perfectionism' (2000) 29 *Philosophy and Public Affairs* 5, 29, describing the dependence of many options on social conditions as a 'sociological truism'.

[26] Including the value of autonomy itself: see Charles Taylor, 'Atomism', in his *Philosophy and the Human Sciences: Philosophical Papers 2* (Cambridge University Press, 1985), p. 187, especially pp. 204–5.

[27] Raz, *The Morality of Freedom*, pp. 198–9, 207, 247, 250, 254–5.

[28] *Ibid.*, p. 193.

In light of these observations about the significant contribution that public goods of a cultural character make to the conditions of autonomy, the general point to be made about the connections between charitable purposes and autonomy-promoting goods is this: it is strongly arguable that many if not most of the types of purpose that are regarded as charitable in law tend to generate public goods of a cultural character, and to the extent that these public goods of a cultural character play a role in the framing and constitution of options that may be the subject of autonomous choice, the promotive function of charity law is consistent with the demands of autonomy. A brief look at section 3(1) of the Charities Act 2011 (UK) – a typical modern statutory expression of descriptions of prima facie charitable purpose – should help to illustrate this point. Among the types of purpose listed there are 'advancement of citizenship or community development', 'advancement of the arts, culture, heritage or science', 'advancement of amateur sport', 'advancement of … conflict resolution or reconciliation or the promotion of religious or racial harmony' and 'advancement of environmental protection or improvement'. It is strongly arguable that each of these types of purpose has a tendency to generate public goods of a cultural character, goods that shape and inform many of the options that are available to citizens of England and Wales in the conduct of their lives.

We should take care not to overstate this point about charitable purposes and public goods of a cultural character. It may well be true that the eradication of poverty is a public good of a cultural character in the sense that a poverty-free society is a great place for everyone and not only for those who would otherwise be poor. However, we need not point to any such public good in order to see the point of the state's promotion of purposes within the description 'relief of poverty'; the substantial autonomy-promoting private goods associated with poor relief do that work amply. Similarly, purposes within the description 'advancement of education' almost invariably have a propensity to generate both private and public goods that contribute in various ways to the conditions of autonomy. In short, while the likelihood that a type of charitable purpose will generate autonomy-promoting public goods of a cultural character is sufficient to make a liberal case for the state's promotion of that type of charitable purpose, it is not necessary to make such a case. Nonetheless, it may be that most types of purpose that are regarded as charitable in law do in fact tend to generate autonomy-promoting public goods of a cultural character and, to the extent that this is so, it can only bolster the liberal case for the promotive function of charity law. For example, and again drawing on section 3(1) of the Charities Act 2011 (UK), while purposes within the description 'advancement of animal welfare' seem not to generate private goods that are autonomy-promoting in any obvious way, it is arguable that such purposes contribute to the development and maintenance of a culture characterised by care and compassion, and that this is an autonomy-promoting public good because it is only in a society where virtues such as care and compassion are cultivated and manifested that autonomous lives can flourish.

B The reasoning of state officials and the point of the promotive function

Readers with knowledge of charity law may doubt that this liberal account of the point of the promotive function of charity law is reflected to any substantial degree in the reasoning of the state officials – chiefly judges, but also legislators and administrators – who have, over the years, designed and applied charity law. After all, where are the references to autonomy in charity law? To the extent that what we might for convenience call 'doubt about consistency' is justified, it should not be cause for surprise: the point of the promotive function of charity law is to be understood by reference to the consequences of the pursuit of charitable purposes, not by reference to the reasoning of state officials when applying the legal definition of charity. But is doubt about consistency even justified? That depends on the extent to which state officials, when working with the legal definition of charity, offer reasons that are consistent with a sound understanding of the political demands of the value of autonomy. I want to consider whether doubt about consistency is justified in respect of the reasoning of state officials in relation to one aspect of the legal definition of charity: the 'benefit' component of the public benefit test.[29] Obviously, I cannot evaluate every act of reasoning in the charity law setting that bears on the question of benefit. Nonetheless, I want to make three observations of a general nature. These observations suggest that, in some important respects, the reasoning of state officials on the question of benefit is consistent with a liberal account of the point of the promotive function of

[29] In England and Wales, the jurisprudence now refers to the 'benefit' component of the public benefit test as the requirement of 'public benefit in the first sense': see generally *R (Independent Schools Council)* v. *Charity Commission for England and Wales* [2012] Ch 214 (TCC); *Charity Commission for England and Wales* v. *Her Majesty's Attorney-General* [2012] UKUT B19 (TCC).

charity law. To that extent, there are reasons to think that doubt about consistency is not justified.

First, some more philosophy. I want to consider the value of autonomy in more depth, with reference once again to Raz. For Raz, autonomy is the core personal and political value, but it is not the only one, nor is it ultimate. Rather, according to Raz, autonomy is an 'enabling' value, the point of which is to 'enable people to engage with other values'.[30] In Raz's thinking, the value of enabling values such as autonomy is derivative; they derive their goodness from the values with which they enable engagement.[31] In the case of autonomy, its value is derived from the value of options chosen. In light of Raz's understanding of autonomy as an enabling value, we may draw out three important elements of his thinking on autonomy. First, as it is only possible to conceive of an enabling value such as autonomy if one accepts the objective existence of values other than autonomy – for how else can autonomy serve its point of enabling engagement with such other values? – it is clear that, for Raz, autonomy is not a matter of unfettered choice or the satisfaction of personal preferences.[32] Instead, autonomy for Raz is a matter of self-directed engagement with goods whose goodness is established independently of their being chosen. Thus, autonomy depends on the existence of what Derek Parfit calls 'facts about value';[33] it depends on objectivity in matters of value.[34] A second element of Raz's thinking on autonomy is related to his objectivity about value. While, in Raz's conception, in general terms it may be said that autonomy is an ideal of great value, the autonomy of a person who chooses valueless or base options is itself without value to that extent. It follows that, for Raz, an adequate

[30] Joseph Raz, *The Practice of Value* (Oxford University Press, 2003), p. 36. See also Jeremy Waldron, 'Autonomy and Perfectionism in Raz's *Morality of Freedom*' (1989) 62 *Southern California Law Review* 1097, 1128–9, discussing the 'aspiration to value' that is implicit in autonomous choices.

[31] Raz, *The Morality of Freedom*, pp. 16–17, 380–1; Raz, 'Autonomy, Toleration and the Harm Principle', p. 330; Raz, *The Practice of Value*, pp. 35–6.

[32] See also George Sher, *Beyond Neutrality: Perfectionism and Politics* (Cambridge University Press, 1997), Chapter 3.

[33] Derek Parfit, *Reasons and Persons* (Oxford: Clarendon Press, 1984), p. 499.

[34] Raz's thinking on objectivity and value is more complex than this statement might suggest, largely on account of his beliefs about the social dependence of value: see Raz, *The Practice of Value*; Joseph Raz, *Engaging Reason: On the Theory of Value and Action* (Oxford University Press, 1999), Chapters 6–9; Joseph Raz, *Between Authority and Interpretation: On the Theory of Law and Practical Reason* (Oxford University Press, 2009), pp. 305–6. Nonetheless, Raz's account of autonomy as an enabling value depends on there being facts about value, even if those facts are (as Raz thinks they are) heavily qualified by social contingencies.

range of options need never include such valueless or base options, and this has implications for both personal ethics and political morality.[35]

A third element of Raz's thinking that emerges from his understanding of autonomy as an enabling value is his commitment to value pluralism. Value pluralism, as a philosophical position, is associated with acceptance of two related propositions: first, that there are many types of value; and second, that values can sometimes conflict.[36] Thus understood, value pluralism may be contrasted philosophically with monism about value, which entails acceptance of the proposition that all values are to be understood as instances of some master-value, as well as the proposition that values can never be incompatible or incommensurable. Perhaps the best-known examples of monist theories of value are the various strands of utilitarianism, according to which all questions of value may be reduced to questions about utility understood in one way or another. In contrast, value pluralism characterises a range of theories of the good, from natural law theories, to objective list theories of other kinds, to Raz's liberal conception of the good. For Raz, acceptance of value pluralism is necessary to understanding how autonomy works as an enabling value;[37] it is only in light of value pluralism that a person can ever stand to make genuine choices among genuine options, as opposed to illusory choices among what are only ostensibly options. From a Razian perspective, a person whose only options were to realise one master-value in a variety of ways would lack an adequate range of options; indeed, in a sense he/she would lack any options at all.[38]

To reiterate: from Raz's understanding of autonomy as an 'enabling' value, three elements of his thinking on autonomy emerge: first, objectivity about value; second, acceptance of the proposition that an adequate range of options need never include valueless or base options; and finally, value pluralism. To what extent does the reasoning of state officials in the charity law setting reflect these three elements? There are reasons to think that when designing and applying charity law, state officials reason in ways that are substantially consistent with all three.

[35] Raz, *The Morality of Freedom*, pp. 380–1.

[36] See generally Isaiah Berlin, 'The Decline of Utopian Ideas in the West' and 'Alleged Relativism in Eighteenth Century European Thought', both in his *The Crooked Timber of Humanity: Chapters in the History of Ideas* (London: Pimlico, 2003), p. 20 and p. 70 respectively; Charles Taylor, 'The Diversity of Goods', in his *Philosophy and the Human Sciences: Philosophical Papers 2* (Cambridge University Press, 1985), p. 230; Raz, *The Practice of Value*.

[37] Raz, *The Morality of Freedom*, p. 161.

[38] See Berlin, 'Two Concepts of Liberty', pp. 216–7.

To begin with, state officials mostly insist on adopting an attitude of objectivity when making findings of benefit in the setting of the public benefit test. This objectivity is manifested in the refusal of decision-makers to defer to the beliefs about benefit of those who would do charity.[39] In *National Anti-Vivisection Society* v. *Inland Revenue Commissioners*, a case about the purposes of a society formed to campaign for the banning of medical experimentation on live animals, the House of Lords endorsed an objective approach to the 'benefit' component of the public benefit test, overruling an earlier decision in which a judge had made a finding of benefit by deferring to the beliefs of the testatrix of a testamentary trust for anti-vivisection purposes.[40] This objective mindset was again on display in *Gilmour* v. *Coats*, in relation to the purposes of a Carmelite order of nuns who spent their lives in intercessory prayer and other spiritual exercises within their convent.[41] On the question whether or not the intercessory prayer of the nuns was of public benefit, the House of Lords had evidence from the Roman Catholic Archbishop of Westminster as to his church's teaching that such prayer generated spiritual benefit in the form of God's blessing on the whole world. Rather than defer to this teaching, Their Lordships insisted that a finding of benefit was for the court itself to make, before concluding that a finding of spiritual benefit was not possible on the available evidence.[42] And in *Re Hummeltenberg, Beatty* v. *London Spiritualistic Alliance*, Russell J endorsed an objective approach to the question of benefit, stating that '[i]f a testator by stating or indicating his view that a trust is beneficial to the public can establish that fact beyond question, trusts might be established in perpetuity for

39 I say 'mostly' because in Ireland and (to a certain extent) Australia, decision-makers do defer to beliefs about benefit in 'advancement of religion' cases: *O'Hanlon* v. *Logue* [1906] 1 IR 247; *Attorney-General* v. *Becher* [1910] 2 IR 251; *Nelan* v. *Downes* (1917) 23 CLR 546; Charities Act 2009 (Ireland) s. 3(6).

40 [1948] AC 31 at 44–7 (Lord Wright), at 65–6 (Lord Simonds). The earlier case was *Re Foveaux* [1895] Ch 501. At 49, Lord Wright suggested that in forming an objective view as to benefit, at least where a claimed benefit is intangible, a decision-maker should accept only propositions that have earned 'approval by the common understanding of enlightened opinion for the time being'. This might be thought to dilute the objectivity to which I refer in the text. However, when we look across charity law as a whole, we find that reference to public opinion is seldom a characteristic of the inquiry into benefit. Moreover, Lord Wright endorsed reference only to 'enlightened' opinion; presumably what constitutes 'enlightened' opinion can be determined only by a decision-maker adopting an objective mindset.

41 [1949] AC 426.

42 *Ibid.*, at 446 (Lord Simonds), at 452 (Lord du Parcq), at 456–60 (Lord Reid).

the promotion of all kinds of fantastic (although not unlawful) objects, of which the training of poodles to dance might be a mild example'.[43]

Moreover, the objectivity of decision-makers when considering the question of benefit sometimes leads them to find that a purpose is not charitable because it stands to generate disvalue; this sort of reasoning is consistent with the proposition that certain purposes are likely to produce consequences that should not be promoted by the state in view of the demands of autonomy. For example, in the case of *Re Pinion (deceased)*, the English Court of Appeal refused to recognise a testamentary trust as charitable because its purpose was to display to the public a collection of art and furniture that in the opinion of one of the judges was 'junk'.[44] In the same case, Harman LJ expressed the view, *obiter dicta*, that a library of pornography could not be charitable.[45]

Finally, not only do state officials typically adopt an attitude of objectivity when applying the 'benefit' component of the public benefit test, they also refuse to reason reductively about benefit when applying that component of the test. This means that they do not frame their thinking about benefit in accordance with monistic accounts of value such as utilitarianism. Instead, their reasoning is consistent with the general proposition that many types of value can ground findings of benefit, and that sometimes in making findings of benefit it is necessary to choose among conflicting values.[46] Decision-makers considering the question of public benefit have pointed to an array of (usually non-excludable public) goods such as a humane culture,[47] the market economy,[48] free political expression,[49] improved moral standards[50] and the rule of law[51] in making

[43] [1923] 1 Ch 237 at 242.

[44] [1964] 1 All ER 890 at 893–4 (Harman LJ).

[45] *Ibid.*, at 893.

[46] This is a reason to reject Cohen's interpretation of charity law as utilitarian in inspiration: Harvey Cohen, 'Charities – A Utilitarian Perspective' (1983) 36 *Current Legal Problems* 241. Donovan Waters, 'The Advancement of Religion in a Pluralist Society (Part II): Abolishing the Public Benefit Element' (2011) 17 *Trusts and Trustees* 729, has suggested that charity law ought to be reformed to bring it into closer alignment with utilitarianism; the merits of that suggestion turn ultimately on the merits of utilitarianism, a question that I cannot address here.

[47] *Re Wedgwood* [1915] 1 Ch 113.

[48] *Crystal Palace Trustees* v. *Minister of Town and Country Planning* [1951] Ch 132 (Danckwerts J).

[49] *Aid/Watch Incorporated* v. *Commissioner of Taxation* (2010) 241 CLR 529.

[50] *Joyce* v. *Ashfield Municipal Council* [1975] 1 NSWLR 744.

[51] *Incorporated Council of Law Reporting of the State of Queensland* v. *Federal Commissioner of Taxation* (1971) 125 CLR 659.

findings of benefit, and – with one possible exception – they have nowhere suggested that a single measure of value might animate or underpin these ostensibly diverse goods. In this way, the reasoning of state officials when applying the 'benefit' component of the public benefit test is consistent with value pluralism.

The possible exception is the *Anti-Vivisection* case, where the question of benefit turned on two competing propositions: one that pointed to the value of a humane culture, and one that pointed to public goods associated with advances in medical research.[52] The House of Lords found that, in the circumstances of the case, the former value was far outweighed by the latter ones, and on that basis refused to make a finding that the purposes of the anti-vivisection society were of public benefit. On one view, this preparedness to weigh competing values against each other and choose among them suggests a mindset that is reductive about value. There is some support for this view in the reasoning of Lord Wright, referring to 'conflicting moral and material utilities'; this reference to 'utilities' obviously suggests a monistic approach to value.[53] However, on another view, the choice among values disclosed by the reasoning in the *Anti-Vivisection* case was experienced by the judges in that case as a choice among conflicting incommensurable values, and there is also support for this view in the reasoning of Lord Wright, in a passage where he explicitly declined to form a view on whether 'utilitarianism or intuitionist ethics is the truer theory'.[54] In light of the demonstrated refusal to reason reductively about benefit in other cases in charity law, it is strongly arguable that this latter view of the *Anti-Vivisection* case is the more plausible one.

4 The creative function of charity law

The facilitative and promotive functions of charity law suggest that the point of charity law is nothing more nor less than to assist and encourage people to do good. From a perfectionist liberal perspective, we might add to this suggestion by pointing out that the good that charity law assists and encourages people to do is best understood in light of the ideal of autonomy. However, such an account of the point of charity law would be incomplete, because charity law has its limits and not all of these limits are set by reference to whether or not the purposes that people pursue

[52] *National Anti-Vivisection Society* v. *Inland Revenue Commissioners* [1948] AC 31.
[53] *Ibid.*, at 49. See also 43.
[54] *Ibid.*, at 48.

promise to generate value. After all, very many value-generating purposes that are pursued in the family, associational and commercial spheres of human interaction are not regarded as charitable in law. The main limits of charity law emerge not from those elements of charity law that test purposes against judgments or assessments of what is of value and what is not of value: that is, the 'benefit' component of the public benefit test and the criterion that purposes, in order to be charitable, must fall within one or more of a set of descriptions of prima facie charitable purpose. The main limits of charity law emerge from the 'public' component of the public benefit test.[55]

The 'public' component of the public benefit test polices the boundaries of charity law in several ways. First, it ensures that purposes are not regarded as charitable where the class of persons that they stand to benefit is composed of individuals who are members of a family, employees of a company, members of an association or club, or connected to each other in some other way that, from the perspective of charity law, is cause for concern.[56] Such a problematic connection may exist where an organisation has a primary purpose of benefiting its members, even if the organisation in question also carries out secondary purposes of public benefit,[57] or where a group of individuals pursues a common purpose of assisting those of their number who might need help.[58] A second way in which the 'public' component of the public benefit test circumscribes charity law is by excluding from it purposes that aim at the generation of private profit, whether or not such purposes are likely incidentally to generate benefit to the public.[59] Finally, and perhaps more controversially, in at least some jurisdictions the 'public' component of the public benefit test serves to ensure that purposes that exclude the poor, because they entail the

[55] In the jurisprudence of England and Wales, this is now referred to as the requirement of 'public benefit in the second sense': *R (Independent Schools Council)* v. *Charity Commission for England and Wales* [2012] Ch 214 (TCC); *Charity Commission for England and Wales* v. *Her Majesty's Attorney-General* [2012] UKUT B19 (TCC).

[56] *Re Compton* [1945] 1 Ch 123; *Oppenheim* v. *Tobacco Securities Trust Co. Ltd* [1951] AC 297; *Re Cox, Baker* v. *National Trust Company Limited* [1953] 1 SCR 94 (SCC); *Thompson* v. *Federal Commissioner of Taxation* (1959) 102 CLR 315; *Davies* v. *Perpetual Trustee Company Ltd* [1959] AC 439; *Caffoor* v. *Commissioner of Income Tax (Colombo)* [1961] AC 584; but contrast *Re Koettgen's Will Trusts* [1954] 1 Ch 252 (Upjohn J).

[57] *Inland Revenue Commissioners* v. *City of Glasgow Police Athletics Association* [1953] AC 380 (HL).

[58] *Re Hobourn Aero Components Limited's Air Raid Distress Fund* [1946] 1 Ch 194 (CA).

[59] *R* v. *Assessors of the Town of Sunny Brae* [1952] SCR 76 (SCC); cf. *Federal Commissioner of Taxation* v. *Word Investments Ltd* (2008) 236 CLR 204 (HCA).

provision of goods or services in exchange for fees that the poor cannot afford, are beyond the limits of charity law.[60]

Why limit charity law in these ways? Various answers might be given to this question. Confining the facilitative and promotive functions of charity law only to cases where purposes include the poor might be thought desirable, even necessary, in light of sound principles of social justice.[61] It might be argued that confining at least the promotive function of charity law only to cases where purposes are 'not for profit' is, relatively speaking, economically efficient because people require incentives to pursue 'not-for-profit' purposes that they do not require to pursue the purpose of generating private profit, and therefore the provision of such incentives to those pursuing 'for-profit' purposes is redundant.[62] And it might be argued that where people seek to benefit members of a family, or employees of a company, or members of an association or club, or themselves (whether as members of an organisation or as participants in a self-help arrangement), their purposes in some way lack altruism and for this reason do not warrant charitable status in law. To my mind, there is merit to each of these arguments, but for present purposes I want to concentrate on the last one, appealing to altruism. The thought that I want to pursue is that through the 'public' component of the public benefit test, the state limits charity law in ways that are best understood with reference to a notion of altruism. I want to spend the rest of this part of the chapter illuminating this notion of altruism and showing how the 'public' component of the public benefit test, even though it circumscribes charity law, serves what might be called the creative function of that body of law.

Altruism entails doing good for others in a particular way: it entails doing good for others *as such*.[63] Thus, altruism is a simple response to the humanity in other people, unmediated by any notion of reciprocity or personal advantage: in this, altruism is donative, and may be contrasted

[60] See Charities Act 2009 (Ireland) s. 3(7); Charities Act (Northern Ireland) 2008 (Northern Ireland) s. 3(3); Charities and Trustees Investment (Scotland) Act 2005 (Scotland) s. 8(2)(b); *R (Independent Schools Council)* v. *Charity Commission for England and Wales* [2012] Ch 214 (TCC), especially at [178].

[61] Consider, for example, John Rawls' famous 'difference principle': '[s]ocial and economic inequalities are to … be to the greatest benefit of the least-advantaged members of society': John Rawls, *Justice as Fairness: A Restatement*, Erin Kelly (ed.) (Cambridge, MA: Belknap Press, 2001), [13.1].

[62] See Henry Hansmann, 'The Rationale for Exempting Nonprofit Organisations from Corporate Income Tax' (1981) 91 *Yale Law Journal* 54.

[63] See generally Thomas Nagel, *The Possibility of Altruism*, paperback edition (Princeton University Press, 1978).

with actions that take the form of exchange or that are characterised by mutuality.[64] Similarly, altruism is unmediated by complicating moral factors such as duties or special obligations; as such, it may be contrasted with many types of action that we ordinarily associate with charity (in the non-legal sense), from discharging one's responsibilities towards a needy relative, friend or neighbour, to caring for others because, in one's religious worldview, one has been commanded to do so.[65] I think that it is altruism in the sense of doing good for others as such in which the 'public' component of the public benefit test takes an interest when it aims to limit the range of charity law.

We must be careful to isolate exactly the way in which the 'public' component of the public benefit test takes an interest in altruism, lest we fall into the trap of thinking that decision-makers use that component of the public benefit test to categorise actions according to whether or not they are altruistic and then to exclude non-altruistic actions from the law of charity. That is not true. Actions are altruistic or not depending on the motives that animate them, but it is a fundamental principle of charity law that in ascertaining whether or not a purpose is charitable, a decision-maker must not have regard to the motives of the person or people whose purpose it is. This, of course, rules out any inquiry into whether or not those who claim that their purposes are charitable pursue those purposes

[64] Much of the scholarly literature on gifts assumes that gifts invariably entail exchanges of one sort or another. However, there are reasons to doubt that this is so. For example, the influential anthropological account of gifts as exchanges of Marcel Mauss, *The Gift: The Form and Reason for Exchange in Archaic Societies*, W. D. Halls (trans.) (New York: W. W. Norton, 1990, first published in French in 1950), studied gifts in pre-modern societies where altruism in the sense of doing good for others as such with no expectation of return would have been entirely foreign given prevailing cultural norms. To point out that gifts entailed exchanges in such pre-modern societies tells us nothing about whether or not gifts entail exchanges in modern societies. See further Michael Walzer, *Spheres of Justice: A Defense of Pluralism and Equality* (New York: Basic Books, 1983), p. 128; Jacques T. Godbout and Alain Caillé, *The World of the Gift*, Donald Winkler (trans.) (Montreal and Kingston: McGill-Queen's University Press, 1998), p. 78. Similarly, the commitment of many economists to analysing all human phenomena in terms of self-interest leads to thinking about gifts that reduces them to exchanges. Perhaps the best example is Andreoni's claim that people are assumed to derive a 'warm glow' from giving, and that this personal advantage is part and parcel of altruism: James Adreoni, 'Giving with Impure Altruism: Applications to Charity and Ricardian Equivalence' (1989) 97 *Journal of Political Economy* 1447. But as Godbout and Caillé point out (*The World of the Gift*, p. 213), there is no reason to insist on such reductive thinking about a phenomenon such as giving that, on its face, is both *sui generis* and basic.

[65] See Ontario Law Reform Commission, *Report on the Law of Charities: Volume 1* (1996), pp. 150–2.

altruistically, given that the only way in which it can be known whether or not an action is altruistic is via an inquiry into motives.[66] It is entirely possible that many charitable purposes are in fact pursued non-altruistically, whether self-interestedly or from a sense of duty; but, if this is the case, it is simply irrelevant in the setting of the 'public' component of the public benefit test.

I think that the 'public' component of the public benefit test takes an interest in altruism in a more subtle way. Through that component of the public benefit test, charity law promotes a conception of charity in the legal sense that distinguishes it from notions of reciprocity and personal advantage and from notions of duty or special obligation, and to that extent charity law aims to ensure that the public meaning of charity in the legal sense is associated closely with the other-regarding character of altruism. By giving shape and content in this way to the public meaning of charity in the legal sense, charity law performs a creative function, in addition to its facilitative and promotive functions. Moreover, by creating public meaning for charity in the legal sense, charity law also assists in creating a culture in which those who are altruistic are encouraged to express that altruism via the pursuit of charitable purposes. After all, that close association gives the altruistic reasons to expect that their pursuit of charitable purposes will be interpreted – perhaps by those whose interests are associated with that pursuit, perhaps by others – as altruistic; and this in turn may give assurance to the altruistic that their altruism will be successful should they express it via the pursuit of charitable purposes. That the public meaning of charity in the legal sense has a close association with altruism may also assist in creating a culture in which those who pursue charitable purposes are encouraged to do so altruistically.

This point about public meaning should not be overstated; in some respects, the public meaning of charity in the legal sense departs from the notion of altruism. For example, it is well known that purposes meeting the description 'relief of poverty' need not satisfy the 'public' component of the public benefit test in order to be regarded as charitable in law;[67] to that extent the public meaning of charity appears to be informed as much by notions of duty and special obligation as by regard for others as such. Moreover, so long as they do not exclude the poor, purposes may be regarded as charitable in law even though they entail the provision of

[66] *Ibid.*
[67] See *Charity Commission for England and Wales* v. *Her Majesty's Attorney-General* [2012] UKUT B19 (TCC) for the most recent affirmation of this proposition.

goods or services in exchange for the payment of fees or some other form of 'bargain';[68] once again, the recognition of such purposes as charitable in law notwithstanding their element of exchange suggests that the public meaning of charity in the legal sense is not exhausted by the donative character of altruism. That said, the case of 'relief of poverty' has often been regarded as an anomaly in charity law, and charity law tolerates fee-charging only to the extent that it is not in the pursuit of a purpose of making private profit and thus is not coupled with any element of personal advantage. Perhaps more importantly, assuming that there is a state project of creating for charity in the legal sense a public meaning associated with altruism, it may not matter much that some charitable purposes seem not to lend themselves to such a meaning. So long as *most* charitable purposes do so lend themselves, the creative function of charity law may be consistent with the recognition as charitable of certain types of purpose that are most readily interpreted as non-altruistic.

Why does any of this matter? What is the point of the creative function of charity law? One last time I want to return to the liberal outlook that I introduced earlier, according to which the key personal and political value is autonomy. Recall that autonomy demands the provision of an adequate range of options to choose from in forging a path of self-determination and self-disclosure in life. Now, by performing its creative function and generating for charity in the legal sense a public meaning that is closely associated with altruism, charity law enhances the options available to individuals by making available options with that distinctive public meaning that would not otherwise be available. This is a substantial contribution to the conditions of autonomy, given that options make little sense as options except in light of the public meaning that they have. In performing its creative function, charity law thus makes possible richer understandings of social interaction than would otherwise be possible.

Moreover, to the extent that the public meaning of charity in the legal sense encourages those who are altruistic to pursue charitable purposes and encourages those who pursue charitable purposes to be altruistic, charity law may be said to promote altruism, and an argument is available to the effect that this, too, is a substantial contribution to the conditions of autonomy. Of course, there is no a priori reason why individuals must invariably have options to act altruistically if they are to enjoy

[68] *Re Resch's Will Trusts, Le Cras* v. *Perpetual Trustee Co Ltd* [1968] 1 AC 514; *Joseph Rowntree Memorial Trust Housing Association Ltd* v. *Attorney-General* [1983] Ch 159.

autonomy. Theoretically, an adequate range of options might be composed in a variety of ways,[69] and it is quite conceivable that such a range might lack options that entail the expression of altruism in action. That said, there might be available a liberal argument for the state promotion of altruism, given prevailing social conditions. Some have argued that the emphasis placed on norms of exchange associated with markets in the public culture of many contemporary societies threatens to 'crowd out' altruism and other modes of social interaction that are inconsistent with market norms.[70] If this argument is sound, then in such societies there is a risk that the options available to citizens in their dealings with each other will shrink and that diverse modes of social interaction will increasingly be replaced by just one such mode: the market. By promoting altruism, the state may play a role in resisting this narrowing of citizens' options, and this is of obvious value in light of the demands of autonomy.

An argument of this sort, about the value of state promotion of altruism in light of the demands of autonomy and prevailing social conditions, might be invoked against those who would argue for the watering down of the 'public' component of the public benefit test of charity law. For example, it has been proposed that charities should be permitted to pursue their purposes 'for profit', given that the beneficial consequences of carrying out charitable purposes do not necessarily vary according to whether those purposes are pursued 'for profit' or 'not for profit'.[71] In light of the promotive function of charity law that I discussed earlier, such proposals may appear to make sense, at least to the extent that the consequences of pursuing charitable purposes are the same irrespective of whether the purposes are pursued 'for profit' or 'not for profit'. But once the creative function of charity law is brought into view, proposals to permit 'for-profit' charity must be viewed with greater suspicion, given that part of the point of charity law is to carve out a space for charity in the legal sense that is free of the sort of self-interested motives that typically characterise 'for-profit' endeavours.

[69] Raz, *The Morality of Freedom*, p. 410.

[70] See, e.g., Richard M. Titmuss, *The Gift Relationship: From Human Blood to Social Policy* (London: Allen and Unwin, 1970); Peter Singer, 'Altruism and Commerce: A Defence of Titmuss against Arrow' (1973) 2 *Philosophy and Public Affairs* 312; Michael Sandel, *What Money Can't Buy: The Moral Limits of Markets* (London: Allen Lane, 2012).

[71] Anup Malani and Eric A. Posner, 'The Case for For-Profit Charities' (2007) 93 *Virginia Law Review* 2017.

5 Conclusion

In this chapter I have sought to illuminate the point of charity law from a liberal philosophical perspective, by considering the point of three functions that charity law may be seen to perform: a facilitative function; a function of promoting charitable purposes; and a creative function. Reflection on the point of these three functions of charity law reveals that there is arguably a point to charity law in light of the liberal ideal of autonomy. To say this is not to say that every aspect of charity law is justified as a matter of political morality. When approaching a body of law as complex and inconsistent as charity law, to make such a sweeping claim would be simply foolish. But it is to say that the project of charity law – the project of marking out certain purposes as charitable in the legal sense and extending legal privileges to those who pursue such purposes – might in a general sense be defensible in light of liberal commitments.

6

Public benefit, discrimination and the definition of charity

ADAM PARACHIN

1 Introduction

Discriminatory charitable trusts represent an interesting context in which to study the relationship between public law values pertaining to equality and private law. The unique juridical features of charitable trusts, especially the public benefit requirement exclusive to charitable trusts, have been thought to mitigate the controversies normally arising when the extension of public law equality values to branches of private law is mooted. So while Lorraine Weinrib and Ernest Weinrib have concluded that constitutional equality values enshrined in the Canadian Charter of Rights and Freedoms[1] should not be invoked to invalidate discriminatory clauses in non-charitable trusts, they have drawn just the opposite conclusion in relation to charitable trusts.[2] Specifically, they have concluded that '[b]ecause public benefit constitutes the entire range of application for testamentary freedom in charitable trusts, that freedom has no application inconsistent with Charter values'.[3] Elsewhere, it has been argued that a discriminatory charitable trust is a 'contradiction in terms'.[4] Likewise, discrimination has been said to be 'intrinsically incompatible'[5] with legal

The helpful comments of Debra Morris on an earlier draft of this chapter are acknowledged.

[1] The Constitution Act 1982 (being Schedule B to the Canada Act 1982 (UK) 1982, c 11), pt. I (Canadian Charter of Rights and Freedoms) (Canadian Charter).

[2] L. Weinrib and E. Weinrib, 'Constitutional Values in Private Law in Canada', in Daniel Friedmann and Daphne Barak-Erez (eds.), *Human Rights in Private Law* (Oxford: Hart Publishing, 2001), p. 68.

[3] *Ibid.* Though the quote references 'Charter values' generally rather than constitutional equality values specifically, it is taken from a context in which the argument is made out that discriminatory trust provisions should be struck.

[4] P. S. A. Lamek, Case Comment (1966) 4 *Osgoode Hall Law Journal* 113, 119.

[5] N. Mirkay, 'Is It "Charitable" to Discriminate?: The Necessary Transformation of Section 501(c)(3) into the Gold Standard for Charities' (2007) *Wisconsin Law Review* 45, 84.

charity and 'at odds with the common community conscience and the notion of what constitutes a charity'.[6] One of the leading cases went so far as to conclude that it was to 'expatiate the obvious' to say that the discriminatory trust under review lacked the character of a charitable trust.[7] More recently, an esteemed charity law scholar observed that the charity law 'requirement to provide public benefit clearly links very neatly with the duty to avoid discrimination' and that 'it could be argued that public benefit cannot be achieved through discrimination'.[8] The implication of this is that charity law is an area where private law and public law values dovetail such that 'equality' is not a foreign public law value per se but rather a value inhering in the internal logic and reasoning of charity law, and, in particular, the charity law requirement for public benefit.

This chapter critically reflects upon this view of discriminatory charity. I will not challenge the claim that discrimination is non-charitable, at least not in the sense of building a normative case in support of the charitableness of discrimination. I will instead seek to understand the nature of the claim that charity and discrimination are incompatible. Does this claim appeal to ideals and doctrines originating in the law of charity such that it is cognisable to the internal logic of charity law or does it use, consciously or otherwise, the public benefit requirement to import into charity law equality values originating in public law or elsewhere? When people say that it is not charitable to discriminate, are they doing private law in the sense of attempting to understand a branch of private law on its own terms or are they, in effect, subjecting the law of charitable trusts to a form of public law scrutiny? One might say they are doing both and that framing the question as 'either/or' misses the very point that the public benefit requirement applied in charity law shares a concern for equality in common with public law. Fair enough. My question is whether this view supplies an accurate depiction of the public benefit requirement. Focusing specifically on how the public benefit requirement is currently applied under Canadian law, I argue that it is more difficult to defend the idea that it is not charitable to discriminate from a perspective internal to the logic and doctrines of charity law than tends to be recognised.[9] Neither

[6] *Ibid.*, 86.

[7] *Canada Trust Co.* v. *Ontario Human Rights Commission* (1990) 69 DLR (4th) 321 (*Canada Trust Co.*) at [37] (Robins J).

[8] Debra Morris, 'Charities and the Modern Equality Framework – Heading for a Collision?' (2012) 65 *Current Legal Problems* 295, at 299 and 300, respectively.

[9] See also François du Toit, 'Constitutionalism, Public Policy and Discriminatory Testamentary Bequests – A Good Fit Between Common Law and Civil Law In South Africa's Mixed Jurisdiction?' (2012) 27 *Tulane European and Civil Law Forum* 97 for

component of the public benefit requirement – the public component nor the benefit component – firmly establishes the proposition that discrimination is necessarily a bar to charitable status.

The argument developed in this chapter matters for at least two reasons. First, it seeks to enhance understanding of the public benefit requirement, which is a difficult and often misunderstood feature of charity law.[10] Second, and more to the point of this edited collection, it responds to the suggestion that charity law – owing to the public benefit test's alleged embodiment of equality values – represents an exceptional context in which the transmission of values between public law and private law is uncontentious. While it could, of course, be said that the charity law requirement of public benefit supplies a basis for concluding that it is not charitable to discriminate, this is arguably an aspirational argument about what public benefit could and perhaps even should come to mean more than it is an argument about what the cases to date reveal about the public benefit requirement.[11] A study of the public benefit jurisprudence suggests that public law equality norms lack the innate and obvious compatibility that they have at times been assumed to have with the public benefit requirement.[12] It follows that the considerations governing when, if at all, public law equality norms should be applied to trusts generally versus charitable trusts specifically might not be as dissimilar as they are sometimes thought to be. Those suggesting otherwise are not rooting their argument in how courts have developed the charity law requirement for public benefit so much as they are deferring to public law equality norms to determine the proper boundaries of public benefit.

an analysis casting the regulation of both charitable and non-charitable trusts as an exercise in weighting constitutional and public policy equality prescripts against traditional private law values such as testamentary freedom.

10 The public benefit jurisprudence has, for example, been described as 'capricious', 'arbitrary' and 'sometimes impossible to reconcile'. See G. H. L. Fridman, 'Charities and Public Benefit' (1953) 31 *The Canadian Bar Review* 537, 539.

11 The above quote from Debra Morris very clearly acknowledges this point, as she expressly observes that it '*could* be argued that public benefit cannot be achieved through discrimination': Morris, 'Charities and the Modern Equality Framework', 300 (emphasis added). Her argument, rooted as it is in recent statutory reforms to English equality law, is not intended to develop a general theory of public benefit for jurisdictions lacking analogous statutory rules.

12 See, however, the chapter in this collection by Matthew Harding for an appeal to the value of autonomy as a way of understanding and justifying the legal phenomenon of charity. Harding argues that discriminatory charitable trusts could be struck on the ground that they undermine the conditions for autonomy and thus undermine the very basis for the legal recognition and promotion of charity in the first place (p. 147 of this volume).

The chapter begins with an analysis of the authorities dealing with discriminatory charitable trusts. It then proceeds to examine the claim that it is not charitable to discriminate in light of how each component of the public benefit requirement – the public component and the benefit component – has been developed in the jurisprudence.

2 Leading authorities dealing with discriminatory charitable trusts

The starting point of the analysis is Lord Simonds' observation in *National Anti-Vivisection Society* v. *Inland Revenue Commissioners* that a 'purpose regarded in one age as charitable may in another be regarded differently'.[13] Given the responsiveness of the meaning of charity to social change, one might anticipate that the stance of charity law on the validity of discriminatory charitable trusts might have changed as human rights have increasingly become a reference point for evaluating law and social policy. In fact charity law has indeed moved in the direction of a more restrictive approach to the regulation of discriminatory charitable trusts. Interestingly, however, the law has not accepted as a categorical rule the idea that it is not charitable to discriminate. Instead, the denouncement of discrimination as incompatible with charitable status in some authorities continues to coexist with the acceptance of discriminatory charitable trusts in others.

Several early American authorities upheld overtly discriminatory charitable trusts on the theory that such trusts (at least when the trustees are not public officials) are entirely private arrangements completely unaffected by public law equality norms. Other authorities took a more restrictive approach but did not expressly do so under the guise that discrimination is somehow incompatible with charitable status. For example, in *Re Lysaght*,[14] a testatrix established a testamentary scholarship fund that restricted eligible scholarship candidates to male medical students 'not of Jewish or Roman Catholic faith'. The Royal College of Surgeons, the named trustee of the fund, refused to administer the fund due to the religious restriction.[15] Notwithstanding the well-established principle that no trust can fail for want of a trustee, the Court characterised the College's refusal as something rendering the fund impossible to administer. Relying upon the doctrine of cy-près, the Court was then able to

[13] [1948] AC 31 (*National Anti-Vivisection Society*) at 74.
[14] [1966] Ch 191.
[15] Curiously, no objection was made over the gender restriction.

modify the terms of the trust so as to remove the discriminatory restriction.[16] Similarly, in *Re Dominion Students Trust*,[17] the Court considered a charitable trust to provide a student hostel for male students 'of European origin'. The trustees sought a cy-près order to remove the ethnic restriction.[18] The Court concluded that the ethnic restriction made the purpose of the fund, promoting community of citizenship, impracticable and thus used its cy-près jurisdiction to remove the ethnic requirement.

The reasoning of *Re Lysaght* and *Re Dominion Students Trust* has an air of artificiality. It is by no means clear that either case involved an impossibility or impracticability as those terms are normally understood in cy-près jurisprudence. Given the somewhat strained reasoning of *Re Lysaght* and *Re Dominion Students Trust*, it has been speculated that both cases were driven by an unspoken concern to rid the trusts of their discriminatory provisions.[19]

However, as time went on courts came to more overtly recognise the potential discordance between discrimination and charitable status. The leading US decision is *Bob Jones University* v. *United States*.[20] In 1970, after a court issued an injunction prohibiting the Internal Revenue Service (IRS) from awarding tax-exempt status to racially discriminatory schools,[21] the IRS released a revenue ruling indicating that such schools could no longer qualify as charities under US tax law.[22] Further to this revenue ruling, the IRS concluded that two religious schools (Bob Jones University and Goldsboro Christian Schools) could not qualify as educational charities under federal income tax law on the grounds that they were discriminatory. These schools engaged in racially discriminatory practices further to sincerely held religious beliefs against interracial dating and marriage.

[16] The Court expressly rejected (at 206) the argument that the impugned provisions of the trust were contrary to public policy. Buckley J acknowledged that the exclusion of Jews and Roman Catholics was 'undesirable' and 'unamiable' but not against public policy.

[17] [1947] 1 Ch 183.

[18] Once again, no objection was made to the gender restriction.

[19] See J. Phillips, 'Anti-Discrimination, Freedom of Property Disposition, and the Public Policy of Charitable Educational Trusts: A Comment on *Re Canada Trust Company and Ontario Human Rights Commission*' (1990) 9(3) *Philanthropist* 3, 19–20; B. Ziff, *Unforeseen Legacies: Reuben Wells Leonard and the Leonard Foundation Trust* (University of Toronto Press, 2000), p. 117; J. Colliton, 'Race and Sex Discrimination in Charitable Trusts' (2002–03) 12 *Cornell Journal of Law and Public Policy* 275, 284; F. H. Newark, 'Trustees Who Dislike the Terms of the Trust' (1966) 17 *Northern Ireland Legal Quarterly* 123; Morris, 'Charities and the Modern Equality Framework', 308.

[20] 461 US 574 (1983) (*Bob Jones*).

[21] See *Green* v. *Kennedy (Secretary of the Treasury)* 309 F Supp 1127.

[22] IRS, Rev. Rul. 71–447, 1971–2 CB 230.

The US Supreme Court agreed that neither of these educational institutions could qualify as charities for tax purposes.

The majority judgment of Burger CJ drew upon the charity law requirement for public benefit. He observed that a 'corollary to the public benefit principle is the requirement, long recognised in the law of trusts, that the purpose of a charitable trust may not be illegal or violate established public policy'.[23] While emphasising that a charitable trust should be found to violate public policy 'only where there can be no doubt that the activity involved is contrary to a fundamental public policy',[24] he concluded that this test was met in the facts of the case as there could be 'no doubt' that a public policy against racial discrimination existed.[25] There are, he observed, 'few social or political issues' that have 'been more vigorously debated and more extensively ventilated than the issue of racial discrimination'.[26]

The leading Canadian decision, *Canada Trust Co.*,[27] dealt with a scholarship fund (the Leonard Fund) established in 1923 by the late Colonel Reuben Wells Leonard. The recitals in the trust instrument set out the unabashedly discriminatory views of Colonel Leonard on race, religion and citizenship. They stated his belief that 'the White Race is, as a whole, best qualified by nature to be entrusted with the development of civilization and the general progress of the World', that the 'progress of the World depends in the future, as in the past, on the maintenance of the Christian religion' and that 'the advancement of civilization depends very greatly upon the independence, the stability and prosperity of the British Empire'.[28] The terms of the fund provided that a student could qualify for a scholarship only if he or she was a 'British subject of the White Race and of the Christian Religion in its Protestant form' and only if 'without financial assistance' he or she 'would be unable to pursue a course of study'.[29] No more than one quarter of the scholarship moneys awarded in any given year could be given to women.[30] The racial and religious restrictions also limited who could participate in the management and administration of the fund.[31] In addition, the trustees were directed to

[23] *Bob Jones* 461 US 574 (1983) at 591.

[24] *Ibid.*, at 592. [25] *Ibid.*, at 588. [26] *Ibid.*, at 596.

[27] (1990) 69 DLR (4th) 321. For thorough analyses, see Ziff, *Unforeseen Legacies*; Phillips, 'Anti-Discrimination'; J. C. Shepherd, 'When the Common Law Fails' (1988–89) 9 *Estates and Trusts Journal* 117.

[28] *Canada Trust Co.* (1990) 69 DLR (4th) 321 at [12].

[29] *Ibid.*, at [16]. [30] *Ibid.* [31] *Ibid.*, at [14].

give preference to scholarship candidates whose parents were employed as clergy, teachers, engineers, military personnel or metallurgists.[32]

The Leonard Fund operated for many years without complaint. In fact, after his death, Colonel Leonard was heralded as 'one of Canada's finest citizens'.[33] Over time several Canadian universities declined to participate in the administration of the Leonard scholarships.[34] The controversy culminated in 1986 when the Ontario Human Rights Commission filed a formal complaint against the Leonard Fund alleging that it violated the Human Rights Code.[35] The trustee of the Leonard Fund sought advice and direction of the court 'as to the essential validity' of the trust.[36]

While the court of first instance upheld the trust,[37] the Ontario Court of Appeal unanimously concluded that the Leonard Fund's discriminatory provisions could not stand. The doctrine of cy-près was applied to remove both the recitals and the eligibility criteria based on race, gender, religion and nationality. The Court declined (without explanation) to remove the direction to prefer candidates on the basis of parental occupation.[38] Perhaps because the invalidity of the trust's discriminatory provisions was perceived to be 'obvious',[39] the majority judgment did not very clearly isolate what specific requirement of charity law was breached by the trust. The majority judgment appears to have been oriented around the idea of public benefit, although, curiously, it does not make use of the phrase public benefit. The judgment instead makes use of the phrase 'public interest' notwithstanding that this phrase lacks any established meaning in charity law. Writing for the majority, Robins JA emphasised that, although the fund 'may have been privately created', it had a 'public or, at the least, a quasi-public character'.[40] He went on to describe the trust's discriminatory provisions as being 'so at odds with today's social values as to make its continued operation in its present form inimical to the public interest'.[41] Since they were not 'conducive to the public interest',[42] the trust's discriminatory provisions were struck.

32 *Ibid.*, at [16].

33 *Telegram* (Toronto), 17 December 1930. Quoted in Shepherd, 'When the Common Law Fails', 117.

34 See Ziff, *Unforeseen Legacies*, pp. 120–1.

35 SO 1981, c 53.

36 *Canada Trust Co.* (1990) 69 DLR (4th) 321 at [28].

37 *Re Canada Trust Co and Ontario Human Rights Commission* (1987) 61 OR (2d) 75.

38 *Canada Trust Co.* (1990) 69 DLR (4th) 321 at [46], [98].

39 *Ibid.*, at [37]. 40 *Ibid.*, at [33].

41 *Ibid.*, at [35]. 42 *Ibid.*, at [38].

Although the concurring judgment of Tarnopolsky J went somewhat further in addressing the conflict posed by the trust's discriminatory provisions with the legal requirements for charitable status, it too was not as clear on this point as one might have anticipated. Interestingly, Tarnopolsky J expressly concluded that the trust met the essential requirements for charitable status, holding that it was not only established for an exclusively charitable purpose, namely the advancement of education, but also that it met the requirement for public benefit even if this requirement were defined negatively as meaning 'not harmful'.[43] The judgment went on, however, to find that the trust's discriminatory provisions were nevertheless invalid on the basis that they were contrary to the public policy against discrimination.[44] The difficulty is that Tarnopolsky J did not expressly elaborate on exactly how such public policy considerations factor into the test for charitable status. Since conformity with the public policy against discrimination was not included by Tarnopolsky J in the list of specific requirements for charitable status,[45] one might conclude that public policy was assumed to have relevance to all trusts (charitable and otherwise). However, Tarnopolsky J expressly rejected the idea that non-charitable trusts must conform with the public policy against discrimination.[46] It would therefore appear that the judgment treated such public policy considerations as being relevant only inasmuch as they factor into the test for charitable status perhaps by informing the test for the public benefit requirement.[47] Once again, this was not explicit in the text of the judgment and is inconsistent with Tarnopolsky J's conclusion that the trust met the public benefit requirement.

Tarnopolsky J made clear in *Canada Trust Co.* that not all beneficiary restrictions in charitable trusts will vitiate charitableness.[48] Subsequent decisions have embraced this idea by finding that charitable trusts possess a scope for permissible discrimination. For example, in *Re Ramsden Estate*[49] the Court upheld a scholarship fund restricted to Protestants. *Canada Trust Co.* was distinguished on the basis that that case dealt with a trust 'based on blatant religious supremacy and racism'.[50] Likewise,

[43] *Ibid.*, at [79–80]. [44] *Ibid.*, at [95].

[45] *Ibid.*, at [79]. [46] *Ibid.*, at [100].

[47] Debra Morris likewise observes that '[a] trust contrary to public policy should not be for the public benefit': Morris, 'Charities and the Modern Equality Framework', 309.

[48] *Canada Trust Co.* (1990) 69 DLR (4th) 321 at [98].

[49] (1996) 139 DLR (4th) 746 (*Ramsden Estate*).

[50] *Ibid.*, at [13] (MacDonald CJTD).

University of Victoria v. *British Columbia (A.G.)*[51] upheld a scholarship for practising Roman Catholics. The Court reasoned that a 'scholarship or bursary that simply restricts the class of recipients to members of a particular religious faith does not offend public policy'.[52] The Court explicitly rejected the idea that only ameliorative trusts can prefer one segment of society.[53] In addition, the Court emphasised that even scholarship funds restricted to persons of particular faiths have social utility inasmuch as they provide educational opportunities to a segment of society.[54] The importance of protecting testamentary freedom from erosion was also identified as a relevant consideration.[55] Similar to *Ramsden Estate*, *Canada Trust Co.* was distinguished without elaboration on the basis that it dealt with a trust whose provisions were 'clearly offensive'.[56]

Even racial preferences have been upheld since *Canada Trust Co.* In *Kay* v. *South Eastern Sydney Area Health Service*[57] an overtly discriminatory fund for the treatment of white babies was somewhat astonishingly upheld as a valid charitable trust by the Supreme Court of New South Wales. The Court relied upon exemptions from Australian anti-discrimination legislation for institutions providing 'charitable benefits'. Given that this phrase is statutorily defined to mean 'benefits for purposes that are exclusively charitable', these exemptions could apply only if the restricted nature of the fund under review did not disqualify it as charitable in the first place.[58] The Court concluded that the fund fell 'squarely' within the statutory exemptions on the grounds that its essential purpose – to 'treat sick children in hospital' – was indeed charitable at law.[59] On the specific issue of whether it is charitable to discriminate, the Court observed that 'testators can be as capricious as they like and that if they wish to benefit a charity in respect of, or even of, a discriminatory group, they are at liberty to do so'.[60]

More recently, the Civil Marriage Act,[61] which extended the meaning of marriage to include same-sex relationships under Canadian federal law, enacted a new provision (s. 149.1(6.21)) to the Income Tax Act[62] of

[51] [2000] BCJ No. 520. [52] *Ibid.*, at [25] (Maczko J).
[53] *Ibid.*, at [17]. [54] *Ibid.*
[55] *Ibid.* [56] *Ibid.*, at [25].
[57] [2003] NSWSC 292 (*Kay*).
[58] See subss. 8(2) and 8(3) of the Racial Discrimination Act 1975 (Cth) and subss. 55(1) and 55(2) of the Anti-Discrimination Act 1977 (NSW).
[59] *Kay* [2003] NSWSC 292 at [18], [19].
[60] *Ibid.*, at [18]. [61] SC 2005, c 33.
[62] RSC 1985, c 1 (5th Supp) (ITA).

relevance to charities. This provision provides that, subject to the usual restrictions on political advocacy, charities organised for the advancement of religion will *not* have their charitable registration revoked solely because they or any of their members exercise freedom of conscience and religion in relation to the meaning of marriage.[63] We can abstract from s. 149.1(6.21) the general principle that there is absent a direct link between the restrictions against discrimination applied in charity law (either via the public benefit requirement or via a discrete doctrine of public policy) and the concept of discrimination developed in constitutional equality jurisprudence. The implication is that a charity should not necessarily risk losing its charitable status by taking positions on issues and engaging in practices that constitutional equality jurisprudence prohibits the state from taking. Like *Ramsden Estate*, *University of Victoria* v. *British Columbia (A.G.)* and *Kay*, this reveals that there exists a scope for permissible discrimination by charities.

Recent statutory reforms to English anti-discrimination law impact upon the scope of permissible discrimination by English charities. Under s. 193 of the Equality Act 2010 (UK), charities are prohibited from restricting benefits on the basis of a 'protected characteristic'[64] except where: (1) they are acting in pursuance of a charitable instrument; and (2) they are either redressing historical disadvantage or using proportionate means to achieve a legitimate end.[65] The first point to note is that this statutory rule does not on its face restrain the legal meaning of charity. To the contrary, it speaks to the circumstances in which charities may lawfully discriminate, which is not the same as determining the specific circumstances in which it is charitable to discriminate in the first place. Admittedly, it makes little difference as a practical matter whether discrimination is prohibited at the stage of defining charity or at the stage of applying statutory law to charities, since either way discrimination is restrained. However,

[63] Subs. 149.1(6.21) of the ITA provides as follows: '**(6.21) Marriage for civil purposes** – For greater certainty, subject to subsections (6.1) and (6.2), a registered charity with stated purposes that include the advancement of religion shall not have its registration revoked or be subject to any other penalty under Part V solely because it or any of its members, officials, supporters or adherents exercises, in relation to marriage between persons of the same sex, the freedom of conscience and religion guaranteed under the *Canadian Charter of Rights and Freedoms*.'

[64] Defined in s. 4 of the Equality Act 2010 (UK) to mean age, disability, gender reassignment, marriage, civil partnership, pregnancy, maternity, race, religion, belief, sex and sexual orientation.

[65] Section 193. References to colour are nevertheless ignored further to s. 193(4).

the distinction matters greatly to those studying discriminatory charity from the standpoint of the definition of charity.[66]

The second point to note is that s. 193 of the Equality Act 2010 presupposes the possibility of a trust that is discriminatory but nevertheless charitable at law. This is the only way to make sense of the requirement that discrimination is permissible if it is authorised by a '*charitable* instrument'. If a charitable instrument could not as a matter of law authorise discrimination, the provision would not and could not have application. It is therefore interesting to note that the public benefit requirement is now being interpreted by the Charity Commission in light of s. 193. Conflating the public benefit test with the statutory circumstances in which discrimination is lawful, the Charity Commission has specified that public benefit can coexist with discrimination *only* when it can be justified as either an attempt to redress historical disadvantage or as a proportionate means to achieve a legitimate end.[67] Not surprisingly, this approach to defining charity has militated against the prospect of discrimination passing the test for charitable status under English law. It was, for example, just recently concluded in *Catholic Care (Diocese of Leeds)* v. *Charity Commission for England and Wales* that a Roman Catholic adoption agency could not amend its governing document to expressly provide that adoption services would only be provided to heterosexual couples.[68]

In sum, the cases have progressed from initially ignoring discrimination in charitable trusts to overtly recognising that discrimination can (though does not necessarily) vitiate charitable status. The analysis of discriminatory charity in the authorities has largely been centred around the concept of public benefit. The authorities finding against the charitableness of discriminatory trusts have generally done so on the basis that such trusts lack public benefit in the charity law sense of the term. Given the centrality of the public benefit requirement to this issue, the remaining sections of this chapter consider in greater detail the implications of this requirement for discriminatory charitable trusts.

[66] The distinction is particularly noteworthy in Canada where English authorities regarding the meaning of charity are liberally drawn upon. If English authorities continue in future to define charity with a view to English statutory law, it will be necessary for Canadian authorities to reconsider the authoritative weight of English precedents.

[67] Charity Commission, *Equality Act Guidance for Charities*, December 2012, p. 10, available at: www.charitycommission.gov.uk/detailed-guidance/protecting-your-charity/equality-act-guidance-for-charities-restricting-who-can-benefit-from-charities/ (last accessed 23 May 2013).

[68] [2012] UKUT 395 (TCC) (*Catholic Care*).

3 The *public* component of the public benefit requirement

There are two components to the public benefit test: (1) the public component and (2) the benefit component. The public component is considered in this section and the benefit component is considered in the next.

There are different senses in which one could conceive of the public requirement. One could, for example, say that charities have to be public in the sense of the kind of goods and services they provide, that is, charities must provide goods and services of a public character. Alternatively, one could say that charities have to be public in the sense of whom they benefit, that is charities must benefit 'the public'. Both senses of the term public could in theory be viewed as providing an entry point for equality considerations. If the goods and services provided by charities must be of a public character, one might say that there exists a parallel of sorts between governmental and charitable purposes. Inasmuch as discriminatory purposes and discriminatorily targeted goods and services are beyond the purview of government, they would on this logic likewise fail to qualify as charitable at law. Alternatively, if the goods and services provided by charities must benefit 'the public', then one might say that charities cannot target goods and services to factions of the public on the basis of discriminatory selection criteria since doing so would not benefit the public but rather an inappropriately restricted section of the public.

Putting aside the policy merits (or lack thereof) of such an aspirational understanding of the public requirement, the established jurisprudence is notable for not very clearly supporting it. The cases do not support, at least not formally, the idea that the public requirement means that charities must serve public purposes in the sense of purposes necessarily analogous to governmental purposes. The required character of charitable purposes is taken up by another aspect of the common law test for charitable status, namely the requirement that the purposes being pursued must fall within the four *Pemsel* 'heads' of charity: the relief of poverty; the advancement of religion; the advancement of education; and other purposes beneficial to the community.[69] Admittedly, there is some overlap between purposes falling within these categories and purposes pursued by governmental programming under the modern welfare state. The overlap is exposed by the practice of governments, at times, to deliver charitable programming

[69] *Income Tax Special Purpose Commissioners* v. *Pemsel* [1891] AC 531 (*Pemsel*).

through charities.[70] However, there are reasons to be wary of embracing an understanding of the public requirement that goes too far in conflating the distinction between charitable and governmental purposes. The single most populous category of legal charity, the advancement of religion, is obviously not of a governmental nature. Further, as the Ontario Law Reform Commission noted in its groundbreaking study of the law of charity, charitable purposes are public not in the sense of being governmental but rather in the sense of being universal.[71] That is, the appeal of charitable goods and services is common in that charitable purposes are concerned with universal forms of human flourishing. The organising principle behind the identification of charitable purposes is universality, not 'governmentality'. As such, charity law itself does not recognise a strong parallel between charitable and governmental purposes.[72] A trust with an express or implied governmental purpose can for that reason alone be disqualified as charitable at law.[73] For these (and other) reasons a conception of charitable programming as public or governmental in nature supplies a tenuous basis for importing equality principles into charity law.

The jurisprudence dealing with the public component of the public benefit test is more concerned with who is to receive a benefit, and, more specifically, the criteria used to determine who is to receive a benefit, rather than with the kind of benefit conferred. The public requirement means that there must be an identifiable public – a community or section of community – benefited by the trust. If it is unclear who benefits from a putative charitable trust, then charitable status will be withheld.[74] The public requirement speaks to the criteria that may be used to delimit the class of objects for a charitable trust. Most of the cases dealing with the public requirement are concerned with differentiating legal charity from private benevolence. What differentiates the two in the view of the law is that the benefactor in the case of private benevolence can target his or her

[70] I leave aside the question of whether charities delivering goods and services on behalf of government should be regulated as though they are government.

[71] Ontario Law Reform Commission, *Report on the Law of Charities* (Toronto: Ontario Law Reform Commission, 1997), Chapter 6.

[72] See, e.g., Matthew Harding, 'Distinguishing Government from Charity in Australian Law' (2009) 31 *Sydney Law Review* 559.

[73] *Ibid.*, 563.

[74] For example, the trusts in *Keren Kayemeth Le Jisroel Ltd.* v. *Inland Revenue Commissioners* [1932] AC 650 and *Williams' Trustees* v. *Inland Revenue Commissioners* [1947] AC 447 failed to qualify as charitable because, inter alia, it was not clear what community, if any, the trusts would benefit.

benefaction to ascertained persons specifically identified by the benefactor, including such persons connected to him or her (or to anyone else) through family, relationship or any other bond. The truly charitable act, on the other hand, is restricted to the provision of services or benefits to unascertained persons who are remote to the benefactor.

Another way to say this is to note that charities must benefit *a public* (not necessarily *the public*) in the sense of a group of persons identified other than on the basis of personal selection criteria. In practice, all that this tends to mean is that the settlor of a charitable trust is prohibited from either explicitly naming the beneficiaries or restricting the beneficiaries to persons connected to the settlor or any other specific person via private relationship, for example familial, employment or contractual.[75] The public requirement does not therefore speak to who must benefit from a charitable trust so much as it speaks to the *criteria* that may be used to determine who benefits from a charitable trust. The qualifying criteria must be of a public or impersonal nature, hence the phrase '*public* benefit'. Little would be lost if the phrase 'public benefit' were substituted by the more accurate, though admittedly inelegant, phrase 'impersonal benefit'.[76] Capturing a similar idea, the Ontario Law Reform Commission described the public component as being tantamount to a stranger requirement.[77]

It should therefore be no surprise that the vast majority of the cases dealing with the public requirement reveal that it does not represent a positive requirement for publicness so much as a negative prohibition against (excessive) privateness. So what has emerged from the jurisprudence is an approach that tests for publicness by ruling out privateness.[78] Trusts failing the public requirement are almost always trusts that define the class of beneficiaries using private or personal criteria rather than trusts that otherwise fail to live up to positive indicia of publicness.

Even so, the cases reveal that 'public' is not always understood in charity law as something in contradistinction to 'private' or 'personal'. There are a number of exceptions to the principle that trusts using private criteria to

[75] See, e.g., *Oppenheim* v. *Tobacco Securities Trust Co. Ltd.* [1951] AC 297.

[76] Courts have from time to time used the terms 'personal' and 'impersonal' to capture the charity law distinction between public and non-public. See, e.g., *Re Compton* [1945] 1 Ch 123 at 129–30 and *Independent Schools Council* v. *The Charity Commission for England and Wales* [2011] UKUT 421 (*Independent Schools Council*) at [141] and [146].

[77] Ontario Law Reform Commission, *Report on the Law of Charities*, pp. 150–2.

[78] Note how Lord Simonds equates public with not private in the following quote from *Williams' Trustees* v. *Inland Revenue Commissioners* [1947] AC 447 at 457: '[T]he principle has been consistently maintained, that a trust in order to be charitable must be of a public character. It must not be merely for the benefit of private individuals.'

restrict or define the class of beneficiaries fail the public requirement. It is well established in Canadian law that it is possible to use private criteria to delimit the class of beneficiaries for trusts established for the relief of poverty. For reasons that courts have never made clear, funds established for the relief of poverty have been upheld as charitable even where the class of beneficiaries has been defined on the basis of familial,[79] employment[80] or other private relationships.[81] Nor has the lenient treatment been exclusive to poverty trusts. An orphanage restricted to children of deceased railway employees and a fund for the benefit of widows and children of seamen in Liverpool have been held to be charitable.[82] Similarly, scholarship funds with a direction to prefer descendants of the settlor[83] or employees (or family members of employees) of a particular employer[84] have been upheld as charitable. So too have funds designed to benefit the residents of a particular locality *and their descendants*[85] and trusts for the resettlement of soldiers.[86] So the public requirement does not mean that private selection is categorically inconsistent with charitable status.

What, if anything, does this understanding of the 'public' requirement say about trusts restricting the class of beneficiaries on the basis of discriminatory criteria? Might it be said, consistently with the existing jurisprudence, that discriminatory trusts define their beneficiaries too narrowly to qualify as 'public'? The cases could at least be said to provide a toehold (though a tenuous one) for this line of reasoning. What these cases ultimately establish is that the status of a trust as charitable or non-

[79] See, e.g., *Re Segalman* [1996] Ch 171; *Re Scarisbrick* [1951] Ch 622; *Re Cohn* [1952] 3 DLR 833 (NSSC).

[80] See, e.g., *Dingle* v. *Turner* [1972] AC 601; *Re Gosling* (1900) 48 WR 300; *Gibson* v. *South American Stores Ltd.* [1950] Ch 177; *Jones T. Eaton Co.* [1973] SCR 635.

[81] A trust for the relief of poverty may be limited on the basis of membership in a club (see *Re Young's Will Trusts* [1955] 1 WLR 1269), association (see *Re Lacy* [1899] 2 Ch 149) or society (see *Pease* v. *Pattinson* (1886) 32 Ch D 154).

[82] *Hall* v. *Derby Borough Urban Sanitary Authority* (1885) 16 QBD 163; *Powell* v. *Attorney General* (1817) 3 Mer 48. Charity law apparently distinguishes common employment from a common employer. See, though, *Oppenheim* v. *Tobacco Securities Trust Co. Ltd.* [1951] AC 297 at 307.

[83] *Caffoor* v. *Income Tax Commissioner* [1961] AC 584; *Permanent Trustee Co. (NSW)* v. *Presbyterian Church (NSW) Property Trust* (1946) 64 WN (NSW) 8; *Herbert* v. *Cyr and Lynch* [1944] 2 DLR 374.

[84] *Re Koettgen's Will Trusts* [1954] Ch 252; *Public Trustee* v. *Young* (1980) 24 SASR 407.

[85] *Re Tree* [1948] Ch 325.

[86] *Verge* v. *Somerville* [1924] AC 496. This arguably represents an exception to the public criterion inasmuch as the class of beneficiaries – soldiers – is defined on the basis of common employment, something that would normally privatise the trust and disqualify it as charitable.

charitable can turn on the criteria used to define the class of beneficiaries. A fund that would ordinarily be considered charitable, for example a scholarship fund, will instead be considered non-charitable for no other reason than that the class of persons eligible to benefit is restricted in a way, for example on the basis of family or employment relationships, that contradicts the legal conception of charity as something other than private benevolence. Adopting similar reasoning one could posit that a trust using discriminatory criteria to identify eligible beneficiaries should be non-charitable if for no other reason than that allocating goods and services on the basis of such criteria is (or at least should be) inconsistent with the legal concept of charity. The common denominator with the public benefit jurisprudence, so the argument would go, is that charitable status is unavailable where the criteria used to identify eligible beneficiaries departs in some fundamental way from the essence of the truly charitable act.

The question is whether the principle emerging from the public benefit cases is really this broad under current law. I do not think that it is, at least not under established Canadian law. My point is not that discriminatory trusts are necessarily charitable, but rather that, if they are non-charitable, it is not because they clearly fail the public aspect of the public benefit requirement. The public requirement does not exist to police every departure from the law's conception of charity. The cases have assigned it a more limited function. As I have said, the most clearly established goal of the public requirement is to restrict charitable status to trusts benefitting persons constituting *a public* in the sense of persons identified other than on the basis of personal criteria. Restricting the class of beneficiaries on the basis of discriminatory criteria does not obviously fall offside the public requirement because such criteria do not by their nature personalise or privatise the trust.

There has been some suggestion, particularly of late, that the public requirement goes further and also requires that a link exist between the purposes of a charitable trust and the persons eligible for goods and services under the trust. This reasoning evolves out of the dictum of Lord Simonds in *Inland Revenue Commissioners* v. *Baddeley*, where he contemplated a hypothetical trust providing a bridge for impecunious Methodists only.[87] He reasoned that such a trust is 'clearly not a charity' because it fails the public requirement.[88] According to Lord Simonds, '[i]t is not of

[87] [1955] AC 572 (*Baddeley*) at 592.
[88] *Ibid.*

general public utility: for it does not serve the public purpose which its nature qualifies it to serve'.[89] The implication is that a charitable trust's class of direct beneficiaries must somehow correspond with the trust's purposes. The UK Charity Commission has interpreted this liberally as a prohibition against a charitable trust defining its class of direct beneficiaries using criteria unrelated to its charitable purpose.[90] In the view of the Commission, a link must exist between the class of direct beneficiaries and the purposes of the fund. Similarly, the Canada Revenue Agency has opined that '[w]hen a charity proposes to restrict the beneficiaries of the undertaking in any way, the nature of the restriction must be clearly linked to the proposed benefit'.[91]

Accepting that this accurately reflects established law, this understanding of the public requirement could pose a potential hurdle for the charitableness of discriminatory trusts. Rather than rationally correspond with a fund's charitable purposes, discriminatory eligibility criteria could more readily be viewed as aberrations from those purposes. An educational trust restricted to 'whites only' would, for example, have to contend with the argument that it fails the public requirement because its restricted class of beneficiaries is discordant with its charitable purpose.[92] Such a trust would be similar to a bridge for impecunious Methodists because just as class and religion have no intrinsic link with the purposes served by a bridge, neither does colour have any intrinsic link with education.

[89] *Ibid.* In the same case, Lord Somervell of Harrow observed (at 582) that: 'I cannot accept the principle submitted by the respondents that a section of the public sufficient to support a valid trust in one category must as a matter of law be sufficient to support a trust in any other category. I think that difficulties are apt to arise if one seeks to consider the class apart from the particular nature of the charitable purpose. They are, in my opinion, interdependent.' Various other cases of high authority contain statements to the effect that the specific requirements of the public criterion vary among the four heads of charity. See, e.g., *Dingle* v. *Turner* [1972] AC 601 at 624 (Lord Cross); *Gilmour* v. *Coats* [1949] AC 426 at 449 (Lord Simonds).

[90] Charity Commission, *Analysis of the Law Underpinning Charities and Public Benefit* (London: Charity Commission, 2008), p. 18, available at: www.charitycommission.gov.uk/Library/guidance/lawpb1208.pdf (last accessed 23 May 2013).

[91] Canada Revenue Agency, *Guidelines for Registering a Charity: Meeting the Public Benefit Test*, CPS-024 (10 March 2006), s. 3.2.2, available at: www.cra-arc.gc.ca/chrts-gvng/chrts/plcy/cps/cps-024-eng.html (last accessed 24 June 2013).

[92] The reference to colour would be struck under English law further to s. 193(4) of the Equality Act 2010 (UK). There is no analogous provision in Canadian law, which is not to say that such a trust would be upheld as charitable in Canada.

There are, however, limits to how far such an expanded understanding of the public requirement would go in establishing the non-charitableness of discrimination. Under a rule requiring a link between charitable purposes and class of beneficiaries the most proximate cause of non-charitableness for a discriminatory trust would not be discrimination per se, but rather the mismatch between the fund's purposes and its beneficiary class.[93] Such a rule would not therefore directly establish the non-charitableness of discrimination so much as it would pose an impediment to the charitableness of discriminatory trusts. The impediment would not even be insurmountable as there will presumably be contexts in which the rule would actually vindicate charitable programming that might at first appear to be discriminatory. Distinctions that might be suspect in, say, the educational context may have intrinsic relevance to, say, a fund for the advancement of a particular religious dogma.

Compare, for example, a church choosing to perform marriage ceremonies only for heterosexual couples with a scholarship fund restricting eligible recipients to persons in heterosexual marriages. Though both funds share a common concern for the 'true' view of marriage, we might draw very different conclusions about whether they both qualify as charitable at law. Since a theology of marriage is arguably intrinsically related to advancing religious belief, the church meets the requirement for a link between its essential purposes and its beneficiary class.[94] However, since this issue has no obvious relevance to a scholarship fund, the latter might be said to fail the public requirement.

Things get increasingly complicated the more that charitable programming straddles multiple categories of charitable purposes. Does a particular church outreach programme lose the cloak of its religious character when the services being provided dovetail with one or more of the other heads of charity, such as a church soup kitchen relieving poverty or a church orphanage providing adoption services, as in *Catholic Care*? There are limits as to how far a religious link can go in inoculating distinctions that might otherwise be viewed as discriminatory. It is submitted that those limits were exceeded in the facts of *Bob Jones*,[95] but in other cases the determination will be more difficult, drawing upon judgments that go well beyond the proper meaning of charity and extend to policy

[93] Of course, one could say that these are not separate issues, arguing that the mismatch between purpose and beneficiary class is perhaps what makes the fund discriminatory in the first place.

[94] This is presumably one of the rationales behind s. 149.1(6.21) of the ITA.

[95] 461 US 574 (1983).

preferences pertaining to the relative priority to be assigned to religion versus equality.

Be that as it may, it is not altogether clear that the law actually requires that a charitable trust's class of beneficiaries necessarily correlate with its charitable purposes. It is perhaps helpful to consider the dictum of Lord Simonds in *Baddeley*[96] in greater detail. *Baddeley* dealt with a trust promoting the religious, social and physical well-being of residents of named localities who were (or were likely to become) members of the Methodist church. The majority ruled against the charitableness of the fund on the grounds that its purposes were not charitable. Lords Simonds and Somervell also reasoned that the trust's narrowly defined class of beneficiaries meant that it failed the public requirement. In the course of judgment, Lord Simonds famously commented as follows on the struggle of courts and commentators to come to terms with what precisely it means to say that a charitable trust is 'public':[97]

> the difficulty has sometimes been increased by failing to observe the distinction ... between a form of relief extended to the whole community yet by its very nature advantageous only to the few and a form of relief accorded to a selected few out of a larger number equally willing and able to take advantage of it.

From the context it is clear that Lord Simonds' essential point was that the public requirement does not mean that every member of the public must directly benefit from the fund. A trust may pass the public test even though some members of the public are not within the class of direct beneficiaries. He reasoned, though, that it is necessary to consider the kind of exclusion because some (though not all) exclusions are inconsistent with the public requirement.

Lord Simonds was in effect contemplating two kinds of exclusions – informal and formal. Informal exclusions pose no bar to charitable status. This kind of exclusion is not explicitly provided for in the trust instrument but rather inheres in the nature of the charitable purposes being pursued. This is what Lord Simonds meant when he contemplated a 'form of relief extended to the whole community *yet by its very nature* advantageous only to the few'. Some charitable purposes, though they are formally open to everyone, by their nature exclude those who lack the interest, capability or life circumstances to benefit directly from the purpose. Lord Simonds cited as examples trusts for the provision of sea

[96] [1955] AC 572. [97] *Ibid.*, at 592.

walls, child welfare and the repatriation of soldiers since these funds are charitable though by their nature they exclude, respectively, inland residents, adults and civilians.

Formal exclusions are different. These kinds of exclusions exist where a good or service that would in the ordinary course correspond with the interests, capabilities or life circumstances of a broad class of beneficiaries is formally restricted to a narrower class by the express terms of the trust. Rather than inhere in the purpose being pursued, formal exclusions restrain the class of direct beneficiaries relative to the class that the trust's purposes (broadly construed) could by their nature support. The concern raised by this kind of exclusion is that it is discordant with the purposes of the trust. This is the context in which Lord Simonds cited the example of a bridge restricted to impecunious Methodists.[98] He observed that such a trust fails the public requirement because the formally restricted class of beneficiaries means that the trust 'does not serve the public purpose which its nature qualifies it to serve'.[99]

There are two interpretations of Lord Simonds' dictum regarding formal exclusions. Under one interpretation, formal exclusions are absolutely prohibited only in connection with charitable purposes of general public utility. A more liberal interpretation (adopted by the Charity Commission) is that Lord Simonds' reasoning supports a general rule against formally restricting the class of beneficiaries using criteria unrelated to the trust's charitable purposes. On this view, the class of beneficiaries for, say, an educational trust can only be defined using educational criteria. This might include demonstrated aptitude for education or evidence of a barrier, for instance a financial barrier, to education. Formal exclusions that go any further fail the public requirement even where the good or service in question is not of general public utility.

I contend there are sound reasons to restrict Lord Simonds' dictum to trusts established for purposes of general public utility. A broader interpretation is arguably not supported by the case law.[100] Lord Simonds' reflections were neither adopted by a majority of the court in *Baddeley*, nor have they subsequently spawned a body of supporting authorities.

[98] *Ibid.* [99] *Ibid.*

[100] Debra Morris makes a similar point: Debra Morris, 'The Long and Winding Road to Reforming the Public Benefit Test for Charity: A Worthwhile Trip or "Is Your Journey Really Necessary?"', in M. McGregor-Lowndes and K. O'Halloran (eds.), *Modernising Charity Law: Recent Developments and Future Directions* (Cheltenham: Edward Elgar Publishing, 2010), p. 108.

In fact, numerous cases have upheld charitable trusts using exclusionary criteria with no obvious relevance to the trusts' charitable purposes. For example, religious affiliation,[101] parental occupation[102] and nationality[103] are among the criteria courts have upheld for educational trusts. Perhaps in some cases these criteria might be positively correlated with a barrier to education and thus related in at least some way to education, but by and large they seem to have no inherent or logical 'link' with education. A similar point may be made of a home for old Christian Scientists,[104] a home of rest exclusive to seamen,[105] a trust exclusive to poor lawyers and their families,[106] a fund to promote marriage among persons of a specified religion,[107] a fund to benefit wounded foreign soldiers of a particular nationality[108] and a fund restricting access to an oyster fishery to freeholders in a particular locality.[109] Whatever else may be said about why courts have upheld these funds (and others like them), it seems apparent that rather than strictly requiring a link between a trust's charitable purpose and its class of beneficiaries, courts have instead tended to protect to at least some degree the freedom of settlors to target the delivery of charitable goods and services.

Another difficulty with applying Lord Simonds' dictum to all charitable purposes is that doing so seems to require something generally absent from charity law – an idealised class of beneficiaries against which to compare and evaluate the settlor's chosen class. It can only be said that a trust's designated class of beneficiaries does not match the trust's charitable purposes where the designated class is narrower than or altogether discordant with the normative class corresponding with those purposes.

[101] *Pemsel* [1891] AC 531; *Ramsden Estate* (1996) 139 DLR (4th) 746; *University of Victoria* v. *British Columbia (A.G.)* [2000] BCJ No. 520.

[102] *Canada Trust Co.* (1990) 69 DLR (4th) 321 (preference to children of clergy, teachers, engineers, military personnel or metallurgists); *German* v. *Chapman* (1877) 7 Ch D 271 (restricted to daughters of missioners); *Hall* v. *Derby Borough Urban Sanitary Authority* (1885) 16 QBD 163 (restricted to children of railway workers).

[103] *Attorney-General (NSW)* v. *Perpetual Trustee Co. Ltd.* (1940) 63 CLR 209 (restricted to Australians); *Re Koettgen's Will Trusts, Westerminster Bank Ltd.* v. *Family Welfare Association Trustees Ltd.* [1954] Ch 252 (restricted to British subjects).

[104] *City of Hawthorn* v. *Victoria Welfare Association* [1970] VR 205; *Re Hilditch* (1985) 39 SASR 469.

[105] *Finch* v. *Poplar Corp.* (1967) 66 LGR 324.

[106] *Re Denison* (1974) 42 DLR (3d) 652.

[107] *Re Cohen* (1919) 36 TLR 16.

[108] *Re Robinson* [1931] 2 Ch 122.

[109] *Goodman & Blake* v. *Saltash Corporation* (1882) 7 App Cas 633; [1881–85] All ER Rep 1076.

The problem is that such a normative benchmark is only readily available for a limited category of goods and services – those of general public utility. This is probably why Lord Simonds used the example of a bridge restricted to impecunious Methodists. It seems obvious that the normative class of beneficiaries for a good or service of this kind can be only 'the public' and by extension that any narrower a class of beneficiaries somehow runs contrary to the nature of the good being provided. There is therefore something unique about goods and services of general public utility. We can point to a class of beneficiaries – the public at large – and uncontroversially posit that any narrower a class of beneficiaries is discordant with the fund's purposes.

The same point cannot be unequivocally said in relation to most, if not all, other charitable goods and services. The only thing that can be said with certainty in relation to the first three heads of charity – the relief of poverty, the advancement of religion and the advancement of education – is that these purposes must directly benefit, respectively, the poor, the religious and those seeking knowledge. All that we know for certain is that such trusts may exclude, respectively, the non-poor, the atheistic and those lacking the capacity or interest in the pursuit of knowledge. Unlike the case with goods and services of general public utility, it is difficult to draw on the concept of a link between purpose and beneficiary class to establish any further bright lines in these contexts. If Lord Simonds' dictum is going to be applied across all categories of charity, there simply does not seem to be a way of escaping the necessity for a predetermined list of acceptable and unacceptable exclusionary criteria. The jurisprudence dealing with the public requirement has never clearly produced such a list. Courts have commented adversely on capricious class-defining criteria,[110] but have not otherwise gone very far towards determining when exclusionary criteria are inherently inconsistent with the idea of charity.

It was expressly put to the Privy Council in *Davies* v. *Perpetual Trustee Company* that the trust before the Court failed the public component of the public benefit requirement specifically because the beneficiary class was discordant with the trust's educational purposes.[111] The fund was left 'to the Presbyterians the descendants of those settled in the Colony [of New South Wales] hailing from or born in the North of Ireland to be held in trust for the purpose of establishing a college for the education and tuition of their youth'. Finding against the charitableness of the

[110] *Davies* v. *Perpetual Trustee Co* [1959] AC 439 at 456 (Lord Morton).
[111] *Ibid.*

fund, the Court expressly observed that the class-defining criteria were 'wholly irrelevant to the educational object which the testator had in mind'.[112] While this admittedly lends some support to the view that a link of sorts must exist between the beneficiary class and the purpose being pursued, the broader context of the decision has to be kept in mind. It is clear from the judgment that the Court would have upheld the trust if the class had simply been restricted to Presbyterians. The problem was that the fund went even further and created an arbitrary class within a class through the addition of descendancy and geographic tests to the religious test. So the trust not only distinguished between Presbyterians and non-Presbyterians but further distinguished among Presbyterians using criteria – characterised by the Court as 'capricious'[113] – that would prove highly difficult to administer.[114] The use of a descendancy test was alone sufficient to vitiate the charitableness of the fund because this introduced a personal element to the fund. The case at most reveals that class-defining criteria unrelated to the purpose being pursued *can* cause a trust to fail the public benefit requirement. It does not establish that such criteria necessarily have this effect.

To be clear, my point is not that it would be impossible to refine the public requirement in light of a list of improper exclusionary criteria, including improper discriminatory criteria. Instead, my point is that such a list would not draw upon the logic and doctrines of charity law pertaining to publicness, at least not in the way that is suggested when the exercise is framed as simply requiring a link between charitable purpose and beneficiary class. A children's welfare fund excluding adults is similar to a 'whites only' welfare fund excluding non-whites in the sense that restricting benefits to children and whites, respectively, is clearly linked with the purpose being pursued, at least as that purpose is described in the trust instrument.[115] To be sure, if the purpose is children's welfare, then excluding adults is linked with that purpose in an identical fashion to how excluding non-whites could be said to be linked with the purpose of a whites only welfare fund. Nevertheless, the two funds will be (and should be) viewed quite differently. Why? The disparate reception of these funds will not necessarily be traceable to ideals unique to the charity

[112] *Ibid.* [113] *Ibid.*, at 456.

[114] The Court describes at 453–454 the 'curious' subcategories of Presbyterians contemplated by the fund.

[115] A similar point was argued by the Attorney-General in *Davies* v. *Perpetual Trustee Co* [1959] AC 439 at 451.

law concept of publicness so much as to ideals originating from beyond the law of charity surrounding the kinds of distinctions that should and should not be viewed as harmful. This does not in and of itself reveal a reason why charity law should welcome discriminatory distinctions, but it does go some distance in exposing the true nature of the argument that discrimination fails (or should fail) the charity law requirement for publicness.

4 The *benefit* component of the public benefit requirement

We have seen that the primary function served by the public component of the public benefit requirement is to restrict charitable status to trusts bestowing benefaction not necessarily upon *the public* but rather upon *a public* in the sense of a class of persons delimited other than on the basis of personal selection criteria. Since it is not clear that discriminatorily defined beneficiary classes necessarily fail to qualify as *a public*, at least on the basis of the most well-established meaning of the term public in Canadian charity law, it is not as easy as one might have anticipated to locate within the public jurisprudence a rule clearly establishing the non-charitableness of discriminatory trusts. Turning now to the benefit requirement, one might anticipate the discovery here of a more pronounced hurdle for discriminatory trusts given that this requirement entails a value judgment acknowledging that the trust under review somehow makes the world a better place. The benefit requirement does not require that a court merely tolerate but rather affirm a putative charitable trust as achieving something worthwhile. How could a court endorse in this manner a trust with discriminatory provisions?

The simple answer is that there are circumstances in which courts cannot endorse discriminatory trusts in this manner. Courts have not to date established bright-line rules regarding what specifically the benefit test requires. In *Gilmour* v. *Coats*, Lord Simonds went so far as to observe that '[n]o court would be rash enough to attempt to define precisely or exhaustively what [the public benefit test's] content must be'.[116] However, courts have at least established the baseline principle that a trust injurious to society will not meet the standard.[117] There will be instances in which the harm posed by a discriminatory trust will be so conspicuous

[116] *Gilmour* v. *Coats* [1949] AC 426 at 446–7. Likewise, see *Independent Schools Council* [2011] UKUT 421 at [44].

[117] See, e.g., *National Anti-Vivisection Society* [1948] 1 AC 31 at 65, 69 (Lord Simonds).

that the benefit requirement, even when defined negatively as at the very least meaning 'not harmful', will furnish a ready basis for courts to find against the charitableness of the fund. A trust with invidiously discriminatory provisions, such as the scholarship fund under review in *Canada Trust Co.*, supplies an example. Likewise, the racially discriminatory admissions criteria under review in *Bob Jones*,[118] given that they promoted racial segregation in education, did not meet even a minimal 'not harmful' standard.[119]

Once we move beyond circumstances involving conspicuously harmful discrimination, the obviousness of the impediment to charitableness posed by the benefit requirement begins to wane. One reason why discrimination does not necessarily vitiate charitable benefit is because charity courts have concluded that the requirement for benefit does not amount to a complete prohibition against harm. In *National Anti-Vivisection Society*, Lord Wright observed that courts should 'weigh against each other' detriment and benefit and that the impact of a trust 'must be judged as a whole'.[120] The concept that benefit means net benefit was most recently affirmed in *Catholic Care (Diocese of Leeds)* v. *Charity Commission for England and Wales*.[121] Discrimination inherent in affirmative action style programming could be justified on the basis of this reasoning as the premise of such programming is that the harm of denying opportunity to some is outweighed by the benefit of creating opportunities for members of historically disadvantaged groups.[122] Now, if this were all there was to the idea that benefit in charity law means net benefit, we might be reticent to entertain the conclusion that the benefit requirement goes very far in accommodating harm following from discrimination. After all, affirmative action programming does not balance the harm of discrimination against benefits unrelated to the ideal of equality. To the contrary, since the very goal of such programming is to reduce the harm of discrimination, one would not point to the charitableness of affirmative action measures to demonstrate that harm from discrimination does not vitiate charitable benefit.

118 461 US 574 (1983).

119 Surprisingly, conspicuous harm was not considered to disqualify a health care fund expressly restricted to the treatment of white babies in *Kay* [2003] NSWSC 292.

120 [1948] 1 AC 31 at 47.

121 [2010] 4 All ER 1041. For a statutory articulation of the net benefit concept, see the Charities and Trustee Investment (Scotland) Act 2005, s. 8.

122 The concurring judgment of Tarnopolsky J in *Canada Trust Co.* (1990) 69 DLR (4th) 321 at [96] expressly concluded that such programming can qualify as charitable at law.

It is therefore notable that Lord Wright in *National Anti-Vivisection Society* made clear that benefits and detriments may be balanced even if they are *not* of the same nature.[123] A charitable trust can therefore meet the benefit requirement even if it risks leaving the world worse off in some respect provided that it nevertheless improves the world in some other countervailing though unrelated respect. Since the benefits and detriments need not be of the same nature, it would appear to follow from Lord Wright's reasoning that the harm posed by discrimination can be offset by benefits unrelated to equality. Discrimination is therefore not permissible solely as a means of ameliorating through affirmative action the harm of discrimination. It follows that the specific contexts in which discrimination will not preclude a finding of charitable benefit will be a function of: (1) what charity law considers harmful; (2) what charity law considers beneficial; and (3) how charity law weights benefit versus harm in individual cases.

Dealing first with the issue of harm, we have already discussed the fact that conspicuously harmful discrimination can readily vitiate charitable benefit. At the opposite end of the continuum to such discrimination lies discrimination expressly characterised by human rights law as lawful and, in particular, lawful for charities. Human rights legislation recognises that legal charity represents a protected space in which the usual rules pertaining to discrimination do not apply with the same strictness. For example, s. 18 of Ontario's Human Rights Code[124] expressly allows membership or participation in charitable organisations primarily engaged in serving the interests of persons identified by a prohibited ground of discrimination to be restricted to persons similarly identified.[125] The text of the provision extends to ameliorative programmes in which charitable programming is exclusively targeted at historically disadvantaged groups, but it is not restricted to such programming. Further, s. 24 allows for employment in this kind of organisation to be restricted on the basis of what would ordinarily be considered discriminatory grounds if the nature of the employment makes this a reasonable and bona fide qualification. Section 18.1 dovetails with subsection 149.1(6.21) of the Income

[123] Specifically, Lord Wright observed in *National Anti-Vivisection Society* [1948] 1 AC 31 at 47 that material benefits of vivisection could be weighed against moral benefits of anti-vivisection.

[124] RSO 1990, c H.19.

[125] The prohibited grounds of discrimination include race, ancestry, place of origin, colour, ethnic origin, citizenship, creed, sex, sexual orientation, age, marital status, family status or disability, to be restricted to persons similarly identified.

Tax Act in that it permits a religious organisation to refuse to allow the use of its premises to solemnise a marriage contrary to religious belief. There are somewhat analogous provisions in s. 193 of the Equality Act 2010 (UK).[126]

Since these relieving provisions do not directly speak to the legal definition of charity, they should not be approached as though they are determinative of charitableness. The foremost question for a court to ask is always whether a putative charitable purpose is charitable at law, which is not the same question as whether the circumstances under review entail lawful or unlawful discrimination. Conflating the two issues begs the question by presupposing a direct correspondence between, respectively, what public law identifies as lawful versus unlawful discrimination and what charity law identifies as charitable versus non-charitable. We should not, however, presuppose the non-charitableness of discrimination in the public law understanding of that term any more than we should presuppose the invalidity at common law of discriminatory exercises of property rights. The public law and private law analyses are and should remain distinct.[127] In the charity law context, concluding that discrimination is present goes no further than at most establishing that harm to one degree or another is present. As we have seen, this does not exhaust the analysis but instead leads to a balancing exercise in which the harm of discrimination is balanced against the benefit of the putative charitable programming in order to resolve whether the trust under review is charitable in the sense of conferring a net benefit. Likewise, it does not automatically follow that discrimination regarded by public law (through relieving provisions such as those from the Ontario Human Rights Code[128] identified above) as either not harmful, or not sufficiently harmful to regulate, is for that reason alone incapable of vitiating charitable benefit. The charity law dimension to the problem even here remains one of balancing harm against benefit. Relieving provisions of this sort go no further than (at most) providing an imprecise reference point for considering the amount of weight to be attached to the harm associated with the form of discrimination under review.

[126] See above n. 65 and associated text.

[127] This is not to deny that discrimination can amount to a basis for invalidity in both the charity law and the property law contexts where the harm is conspicuous. The property analogue to *Canada Trust Co.* (1990) 69 DLR (4th) 321 was *Re Drummond Wren* [1945] 4 DLR 674, in which a restrictive covenant prohibiting the sale of land to 'Jews or persons of objectionable nationality' was held void as against public policy.

[128] SO 1981, c 53.

Of course, the balancing exercise inherent in the charity law concept of net benefit requires a reference point for identifying and weighting not only harm but also benefit. One reason why the topic of discriminatory charity is so challenging is because the charity law concept of benefit is itself shrouded in mystification. A useful, though perhaps counter-intuitive, starting point for understanding the charity law concept of benefit is to lead off by questioning whether benefit is indeed a discrete requirement for charitable status. As it might prove controversial even to ask such a question, let me make clear that I am not implying that purposes altogether lacking benefit or of utterly dubious benefit can and should qualify as charitable at law. All that I am critically reflecting upon is whether the requirement for benefit is necessarily separate and discrete from the requirement that all of a charitable trust's purposes fall within one or more of the established heads of charity.

Although the need for benefit is so well established as to be beyond dispute, the cases are interesting for the fact that they do not as a standard practice expressly consider whether a putative charitable trust's purposes are both: (1) within the established heads of charity; and (2) also of benefit.[129] Periodically a court will expressly comment upon the benefit, or lack thereof, associated with a putative charitable trust. Such was the case in *Re Pinion*, where Lord Harman left no room for doubt when he famously described the art collection under review as 'worthless', 'atrociously bad' and a 'mass of junk'.[130] Likewise, in *Re Hummeltenberg*,[131] the Court concluded that no benefit could be found in a trust established for 'training and developing, suitable persons, male and female, as mediums'. But such cases are the outliers. It is far more commonly the case for the benefit analysis to be subsumed into the analysis of whether the purposes under review amount to poverty relief, religion, education or some other charitable purpose. In other words, the benefit requirement tends to be built into what qualifies as poverty relief, religion or education, in the first place far more than it is approached and enforced as an altogether separate requirement.[132] So, it is not as though benefit is not required. To the contrary, one might say that the test for charitable status is reducible to a

[129] Statutory reforms in England mean that English charities must establish that they achieve *both* a purpose recognised as charitable *and* a public benefit. See Charities Act 2011 (UK), s. 2. Canadian law continues to operate under the common law approach where the two requirements are not clearly treated as separate.

[130] [1965] 1 Ch 85 at 106–7.

[131] [1923] 1 Ch 237.

[132] The recent holding in *Independent Schools Council* [2011] UKUT 421 at [42] suggests that the benefit requirement has in 'more recent times' been treated by courts as a 'separately

public benefit test and that the *Pemsel* categories of charitable purposes are significant only because they represent pursuits considered beneficial by charity law.[133] But regardless of whether we are willing to go quite that far, it should not prove controversial to posit that the various categories of legal charity represent, if nothing else, things considered beneficial by charity law.

This does not exhaust the analysis of the benefit requirement, but it does tell us something about the circumstances in which the charity law requirement for benefit might not altogether disallow discrimination. If harm can be balanced against benefit, and there is high authority to say that it can, and if the charity law understanding of benefit is implicit in each of the heads of charity, and it would be difficult to suggest otherwise, then it would seem that the harm following from discrimination need not vitiate benefit where it can be understood as relating in some way to the particular head of charity being pursued.[134] In such circumstances, the benefit against which to balance the harm of discrimination may be located in the charitable purpose itself. One might condemn this reasoning as amounting to the tautological proposition that it is charitable to discriminate when the definition of charity extends to discrimination. While there is admittedly an element of circularity to the reasoning, there is arguably more structure to it than this retort acknowledges.

For example, this view of the benefit requirement helps make sense of the decision in *Canada Trust Co.* Apart from its conspicuously harmful nature, one reason why the discrimination at issue in that case posed such a problem vis-à-vis the benefit requirement is that it could not very easily be brought within the umbrella of the benefit normally resulting from the advancement of education. The recitals to the trust made clear that scholarships were being used (arguably) not to achieve the charitable purpose of advancing education but rather to achieve the non-charitable goal of perpetuating racial and ethnic privilege. At the very least the trust

identified requirement' for charitable status. The judgment nevertheless acknowledges at [53] that it is 'not clear' whether the authorities truly establish that benefit is indeed a separate and discrete requirement.

133 See, e.g., P. Luxton, 'Opening Pandora's Box: The Upper Tribunal's Decision on Public Benefit and Independent Schools' (2012) 15 *Charity Law and Practice Review* 27.

134 It was observed in *Independent Schools Council* [2011] UKUT 421 at [106] that, when balancing harm against benefit, 'great weight is to be given to a purpose which would, ordinarily, be charitable' and that 'before the alleged disadvantages can be given much weight, they need to be clearly demonstrated'.

revealed that a charitable purpose, the advancement of education through scholarships, coexisted with a collateral non-charitable purpose. Either way the fund fell short of the requirement that it be established for exclusively charitable purposes, which in turn foreclosed the possibility of the discrimination at issue in that case being balanced against the benefit of education.[135] This reasoning does not derive from the blunt proposition that it is simply not charitable to discriminate so much as from the idea that the terms of the trust could not be understood solely in terms of what it means to advance education. Education was not the goal but rather the means to a non-charitable goal.[136]

In other contexts, however, it may be possible to situate that which seems discriminatory squarely within a recognised charitable purpose. Religious charities may, for example, teach doctrines or engage in practices that seem inconsistent on some level with conceptions of equality reflected in public law. They might advance highly traditional teachings on issues such as family, abortion and sexuality that some may say run contrary to the progressive nature of equality rights. As already discussed in this chapter, some churches teach heterosexual theologies of marriage and restrict marriage ceremonies accordingly. In some denominations, women may not be considered eligible for certain leadership positions. Traditional gender roles may be framed by some churches as part of God's intended plan for humanity. These sorts of issues may lead some to question whether certain religious charities truly meet the benefit requirement for charitable status. However, charity law furnishes a basis for concluding that that which falls within the domain of religion can be conceived of as possessing the benefit assumed by charity courts to inhere in religion.[137]

[135] If I am right on this point, it calls into question the Court's use of the doctrine of *cy-près* to correct the defect in the trust as this doctrine is not normally applied to make charitable a fund that fails to meet the requirements for charitable status. Perhaps the case reveals an exception where the fund was considered charitable at the time of its creation and only became non-charitable on a supervening basis.

[136] A similar point could perhaps be made in relation to the health care fund restricted to 'white babies' upheld in *Kay* [2003] NSWSC 292. Was this a fund established for a health care purpose or a fund using health care to achieve a discriminatory purpose? In upholding the fund as charitable, the Court revealed a willingness to balance harm against benefit. Specifically, the Court reasoned at [19] that 'the receipt of a fund to benefit white babies would just mean that more of the general funds of the hospital would be available to treat non-white babies so that, in due course, despite the testatrix's intention things will even up'.

[137] Note the use of the word '*assumed*' rather than '*presumed*'. While courts have assumed as a starting point the benefit of poverty relief, education and religion, they have not gone

So, in this context the central question might not be whether a particular doctrine or practice is discriminatory per se, but instead whether it is truly religious.[138]

Indeed, this is the very technique by which courts have avoided the conflict posed by the need to find benefit in religion, on the one hand, versus the desirability of remaining neutral on the efficacy of individual religious doctrines, on the other hand. Since religion is accepted by charity law as a universal good, courts have usually been content to go no further than considering whether what is before them qualifies as religion.[139] If it meets this standard, the existence of benefit has tended to be accepted without each doctrine being individually scrutinised. This is the basis on which a particular church or religious institution might meet the benefit requirement, even if some of its teachings and practices do not exactly reveal an enthusiastic acceptance of equality norms developed in the public law context.

There are even recent cases that have upheld what some might regard as discriminatory distinctions, notwithstanding that the discrimination under review could not very readily be said to inhere in the charitable purposes being pursued. Canadian examples include *Ramsden Estate*[140] and *University of Victoria* v. *British Columbia (A.G.)*,[141] both of which upheld academic scholarships restricted on the basis of religious criteria. There was no attempt in these cases to benefit a disadvantaged group, nor was there any rational link between the religious restriction and the nature of the good being provided. These cases and others like them reveal that courts are willing to allow settlors of charitable trusts to manifest a degree of favouritism provided at least that the trust is not invidiously discriminatory. Relating this back to the benefit requirement, it would appear that the requirement for charitable benefit accommodates within limits what,

so far as to establish a formal presumption of benefit. See, e.g., J. Hackney, 'Charities and Public Benefit' (2008) 124 *Law Quarterly Review* 347, 348; *Independent Schools Council* [2011] UKUT 421 at [42]–[113].

138 See, e.g., Hackney, 'Charities and Public Benefit', 348.

139 In *Gilmour* v. *Coats* [1949] AC 426 at 459, Lord Reid articulated the orthodox principle that '[t]he law must accept the position that it is right that different religions should each be supported irrespective of whether or not all its beliefs are true'. Nevertheless, the religious organisation under review was held to be non-charitable on the grounds that the Court could only find benefit if it were to accept Catholic doctrine regarding intercessory prayer, something the Court was not willing to do. The judgment has been much criticised for its seemingly inconsistent reasoning.

140 (1996) 139 DLR (4th) 746.

141 [2000] BCJ No. 520.

for lack of a better phrase, might simply be described as settlor preference. At the least, there is a demonstrated reluctance to balance benefits and disadvantages where the suggested disadvantages 'depend on value judgments influenced by social and political agendas'.[142]

Now, some might say that I find myself in a contradiction, having cautioned in the previous section against requiring a link between beneficiary class and charitable purpose but nevertheless having accepted in this section the idea that discovering such a link might somehow be relevant to determining whether discrimination passes the benefit requirement. Why acknowledge the potential relevance of a link in the context of the benefit requirement but not in the context of the public requirement? The primary reason is that this way of understanding the cases does a better job of exposing the discretionary nature of the judgments being drawn in this area of the law. The shortcoming of saying that the *public* requirement *necessitates* a link between the beneficiary class and the charitable purpose is that this frames the principle too concretely. Such a rule, on its face, categorically forbids charitable status where the requisite link between purpose and beneficiary class is absent. So if such a rule does indeed exist, we would not expect to discover, as we do, that courts have upheld charitable trusts targeting charitable goods and services on the basis of criteria unrelated to the charitable purposes being pursued. However, if we instead recognise that the search for a link occurs at the stage of evaluating benefit, and, in particular, as part of the *discretionary* weighting of benefits versus harms implicit in the search for net benefit, then the cases upholding the charitableness of seemingly discriminatory trusts no longer seem as difficult to understand. To the contrary, the existence of such cases would simply reveal that balancing benefits against harms is a highly discretionary and context-sensitive way of evaluating the presence or absence of net benefit. The discretionary nature of the analysis allows charitable trusts to be upheld from time to time, notwithstanding that the beneficiary class seems discordant with the underlying charitable purpose, provided there is at least a net benefit.

More to the point of this chapter, exposing the discretionary nature of charity law's benefit requirement is important because it reveals just how difficult it is to demonstrate clearly that this requirement – unassisted by equality ideals originating from beyond the law of charity – forbids discrimination. The recent decision in *Catholic Care*[143] illustrates the point.

142 *Independent Schools Council* [2011] UKUT 421 at [107].
143 [2012] UKUT 395 (TCC).

As mentioned above, at issue was whether the Roman Catholic charity in question could continue its practice of restricting the provision of adoption services to heterosexual couples. Changes to English equality law meant that this practice could be continued by the charity only if, among other things, the practice was expressly authorised by its charitable instrument.[144] The case centred on whether the charity could amend its charitable instrument accordingly, which in turn required a determination of whether the practice was charitable in the first place. The judgment, which went against the charity, weighed a number of competing values, including the value of religious beliefs in support of the traditional family versus the value of equality for same-sex couples. In deciding the case against the charity, Sales J very clearly prioritised equality rights over the other competing considerations.

Notably, the decision in *Catholic Care* made no appeal to any particular ideal of 'charity', but instead drew heavily upon equality principles developed in the public law context. In part this was because counsel for both sides agreed that the case should not be decided independently of whether the charity's practices amounted to lawful discrimination under s. 193 of the Equality Act 2010.[145] This resulted in the case becoming consumed with whether the charity's practices could be objectively justified as a proportionate means of achieving a legitimate aim.[146] Even if counsel had insisted that the charitableness of the charity's practices be addressed as a discrete issue, which would have been more analytically sound, it is submitted that the case, requiring as it did that the harm of discrimination be balanced against the benefit of a religiously inspired conception of the family, could not in any event have been decided solely on the basis of the doctrines and logic of charity law. From a charity law perspective, there is no magic to the decision as it could just as well have gone the other way without doing violence to any as yet clearly established principle or doctrine of charity law. In and of itself this does not establish that the case was incorrectly decided, but it does reveal a certain shortcoming to the claim that charity law is equipped through its own logic and doctrines to establish the non-charitableness of discrimination. There does not seem

[144] Equality Act 2010 (UK), s. 193.

[145] [2012] UKUT 395 at [7].

[146] Demonstrating that discrimination is a proportionate means for a charity to achieve a legitimate aim is one of the ways for a charity to engage in lawful discrimination under s. 193(2) of the Equality Act 2010.

to be any escaping the conclusion that values external to charity law play an enormous role in discussions and analyses of discriminatory charity.

5 Conclusion

A distinguishing feature of charitable trusts is that they are alone in the world of trusts for having to conform to a public benefit standard. Notwithstanding the centrality of the concept of public benefit to charitable trusts, it represents one of the least well understood aspects of the law of charity. At least one reason for this is that public benefit is a somewhat loaded phrase in the sense that it conjures up ideals lacking correspondence with how courts have developed it as a concept with meaning distinctive and peculiar to the law of charity. Indeed, the topic of discriminatory charity reveals a discordance between what public benefit is sometimes assumed to mean, or could very well be interpreted to mean without doing violence to conceivable meanings of the terms 'public' and 'benefit', and how charity courts have over time developed the concept. So although the public benefit requirement might be assumed to readily furnish charity courts with a tool uniquely capable of prohibiting discrimination through charitable trusts, the public benefit jurisprudence does not supply a particularly robust impediment directly aimed at curtailing the charitableness of discriminatory trusts. This raises some interesting questions about the nature of the claim that it is not, or should not be, charitable to discriminate.

The point I have attempted to make in this chapter is neither that there is absent any restriction under existing law against discriminatory charity, nor that there should be no such restriction. My point is instead that the elaboration of such a restriction in individual circumstances is in a great many instances not going to be an exercise drawing solely on the logic and doctrines of charity law, at least not as they pertain to the public benefit requirement. It is instead an exercise heavily influenced by discretionary judgments surrounding the relative priority to be assigned to equality versus other competing values vying for consideration. The balancing exercise whereby courts weigh the harm inflicted by a discriminatory charitable trust against its anticipated benefit would seem to take courts beyond the traditionally conceived boundaries of the judicial realm and involve them in what is arguably a legislative-like policy-making exercise. Whatever else might be said of a holding such as that in *Catholic Care*,[147] the reasoning of this case ultimately boils down to the

[147] [2012] UKUT 395.

value judgment that equality, or at least a particular conception of equality, should take priority over other competing considerations. Likewise, the conclusion in *Kay*[148] reveals an underlying value judgment to prioritise traditional property rights and testamentary freedom over equality. So rather than maintain that charity law is somehow unique in the sense of furnishing courts with the normative resources to prohibit discrimination through charitable trusts, it might be more accurate to posit that charity law simply supplies courts with the means through which equality-oriented considerations may (or just as easily may not) be brought to bear at the discretion of the court. In this sense, the regulation of discriminatory charity does not represent the categorically distinct context that it is sometimes assumed to represent. To the contrary, the kinds of value judgments ultimately being drawn are apt to be very similar to those arising when the relevance of public law equality norms to other branches of private law is considered.

The analysis in this chapter is admittedly not exhaustive as it has not considered all dimensions of the topic. For example, although the idea that it is not charitable to discriminate requires a referent for identifying that which is truly discriminatory, no analysis was offered of how discriminatory charitable trust provisions may be identified in the first place. Neither have all features of charitable trusts that might be construed as posing a unique incompatibility with discrimination been discussed. The state support of charities, especially through income tax concessions, might, for example, be construed as supplying an additional basis on which to conclude against the charitableness of discrimination.[149] In addition, the doctrine of public policy – through which charitable trusts may be struck if they run contrary to public policy – has not been directly analysed, notwithstanding that it has been factored into the judicial analysis of discriminatory charity.[150] The failure to address these facets of the topic is not a denial of their relevance so much as an acknowledgement that the topic of discriminatory charity is so complex and multifactorial

[148] [2003] NSWSC 292.

[149] See, e.g., L. Sugin, 'Tax Expenditure Analysis and Constitutional Decisions' (1998–1999) 50 *Hastings Law Journal* 407 at 407; E. Zelinsky, 'Are Tax "Benefits" Constitutionally Equivalent To Direct Expenditures?' (1998) 112 *Harvard Law Review* 379; Donna D. Adler, 'The Internal Revenue Code, The Constitution, and The Courts: The Use of Tax Expenditure in Judicial Decision Making' (1993) 28 *Wake Forest Law Review* 855; Mirkay, 'Is It "Charitable" to Discriminate?'.

[150] See, e.g., *Bob Jones* 461 US 574 (1983).

that no single chapter could adequately address all relevant dimensions to the problem.

It is not clear, however, that taking these additional issues into account would ultimately go very far in assuaging my scepticism over whether the law of charitable trusts, unassisted by equality considerations imported from beyond the law of charity, is uniquely equipped precisely to establish either the reasons why or the precise circumstances in which discrimination is unacceptable. To be sure, the search for a referent for what constitutes discrimination in the first place will only lend support to the idea that values external to the law of charity are playing a role here, since such a search will just raise questions over the extent to which, if at all, equality values drawn from public law generally and constitutional law specifically should be imported into charity law. Further, an analysis of the doctrine of public policy will not necessarily yield insights specific to the law of charitable trusts because, unlike the requirement for public benefit, which is unique to charitable trusts, the principle that dispositions offending public policy are invalid applies across various branches of private law. Likewise, an analysis of the various legal privileges exclusive to charitable status, assuming that the extension of such privileges does not in and of itself amount to constitutionally reviewable state action, will not necessarily change the essential questions, which remain whether, when and why discrimination is incompatible with legal charity. It seems unavoidable that the answers to these questions will ultimately turn not solely on principles finding expression in the doctrines of charity law, but will instead entail a balancing exercise in which values originating from beyond the law of charity are pitted against competing considerations. The nature of the analysis therefore shares a surprising amount in common with the analysis of discriminatory provisions in non-charitable trusts. This does not mean that discriminatory charity should be permitted to go without restriction, but it does tell us something about the kinds of considerations informing the conclusion that charity is incompatible with discrimination.

7

Private law and its normative influence on human rights

MICHELLE FLAHERTY

1 Introduction

There has been a great deal of discussion in recent academic literature about the role of human rights in private law. Although it is generally agreed that private law concepts have been significantly impacted by human rights principles, there has been less discussion about whether human rights principles have themselves developed in consonance with traditional private law concepts and traditions.

This chapter argues that there has been a cross-pollination of sorts between human rights and private law and that, in a number of significant ways, private law concepts and rights have influenced and even defined the scope and development of human rights protections.

Private law and human rights share some basic legal principles and objectives and, in some ways, they draw from some of the same legal traditions.[1] I will argue that, well before the advent of human rights legislation, private law already reflected some of the values and morals later enshrined in human rights statutes.[2] In this way, the line between human rights and

The author wishes to thank Sébastien Grammond and Adam Dodek for support and helpful comments.

[1] Mayo Moran, 'The Mutually Constitutive Nature of Public and Private Law', in Andrew Robertson and Tang Hang Wu (eds.), *The Goals of Private Law* (Oxford: Hart Publishing, 2009), p. 17; Mark D. Walters, 'Incorporating Common Law Into the Constitution of Canada: *EGALE* v. *Canada* and the Status of Marriage' (2003) 41 *Osgoode Hall Law Journal* 75; Peter Benson, 'Equality of Opportunity and Private Law', in Daniel Friedmann and Daphne Barak-Erez (eds.), *Human Rights in Private Law* (Oxford: Hart Publishing, 2001), p. 201.

[2] The focus of this chapter is not the dichotomy between individual and group rights. Rather, the issue I wish to raise is whether there are shared values that underlie both private law and human rights; whether the latter are exercised in a way that is individual or collective in nature. I argue that some of the same public policy considerations and expressions of the

private law is blurred and porous to reciprocal influences.[3] Not only do some private law principles underpin human rights thinking, but in some circumstances human rights law has evolved around and in light of long-standing private law principles and protections. I consider two examples from a Canadian perspective: human rights protection for property law rights and the limits that human rights have placed on the freedom to bequeath. I hypothesise that private law concepts have played a substantive role in shaping human rights law thinking in these two areas.

First, any property rights afforded through constitutional human rights legislation in Canada derive from – and are consistent with – existing protections for private property. In regard to expropriation, in particular, any human rights protections available largely mirror rights available under ordinary, non-constitutional statutes. As I discuss in more detail below, human rights protection of property in Canada has essentially adopted the existing private law-inspired framework and has added little to the rights of property holders. While the language of human rights statutes suggests that property rights be approached differently under private law and in human rights, the courts appear to favour the private law approach and have imported it into human rights law. I argue that this confluence, which is unsupported by the language of human rights statutes, is a testament to the influence of private law principles on human rights.

collective interest (for example, the desire to protect vulnerable individuals from harm) underlie both human rights legislation as well as some jurisprudential developments in private law. Regarding the dichotomy between individual and group rights, I note in passing that the Canadian approach to the group rights and individual rights dichotomy has not followed the standard liberal model of rights. Canadian courts and academics speak of human rights that encompass both individual and collective aspects, the content of which is informed by collective interests. There are historic reasons behind the notion that collective interests and values must inform the development of human rights: see, e.g., Claire L'Heureux-Dubé, 'It Takes A Vision: The Constitutionalization of Equality in Canada' (2002) 14 *Yale Journal of Law and Feminism* 363, 366; Will Kymlicka, 'Human Rights and Ethnocultural Justice' (1998) 4(2) *Review of Constitutional Studies* 213; Jane Jenson and Martin Papillon, *The 'Canadian Diversity Model': A Repertoire in Search of a Framework (CPRN Discussion Paper No. F19)* (Ottawa: Canadian Policy Research Networks, 2001), pp. 12–13, available at: www.cccg.umontreal.ca/pdf/CPRN/CPRN_F19.pdf (last accessed 24 May 2013).

[3] See Lorraine E. Weinrib and Ernest J. Weinrib, 'Constitutional Values and Private Law in Canada', in Daniel Friedmann and Daphne Barak-Erez (eds.), *Human Rights in Private Law* (Oxford: Hart Publishing, 2001), p. 43, Ernest J. Weinrib, *The Idea of Private Law* (Cambridge, MA: Harvard University Press, 1995); Hugh Collins, 'Utility and Rights in Common Law Reasoning: Rebalancing Private Law Through Constitutionalization' (2007) 30 *Dalhousie Law Journal* 1; Lorenz Fastrich, 'Human Rights and Private Law', in Katja S. Ziegler (ed.), *Human Rights and Private Law: Privacy as Autonomy* (Oxford: Hart Publishing, 2007), p. 23.

Second, we consider the private law limits placed on the freedom to bequeath. I will argue that, long before human rights legislation prohibited certain forms of discrimination, private law had refused to give effect to testamentary clauses that were deemed to be against the public interest. In this regard, private law had long accepted that broader public policy considerations[4] had a role to play in determining the validity of testamentary conditions. The limits on the freedom to bequeath currently imposed through human rights legislation may be different from the early private law limits. However, private law served as an important precursor to human rights legislation in this area and, to some extent, it continues to influence the human rights analysis.

I argue that, in these two examples at least, private law and human rights have a shared goal: although they may go about it differently, both seek to provide a level of protection to vulnerable individuals. In both examples, whether a human rights or a private law analysis is applied, there is some degree of congruence in the rights that result. This suggests that, in at least these two cases, private law and human rights have cross-pollinated and there have been reciprocal influences.

2 The interplay between private law and human rights

Terms such as 'private law', 'public law', 'human rights' and 'constitutional values' are difficult to define conclusively. These expressions are nuanced and can take on different meanings depending on the context in which they are used. Indeed, the very purpose of this chapter is to show that, in some instances, the distinctions between these spheres are blurred because of mutual and reciprocal influences. Although it may have been traditionally viewed as such, I argue that there is no purely private law sphere that is entirely isolated from the influence of the values that underpin human rights legislation.[5] Accordingly, 'private law' cannot be defined without regard to some of these principles. Similarly, I argue that there is no purely human rights sphere, because human rights values are also shaped by and incorporate some elements of private law.[6]

4 In the case of testamentary conditions, at least, these include concern for vulnerable individuals and a desire to protect them against unfairness and hardship. Similar policy considerations are also at the root of human rights legislation.

5 Weinrib, *The Idea of Private Law*. See also Frances Raday, 'Privatising Human Rights and the Abuse of Power' (2000) 13 *Canadian Journal of Law and Jurisprudence* 103, paras. 50–52.

6 In the common law, at least, it is difficult to draw clear boundaries around what is meant by 'public' and 'private'. As the Supreme Court of Canada has explained, this makes

A *The tension between private law and human rights*

Although private law and human rights[7] each appears to regulate its own, separate set of relationships, they can both apply to a particular set of relationships or transactions. In some Canadian jurisdictions, human rights statutes apply specifically to private actors in the course of their private transactions.[8] This means that, in their private legal relationships, parties are governed by more than just their own interests and are required to respect the human rights of others.

In the same way that human rights law has introduced itself into individual relationships, private law has also played a role in the regulation of relationships between individuals and the state. An example of the latter flows from the British House of Lords' decision in *Anns* v. *Merton London Borough Council*,[9] which has been adopted by the Supreme Court of Canada in, inter alia, *Kamloops (City)* v. *Nielsen*.[10] In cases applying *Anns*, Canadian courts have found that public officials exercising a purely public function may owe a private law duty of care. In this way, state actors can be held responsible for damages based on the negligent exercise of their public function.[11]

Arguably, there are two main sources of tension between human rights and private law. First, the tension between the two spheres may be most pronounced in transactions or relationships that engage both private law and human rights elements. It is particularly apparent in those

it difficult for civil law jurists in our bi-juridical legal system to determine what elements of the common law are 'public'. For an application in the civil law context, see *Prud'homme* v. *Prud'homme* [2002] 4 SCR 663; 221 DLR (4th) 115 at [46].

[7] In this chapter, 'human rights' is also used to refer to the civil and political rights and fundamental freedoms that are constitutionally protected within Canada. In Canadian common law jurisdictions, these rights do not generally include any right to property. However, in human rights instruments in Quebec, property rights are included in the list of protected civil rights.

[8] See, e.g., the Charter of Human Rights and Freedoms, RSQ, c C-12 (Quebec Charter), s. 13 and the Ontario Human Rights Code, RSO 1990, c H.19 (Ontario Code).

[9] [1978] AC 728 (*Anns*).

[10] [1984] 2 SCR 2. While *Anns* [1978] AC 728 continues to reflect the Canadian approach, the British House of Lords has since departed from this jurisprudence: *Murphy* v. *Brentwood District Council* [1991] 1 AC 398.

[11] See, e.g., *Childs* v. *Desormeaux* [2006] 1 SCR 643; 266 DLR (4th) 257; *Design Services Ltd.* v. *Canada* [2008] 1 SCR 737; 293 DLR (4th) 437. It is noteworthy that the existence of a private law duty regarding the exercise of public functions is somewhat exceptional and the courts have taken pains to restrict the circumstances in which a public function will engender civil liability. For example, when the issue is the liability of a public authority exercising a public function, the legal threshold for negligence is more exacting.

circumstances that private law and human rights must somehow operate in concert. While there may be nuances in their underlying values and the extent to which they seek to embody collective versus individual interests, each system must somehow reflect the same fundamental societal values and norms. Each, after all, operates within the same society and while there may be structural and historical differences between the two spheres, society's values and morals exert a similar normative pressure on both.

Second, while private law and human rights have some objectives and values in common, conflict may arise where the private law notion of a particular right is different from its human rights counterpart. In other words, the private law values of self-determination and autonomy can be at odds with the values that give rise to human rights statutes, which relate not only to individuals' rights, but also to collective interests.[12] This is not to say that collective interests are not a factor in private law. Arguably, however, as the private law limits on the freedom to bequeath (which we will discuss later) demonstrate, there can be nuanced differences in the values that underlie the private law and human rights.

This tension reveals itself when we consider the role that human rights principles have played in the development of private law doctrine. The general consensus is that human rights play a significant role in shaping private law.[13] In this regard, the Supreme Court of Canada has used increasingly clear language (in both common law and civil law contexts) to explain that private law must develop in concert with human rights principles. Where the two conflict, the Court has stated that private law must yield to accommodate human rights values. Thus, even where legislation does not explicitly require a private party's compliance with the human rights legislation in a particular transaction, the private law doctrine and principles that govern that relationship must themselves be consonant with – or at least balanced against – human rights principles.[14]

[12] See, e.g., William Lucy, 'What's Private about Private Law?', in Andrew Robertson and Tang Hang Wu (eds.), *The Goals of Private Law* (Oxford: Hart Publishing, 2009), p. 49.

[13] See, e.g., *ibid.*; Moran, 'The Mutually Constitutive Nature of Public and Private Law'; Collins, 'Utility and Rights in Common Law Reasoning'; Fastrich, 'Human Rights and Private Law'; Raday, 'Privatising Human Rights'; Aharon Barak, 'Constitutional Human Rights and Private Law', in Daniel Friedmann and Daphne Barak-Erez (eds.), *Human Rights in Private Law* (Oxford: Hart Publishing, 2001), p.13.

[14] *RWDSU* v. *Dolphin Delivery Ltd.* [1986] 2 SCR 573; 33 DLR (4th) 174. More recently, *Dagenais* v. *Canadian Broadcasting Corp.* [1994] 3 SCR 835; 20 OR (3d) 816; 120 DLR (4th) 12; *Hill* v. *Church of Scientology of Toronto* [1995] 2 SCR 1130; 24 OR (3d) 865; 126 DLR (4th) 129; *Grant* v. *Torstar Corp.* [2009] 3 SCR 640. See also *Gilles E. Néron*

In addition to the circumstances we have discussed, private law and human rights interact in a number of more subtle ways. For instance, legislation has increasingly served to define the principles that govern the resolution of all legal relationships, including private law disputes. In this regard, Hugh Collins speaks of the historic evolution of private law in response to government intervention that brings collective considerations to the private sphere. He writes:

> The private law of tort, contract, and property rights that emerged in the nineteenth century provided a fortress of protections for individual rights, but the consequences for collective welfare were quickly found wanting. These consequences were addressed by the welfare state, regulation, and the separation of new spheres of private law such as consumer law and labour law from mainstream doctrine. By the second half of the twentieth century, however, these regulatory measures had triggered a marked shift in private law reasoning as a whole, which became more instrumental or policy oriented. It evolved into a hybrid of the old private interest reasoning and modern policy oriented regulatory reasoning.[15]

We will turn shortly to a discussion of the role of the Constitution, which is a more direct and overt means of bringing collective interests to bear in private transactions. It is important to note, however, that the above discussion relates to something different: the very significant influence of ordinary, non-constitutional legislation. While these statutes may not speak overtly of human rights, they bring a public dimension to private law, in some instances infusing it with policy-oriented considerations that may also underpin human rights legislation.[16]

When we consider public influences on private law, it is important to keep in mind the public nature of the decision-making process and the role this may play in shaping private law considerations. This phenomenon has been described by the American legal realist movement, which posits that judges decide cases not only on legal principles, but also for

Communication Marketing Inc. v. *Chambre des notaires du Québec* [2004] 3 SCR 95; 241 DLR (4th) 577; *Prud'homme* v. *Prud'homme* [2002] 4 SCR 663; 221 DLR (4th) 115.

[15] Collins, 'Utility and Rights in Common Law Reasoning'.

[16] The incorporation of human rights-like principles into the private law through ordinary, non-constitutional legislation is perhaps most prominent in the civil law tradition. For example, the Civil Code of Québec, LRQ, c C-1991 (Civil Code), which governs most legal transactions, embodies a number of values that relate closely to those enshrined in human rights statutes. Title One of the Civil Code is entitled 'Enjoyment and exercise of civil rights' and includes protection for, inter alia, patrimony, the right to life, the inviolability and integrity of the person, and the right to the respect for one's name, reputation and privacy.

policy reasons.[17] According to legal realists, a decision is not the inevitable outcome of the application of legal principles but rather is based on what outcome the judge thinks is fair in the circumstances. In this context, the law is considered to be indeterminate: the law does not, in and of itself, justify a conclusion. The courts' idea of fairness is an important factor and the law is not so much a system of defining or determining principles as it is an instrument for furthering collective interests.[18] Collins writes that, in reality, 'decisions have to be justifiable by reference to [two] criteria – legal principle and social policy'.[19]

B Human rights influence over the private sphere

The purpose of this chapter is to look at private law's influence on human rights; its objective is not to consider in great detail the influence of human rights on private law. However, because this latter influence effectively mirrors the subject matter of this chapter, it does warrant some consideration. To the extent that human rights may serve to guide private law developments, it may be useful to consider whether there is a theoretical basis for reciprocal influences. Put differently, if human rights influence the private sphere, to what extent is the reverse also theoretically legitimate?

As we have seen, it is generally accepted that human rights have had a long-standing and normative influence on private law. The general consensus in both Canada and Europe is that private law relationships should be governed in a manner that incorporates consideration for human rights principles.[20] The Supreme Court of Canada addressed the issue shortly after the Canadian Charter[21] came into effect.[22] The Court's position seems to rest on the presumption that human rights law is of overarching

[17] See also Brian Leiter, 'American Legal Realism', in M. Golding and W. Edmundson (eds.), *The Blackwell Guide to Philosophy of Law and Legal Theory* (Oxford: Blackwell, 2005), pp. 50–66.

[18] Collins, 'Utility and Rights in Common Law Reasoning'. See also Leiter, 'American Legal Realism'.

[19] Collins, 'Utility and Rights in Common Law Reasoning'.

[20] See above n. 13.

[21] The Constitution Act 1982 (being Schedule B to the Canada Act 1982 (UK) 1982, c 11), pt. I (Canadian Charter of Rights and Freedoms) (Canadian Charter).

[22] *RWDSU* v. *Dolphin Delivery Ltd.* [1986] 2 SCR 573; 33 DLR (4th) 174. More recently, *Dagenais* v. *Canadian Broadcasting Corp* [1994] 3 SCR 835; 20 OR (3d) 816; 120 DLR (4th) 12; *Hill* v. *Church of Scientology of Toronto* [1995] 2 SCR 1130; 24 OR (3d) 865; 126 DLR (4th) 129; *Grant* v. *Torstar Corp.* [2009] 3 SCR 640.

importance. Put differently, because human rights are derived from the highest laws in the land, they should at least indirectly influence legal developments that engage the values human rights law enshrines.

Mayo Moran speaks of a 'public law positive' approach to private law. This approach places human rights at the top of the hierarchy of laws and views private law essentially as the mechanism for implementing key human rights values. Moran writes that, considered in this context, human rights is 'corrective' of private law. Problems with the traditional approach to private law, including its vulnerability to improper discrimination, can and should be remedied by applying collective and human rights considerations to traditional private law principles.[23]

Ernest Weinrib approaches the same theoretical question from a somewhat different perspective. He rationalises the influences of human rights law on the private sphere, not from the public law positive approach, but in terms of the exercise of private rights. In other words, he considers how and whether the principles of private law are receptive to human rights values.[24]

This theoretical issue is addressed more directly in the Quebec civil law. There, a number of principles consistent with collective interests (such as the protection of vulnerable members of society) are incorporated directly into the private law through the Civil Code. In this way, the private law in Quebec already contains explicit mechanisms to ensure a balancing of sorts between the exercise of individual rights and the collective good.[25]

Regardless of the paradigm of the analysis, however, it seems that the theoretical basis for the influence of human rights on the private law can be found, at least in part, in the particular role and importance of freedoms and human rights values in a constitutional democracy. Importantly, a number of academics caution against a view of private law as secondary to, or an instrument of, human rights law. In their view, private law is much more than a mechanism for implementing human rights principles. It is a key component of the legal system and houses important rights and values of its own. As a result, they argue that there must be limits to the extent to which private law can be made compliant with human rights law. The trend towards constitutionalising private law requires new techniques for ensuring that the human rights principles

[23] Moran, 'The Mutually Constitutive Nature of Public and Private Law', 17, 19.
[24] Weinrib and Weinrib, 'Constitutional Values and Private Law in Canada', pp. 46–9.
[25] For example, Arts. 1, 3, 6–9.

that are imported into private law continue to make sense in the terms of relationships between private individuals.[26]

As we shall see, however, regardless of the direction in which the influence flows, much of the interplay between private law and human rights focuses on achieving balance between individual interests and the public good. While there may be recognition that each must, to some degree, operate in concert, the fact remains that each has an important role to play, one that cannot be entirely subsumed by the other.

C *Private law's legitimate role in shaping human rights principles*

There are a number of important similarities between human rights and private law. Principal among these is that, like human rights, private law is itself the source of important values and rights. While private law rights may not have the same overarching quality or constitutional status as human rights, they do form a fundamental part of our legal tradition.

Indeed, private law has always had, at its base, a series of governing principles. To understand the nature of these principles, we need to consider how private law has evolved over time, what values it embodies, and what freedoms it has consistently protected. Of course, when we reflect on what values private law seeks to protect, we do not (as in the case of human rights) have the benefit of a constitution or other singular document that delineates the protected freedoms. Instead, we have to look more generally at trends in legal thinking and decision-making to understand the governing principles on which private law is based. Ordinarily, non-constitutional statutes can also be of assistance in that they can be an expression of private law values, either explicitly – as in the case of the Civil Code[27] – or implicitly, to the extent that they rest on private law principles.[28]

[26] Collins, 'Utility and Rights in Common Law Reasoning'. See also Fastrich, 'Human Rights and Private Law', 30; Moran, 'The Mutually Constitutive Nature of Public and Private Law'; Dagmar Coester-Waltjen, 'Discrimination in Private Law – New European Principles and the Freedom of Contract', in Katja S. Ziegler (ed.), *Human Rights and Private Law: Privacy as Autonomy* (Oxford: Hart Publishing, 2007), p. 123.

[27] See, e.g., Arts. 1–9.

[28] Consider, e.g., expropriation legislation in Canada, which provides compensation where an individual's property interests are interfered with by the state. Implicitly, the idea of compensation for interference with a right rests on the private law values of autonomy and self-determination. The state can only interfere with an individual's right to manage his her affairs according to his/her own will in limited circumstances, where the statutory criteria are met and fair compensation is provided.

A wide range of terms have been used to describe the fundamental freedoms that form the basis of private law. These include autonomy, freedom of will, freedom of contract and the ability to regulate one's own affairs at will and without interference.[29] To understand what is meant by private law freedoms, it may be useful to compare and contrast these to human rights. In this regard, Hugh Collins writes:

> Private law delivers on the liberal state's promise to respect the freedom of individuals. Protection of civil liberties through public law secures for citizens freedom from the misuse of state force. Thus public law provides negative freedom for individuals.
>
> In contrast, private law enables members of the society to use this freedom in constructive ways – to make a home, to earn an income from business activities or a job, and to acquire possessions and enjoy services. The regulatory mechanisms, institutions, and facilitative rules of private law – the rules of contract law, property rights, and rules that protect personal interests against infringement by other individuals – enable personal liberty to become a fruitful experience. Private law constructs a framework of opportunities for individuals in cooperation with others to become authors of their own lives.[30]

When we speak of the interplay between private and human rights law, it is important to consider that the two regimes share some fundamental principles and, in many ways, operate to protect some of the same basic freedoms. This is, arguably, the case with the right to basic human dignity, which forms a critical part of human rights principles. It also underlies the notion of autonomy, which is all-important in the private law sphere. In private law, the notion of dignity is fundamentally connected to the value of individual autonomy. As Roger Brownsword explains, there is a clear nexus between human dignity and the right to autonomy: without the right to make contracts, to dispose of property and to arrange our affairs according to our own will, we cannot fulfil our human potential, assert self-determination or achieve our full level of self-worth.[31] This private law conception of dignity requires not only protection from interference by state actors, but also includes the ability to exercise one's will in one's own private dealings. Or as Dagmar Coester-Waltjen explains, while the

[29] Lucy, 'What's Private about Private Law?'; Fastrich, 'Human Rights and Private Law', 28–30; Roger Brownsword, 'Freedom of Contract, Human Rights and Human Dignity', in Daniel Friedmann and Daphne Barak-Erez (eds.), *Human Rights in Private Law* (Oxford: Hart Publishing, 2001), p. 189; Coester-Waltjen, 'Discrimination in Private Law', p. 123.

[30] Collins, 'Utility and Rights in Common Law Reasoning'.

[31] Brownsword, 'Freedom of Contract'. See also Moran, 'The Mutually Constitutive Nature of Public and Private law'.

right not to be discriminated against on improper grounds is an important element of human dignity, it is only one aspect of the dignity rights related to personhood.[32]

Equality is another, related example that illustrates the parallels between private and human rights law. Private law has long been concerned with transactional equality and ensuring that participants in private relationships have equal status and equal opportunities within the transaction. Fundamentally, the concern is that one party not be in a position to unfairly dominate or determine the relationship.[33] Of course, equality is also critical in the human rights context. There, while there are transactional equality safeguards, the principal concern is substantive equality.[34]

When considered in this light, it becomes apparent that private law and human rights have an important element in common: to some extent, both are concerned with the protection of rights and freedoms fundamentally related to personhood. Arguably, however, they begin to diverge from that point. For even where they share an objective or value, private and human rights law often find themselves at odds about how to express that value.

To illustrate this idea, let us return to the example of a testator wishing to dispose of her belongings in a way that distinguishes among beneficiaries on the basis of their marital status. Provisions of this nature in the testator's will are clearly an exercise of the testator's private law rights to autonomy – her freedom to dispose of her belongings according to her own wishes. However, with the influence of human rights principles and, before that, with the influence of collective values in private law principles, that freedom or autonomy is not absolute: the testator's wishes may not be put into effect because they conflict with the private law notion of fairness or because they offend the beneficiary's human right to freedom from discrimination.

[32] Coester-Waltjen, 'Discrimination in Private Law', p. 123. See also Weinrib, *The Idea of Private Law*, p. 49.

[33] For example, Mark Walters considers whether the common law definition of 'marriage' has given meaning to constitutional values surrounding marriage. See Walters, 'Incorporating Common Law'. Peter Benson considers whether values such as equality (including equality of opportunity) are actually native to private law: Benson, 'Equality of Opportunity'. See also Moran, 'The Mutually Constitutive Nature of Public and Private Law'; Raday, 'Privatising Human Rights', paras. 50–52.

[34] *Andrews* v. *Law Society of British Columbia* [1989] 1 SCR 143; 56 DLR (4th) 1. See also *Law* v. *Canada (Minister of Employment and Immigration)* [1999] 1 SCR 497; 170 DLR (4th) 1; *R* v. *Kapp* [2008] 2 SCR 483; 294 DLR (4th) 1.

This leads to another common characteristic, namely the lexicon shared by private law and human rights. Many private law concepts predate their human rights counterparts and, in fact, form part of the legal framework upon which human rights concepts were built. Cross-fertilisation occurs because concepts are passed from one context to another, and may evolve in the process. Thus, even when considered in a human rights context, the starting point for understanding concepts such as 'person', 'property' or 'marriage' is the meaning attributed to those terms in the private law tradition.[35] As the normative foundation for some of the fundamental concepts shared by both areas, private law has had an important, although sometimes subtle and indirect influence over human rights thinking.

3 Private law as a formative element of the human right to property

The Quebec experience offers an interesting paradigm for considering this issue: in Quebec, property rights are protected under both human rights legislation and ordinary statutes. Importantly, however, there is no greater protection of property rights through human rights than there is through private law. I argue that this is indicative of the influence of private law freedoms on human rights notions of property rights. Even though the Quebec Charter arguably allows for additional protections for property, Quebec courts have not significantly interfered with property law rights already developed through the private law and ordinary statutes. This may be because the courts recognised that the appropriate balancing of private law rights and collective interests had already been achieved.

Property rights under the Quebec Charter are, on their face, very broad: they include, inter alia, the right to the peaceful enjoyment of property, free disposition of property and the inviolability of the home.[36] All of these rights are found under the heading 'Fundamental Freedoms and Rights'. Their location in the Quebec Charter is important in that, unlike social and other economic rights, property rights cannot be derogated from by the legislator.[37] While the state can derogate from social and

[35] See Walters, 'Incorporating Common Law'; Benson, 'Equality of Opportunity'.

[36] Section 6 states: 'Every person has a right to the peaceful enjoyment and free disposition of his property, except to the extent provided by law.' While the source of substantive property rights has generally been s. 6, there are two further provisions (ss. 7 and 8) that relate directly to property and fall under the heading 'Fundamental Freedoms and Rights'.

[37] See s. 52 of the Quebec Charter. There is, however, an internal limit to the Quebec Charter right to property. See below n. 38.

most economic rights, it may not abridge fundamental freedoms, which include the right to property at ss. 6, 7 and 8 of the Quebec Charter. This suggests that, in the hierarchy of rights, property rights have the same status as rights traditionally viewed as 'fundamental', including political and civil rights. This positioning implies that Quebec legislators saw the exercise of property rights as part of fundamental rights, either because they are necessary for the exercise of traditional civil and political rights or because, on a stand-alone basis, they are on par with them.

From the start, however, property rights took on a very different meaning. This is largely because the Quebec judiciary adopted a narrow interpretation of property rights, giving full weight to the internal limits contained in the provisions setting out property law protections. Section 9.1, in particular, has been a vehicle for including non-constitutional principles in setting out parameters to fundamental freedoms. It has also been used as a tool to balance competing constitutional rights.[38] In many ways, the analytical framework for s. 9.1 resembles the test developed under s. 1 of the Canadian Charter, which requires a balancing exercise and consideration of (a) whether there is a rational connection between the limit placed on the fundamental right and the legislative purpose; and (b) whether there is proportionality between the legislative means and the end it serves.[39]

However, the language of s. 9.1 of the Quebec Charter contrasts in important ways with s. 1 of the Canadian Charter.[40] Under s. 9.1, to show

[38] See, e.g., *Syndicat Northcrest* v. *Amselem* [2004] 2 SCR 551 (*Amselem*). In the context of social rights, a similarly restrictive view of Quebec Charter protection was adopted in *Chaoulli* v. *Quebec (Attorney General)* [2005] 1 SCR 791; 254 DLR (4th) 577. These cases found significant limits to rights based on ss. 9.1 and 6 of the Quebec Charter. Section 9.1 states: 'In exercising his fundamental freedoms and rights, a person shall maintain a proper regard for democratic values, public order and the general well-being of the citizens of Québec. In this respect, the scope of the freedoms and rights, and limits to their exercise, may be fixed by law.' The internal limit included in s. 6 ('to the extent provided by law') is a further restrictive dimension that does not exist for other fundamental rights under the Quebec Charter. Much like s. 9.1, the language of s. 6 does not necessarily lead to a restrictive view of property rights and much turns on the meaning given by the courts to the expression 'provided by law'. Scrutiny has been focused on the narrow issue of whether the right has been limited through the operation of a statutory instrument. The very existence of a statute is often seen as sufficient justification for the infringement of property.

[39] For the test under s. 1 of the Canadian Charter, see, e.g., *Ford* v. *Quebec (Attorney General)* [1988] 2 SCR 712; 54 DLR (4th) 577.

[40] Section 1 of the Canadian Charter states: 'The Canadian Charter of Rights and Freedoms guarantees the rights and freedoms set out in it subject only to such reasonable limits prescribed by law as can be demonstrably justified in a free and democratic society.'

that one's rights have been breached, an individual has the onus of establishing that he or she exercised rights in a manner consistent with certain values, including the collective well-being of others. Rights seekers have no such obligation under s. 1 of the Canadian Charter. Instead, at s. 1 of the Canadian Charter it is the state (not the person claiming a right) that is required to act within the parameters of the values accepted within a democratic society. This difference means that s. 9.1 is a more potent justificatory clause than s. 1 of the Canadian Charter.

This was illustrated most recently in *Amselem*,[41] where s. 9.1 was a critical part of reconciling opposing constitutionally protected rights. The result of this exercise was that s. 9.1 was interpreted by the Supreme Court of Canada in a way that subordinates property rights to more traditional civil and political rights, such as freedom of religion.

The appellants in *Amselem* had, for religious reasons, erected structures on the balcony of their condominium units. The structures (called 'succahs') were to be in place for nine days a year, the duration of a Jewish religious festival. The respondent, the condominium corporation, asked that the succahs be removed because they violated the condominium's by-laws, which prohibited decorations, alterations and constructions on the balconies.

At issue in *Amselem* was whether the contractual terms governing the appellants' relationship with the condominium corporation (prohibiting constructions on balconies) infringed the appellants' freedom of religion protected under the Quebec Charter.

The Court was divided, essentially along the lines of the judges' legal traditions.[42] The majority was composed principally of common law-trained jurists.[43] It held that the appellants were exercising a freedom of religion protected by human rights legislation. It then considered to what extent the provisions of the condominium agreements breached this right. The rights of the other condominium unit holders to the peaceful enjoyment of their property and to personal security, protected under ss. 6 and 1 of the Quebec Charter, respectively, were mentioned almost in passing. Iacobucci J, writing for the majority, held that the alleged breach

[41] [2004] 2 SCR 551.

[42] See Sébastien Grammond, 'Conceptions canadiennes et québécoise des droits fondamentaux et de la religion: convergence ou conflit?' (2009) 43 *Revue Juridique Thémis* 83. Grammond theorises that this divergence among judges is due not so much to differences in their legal background, but to differences (between Quebeckers and other Canadians) in cultural and religious conceptions of religion and its relationship to the state.

[43] With the exception of Fish J.

of the condominium unit holders' rights were minimal at most and did not impose valid limits on the appellants' attempts to exercise their freedom of religion.[44]

Bastarache J, writing for the minority,[45] adopted an analysis centred on the provisions of the Quebec Charter and their role in defining rights. He held that the respondents' freedom of religion must be interpreted in light of s. 9.1 of the Quebec Charter, which requires that the rights and freedoms be exercised in respect of each other with 'a proper regard for democratic values, public order and the general well being of the citizens of Quebec'. Bastarache J found that s. 9.1 of the Quebec Charter requires more than a balancing of the rights of different parties. Rather, it contemplates a reconciliation of those rights in a way that accounts for the general interests of the citizens of Quebec. He wrote that the appellants' rights to freedom of religion conflicted with the rights of each unit holder to, inter alia, the peaceful enjoyment of property under s. 6 of the Quebec Charter.[46] Bastarache J rejected the majority's view that the s. 6 rights of the other condominium unit holders had suffered a *de minimis* violation. He also rejected the notion, implicit in the majority's conclusion, that rights exist in a hierarchy. Rather, in defining the content of the respondents' right to freedom of religion, he considered the scope of the other rights involved. He concluded that, since the right to freedom of religion could not be exercised in harmony with the rights and freedoms of others or with the 'general well-being', the infringement of Mr Amselem's right was legitimate.[47]

The facts in *Amselem* placed two competing rights in opposition: on the one hand freedom of religion, and on the other the right enshrined in the Quebec Charter to peaceful enjoyment and free disposition of property. The decision begs a number of questions: can the exercise of individual property rights, when in conflict with other rights held by the majority, ever meet the requirements of s. 9.1 of the Quebec Charter? How can the exercise of individual property rights interface with the general interests of the citizens of Quebec, particularly where the individual bears the onus of reconciling the two? The nature of property rights and the potency of s. 9.1 present challenges to anyone seeking to assert a constitutional right to property. Indeed, the majority's conclusion in *Amselem* suggests that,

44 *Amselem* at [84].
45 Consisting of Lebel J and Deschamps J. Binnie J wrote a separate dissent.
46 *Amselem* at [165]. For the text of Section 6, see note 36, above.
47 *Amselem* at [180].

in the gradations of constitutional protection under the Quebec Charter, property rights will play a subordinate role.

The further implication is that the broader the views on possible justifications for state interference with a right, the narrower will be the scope of the right that is ultimately recognised. Given the internal limit to property rights contained in s. 6 of the Quebec Charter, the simple existence of a statutory instrument may be sufficient to defend state interference. If so, the right is effectively devoid of any real constitutional protection.[48] If it can be abridged or derogated from through the application of a statutory instrument, how is the human right to property different from the right to fair compensation for expropriation that exists outside the constitutional framework?

In this regard, the rights and remedies afforded for breach of property law rights under the Quebec Charter are consistent with those already available through non-constitutional expropriation statutes in most jurisdictions (including Quebec). Expropriation statutes generally protect against expropriation by the state without fair compensation.[49] Expansively worded human rights legislation has not interfered with or expanded upon rights because the Quebec judiciary has generally adopted a narrow interpretation of rights, giving full weight to the internal limits contained in the provisions setting out property law protections.[50]

[48] The internal limit included in s. 6 ('to the extent provided by law') is a further restrictive dimension to the right of property. This internal limit does not exist for other fundamental rights under the Quebec Charter and has led Professor Debruche to comment that: 'This specific limitation is thus substituted to the general limit set out in section 9.1 of the Charter for the rest of the protected rights and liberties. It is thus an ad hoc limitation applying only to the right of property, which in turn has led to considering property as a right stripped of any supra-legal status, inferior in rank to the other rights and liberties entrenched in the Quebec Charter.' See Anne-Françoise Debruche, 'Property in the Archipelagos of Human Rights: Comparative Thoughts on Judicial Exploration in Europe and Canada', in Josep Ma. Castellà Andreu and Sébastien Grammond (eds.), *Diversidad Derechos Fundamentales y Federalismo* (Barcelona: Atelier Libros Juridicos, 2010), p. 217.

[49] In Quebec, the Expropriation Act, RSQ, c E-24, s. 38 stipulates that expropriation must be authorised by the state and that 'no other authorization shall be required, notwithstanding any law'. Section 58 requires the payment of a fair indemnity fixed according to the value of the expropriated property plus any damage directly caused by expropriation. In Canada, the Expropriation Act, RSC 1985, c E-21 provides a general power for the state appropriation where necessary for a public work or other public purpose. There are a number of exceptions to this right, most notably regarding first nations' land.

[50] See *Amselem* [2004] 2 SCR 551. See also *Chaoulli* v. *Quebec (Attorney General)* [2005] 1 SCR 791; 254 DLR (4th) 577. These cases found significant limits to rights based on ss. 9.1 and 6 of the Quebec Charter.

4 Constitutional and private law limits on the freedom to bequeath

Unlike with the right to property, where they seem to agree as to the appropriate framing of the right, human rights and the private law have taken different approaches to the freedom to bequeath. As a result, the extent of the freedom to bequeath appears to differ according to whether it is being considered in a private law or a human rights context. Notwithstanding this, limits placed on the freedom to bequeath within both human rights and private law illustrate that collective interests, such as the interest in safeguarding the institution of marriage, have long been a factor in both contexts. They showcase a common ground between human rights and private law: while they may approach the issue differently, both have long expressed concern for fairness and, at least indirectly, for collective interests.

As in other areas of private law, tension has existed between the courts' urge to address unfairness in private contractual arrangements and their desire to respect basic private law principles, such as autonomy and parties' need for certainty in managing their affairs. Testamentary clauses that distinguish among beneficiaries on the basis of marital status throw these issues into sharp relief.

A Intention and the traditional approach to testamentary conditions

Human rights legislation in Canada generally prohibits distinctions on the basis of marital status. However, long before the existence of any such human rights prohibition, the courts had already perceived viduity (widowhood) testamentary clauses to be unfair in certain circumstances. They regularly refused to uphold such clauses on the grounds that they were contrary to the public interest or the public order. Even though they were operating in a purely private law context, the pre-human rights courts explicitly looked to collective interests as a factor for invalidating these provisions.

Before the advent of human rights legislation, the legality of remarriage conditions hinged on the testator's intentions. Where the courts deemed the testator's intentions to be consistent with their interpretation of the 'public values' prevailing at the time, the conditions were upheld, no matter what their ultimate effect.[51]

[51] In Quebec, the analysis revolved around the notion of 'public order'. See *Kria* v. *Abraham* [1988] RJQ 1831. The use of 'public interest' in this chapter refers generally to both the

As the following examples show, the notion of 'public values' and, to some extent, 'public order' was very subjective. For example, when a testamentary condition's principal objective was to protect the widow against opportunists, the condition was deemed to be a valid exercise of the testator's right to dispose of his or her property. However, where the testator's principal object was to prevent the widow's remarriage or to bring about a marriage break-up, the condition was generally invalid because it was deemed to be against the collective interest in the institution of marriage.[52]

This disregard for the ultimate effect of the testamentary condition resulted in a strange dichotomy. While in both the above examples the effect of the testamentary clause was to prevent remarriage, only the 'good faith' clause was upheld.[53] Thus, the issue for the Court was not whether marriage was restrained, but rather a question of morality: did the testator mean good or ill in restraining the marriage? This approach raises obvious concerns, including the difficulty of determining the intentions of an individual who is (necessarily) no longer alive, as well as the challenge of attributing moral value to that intention. The analysis may be so subjective as to approach guesswork.[54]

Historically, concepts such as 'public good' and 'public order' were, arguably, more fluid then than they are today. In the absence of guiding constitutional and human rights legislation, judges were left largely to their own morals, ideals and experiences to guide them in expressing what was in the collective interest.

Our values have evolved considerably since the traditional approach to testamentary conditions was developed. Certainly, the basis upon which courts consider conditions invalid today draws little from earlier visions of the 'public good'. Our interest in the traditional analysis arises not from the nature of the values it ultimately protected, but from the fact that it did incorporate collective values such as the public good. Indeed, the idea

civil law notion of 'public order' and the common law notion of 'public values'.

[52] Christine Morin, 'La Liberté de Tester: Évolution et Révolution dans les Représentations de la Doctrine Québécoise' (2008) 38 *Revue de Droit de l'Universite de Sherbrooke* 339, para. 7; Madeleine Cantin Cumyn, 'La Liberté Testamentaire et la Charte des Droits et Libertés de la Personne' (1982) 84(5) *Revue du Notariat* 223; *Re Petit, succession* [1988] JQ 1241 (CS) (*Re Petit*) at [11]; *Kria* v. *Abraham* [1988] RJQ 1831; *Re Muirhead Estate* [1919] SJ 47 (KB).

[53] For example, the court in *Re Muirhead Estate* [1919] SJ 47 (KB) found that it was in the public interest to encourage a first marriage, but not in the public interest to facilitate a second marriage.

[54] See Cantin Cumyn, 'La Liberté Testamentaire'.

that the enforceability of a testamentary clause depends upon whether a party meant good or ill in the disposition of property is not part of a traditional private law analysis.

For our purposes, the importance of the traditional approach is its openness to considering the public interest in determining the validity of a testamentary provision. In theory at least, the traditional approach could accommodate evolving values. It focuses on the intention of the testator and its compatibility with the public interest, as that notion is understood over time. Arguably, the private law can offer anti-discrimination protection that rivals what is available under human rights legislation.

To illustrate this idea, we turn to two examples that arise within Canada: the civil law approach in Quebec, where human rights legislation has been applied to testamentary clauses, and the common law approach in other Canadian jurisdictions, where human rights legislation does not apply to testaments.[55]

B Quebec: the civil law approach and the emerging importance of collective values

While the general framework of estates law in Quebec flows from French civil law, the approach and importance attributed to freedom to bequeath is derived from the common law.[56] In its initial permutation, the Civil Code provided for absolute freedom to bequeath.[57] However, the academic discussion as early as the 1930s shows that, as with the common law, the notion of public order was soon seen as an appropriate limit to this freedom.[58]

[55] Consider, for example, s. 3 of the Ontario Human Rights Code, RSO 1990, c H.19, which states: 'Every person having legal capacity has a right to contract on equal terms without discrimination because of race, ancestry, place of origin, colour, ethnic origin, citizenship, creed, sex, sexual orientation, age, marital status, family status or disability.' Because testaments do not have the common law characteristics of a contract, the Ontario Human Rights Code and its equivalent in other Canadian jurisdictions have not generally factored into the analysis of whether testamentary conditions ought to be upheld. The Quebec Charter is worded more broadly and has been applied to testaments. Section 13 of the Quebec Charter states: 'No one may in a juridical act stipulate a clause involving discrimination.'

[56] Morin, 'La Liberté de Tester', para. 9.

[57] Code civil du Bas Canada, Quatrième et Cinquième Rapports, Québec, 1865.

[58] Morin, 'La Liberté de Tester', paras. 5, 14–34.

Ultimately, the Quebec Charter enshrined limits on the freedom to bequeath.[59] While the starting point, the testator's intention, was initially similar in both jurisdictions, the Quebec Charter shifted (or ought to have shifted) the Quebec courts' approach away from this intention-based analysis.[60] This is because, fundamentally, human rights principles in Canada focus on the effect of the discrimination and the intention of the actor is immaterial.[61] Canadian courts have long recognised that intention is not a necessary element of discrimination.[62] It follows that an intention-based analysis, where a testamentary condition is void only if adopted in bad faith, is inconsistent with the Quebec Charter and the human rights principles it encompasses. The Quebec Charter requires an analysis of the effect of the testamentary condition. If its effect is discriminatory, it should be struck down, regardless of whether it was adopted in good or bad faith.[63]

The courts have struggled to reconcile the traditional approach to testamentary conditions with the constitutional protections that became available with the Quebec Charter. Courts have yet to achieve a clear consensus as to the appropriate approach and, while the Quebec Charter has been the focus, the testator's intention has continued to creep into the analysis.

For example, in *Re Petit*,[64] Savoie J looked primarily to human rights legislation to resolve the issue of the validity of a remarriage condition. Savoie J applied the Quebec Charter and concluded that requiring someone to remain a widow constitutes discrimination under the Quebec Charter and is invalid, regardless of the intention of the testator.

In *Central Guaranty Trust Co.* v. *Lefebvre-Gervais*,[65] the Court adopted a hybrid form of reasoning, one that considered both the rights protected

[59] See, e.g., s. 10 of the Quebec Charter. Notably, under Quebec civil law a testament is a contract that is subject to the Quebec Charter. See *Re Petit* [1988] JQ 1241 (CS); Pierre-Gabriel Jobin, 'Peut-on, grâce au contrat, se faire justice soi-même en droit québécois?' (2009) 3 *Revue Trimestrielle de Droit Civil* 481.

[60] Cantin Cumyn, 'La Liberté Testamentaire', 223.

[61] See, e.g., *British Columbia (Public Service Employee Relations Commission)* v. *BCGSEU* [1999] 3 SCR 3; 176 DLR (4th) 1 at [27]–[29]. See also Cantin Cumyn, 'La Liberté Testamentaire'.

[62] *Ont. Human Rights Comm.* v. *Simpsons-Sears* [1985] 2 SCR 536; 52 OR (2d) 799; 23 DLR (4th) 321.

[63] Cantin Cumyn, 'La Liberté Testamentaire'.

[64] [1988] JQ 1241 (CS) at [21].

[65] 47 ETR 257; [1992] RJQ 2264; JE 92–1441.

in the Quebec Charter and the testator's intention. The will in that case contained the following clause:

> My trustees are directed to stop all or part of the pension to my wife Iona should she elect to remarry and this the month following her wedding should her new husband not be working or be without a substantial income.

The Court found that the remarriage condition did not create a distinction based on civil status, but rather one based on the ability of the new husband to provide for the widow. It concluded that the clause was not discriminatory, basing this conclusion not on the effect of the testament but on the testator's apparent intent to protect the widow rather than to prevent a remarriage. This is an example of the private law's intention-based analysis influencing the courts' approach to human rights.

C *The common law approach*

While common law jurisdictions in Canada also have human rights legislation, these statutes do not apply to testaments.[66] Thus, in contrast with the Quebec approach, common law courts in Canada continue to review remarriage conditions based on the testator's intentions.

The case law in common law jurisdictions is such that very few remarriage conditions are held to be against the public interest. Most are upheld as being, in some way, designed to protect the widow or even the other beneficiaries to the will.[67] The courts have generally interpreted the 'public interest' in a way that favours the validity of remarriage conditions. Although the 'public interest' could (and arguably should) be interpreted in light of values enshrined in human rights statutes, these have not generally factored into the analysis.

[66] See, for example, the Ontario Code, above n. 55.

[67] *Re Goodwin* [1969] AJ 65; 3 DLR (3d) 281 illustrates the lengths to which the courts are prepared to go in order to uphold viduity clauses. In that case, the Court considered the validity of a remarriage condition imposed, not on the testator's widow, but on a third-party beneficiary. The testator sought to bequeath a portion of his estate upon his daughter-in-law, provided that she did not remarry. Upon remarriage, the portion of the estate that would have been hers fell to her children. The Court's analysis expanded upon the principle that recognised a husband's interest in his wife's widowhood so as to make it lawful for him to impose a widowhood condition. It found that the testator also had an interest in his daughter-in-law's widowhood to the extent that he sought to protect the interests of his grandchildren.

Re Estate of Philip Brown[68] provides a useful example of the post-human rights analysis typical within common law jurisdictions in Canada. In this case, decided in Nova Scotia in 1995, the Court carried out an extensive review of the case law in the area. Ultimately, it upheld a remarriage clause on the basis of the testator's intention. Without any mention of human rights legislation or values, the Court held that because the testator's intention was not to prevent remarriage but to protect the interests of the widow, the clause was valid.

Where they arise under the Canadian Charter, where the issue is an individual's rights in regard to the state, remarriage provisions have been deemed unconstitutional. In *Bauman* v. *Nova Scotia (Attorney General)*,[69] the Nova Scotia Court of Appeal considered provisions of the Workers' Compensation Act,[70] which terminated certain benefits upon a recipient's remarriage. These provisions were found to be in contravention of the Canadian Charter.

Interestingly, different approaches have been taken in common law jurisdictions, depending on whether or not human rights legislation applies. This showcases the impact of human rights legislation. Where a human rights analysis is applied, and the effect of the clause rather than the intention of the testator is considered, testamentary clauses seem more vulnerable to being struck down.

D Summary

The fact that, to date, the common law has not significantly engaged human rights principles provides some interesting insight into the private law approach to testamentary clauses. In both Quebec and common law jurisdictions, the courts look to public interest factors. In the common law jurisprudence, in particular, these collective interests take on a paternalistic hue, a vestige of the values first incorporated into the traditional approach to testamentary clauses. While society's values may have evolved since the private law doctrine was first developed, the values incorporated into the legal analysis do not appear to have kept pace. The human rights approach is reflected most clearly in the jurisprudence under the Quebec Charter, which focuses on values enshrined in the Quebec Charter.

[68] [1995] NSJ No. 42 (SC).
[69] [2001] 192 NSR (2d) 236; 197 DLR (4th) 644 (NSCA).
[70] Workers' Compensation Act, SNS 1994–95, c 10.

However, even this approach retains vestiges of the traditional, intention-based analysis.[71]

When it comes to widowhood clauses, private law intersects with human rights in at least two ways. First, both areas factor the public interest in protecting vulnerable members of society into their analyses, even though the interests in question are perceived somewhat differently. Second, the traditional private law approach has not been fully supplanted by a human rights analysis, even where human rights statutes apply. Private law factors, such as the paternalistic interest in protecting (often female) beneficiaries and the subjective determination of the testator's intention continue to seep into the analysis.

5 Conclusion

While human rights' influence on private law has recently been in the foreground of much of our legal thinking, the influences are, in fact, reciprocal. Private law has impacted upon our understanding of human rights in a number of ways, some striking, others much more subtle. We have considered two very different examples of this.

In Quebec, property law rights at expropriation are essentially identical, whether they arise in the private or the human rights context. The private law rights developed first. The Quebec Charter came later, using broad language suggestive of expansive and positive protection for property. The courts, however, have generally adopted an approach that parallels the rights already available through ordinary statutes and private law values. Perhaps the courts felt that existing rights were sufficient to achieve any human rights objectives in this area. Or perhaps they were reluctant to give breadth to rights, such as property, that have an important economic element. In any event, it seems clear that the private law of expropriation has helped give shape and meaning to property rights that flow from the Quebec Charter.

Testamentary conditions are a second example of the intersection of private and public law. In this case, however, the result is far from a coherent or shared vision of what is in the collective interest. Under the private law approach, widowhood clauses are most often upheld, the only condition being that the testator's intentions in creating the clause are consistent with what is understood to be the public interest. Human rights values do not generally factor into the interpretation of 'public interest'.

[71] See *Central Guaranty Trust Co. v. Lefebvre-Gervais* [1992] JQ 1735.

Conversely, the human rights approach is not generally tolerant of any distinction based on the marital status of the beneficiary and, under a human rights analysis, these kinds of clauses are most often struck down.

Although private and human rights law generally lead to different results in this context, the two spheres do influence each other in important ways. First, both the private and the human rights approaches consider the public interest as a factor in the analysis, although their perception of the public interest and the extent to which they offer protection is markedly different.

Second, in Canadian common law jurisdictions the private law framework continues to be the main basis for consideration of the issue. Even in Quebec, where the Quebec Charter is the backdrop for the analysis, the testator's intention and the court's subjective assessment of that intention are often a subtle part of the legal reasoning. Thus, the validity of a widowhood clause, which could be analysed in light of human rights values, is often considered based on the private law doctrine. Even where human rights legislation is the basis for the analysis, the private law framework often seeps into the review.

Examples such as these help to illustrate the interrelatedness of private law and human rights. As we have seen, the mutual influences run deep. With property rights, this interplay has meant a similar approach to rights and an importation of principles from one context to the other. In the case of testamentary provisions, however, the cross-pollination has been more subtle. While private law and human rights may have a shared objective, they have adopted contrasting approaches to achieving that goal. Interestingly, even where the traditional private law approach runs contrary to human rights principles, some of its influences persist.

8

The synthesis of public and private in finance law

ALASTAIR HUDSON

1 Introduction

Lawyers create models, in the form of case law, statute and regulation, in an effort to lay a patina of order across the chaos and unpredictability of modern life.[1] These models require constant tweaking and maintenance to keep them serviceable. Periodically they need to be disassembled and rebuilt to accommodate deeper social change. At the present time, one particular model that requires attention is that which purportedly establishes a boundary between the public sphere and the private realm, particularly in relation to banks.

Hitherto, our substantive law has sought to deal differently with two broad areas of human endeavour: on the one hand, the powers of public bodies and their impact on the rights of private persons and, on the other, private law relations between private persons. Broadly speaking, that is the division between public law and private law. This distinction is of limited use, however. As a purportedly rigid boundary, it breaks down when one considers phenomena as diverse as the ability of public bodies to make contracts under private contract law, which involves public bodies using private law, and the impact that private sector institutions such as banks have on economic policy, which involves private banks influencing public bodies and public policy directly. The public is necessarily involved in the private, and the private necessarily impacts on the public. They slip over one another constantly, like wet crabs in a basket.[2]

I am indebted to Professor Kit Barker for his insightful comments on an earlier draft of this chapter.

[1] Lawyers do not tend to talk in this language, but all of those case law tests, statutory mechanisms and regulatory schemes are in truth models for regularising all aspects of social and economic life.

[2] The metaphor comes from Lawrence Durrell, *Balthazar* (London: Faber and Faber, 1958), p. 125, using the narrator to deconstruct the idea of a linear narrative by thinking of events

The existence of any boundary line between the public and the private is therefore primarily ideological. This chapter identifies a challenge to the rigidity of the public–private divide in relation to banks in the global financial system. More particularly, this chapter considers how regulations created and imposed by public bodies can fruitfully come to mould private law principles and rules as they apply to financial transactions;[3] and it also considers how private law models can inform public law principles governing financial regulation.[4]

2 Understanding 'public' and 'private' in finance law

A All law is synthetic

All law is synthetic: by which I mean that all law is a synthesis of legal concepts that are created for use in particular contexts by the courts, legislatures and by legal practitioners. While many legal scholars concern themselves with creating taxonomies of law that attempt to put different legal rules into different baskets labelled 'contract law', 'tort law' and so on, in practice those legal concepts take on lives of their own beyond the limits of that taxonomy as they are developed by practitioners and their clients.[5] After all, there is no taxonomy in the natural world. Instead,

overlapping, crawling over one another like wet crabs in a basket; just as this chapter seeks to argue against linear models of law that prevent the possibilities of ideas from different disciplines overlapping creatively with one another.

[3] The Law Commission considered a different question in its paper 'Fiduciary Duties and Regulatory Rules' (1993) Law Comm Paper 124. This is significant in that the 'regulations' at issue were self-regulatory principles created by the non-statutory Securities and Investment Board (SIB), whereas the regulations in effect in the UK since 2000, being statutory rules and regulations created by the statutory regulator, implement EU legislation, or the principles of UK statutes. Professor Beatson, then a law commissioner, has argued that the principal objection to allowing SIB regulatory principles to govern common law principles was that the SIB regulations were non-statutory: Jack Beatson, 'Financial Services and Fiduciary Duties', in Ewan McKendrick (ed.), *Commercial Aspects of Trusts and Fiduciary Obligations* (Oxford: Clarendon Press, 1992), pp. 58ff. That argument does not apply to Financial Services Authority regulation.

[4] The jurisdictions that are considered here are the United Kingdom in relation to financial regulation, with reference to principles created by the European Union that are implemented in UK financial regulation, and England and Wales in relation to the substantive law.

[5] In the real world, it is commonly impossible to practise law according to the boxes in which legal scholars place it. So, it is impossible to practise 'equity' exclusively (taking that term to encompass constructive trusts, specific performance, and so forth – no matter how interesting a seminar on dishonest assistance may have been); but it is possible to specialise in the drafting of wills, tax avoidance or suing investment advisers for mis-selling derivatives because clients will pay for those services. One can only practise what one's clients will fund.

all taxonomies and the subdivision of legal doctrines are products of the human mind.[6] The division between the public and the private is just such a division. It is vitally important in a democratic society to have a legal field that protects private persons from the power of the state, but along that boundary line there are many crossing points. Ideas from public law combine with ideas from private law constantly. As will emerge below, the development of the law of finance depends upon it. This is a project that requires something different from the divisions and separations of a rigid taxonomy: instead, it requires a blend of ideas.

For the creation of a comprehensive law of finance there is a need for a synthesis of substantive concepts from private law with regulations and statute created specifically for the financial context. Areas of law such as the law of finance are predicated on this synthesis of fundamental *concepts* and rules created for particular *contexts*.[7] The law of finance in the UK is a synthesis of substantive law concepts taken from contract law, tort law, property law, criminal law, equity and private international law,[8] with contextual regulation created by the Financial Services Authority (FSA)[9] further to powers granted to it by the Financial Services and Markets Act 2000 (FSMA 2000).[10]

[6] A good example is P. Birks and R. Chambers, *Restitution Research Resource* (Oxford: Mansfield Press, 1997), which sought to delineate all of the categories of unjust factor giving rise to claims for unjust enrichment, in spite of the torrent of new doctrines emerging in equity. See also G. Samuel, 'Can Gaius Really be Compared to Darwin?' (2000) 49 *International and Comparative Law Quarterly* 297.

[7] As is explored in greater detail in Alastair Hudson, *The Law of Finance*, 1st edition (London: Sweet & Maxwell, 2009), paras. 4–03ff.

[8] As identified in *ibid.*, pp. 1–723 (Section A: General Principles).

[9] The Financial Services Authority is due to be replaced in 2013 (assuming the Financial Services Act 2012 is brought fully into effect according to the current timetable) by new subsidiary entities of the Bank of England, in particular the Financial Conduct Authority and the Prudential Regulatory Authority. The former will have oversight of conduct of business and the latter micro-prudential oversight of individual financial institutions, with the new Financial Policy Committee holding responsibility for the stability of the financial system. However, the bulk of the regulatory provisions considered in this chapter will continue in existence in substantively the same form because they implement EU legislation, which must continue in effect in the UK regardless of which entity acts as the principal regulatory body for the relevant aspects of financial market activity. Strictly, the Financial Services Authority is to be 'renamed' as the 'Financial Conduct Authority' further to the Financial Services Act 2012, s. 6. This chapter was written before any legislative changes were made.

[10] The Financial Services and Markets Act 2000 has been amended over time both to implement EU legislation and to implement changes effected by statutes such as the Companies Act 2006 and the Banking Act 2009, as well as being subject to further amendments so as to accommodate the reforms that are to be introduced to deal with the financial crisis contained in the Financial Services Bill 2012 and the much anticipated Banking Reform

Much of the statutory basis for FSA regulation is EU financial services legislation.[11] Of particular significance for present purposes is the Markets in Financial Instruments Directive 2004[12] (MiFID), which provides the basis for the regulation of 'conduct of business' between financial institutions and their customers. The Financial Services Authority *Conduct of Business Sourcebook* (COBS),[13] which implements MiFID in the UK, places positive obligations on those financial institutions. Amongst other duties are the obligations imposed on 'regulated firms' to classify their customers' level of expertise and to deal with them suitably as a result;[14] the obligation to act in the best interests of the client;[15] the obligation to obtain 'best execution' for the client;[16] and a prohibition on any exclusion clauses that purport to exclude these obligations.[17] The presence of these positive obligations in itself constitutes a different culture from private law in that the courts are typically reluctant to recognise any obligation as binding a person unless, as considered below, it was voluntarily assumed by them. However, these regulations do constitute a regime of positive duties that are imposed on financial institutions.[18] They can be regarded as a statement of the proper behaviour of a financial institution in the conduct of its business. The regulations contained in the FSA Handbook[19] constitute an arm of public law in that they constitute the rules and guidance notes effected by a statutory body further to the powers granted to

Bill 2013. These several sources of law are considered in Hudson, *The Law of Finance*, Chapter 1 ('Components of the Law of Finance').

11 Considered in detail in Hudson, *The Law of Finance*, Chapter 7.

12 2004/39/EC (MiFID).

13 Financial Services Authority, *Conduct of Business Sourcebook* (UK Financial Services Authority) (COBS), available at: http://fsahandbook.info/FSA/html/handbook/COBS (last accessed 11 March 2013).

14 COBS, Chapter 3 generally, especially 3.7.1R. (References to rules within the FSA Handbook contain the suffix 'R', as distinct from guidance notes, which have the suffix 'G'.) The classification process is complex, and firms are required to document their classification decisions: MiFID, Art. 19(7), even though, as considered below, the English courts tend to ignore this regulatory process.

15 MiFID, Art. 19(1) and COBS, 2.1.1R.

16 COBS, 11.2.1R. This may, in itself, constitute a fiduciary duty: see Hudson, *The Law of Finance*, para. 10–44.

17 COBS, 2.12R.

18 In this sense, the term 'positive' connotes an obligation to perform an act, as opposed to a negative duty to refrain from acting, where the former generally involves the expenditure of effort, the taking of risk and possibly the incurring of expense: as explained in the land law context in *Rhone* v. *Stephens* [1994] 2 AC 310 in relation to freehold covenants.

19 UK Financial Services Authority, *The Full Handbook* (FSA Handbook), available at: http://fsahandbook.info/FSA/html/handbook (last accessed 11 March 2013).

it by statute. Many of those same activities, however, have private law consequences too.

Once we accept that these distinctions between public and private are in truth only ideas, then it is possible to deal far more flexibly with other ideas that are otherwise bound up in that distinction. In particular, for the purposes of this book it becomes possible to think of statutory regulation and private law as informing and shaping one another so as to achieve a larger goal. After all, private law (the law governing relationships between individuals) is itself necessarily an emanation of the state in the form of judicially created case law, parliamentary legislation or statute-based regulation by public bodies.

This raises the question as to the goal or goals at which such a synthesised law of finance might be aimed. A full answer to that question is beyond the scope of this chapter. This chapter is intended to be an illustration of how a more coherent legal and regulatory treatment of finance could operate, building on a trend that already exists in the case law, thus synthesising public and private law ideas. The principal focus of this chapter is on the establishment of a *better* law of finance in the wake of the financial crisis that began in August 2007 and that continues to govern all economic and financial services policy in Europe and the USA at present. By 'better' is simply meant a law of finance that is not comprised of a disparate cloud of norms contained separately in substantive private law, in financial regulation and in the extra-statutory practices of the FSA and government (where neither used their legal or regulatory powers before the crisis began as a matter of policy, and where both realised their legal and regulatory powers were inadequate once the crisis hit).[20]

The financial system in the UK needs a single set of private law and regulatory principles that are able to prevent (in the case of financial regulation) and to remedy (in the case of private law and the 'civil penalties' that the FSA is empowered to impose[21]) the worst excesses of a banking system that has indulged in everything from systematic wrongdoing (in the form of fixing benchmark rates such as the London Inter-Bank Offered Rate[22] and mis-selling payment protection insurance to retail customers) and criminal conduct (including insider dealing, money laundering and

[20] Hudson, *The Law of Finance*, paras. 32–09ff. and 29–45ff.

[21] *Ibid.*, para. 12–43; Financial Services and Markets Act 2000, s. 123.

[22] FSA Final Notice, 27 June 2012, 'Barclays fined £59.5 million for significant failings in relation to LIBOR and EURIBOR'.

'sanctions-busting' in the USA), through to straightforward incompetence (such as Barclays misreporting 57.5 million transactions to the FSA in one accounting year[23]). What is really needed more than anything is a synthesised law of finance that can protect customers from the worst excesses of the financial system. The welfare of the end-user of financial services products and of the general economy must be paramount.[24] That requires a regulatory system that can ensure suitable conduct of business and the control of prudential risks in the financial system, and a private law system that can remedy any infractions of those regulations that cause harm to customers. This is only possible if those two, currently disparate social systems (financial regulation and private law) are able to interact.[25]

As is considered below, conduct of business regulation by the FSA in the UK provides an example of an effect on the law governing the creation of contracts between financial institutions and their clients. This is a clear intersection of public law (in the form of financial regulation created further to EU and UK statute) with the rules of private law (in the form of the law on the creation of contracts). This chapter considers examples of an osmosis between public law and private law. The manner in which that interaction should be understood is considered below in relation to the interaction of conduct of business regulation with the law on dishonest assistance and unconscionable receipt; and the possibilities for the interaction of conduct of business regulation with common law claims for negligence and fraud.

B The different objectives of financial regulation and substantive law

For all that they might be capable of synthesis in many contexts, financial regulation and the substantive law have different objectives.[26] In essence, the principal distinctions are the following. Financial regulation can

[23] FSA Final Notice, 19 August 2009, 'Barclays Capital Securities Ltd fined £2.49 million'.

[24] Hudson, *The Law of Finance*, para. 32–28ff.; and Alastair Hudson, 'Financial Regulation and the Welfare State', in A. S. Hudson (ed.), *Modern Financial Techniques, Derivatives and Law* (Kluwer Law International, 2000), p. 235.

[25] Systems theory imagines social systems of this sort as being equivalent to a biological understanding of a cell in which each cell passes information one to another in a particular way: Alastair Hudson, *Towards a Just Society* (New York: Pinter, 1999), p. 105; G. Teubner, *Law as an Autopoietic System* (Oxford: Blackwell, 1993). Systems theorists then analyse the ways in which social systems communicate with one another, and how they overcome different uses of language, different norms and so forth that are particular to their own zones of competence. Such an exercise will be necessary here, as is considered below.

[26] Hudson, *The Law of Finance*, para. 3–03ff.

operate on a 'coercive–regulatory' basis in that the regulator is an overseer and a policeman when, for example, the FSA exercises its statutory powers of investigation and punishment[27] and its powers in relation to market abuse.[28] However, under the FSMA 2000, the FSA (at the time of writing) has further duties to ensure 'market confidence, public awareness, the protection of consumers, and the reduction of financial crime',[29] and – more controversially – to advance the competitive position of the UK economy and financial sector in relation to other jurisdictions, as well as the more mundane business of protecting investors. Therefore, as a regulator, the FSA is not simply concerned with the coercion, oversight or control of regulated firms and employees, but rather it is also concerned with the health of the UK economy as a pivotal market for global financial services. The FSA is thereby an economic actor: a public body that both oversees private bodies and performs a statutory role in relation to the general economy. This dual role, of operating both accelerator in relation to the general economy and brake in relation to activities of financial institutions, contributed to the disastrous light-touch regulatory approach of the FSA before the collapse of Lehman Brothers in September 2008.

There are other functional differences between financial regulation and substantive law. Financial regulation is not created in a vacuum by the regulator, but rather those rules are created after long consultation periods between the FSA and the banking community further to the FSA's statutory obligation to consult with the marketplace.[30] This is a particular feature of commercial, especially financial, regulation. After all, Parliament does not consult with murderers before amending the law on homicide. Therefore, the private sector must be consulted by this public, regulatory body before creating its regulations.

The goals of the substantive law are different, or certainly differently stated, from the goals of financial regulation. The enforcement of contracts is a key part of English law, as is the provision of compensation for wrongs through the common law and equity, and the punishment of wrongs through the criminal law.[31] All of these doctrines are subject to a complex jurisprudence and a body of binding precedent, whereas financial regulations are specific to the financial context, are frequently

[27] *Ibid.*, para. 9–44. [28] *Ibid.*, para. 12–01.

[29] Financial Services and Markets Act 2000, s. 2(2).

[30] Financial Services and Markets Act 2000, s. 8.

[31] Where the criminal law is part of the substantive law in the sense that it is created by statute and by the common law and administered by the courts, as opposed to financial regulation, which is not overseen nor administered by the courts (except in the event of a judicial review action being brought against the FSA).

rewritten as public policy changes and synthesise formal rules with guidance notes. The lack of a formal jurisprudence means that financial regulation is a less reliable body of rules than case law, which, while capable of change, only does so in predictable ways or by reference to earlier rules and principles. The manner in which the FSA will enforce regulations is uneven (occasionally even quixotic) and not capable of clear divination in advance. There is no doctrine of precedent, nor any formal jurisprudence governing its decisions, only the guidance notes in the FSA Handbook.[32] Thus, anticipating regulatory responses to market behaviour is a specific practitioner's art akin to horse whispering. In the wake of the global financial crisis, the approach of regulators around the world transformed from light-touch non-regulation to strict enforcement, at the very least, of high-profile market abuse regulations relating to insider dealing and criminal conspiracies.

C *The quasi-public nature of banking institutions*

One of the key things that changed during the global financial crisis, which began in August 2007 with the failure of Northern Rock and which continues to send out tremors to this day, is that things that had previously been considered to be private indisputably became public. In particular, it is suggested, banks should now be understood as acting as public bodies in four senses that, for reasons of space, can only be stated briefly here.

First, the *ownership* of banks. Northern Rock was nationalised in 2008 further to powers created by the Banking (Special Provisions) Act 2008.[33] The effect was a seismic change in the relationship between the state and the banking industry because the state became the principal shareholder in many banks in the UK and in the EU more generally for the first time. These banks became public bodies in the sense that majority shareholdings in them were owned by the state. Significantly, the remainder of the banking system was supported entirely by public money, such that public money enabled privately owned banks to continue in business. In the USA there were bail-outs of several banking institutions in the sense that

[32] Financial Services Authority, *The Full Handbook*. The FSA Handbook is the document that contains the regulations that are created by the FSA, together with the guidance notes that are interleaved with the formal rules and that indicate the FSA's practice in relation to certain rules.

[33] The 2008 Act was enacted only to provide the regulatory authorities with temporary powers to deal with the Northern Rock and similar crises, before being superseded by the Banking Act 2009.

approximately US$1 trillion was made available to banks to allow them to recapitalise themselves and to fund their businesses.[34] Moreover, governments around the world signalled that the state would support systemically important banking and insurance institutions regardless of the carelessness that had caused their losses in the first place. This demonstrated the new socialisation of risk: that is, a movement of responsibility for private risks into the public sector. The bail-outs of those banks and the use of the money in part to pay bonuses to their employees indicated the continued privatisation of profit. It was a sort of inverted Keynesianism, in which public money was pumped into the economy and then drained directly into the pockets of private individuals (particularly in the form of traders' bonuses) and investment houses, and thus away from an economic stimulus for the real economy.

Second, the *functions* of banks are vital in the operation of the economy generally. The most significant aspect of banks' activities is the maintenance and operation of the banking system, electronic payment systems and so forth, which are essential to the operation of the economy. In this sense, the banks operate as utilities. Salaries and bills are not paid, credit facilities are not available, and so forth, unless the banks continue to function normally. Even welfare benefits and pensions in the UK are paid electronically. Therefore, every citizen and every small business, as well as any large corporate concern, is dependent on the banking system, just as it is dependent on the electricity grid, the water system, the telephone system, and so on. In this vital context, banks function effectively as public bodies.

Third, we must consider the *impact* of banks, investment houses and financial institutions of all stripes on the real economy. It was estimated before the financial crash in the Autumn of 2008 that the financial services industry in the City of London contributed approximately 20 per cent of the total tax take, with over 11 per cent of the total tax take after the crash in 2010.[35] These estimates included the employment taxes levied on the employees of financial institutions in London: it is notorious that those financial institutions themselves paid very little in tax as a percentage of

[34] Andrew Ross Sorkin, *Too Big to Fail: the Inside Story of How Wall Street and Washington Fought to Save the Financial System – and Themselves* (New York: Penguin, 2010).

[35] A study by PwC estimated that the financial sector contributed 11.2 per cent of the total tax take in the UK in the tax year 2009–10, after many redundancies and a downturn in the sector, with the income tax and other tax payments by their employees estimated to have been nearer to 20 per cent before the financial crisis began: PwC, *The Total Tax Contribution of UK Financial Services*, 3rd edition (London: City of London Corporation,

their total profits.[36] The assets held by the largest US investment banks in 2012 accounted for more than half of the entire GDP of the USA.[37] Most significantly of all, the fortunes of governments in the Western world are now dictated by traders in government bonds in finance houses. The democratically elected government in Italy was replaced by a technocratic government at the behest of economists in thrall to the financial system; and the governments of Greece, Ireland and Portugal were required formally to subject their financial policies to the diktat of supranational bodies such as the EU and the International Monetary Fund (IMF) as part of the terms of their bail-outs. Each of these countries saw differing levels of resistance to this anti-democratic displacement of legitimate power in favour of conduits for the views of financial institutions as to the way in which those governments should be run. What emerged was that the private sector came not only to dictate public policy and to constitute a huge part of every national economy, but it also came to displace democracy itself in the EU.

Fourth, we must consider '*financialisation*': a gradual process by which the use of financial instruments and private sector financial models has come to dominate public policy.[38] At the simplest level, the developed economies of the West are dependent on borrowing from private sector banks (principally using the issuance of government bonds to private institutional investors) to pay for their public programmes. In return, before the collapse of Lehman Brothers in 2008 and the near collapse of the global

2010), available at: http://217.154.230.218/NR/rdonlyres/68F49A7E-8255-415B-99A8-1A8273D568D9/0/TotalTax3_FinalForWeb.pdf (last accessed 24 May 2013).

[36] As evidence, see the HMRC updated guidance to banks on their responsibilities in relation to tax avoidance arrangements: HM Revenue & Customs, *The Code of Practice on Taxation for Banks: Updated Guidance on the Terms 'Promote' and 'Facilitate'*, available at: www.hmrc.gov.UK/thelibrary/taxation-banks.pdf (last accessed 24 May 2013).

[37] Bloomberg reported in April 2012 (citing 'central bankers' at the Federal Reserve in New York) that JP Morgan, Bank of America, Citigroup, Wells Fargo and Goldman Sachs together held US$8.5 trillion in assets, which was equivalent to '56% of the total US economy': David J. Lynch, 'Banks Seen Dangerous Defying Obama's Too-Big-to-Fail Move', Bloomberg, 16 April 2012, available at: www.bloomberg.com/news/2012-04-16/obama-bid-to-end-too-big-to-fail-undercut-as-banks-grow.html (last accessed 24 May 2013). Even immediately after the crash, it estimated that in 2010 the six largest investment banks had accounted for 63 per cent of US GDP. See also Kalle Lasn, *Meme Wars* (London: Penguin, 2012); Simon Johnson and James Kwak, *13 Bankers – The Wall Street Takeover* (New York: Pantheon, 2010).

[38] Hudson, *The Law of Finance*, para. 1–71ff.

financial system that followed, governments had used only light-touch regulation of financial institutions and had allowed many cross-border markets, such as that for derivatives, to operate beyond regulation.[39] More specifically, public programmes in the UK were reliant on funding through private sector models, such as the Private Finance Initiative and the Public–Private Partnership, that used financial instruments to procure funding for the building of hospitals and schools, transport infrastructure projects, and so on.[40] The private sector has therefore come to dominate significant aspects of public sector activity in the financial context. The current financial system requires that governments raise money from financial institutions through the issue of government bonds, and that the money supply can be controlled by the issue and repurchase of those bonds. The expectation is that these private financial institutions will disseminate those public funds into the economy more efficiently than direct government spending does by making that cash available to businesses and private individuals through the banking system.[41] As such, financial institutions operate both as lenders to government and as the instruments through which monetary policy is effected in the real economy. Thus, private sector bodies act willingly as agents of public policy.

In these ways, together with the use of public law by means of financial regulation to oversee their activities, financial institutions have come to occupy a public role, in spite of their ownership and their commercial activities being based on private law principles. Necessarily, the public and the private overlap here. What is important, as considered in the next section, is the manner in which principles of public law have come to inform the content of private law in this context of quasi-public activity.

[39] A process towards regulation (as yet incomplete) that is described in Alastair Hudson, *The Law on Financial Derivatives*, 5th edition (London: Sweet & Maxwell, 2012), Chapter 15.

[40] Alastair Hudson, *The Law on Investment Entities* (London: Sweet & Maxwell, 2000), Chapter 15.

[41] The machine broke between the summer of 2007 and 2009 when banks stopped lending to one another and consequently stopped lending into the wider economy. This event was known as the 'credit crunch' in the UK and briefly made the financial crisis appear to be a liquidity crisis rather than a solvency crisis. Thereafter, the quantitative easing initiatives in the Western world saw banks soak up the cheap money that was released by governments so as to replenish their balance sheets. They used this cheap money (issued at negligible interest rates) to hoard on their balance sheets and to fund financial speculation: too little of that money was used to stimulate private business.

3 Circumstances in which regulatory principles have been used to inform private law

A *The general elision of substantive law and regulatory principle*

There are contexts in which the courts are already beginning to use regulatory principles to decide whether or not case law tests are satisfied on any given set of facts.[42] The point is a simple one. Suppose you are a judge, you are deciding a case involving a complex financial instrument and it relates to a question of the substantive law. Perhaps the defendant is alleged to have dishonestly assisted in a breach of fiduciary duty (a common claim in recent years). You are required to decide, for example, whether or not the defendant has been dishonest.[43] The applicable test is whether or not the defendant has failed to act as an honest person would have acted in the same circumstances.[44] FSA regulation stipulates clearly the manner in which business is to be conducted between financial institutions and their customers. It is therefore open to the court to consult the terms of those regulations as a statement of suitable behaviour for a finance professional in those circumstances.

The case of *Bankers Trust International Plc.* v. *PT Dharmala Sakti Sejahtera (No. 2)*[45] is a good indication of how a judge might use financial regulation to develop principles of substantive law. In that case, an investment bank, which specialised in complex financial instruments built on complex mathematical formulae that it guarded jealously, sold interest rate swaps to an Indonesian financial institution that was not a recognised swaps dealer, although it was a market professional in general terms. Those interest rate swaps realised large losses when US interest rates changed. The Indonesian entity claimed that it had not understood that interest rate swaps that were not priced on US interest rates would lose value if US interest rates moved against them. This suggested a remarkable level of naivety for a financial institution, even one that did not deal in swaps in high volumes. The Indonesian entity argued that it had been

[42] See, e.g., *Investors Compensation Scheme* v. *West Bromwich Building Society (No. 2)* [1999] Lloyd's Rep PN 496; *Loosemore* v. *Financial Concepts* [2001] Lloyd's Rep PN 235; *Seymour* v. *Christine Ockwell* [2005] PNLR 39.

[43] The law in this area is considered in detail in Hudson, *The Law of Finance*, Chapter 27.

[44] *Royal Brunei Airlines* v. *Tan* [1995] 2 AC 378; *Barlow Clowes International Ltd* v. *Eurotrust International Ltd.* [2006] 1 WLR 1476; 1 All ER 333.

[45] [1996] CLC 518 (*Bankers Trust*).

subject to misrepresentations, that the enthusiasm that the investment bank's traders had shown for profiting from it indicated fraud, that it had been subject to undue influence, and so forth.

It was held by Mance J, in essence, that because the Indonesian entity fell to be classified under the regulations in force at the time as occupying a mezzanine category between expert market counterparties and inexpert customers, there had been no obligation on the investment bank to have explained to it all of the risks associated with these products. There was therefore no responsibility under the substantive law for the losses that had ensued. By analogy with those regulatory obligations, His Lordship held that there should be no obligation either at common law or in equity on the investment bank to compensate the Indonesian entity for the losses that it had suffered precisely because, in relation to the several applicable tests at common law and in equity, the investment bank could show that it had acted in accordance with its regulatory obligations and – by extension – that it should be taken to have acted suitably under the general law. Thus, by measuring the level of expertise of the Indonesian entity against the applicable code of financial regulation, Mance J was able to decide that the Indonesian entity was not an inexpert client and so Bankers Trust was not required to have treated it as such. If the Indonesian entity had been inexpert, then Bankers Trust would have been obliged to explain all of the risks associated with the swaps to its traders. Thus the decision on the substantive law flowed directly from the application of the financial regulations.

B *Eliding principles of substantive law and regulation in equity – dishonest assistance and unconscionable receipt*

The clearest example of this merger of regulatory and substantive law principles after *Bankers Trust*[46] is in relation to the law on dishonest assistance and on unconscionable receipt. In relation to dishonest assistance, the defendant will be liable to account personally to the beneficiaries of a fiduciary relationship if they have dishonestly assisted a breach of the fiduciary's duties. The principal issue in the decided cases has been whether or not the defendant has acted 'dishonestly'. The leading case in England on the meaning of 'dishonesty' has identified that liability turns on whether or not the defendant failed to act as an honest person would

[46] *Ibid.*

have acted in the circumstances.[47] In relation to financial transactions, it is suggested that there is good authority for the proposition that the court could, and should, look to the content of any regulations that dictate how the defendant should have acted. Somewhat differently, in relation to a claim for unconscionable receipt, a defendant would be liable to account personally to the beneficiaries of a fiduciary relationship if they had received property in circumstances in which there had been a breach of the fiduciary's duty and in which it was unconscionable for them to have done so. Principally, they will be taken to have acted unconscionably if they had the requisite knowledge of the breach of fiduciary duty.[48] Here, financial regulation would be a statement of the information that a regulated person acting properly ought to have known, for example as part of the regulatory know-your-client procedures[49] that financial institutions are required to conduct in relation to their customers.

The link between the substantive law and financial regulation in this context was established in *Cowan de Groot Properties* v. *Eagle Trust*.[50] In that case, Knox J held that the defendant would be held to have acted dishonestly if he had been guilty of 'commercially unacceptable conduct in the particular context'. His Lordship was therefore inviting us to identify what would have been acceptable conduct in the commercial market at issue and then to ask whether or not the defendant had failed to comply with such standards. This, it is suggested, is the root principle here. The standards for commercially acceptable conduct in financial markets are made clear in FSA regulation and the FSA's guidance notes, although there are unregulated markets where commonly understood standards of behaviour can nevertheless be identified through the initiatives of trade associations such as the International Swaps and Derivatives Association (ISDA)[51] or

[47] *Royal Brunei Airlines* v. *Tan* [1995] 2 AC 378; *Barlow Clowes International Ltd* v. *Eurotrust International Ltd* [2006] 1 WLR 1476 as summarised usefully in *Aerostar Maintenance International Limited* v. *Wilson* [2010] EWHC 2032 (Ch) by Morgan J. See also the line of cases culminating in *Starglade Properties Ltd.* v. *Nash* [2010] EWCA Civ 1314; [2011] Lloyd's Rep FC 102, permitting the Court to examine the characteristics of the defendant in so doing, much as financial regulation would require a classification of the parties' comparative expertise.

[48] *Bank of Credit and Commerce International (Overseas) Ltd.* v. *Akindele* [2001] Ch 437; *Charter Plc.* v. *City Index Ltd* [2006] EWHC 2508 (Ch); [2007] 1 WLR 26.

[49] Where the expression 'know your client' is a market colloquialism for the sort of obligations imposed by COBS.

[50] [1992] 4 All ER 700 at 761 (Knox J) (*Cowan de Groot*).

[51] See *Lomas* v. *JFB Firth Rixson Inc.* [2010] EWHC 3372 (Ch); [2011] 2 BCLC 120; Hudson, *The Law on Financial Derivatives*, paras. 2–08ff.

otherwise.[52] Thus a person who treats a customer in a way that would be contrary to conduct of business regulation as required by the FSA, would prima facie be acting unacceptably and would by extension be found to have acted dishonestly or unconscionably, as appropriate. This approach in *Cowan de Groot* has been approved in a number of subsequent cases.

So, in *Heinl* v. *Jyske Bank (Gibraltar) Ltd.*[53] it was considered, inter alia, that contravention of the norms of financial regulation would satisfy the test of knowledge (at that time applicable both to claims based on receipt and on assistance) in that the defendant would be deemed to have knowledge of anything that they ought to have known about if they had complied with the applicable regulation. Similarly, in the complex litigation in *Sphere Drake Insurance Ltd.* v. *Euro International Underwriting Ltd.*[54] there had been trading in the reinsurance market in the losses generated by the US workers' compensation insurance system. The claimant contended that the nature of this market and the arbitrage involved between a small group of traders dealing the same products in a circle was dishonestly represented to him. It was held that this was not a market in which a rational and honest person would have become involved had he understood the nature of the market. The source of the defendants' liabilities was the finding that no honest underwriter in the reinsurance market would have acted in this way in selling these products to these clients, who acted in ignorance of the true nature of the market.

A perception of proper market behaviour will thus guide a court in its decision as to the liability of trustees and investment advisers: it is not even necessary that such perceptions be embodied in formal regulation. Equally, it is suggested, formal regulatory principles should inform a court's perception of what would have constituted proper behaviour in financial markets even by non-regulated persons. In fact in *Manolakaki* v. *Constantinides*[55] Smith J held that such an indication of honest behaviour need not be in formal regulatory principles, but rather could be divined from guidance notes circulated by a regulator (in that case, the Law Society). The courts may interpret the parties' contract as expressly

[52] It is common for parties to litigation to seek expert evidence as to the common practices of financial markets for exactly this sort of claim: on which, see *Lomas* v. *JFB Firth Rixson Inc.* [2010] EWHC 3372 (Ch); [2011] 2 BCLC 120.

[53] [1999] Lloyd's Rep Bank 511 at 535 (Colman J).

[54] [2003] EWHC 1636 (Comm). The bank's principal concern was as to its obligations to assist the police in relation to the contents of a bank account that it had reason to believe had been obtained by fraud, its obligations under criminal law not to 'tip off' its client, and its potential civil law liabilities to its client if it froze the account.

[55] [2004] EWHC 749.

excluding the inclusion of regulatory standards,[56] although the parties may not exclude a number of regulatory obligations (if they are regulated persons), such as the obligations imposed on them under conduct of business regulation.[57]

C *The general ignorance of financial regulation in the case law*

It is interesting that the courts have frequently sought to seem commercially aware while developing principles that are in direct contradiction with financial regulation. For example, in *Polly Peck International Plc.* v. *Nadir (Asil) (No. 2)*[58] Scott LJ held that when a central bank exchanged money that had been taken from a company in breach of a fiduciary duty, and thus received the money, there was no positive obligation on the 'banker' to inquire into the circumstances by which that payment came to be made unless there was something inherently suspicious about it. Similarly, in *Macmillan Inc.* v. *Bishopgate Investment Trust Plc. (No. 3)*,[59] Millett J held somewhat more memorably that account officers in banks are not detectives and therefore that they are not expected to identify payments as being procured in breach of a fiduciary duty, unless there was something about the circumstances that ought to have put that account officer on notice. However, the Money Laundering Regulations 2007 and s. 328 of the Proceeds of Crime Act 2002 do impose positive obligations on banks and their employees to investigate the source of payments made through it by its customers. While Scott LJ and Millett J were concerned not to impose positive obligations on banks that would impose burdens on them that they had not voluntarily assumed, the direction of travel of financial regulation and the criminal law has been in exactly the opposite direction for many years. The law of finance does identify a need for banks to bear a large number of obligations as a result of their sensitive place within our economic life, and the possibility of the banking system being used to fund or facilitate the activities of terrorist or other international criminal organisations.[60]

[56] *Clarion Ltd.* v. *National Provident Institution* [2000] 1 WLR 1888 (Rimer J).

[57] COBS, 2.12R. On which, see Hudson, *The Law of Finance*, para. 10–18.

[58] [1992] 4 All ER 769; 2 Lloyd's Rep 238.

[59] [1996] 1 WLR 387; 1 All ER 585.

[60] In 2012 it was revealed that accounts operated by HSBC in Mexico and in the USA had been used by drug cartels to launder billions of dollars through the New York banking system, and that accounts operated by Standard Chartered Bank had been used to

There is nothing unchallengeable about case law principle. Rather, the principal benefit of a common law system is the ability to redirect its principles when circumstances require it. The radical changes in our approach to international crime and to financial risk in the twenty-first century suggest that it is time for the libertarian drift in the case law to be realigned in parallel with public policy as expressed in financial regulation, so as to create a consistent stream of law and regulation governing financial institutions.

At present, too often private law and financial regulation fail to operate towards any common goal in the UK. While, as was considered above,[61] financial regulation and private law are typically aimed at very different jurisprudential goals, nevertheless it is suggested that ultimately they ought to be directed at a coterminous goal of ensuring the welfare of customers using the financial system, whether by protecting them from abusive practices or maintaining the stability of the financial system beforehand, or by providing them with remedies in the event of such abusive practices after the event. Currently, the law of finance is generally kept a secret among the illuminati of specialist practitioners who service investment banks (especially in relation to complex instruments such as derivatives transactions). One effect of the financial crisis was to put derivatives contracts back into the public eye and back into the courtroom. As interest rate swaps are now being sold to small businesses, it is no longer possible to argue that an elite clientele should be serviced exclusively by an elite cadre of lawyers who have been initiated into the private arts of finance law.[62] Instead, derivatives contracts must be subject to the ordinary law and understanding their workings must be possible for any lawyer: that means that these sophisticated financial markets must be open to view. For the first time there is to be systematic regulation of derivatives markets in the European Union.[63] Consequently, by way of example, there is a common goal in ensuring that the processes of creating and selling complex financial instruments are regulated properly

break sanctions laws in the USA prohibiting payments being made by or on behalf of the government of Iran.

61 As is argued in detail in Chapter 3 of Hudson, *The Law of Finance*.

62 See what promises to be only one in a long line of cases ('Banks set aside £700 million for swaps scandal', *Financial Times*, 31 January 2013) on mis-selling interest rate swaps to small businesses in *Graisley Properties Ltd* v. *Barclays Bank Plc* [2013] EWHC 67 (Comm), and see also *Grant Estates Ltd.* v. *Royal Bank of Scotland* [2012] CSOH 133.

63 European Market Infrastructure Regulation (EMIR) (648/2012/EU) creating an obligation to clear trades through 'central counterparties' and an obligation to report transactions to 'trade repositories'.

and that the private law ramifications of failing to do so are remedied appropriately. This is the principal context in which law and regulation can, and should, combine effectively. However, there are others. The unwieldy process of bringing expensive litigation against the squadrons of lawyers available to financial institutions deters retail customers and small businesses from commencing litigation. Meanwhile the FSA and the Financial Services Ombudsman, both of which were created by the FSMA 2000, are too often prepared to reach settlements of claims with banks (which have been brought by large numbers of disgruntled customers through the statutory ombudsman system) that are contrary to the interests of customers.[64] Again, a commonality of purpose would enable the ultimate goal – the welfare of the customer and of the financial system as a whole – to be achieved. The next section considers how regulatory principles and common law principles can interact fruitfully.

D *Looking to regulatory principles when establishing a common law duty of care*

In relation to the establishment of a duty of care at common law, there have been cases in which the courts have examined the regulatory obligations of regulated firms when deciding whether or not that firm should be treated as owing its client a duty at common law.[65] It was held in *Seymour* v. *Christine Ockwell*[66] that regulatory principles could inform the finding of a common law duty – in that they 'afford strong evidence as to what is expected of a competent advisor in most situations' – although they would not necessarily be dispositive of the matter in themselves because they are merely 'evidence' of what is required to demonstrate that that common law standard of care had been breached. In *Loosemore* v. *Financial Concepts*[67] the Court considered the appropriate conduct in business

[64] A good example of this phenomenon was the agreement reached between the FSA and banks, which had been the subject of hundreds of thousands of complaints by customers who had been mis-sold payment protection insurance, that all claims by customers that crossed an arbitrary threshold of £10 million would be denied (presumably leaving them to be brought under private law) regardless of their merits or the surrounding circumstances: as reported in *The Independent*, 2 February 2013.

[65] See, e.g., *Investors Compensation Scheme* v. *West Bromwich Building Society (No. 2)* [1999] Lloyd's Rep PN 496; *Loosemore* v. *Financial Concepts* [2001] Lloyd's Rep PN 235; *Seymour* v. *Christine Ockwell* [2005] PNLR 39.

[66] [2005] PNLR 39 at [77]; citing with approval *Lloyd Cheyham & Co. Ltd.* v. *Eversheds* [1985] 2 PN 154.

[67] [2001] Lloyd's Rep PN 235.

regulation in formulating the terms of the common law duty. Therefore, evidence of what constituted 'reasonable' behaviour, for example, can possibly be supplied by the appropriate regulations. This has the happy advantage of creating a seamless law of finance in which a defendant's regulatory obligations are complemented by a liability to make compensation, injunction against breach of those obligations, and so forth under private law.

However, the common law will not always release its grip on its legal principles so very easily. So, in cases such as *Beary* v. *Pall Mall Investments*[68] it has been suggested that the common law should continue to apply its traditional principles and not simply rely slavishly on regulatory principles. A different slant on this issue arose in *Gorham* v. *British Telecommunications Plc.*[69] where a financial institution sold pensions advice in such a way as to cause the claimant a loss. The institution argued that its liability under the tort of negligence should be limited to the narrow obligations owed by it under pensions regulation at the time. The Court of Appeal held that the obligations would not be limited to the institution's regulatory obligations when the common law duty of care extended further. Therefore, the position would appear to be that the courts will consider the extent of a defendant's common law duties by reference to the defendant's regulatory obligations, although the defendant will not be able to limit its obligations by relying on a narrower set of obligations in the appropriate context if the common law imposes a higher requirement.

It is true that financial regulation changes in practice too frequently at present to establish itself as a solid jurisprudential set of ideas and concepts comparable to the substantive law. Even the presence of the FSA Markets Tribunal, which rules on questions of infractions of the FSA Handbook, has failed to develop such a body of principle. Nevertheless, it is suggested that the regulatory obligations of financial institutions constitute a justification for imposing liability on them for unreasonable or unsuitable behaviour because that was behaviour in which that institution ought not to have indulged given its obligation to obey its regulatory duties. What must be acknowledged, however, is that many common law courts in recent years have failed to consider or understand the regulatory context in which the defendant was acting when mis-selling complex

[68] [2005] EWCA Civ 415.
[69] [2000] 1 WLR 2129.

financial instruments to their customers. Those cases are considered in the next section.

4 Failures to consider financial regulation and their effect in cases involving mis-selling of derivatives

A *The difference that a synthesis of public and private could make*

That there are differences between private law and financial regulation in practice is self-evident from a survey of the case law, beyond the discussion of the differences set out above. Many judges fail, and some seem to refuse, to consider the regulatory context in which a financial institution operates when considering its common law and equitable liabilities. What emerges, however, is a sense that if the judges had considered the selling financial institution's regulatory obligations, then they might have come to different conclusions about the duties that it should have been deemed to owe to the customers who sued it. By overlooking the positive regulatory obligations imposed on the defendants in mis-selling and other cases, the courts have typically been left to decide on a common-sense basis whether or not they consider that the regulated bank ought to have owed a particular duty to its client. Usually the English courts refuse to recognise the existence of a positive obligation on a financial institution that it had not accepted as part of the contracting process, even though that institution would have borne exactly that obligation under the conduct of business and other regulation applicable to it at the time.

The cases considered in this section all relate to allegations of mis-selling of complex financial products (principally derivatives) to inexpert clients. The clients were businesses or private investors who nevertheless had neither particular experience nor expertise in the derivatives that were sold to them. What is interesting is the way in which the courts restrict themselves to private law norms of contract and tort, which lead them, for the most part, to find that the clients ought to have protected themselves during the contract negotiation process or to have been more diligent in their risk assessment. What the courts fail to do is to consider the norms of financial regulation, which impose positive obligations on banks to do exactly the sort of things that the judges considered that common law did not require them to do. Among those positive, regulatory obligations are (to repeat principles outlined above) conduct of business obligations to identify the client's level of expertise as part of a process of identifying only suitable investment strategies for the client; acting in the client's best interests[70] and to procure the best terms available for the client[71] (which I have argued elsewhere is effectively a fiduciary obligation);[72] and communicating with clients in a way that is fair, clear and not misleading.[73]

If these public regulatory norms had been recognised by the courts, then it could have been understood that the banks bore much more extensive obligations to their clients than the courts were otherwise prepared to admit. It could have been argued that the contracts between the parties were unenforceable because the financial institutions had failed to deal with their customers in a way that was required by regulation, such as explaining the risks associated with the products to those customers, or identifying products that were suitable for customers of their level of sophistication. In essence, what is suggested below as part of contract law theory is that it could be accepted that the financial institutions were effectively unduly influencing their customers into buying products that they did not understand.

B The possibility of using regulatory standards to decide liability under the substantive law

There is a group of cases in which the claimant client was alleging a form of unsuitability in the way in which financial instruments were sold to it. In each case, as outlined above, the defendant financial institution was regulated further to COBS, which required it to identify the client's level of expertise and so forth. These are all positive obligations that the selling institution is required to perform regardless of the terms of their contract.[74] The approach that could have been taken was that of Mance J in *Bankers Trust*,[75] considered above, when His Lordship looked to the Bank of England London Code (the relevant legislation at the time) for a statement of how a bank, acting appropriately, should have acted.

The point here is that it is open to the courts to borrow from financial regulation in establishing whether or not a defendant has crossed the line into unsuitable conduct – whether the applicable test in the general law in those circumstances turns on proof of reasonableness, honesty or good

70 COBS, 2.1.1R. 71 COBS, 11.2.1R.

72 Hudson, *The Law of Finance*, para. 10–44, by reference to the dicta of Asquith LJ in *Reading* v. *R* [1949] 2 KB 232 at 236 that a fiduciary relationship arises where the defendant acts in the claimant's affairs and where the claimant 'relies on the defendant to procure for the plaintiff the best terms available'.

73 MiFID, Art. 19(2). 74 COBS, 2.1.2R.

75 [1996] CLC 518.

conscience. However, as emerges from the cases in the next section, it has been more common in recent cases for the courts to overlook the regulatory standards. It is not clear whether this is because counsel are not leading arguments based on a synthesis of regulatory requirements with common law principles, or whether this is due to a judicial reluctance to do so, or whether this is simply due to an innate habit among English High Court judges of looking at the facts of a case at first instance through the lens of the common law. It is suggested in the discussion to follow that the last of these is the most likely answer, albeit that judges at first instance in England have tended not to apply the common law tests with sufficient assiduity to the facts in front of them.

C Caveat emptor or a duty to act in the client's best interests?

What is clearly observable at first instance in recent cases in England and Wales relating to the liability of banks for mis-selling complex financial products is that the judges spend the vast bulk of their long judgments analysing and finding the facts of the case before them, but very little time setting out the detail of the applicable case law principles in line with the doctrine of precedent. The bulk of the decisions are therefore predicated on a commonsensical appraisal of which obligations the parties had voluntarily assumed by reference to the documents giving expression to their transactions, with a survey of the facts otherwise to see whether any general common law (principally tortious) duties had otherwise been breached. What the judges do not do in these cases is to consider what the financial institutions' positive regulatory obligations were, and in consequence what the common law would dictate that they ought to have done in practice in relation to their clients as a result.

By way of example, in *Titan Steel Wheels Ltd.* v. *Royal Bank of Scotland Plc.*[76] Steel J delivered a, frankly, bad-tempered judgment that was impatient with the claimant's arguments in general and that complained about the unexpectedly long duration of the trial. Here, a bank had sold derivatives (in the form of forward rate agreements intended to control the client's foreign exchange risk) to a manufacturer of specialist wheel products. It was found as a fact that the client could have benefited from a much simpler product (which would also not have generated it such large losses) and still have controlled its foreign exchange liabilities. And yet Steel J chose to blame the client for prioritising a desire for profit (through

[76] [2010] EWHC 211 (Comm) (*Titan*).

the use of derivatives) in creating the transaction, instead of allocating responsibility to the bank for failing to identify its client's level of inexpertise (by reference to COBS) and to explain the risks associated with those derivatives clearly. Indeed, the bank had sought effectively to exclude its liabilities by asserting in its documentation that it was acting only on an 'execution' basis, by which it purported to offer no advice to the client,[77] in spite of its obligations under COBS, which could not be excluded by contract. Moreover, there was evidence that the bank's employees had in fact sought to convince the claimant's finance director of the benefits of the more complex derivative product, which suggested that the bank had gone beyond a mere execution function. More particularly, however, Steel J lapsed into the common law mindset of treating the client as being free to contract 'as a private person' as it saw fit, and then as being beholden to the terms of that contract, instead of recognising the regulatory context in which that transaction ought to have been understood, given the client's inexpertise in complex financial products.

If COBS had been observed strictly, then the risks of the products would have been explained to the finance director clearly and in consequence those transactions might have been executed on different terms, or the finance director might have decided not to enter into them at all. The regulatory approach is to protect the consumer to the limited extent of providing them with sufficient information to enter into a contract on an informed basis. Particularly significantly, the regulations require the financial institution to act 'in the client's best interests'.[78] This is important because it may require that the financial institution must act, to put the matter in private law terms, as a fiduciary.[79] COBS prevents regulated firms from seeking to exclude their obligations by contract. Moreover, if the client suffers a loss, then the fiduciary would be taking a profit on the opposite side of the transaction from which that loss resulted. This, it is suggested, constitutes a conflict of interest between the seller's fiduciary duties and its personal desire to take a profit from the transaction.[80]

[77] An execution function involves merely taking a client's order and completing it without offering any investment advice.

[78] COBS, 2.1.1R.

[79] See Hudson, *The Law of Finance*, para. 10–17.

[80] The provisions of COBS are clear that these obligations cannot be excluded by contract. What is more difficult to know in the absence of decided cases is whether or not these obligations constitute fiduciary obligations in all circumstances. The argument is made in Hudson, *The Law of Finance*, para. 5–26ff. that regulatory obligations such as the obligations to obtain best execution and to act in the best interests of the client should be

Nevertheless, the common law approach is that of *caveat emptor* – let the inexpert buyer of financial products beware – even though conduct of business regulation is supposed to offer them a shield in the form of a right to be treated suitably, to have the risks explained to them in accordance with their level of expertise, and to have their best interests observed by the professional seller of those products. In this vein, the Court of Appeal held in *Peekay Intermark Ltd.* v. *Australia and New Zealand Banking Group Ltd.*[81] that the directing mind of Peekay was at fault for a failure to notice discrepancies in the several documents faxed to him by the defendant bank over time in relation to the sale of derivatives products. It was held, in reliance on much older contract law authority,[82] that the claimant company was bound by the terms of a contract that had been signed on its behalf by its directing mind. Therefore, it could not set the contract aside, nor recover damages from the bank.

At first instance,[83] it had been held that the bank was liable in damages because a lack of communication between its traders and its client account manager had meant that the account manager, who had ordinarily been the liaison between client and bank, had herself failed to appreciate that the nature of the product had changed radically. The change had not been brought consciously to her attention, nor to the client's attention. In the witness box, the account manager, explaining her feelings after having been presented with the discrepancies in the various documents, expressed herself as having been surprised at the changes to the nature of the product that had been sold to the client and said that 'this has got wrong written all over it'.

Nevertheless, the Court of Appeal overlooked these failures on the part of the bank to deal appropriately with its customer by reference to the common law standards. More significantly, perhaps, it overlooked completely the explicit regulatory obligation on the bank to communicate with its customer in a way that was clear, fair and not misleading, as well as the further obligations to identify the client's level of expertise and to act in that client's best interests.

Similarly, the judgment of Gloster J at first instance in *JP Morgan Chase Bank* v. *Springwell Navigation Corporation*[84] (which was later affirmed by

interpreted as being fiduciary duties, which in turn cannot be excluded by contract as required by COBS.

81 [2006] EWCA Civ 386.

82 Culminating in *L'Estrange* v. *Graucob* [1934] 2 KB 394.

83 [2005] EWHC 830 (Comm).

84 [2008] EWHC 1186 (Comm) (*Morgan Chase*).

the Court of Appeal)[85] considered the decision of a wealthy man, acting on behalf of a family investment company, who expanded the company's investment portfolio beyond securities and currency trading into derivatives. It was held that the client was experienced in investment activities, even though he had not dealt in derivatives previously, and that he probably would not have heeded any warnings as to the risks associated with investing in derivatives. Therefore, it was held that the bank bore no liabilities at common law for the losses that were caused to the company by these investments in derivatives. Her Ladyship's judgment did not consider the regulatory obligations on the bank as to client classification, the best interests principle, the best execution principle, and so forth. Because the bank did not conduct the full regulatory client appraisal (and no evidence of such an appraisal is referred to in a lengthy judgment), it cannot be known whether or not the claimant company's directing mind would have been swayed by a warning as to the risks it faced. This was the purpose behind the regulations: to require that warnings be given to clients who required them. Whereas the regulations imposed positive obligations on the bank to explain the risks to its client, Gloster J relied solely on common law concepts of liability, including the need for the parties to have voluntarily assumed any positive obligations in relation to one another. Similarly, the Court of Appeal did not look closely at the regulatory obligations of the bank in relation to conduct of business and know-your-client rules to decide whether or not in that context the bank had acted appropriately. Instead, there is a single phrase in the Court's judgment finding that '[the bank] fulfilled its obligations', without more analysis than that.[86]

The Court of Appeal in *IFE Fund SA* v. *Goldman Sachs International*[87] took a similar approach by looking only at the documentation effected between the parties for the defendant's obligations. The defendant had clearly expressed itself as accepting no responsibility for the content of a prospectus marketing securities for which it was the lead manager. That prospectus contained inaccuracies that the claimant contended had

[85] *Springwell Navigation Corporation* v. *JP Morgan Chase Bank* [2010] EWCA Civ 1221. Reliance was also placed on *Trident Turboprop (Dublin) Ltd.* v. *First Flight Couriers Ltd.* [2008] EWHC 1686, relying ultimately on *Henderson* v. *Merrett Syndicates Ltd.* [1995] 2 AC 145.

[86] *Springwell Navigation Corporation* v. *JP Morgan Chase Bank* [2010] EWCA Civ 1221 at [125] (Aikens LJ).

[87] [2007] EWCA Civ 811; [2007] 2 Lloyd's Rep 449.

induced it into making an unfortunate investment. It was held that the defendant bore no liability because it had explicitly refused to accept any liability from the outset, in spite of its role as lead manager in marketing those securities. In that case, however, all of the parties were market professionals and therefore it could have been held, by reference to the claimants' level of expertise in relation to securities of that type and the issuer's credit worth, that the defendant would have been under no obligation in the conduct of business regulations to have explained the risks to the claimant.

In reaching these decisions, the courts in all of these cases have focused almost exclusively on the documentation between the parties as being expressive of all of the obligations owed between them, in ignorance of any further, regulatory obligations that were also imposed on them. As I have described the point elsewhere:[88]

> The heart of the matter is this. The common law, in particular as exercised through the agency of Commercial Court judges, takes the view that the documentation entered into between parties is decisive of the relationship between them, but that fails to acknowledge that in financial transactions there is a context beyond the traditional concerns of the common law with holding parties to the terms of the agreements which they have signed: in financial transactions the regulated parties are bound by conduct of business regulation out of which they are not permitted to contract. What is remarkable (and familiar) about the transcripts of the telephone conversations which are recorded by Steel J in his judgment [in *Titan*] is just how incoherent they are in a context in which the seller is obliged to make communications to its customer under COBS which are 'fair, clear and not misleading'. The courts did not consider these regulatory requirements in assessing the standards expected of a financial institution in this context.

The purpose of financial regulation is to protect customers from these dangers. Nevertheless, the English common law has yet to accept that these financial regulations constitute a new dimension in contract law as it applies to financial transactions because it imposes positive obligations on regulated firms and those firms may not contract out of those obligations. In essence, this line of cases culminating in the decision in *Titan*,[89] was decided in complete ignorance of the obligations imposed on the defendant by COBS.

[88] Hudson, *The Law on Financial Derivatives*, para. 7–59.
[89] [2010] EWHC 211 (Comm).

D *Other approaches are possible*

A different approach from the common law approach is, however, possible. In *Morgan Stanley UK Group* v. *Puglisi Cosentino*[90] the claimant bank sold a complex derivative to the defendant. The bank was held to have been in breach of the conduct of business regulations then in force in advising the defendant to enter into such a transaction as an inexpert private customer. The documentation that was faxed to the customer identified him as an 'expert customer' despite the fact that he was a retail customer, despite the fact that Morgan Stanley had not dealt with him before (which should have prompted closer know-your-client inquiries), and despite the fact that he had not dealt before in the precise forms of complex derivatives and repo products that had been recommended to him by Morgan Stanley.[91] Longmore J held that the defendant would not have entered into the transaction if he had received proper advice and an appropriate risk warning in accordance with the conduct of business regulations. In consequence, by reference to the applicable regulatory standards that required such advice and warnings to be given, His Lordship held that the contract could not be enforced. This case also illustrates how important it is that the procedure by which documentation is provided to the customer and signed by the customer is conducted appropriately. Longmore J referred to the regulatory concept of 'suitability' in his judgment in much the same way that Mance J had approached the question in *Bankers Trust*.[92]

E *The apparent end of the doctrine of precedent in complex finance law cases*

As was mentioned above, when deciding complex cases in finance law, the High Court judges have tended to lose sight of the detail of the case law authorities that they are supposed to follow, in addition to their tendency to overlook useful parallels in financial regulation. This is true of *Morgan Chase*[93] and *Titan*[94] in particular. Another good example of a judge becoming lost in complex and precise facts in front of him arose

[90] [1998] CLC 481.

[91] There were also questions about his ability to speak English, even though the seller did on occasions provide Italian speakers with whom he could communicate, let alone his ability to understand the products themselves in whatever language.

[92] [1996] CLC 518. [93] [2008] EWHC 1186 (Comm).

[94] [2010] EWHC 211 (Comm).

in the judgment of Hamblen J in *Cassa di Risparmio della Repubblica di San Marino SpA* v. *Barclays Bank Ltd.*[95] That case related to allegations of fraud in the selling by Barclays of a very complex series of CDO and CDS products[96] (which were intended for on-sale to its own customer base) to a small financial institution organised in San Marino. The claimant could only argue fraud because Barclays had excluded its liability by contract for all other default. While these products were initially rated at AAA, they were later downgraded to 'junk' status, and so the claimant sought to recover its loss from Barclays. Ultimately, Hamblen J held that none of the allegations of fraud had been proved on these facts. What is interesting is that, in relation to a claim for fraud, the leading case of *Derry* v. *Peek*[97] is mentioned in only three paragraphs in a judgment of 566 paragraphs. His Lordship preferred to consider each individual allegation of misrepresentation in turn.

These High Court cases have tended to focus far more on recent judgments than on leading cases. They have tended not to trace the legal principles back to leading cases such as the decision of the House of Lords in *Derry* v. *Peek* so as to apply the precise principles established in the highest authorities to the facts before them. There are, for example, many more references made by Hamblen J to the judgment of Gloster J in *Morgan Chase*,[98] which was not even a case exclusively on fraud, than to the principal authority on the law on fraud in *Derry* v. *Peek*: there were seventeen extensive references to the former case and only four passing references to the latter. The loss of respect for the doctrine of precedent is impoverishing finance law by removing much of the certainty from it and by removing observance of centuries of careful jurisprudential development. More to the point, it is more difficult to find that there was no fraud in the *Derry* v. *Peek* sense of that term when constructing this CDO product if one considers the precise dicta of Lord Herschell, who held that an allegation of fraud would be made out if 'a false representation has been made … recklessly, careless whether it be true or false'.[99] The Barclays employees who constructed and marketed this CDO product could certainly have been said to have been 'careless' in their descriptions of it and its profitability, even if they had not been actively 'dishonest'. It is a shame, therefore, that

[95] [2011] EWHC 484 (Comm) (*Cassa*).

[96] See Hudson, *The Law on Financial Derivatives*, para. 7–65 for a detailed description of these products.

[97] (1889) 14 App Cas 337.

[98] [2008] EWHC 1186 (Comm).

[99] (1889) 14 App Cas 337, at 368.

Hamblen J did not consider that carelessness could have been sufficient to make out fraud on a close reading of *Derry* v. *Peek*, instead of tending to assume that it meant conscious, intentional dishonesty as His Lordship appeared to do.

The use of exclusion of liability clauses (as in *Cassa*[100]) in financial contracts is an important issue generally. In *Camerata Property Inc.* v. *Credit Suisse Securities (Europe) Ltd.*[101] Andrew Smith J considered an exclusion of liability clause that provided that a financial institution would not be liable for any loss suffered by its client as a result of following its investment advice except in the event of its gross negligence. The transaction at issue related to a note that had been issued by Lehman Brothers and on-sold by the bank to the claimant. The question arose as to whether or not the bank had been grossly negligent in failing to predict the failure of Lehman Brothers in September 2008, even though the claimant client had contacted the bank several times in the wake of the Bear Stearns collapse in March 2008 and thereafter to express its concerns about financial markets generally and Lehman Brothers in particular. It was held that the bank had not been so negligent as to be grossly negligent, and that, in any event, even if it had been in relation to the credit worth of Lehman Brothers, then, nevertheless, that did not affect the original advice that had been given to the claimant on selling the note. What is interesting, however, is that under the terms of COBS, a selling institution may not exclude its obligations under those regulations[102] and in consequence it could be held that under the common law it should be impossible for the banks to exclude their liabilities for obligations that they are required to perform under the regulations, such as communicating in a way that is not misleading, achieving best execution for the client and acting in the client's best interests.

While Smith J did consider the know-your-client inquiries that the financial institution made of the claimant, as required by regulation, the information that the bank gleaned from those inquiries was not considered by Smith J to have been decisive of either the client's level of expertise or the bank's obligations to that client. This is peculiar because the client had identified a low level of risk tolerance among its investment preferences, and yet the bank recommended high-risk investments. Nevertheless, His Lordship considered that the individual was 'clearly intelligent and

[100] [2011] EWHC 484 (Comm).
[101] [2011] EWHC 479 (Comm); [2011] 2 BCLC 54.
[102] COBS, 2.1.2R.

financially astute'[103] and that he had showed a lively interest in the investments, even though he had expressed himself on the bank's questionnaires to be interested only in conservative investments. This was taken to support a finding that the bank should not bear liability for the claimant's losses. However, on these facts it appears that the bank's relationship manager paid very little attention to the information that was given by the client on the know-your-client questionnaires. It could have been found that the contract between the parties should have been interpreted both in terms of the client's avowed preference for only low-risk investment and also of the bank's regulatory obligations to observe their client classification findings when recommending investments to that client.

5 What financial regulation can learn from private law

This chapter has focused thus far on the ways in which public standards of financial regulation can be absorbed into private law. This section identifies two contexts in which private law mechanisms can inform the development of financial regulation: first, the way in which the doctrine of undue influence can re-energise conduct of business regulation, and, second, the way in which the central principle of 'integrity' should be developed akin to an equitable standard.

A A broader principle of undue influence

The generally overlooked judgment of Lord Denning in *Lloyds Bank Ltd.* v. *Bundy*[104] suggested, in reliance on *Tate* v. *Williamson*,[105] that the actions of a bank that is in possession of all of the knowledge about a banking product on which the inexpert client relies, in a situation in which the client necessarily reposes confidence in the bank as a result, may well result in a finding that the bank had unduly influenced its client. Moreover, the court may even rewrite parts of the contract. As Lord Denning described the principle:

> The fundamental rule is that if the parties have made an agreement, the Court will enforce it, unless it is manifestly unfair and unjust; but if it be

[103] [2011] EWHC 479 (Comm); [2011] 2 BCLC 54 at [114].
[104] [1975] QB 326.
[105] (1866–67) LR 2 Ch App 55, 61. See also *Tufton* v. *Sperni* [1952] 2 TLR 516.

> manifestly unfair and unjust, the Court will disregard it and decide what is fair and just.[106]

The power to impose what is just in these cases could be taken to be power to interpret the contract so as to make it compliant with the seller's regulatory obligations either by setting the contract aside *in toto*, or by ignoring exclusion of liability language in it that contravenes those regulations. The principle was expressed by His Lordship more fully in the following passage:

> Gathering all together, I would suggest that through all these instances there runs a single thread. They rest on 'inequality of bargaining power'. By virtue of it, the English law gives relief to one who, without independent advice, enters into a contract or transfers property for a consideration which is grossly inadequate, when his bargaining power is grievously impaired by reason of his own needs or desires, or by his own ignorance or infirmity, coupled with undue influences or pressures brought to bear on him by or for the benefit of the other. When I use the word 'undue' I do not mean to suggest that the principle depends on proof of any wrongdoing.[107]

Importantly, then, this principle regularises inequality of bargaining power and rebalances the effect of the client's ignorance – just as financial regulation could be thought to do in relation to consumer protection. This principle, it is suggested, offers a much more aggressive basis of principle for the use of financial regulation. Ultimately, regulation is aimed at preventing advantage being taken of one party by another party with greater information. The cornerstone of financial regulation is the provision of information to clients. Once those clients have been given all of the necessary information, then they are free to make their own mistakes.[108] Nevertheless, there is an active assumption here that the court will intervene so as to set aside transactions in which the seller of a product benefits from an unfair advantage over the buyer. This level of interventionism is anathema to free market economists,[109] but in a world that is now acquainted with the LIBOR-fixing scandal and the wholesale mis-

[106] *Lloyds Bank Ltd.* v. *Bundy* [1975] QB 326; referring to *Akerblom* v. *Price* (1881) 7 QBD 129 at 133 (Brett LJ).

[107] *Ibid.*, at 339.

[108] This is the heart of securities regulation, for example. See Financial Services and Markets Act 2000, s. 87A, which requires that all 'necessary information' in relation to an issue of prescribed types of securities be given to potential investors by way of a prospectus.

[109] See, e.g., Milton Friedman, *Capitalism and Freedom* (University of Chicago Press, 1962).

selling of PPI products by high street banks in the UK – both of which have resulted in fines of billions of pounds in the aggregate being imposed on banks by the FSA – there is a genuine need for financial regulation to be proactive in the defence of retail customers and for private law to support that initiative by setting aside inappropriate contracts that were formed on the basis of inequalities of bargaining power and insufficient provision of information to the customer.

B The development of an equitable concept of 'integrity'

The core principle of financial regulation in the UK, having been present since the Securities and Investment Board self-regulatory principles in effect before 2000, is a requirement that regulated firms act with 'integrity'. The *Principles for Businesses* Rulebook[110] in the FSA Handbook[111] presents this requirement of integrity as its first principle. The remainder of the rulebook is to be interpreted in accordance with that principle. However, financial regulation still has no developed understanding of how the idea of 'integrity' is to be understood.

By contrast, English equity is predicated on a principle of 'conscience',[112] which, it is suggested, is similar to that of integrity. Both codes of rules are deontological in that they purport to set out a high-level moral principle by reference to which individual cases are to be decided.[113] Much financial regulation created under the Lamfalussy methodology[114] at the level of the European Union was created in the first place on the basis of high-level principles that the individual Member States could implement into their national law by whatever mechanism was most effective, and always on the basis that they could make their domestic legislation more stringent

110 Financial Services Authority, *Principles for Businesses (PRIN)* (UK Financial Services Authority) (PRIN), available at: http://fsahandbook.info/FSA/html/handbook/PRIN (last accessed 24 May 2013).

111 Financial Services Authority, *The Full Handbook*.

112 See, e.g., *Westdeutsche Landesbank Girozentrale* v. *Islington London Borough Council* [1996] AC 669.

113 In truth, equity, with its adherence to the doctrine of precedent, is probably best understood as a combination of an overarching moral principle with a consequentialist mechanism for allowing decided cases to influence the central moral principle; that is, the idea of conscience is best understood by reference to the decided cases that have provided contextual applications of the idea of conscience.

114 As explained in the Lamfalussy Report: Committee of Wise Men, *Final Report of the Committee of Wise Men on the Regulation of European Securities Markets* (Brussels, 15 February 2001), available at: http://ec.europa.eu/internal_market/securities/docs/lamfalussy/wisemen/final-report-wise-men_en.pdf (last accessed 24 May 2013).

than the EU statutory principles. Latterly, the Larosière Report[115] for the EU has meant that financial services legislation will, in future, be created by directly enforceable EU Regulations. However, what equity indicates is significant is that domestic UK financial regulation, which has a deontological core in the form of the PRIN regulations, needs a clear jurisprudence as to the meaning and application of the concept of 'integrity' in these contexts. The absence of guidance notes or any commentary from the FSA itself in this context does not help matters.

6 Conclusion

In many senses, the very idea of a rigid boundary between public and private is very old hat. To take one example, the Wikileaks revelations have laid bare many minor secrets of many states. After all, the existence of security services and spies demonstrates that the state has its own private information. The law on super-injunctions and the new tort of 'privacy' have redrawn the ability of private law to keep private matters private. At the same time, the most tedious aspects of many people's private lives (perhaps as they seek public notoriety) are documented on Twitter, on internet blogs and so on. In this new virtual world, what is public and what is private?

Less well known than these movements in the tectonic plates of private and public is the steady acquisition of the public space by financial institutions. Not just in terms of their dreadful size as they become too big to fail and too big to regulate, but also in terms of their control of economic policy and their ability to displace the democratic process in Italy, Greece, Ireland, Portugal and so on. The legal treatment of banks is a combination of public law (through financial regulation) and private law transactions between bankers and customers of various stripes.[116] In consequence, the law of finance requires a synthesis between those two legal sources.

There is a sense of the word 'synthetic', which is taken to suggest something unnatural, forced and inauthentic. And yet, most of life is made up of combinations of elements, compounds and useful interactions

[115] Jacques de Larosière *et al.*, *The High-Level Group on Financial Supervision in the EU Report* (Brussels, 25 February 2009), available at: http://ec.europa.eu/internal_market/finances/docs/de_larosiere_report_en.pdf (last accessed 24 May 2013).

[116] It was argued in Beatson, 'Financial Services and Fiduciary Duties', 58 that 'any separation of regulatory rules and "ordinary" law could be an impediment to the achievement of a clearly understood body of law': a task which is taken on throughout Hudson, *The Law of Finance*.

between different substances. There is a school of legal scholarship that is concerned with separations of law into different elements by way of taxonomy. The trouble with such taxonomies is that they value difference and separation over blending ingredients together. They insist on difference where maybe none exists. In consequence, it is difficult to adapt to social change when such change cuts across those taxonomic boundaries. The world, however, is infinitely more complex than these taxonomies. A taxonomy is simply an attempt by a human mind to order an understanding of the world. But that does not stop the world from turning. The law of finance that is slowly emerging in the wake of the financial crisis is just such a synthesis of public and private elements into a coherent whole, with the ultimate aim of keeping the economic world turning.

9

Discerning public law concepts in corporate law discourse

ANITA K. KRUG

1 Introduction

Tell many an academic that you are a scholar of corporate governance or that your research interests centre on corporate law, and, in return, the suggestion will likely be made, at some point, that your work falls within the realm of 'private law'. Indeed, among both scholars and policy-makers there remains a widely shared, and apparently stubborn, assumption that corporate law and its myriad permutations are firmly anchored in the realm of private law, alongside a group of other fields considered to be on the private law side of the public law/private law dichotomy. Accordingly, corporate law is grouped with the fields of tort law, property law and contract law and, therefore, placed in contrast with constitutional law, administrative law and criminal law, and other classic public law fields – the latter so labelled because these fields of law govern the relationship between the state, as the representative of the 'public', and its subjects. The basis for this classification is not particularly difficult to discern. However, its persistence *is*, particularly given global legal and regulatory developments in the past eighty-plus years.

Corporate law is private law, in the sense that, much like the relationships between contracting parties and between tortfeasor and victim, corporate law concerns itself with the core relationships of business enterprises, which are, in turn, relationships among private parties – managers (directors and officers) and owners (shareholders). We might even say that corporate law is a special variation of contract law, one that – in the United States, for example – has as its starting point the default rules of the corporate 'codes' (statutes) established locally in each US state. Corporate law, however, stretches beyond the boundaries of private law into the realm of public law. There are a couple of perspectives from which this is so – one fairly evident, the other less so. The former perspective focuses on the myriad ways in which the state has come to regulate corporations with a view towards achieving public policy goals. Lest there be any doubt, moreover, this regulation is fundamentally *corporate* law, imposed on corporations by virtue of their status as such (albeit the publicly traded variety) rather than based on the particular activities certain corporations might pursue. This public policy-based regulation encompasses disclosure requirements in connection with, among other things, a corporation's solicitation of shareholder votes; procedural requirements relating to tender offers; and requirements that certain board committees meet specified independence thresholds.

The less-evident perspective encompasses a more subtle, and arguably more interesting, basis for the 'blurring' of the public law/private law distinction in corporate law and stems from the increasingly transnational character of corporate law. In particular, as some comparative corporate governance scholars have observed, there has been an ongoing global (and implicit) 'conversation' among jurisdictions regarding the nature and content of the laws, rules, practices and ideologies ('norms and rules', for simplicity) of corporate governance. That is, corporate norms and rules have been transplanted from jurisdiction to jurisdiction and imitated among jurisdictions as they have evolved over time.[1] In light of that perceived phenomenon, there has arisen the suggestion that jurisdictions may shape their norms and rules in a manner that causes them to 'converge' on the dominant system of corporate governance. A subtheme of that suggestion is the notion that convergence is desirable, in that it tends to centre on those norms and rules that are most efficient, however 'efficiency' might be measured. These considerations, more broadly, have made their mark on corporate law scholarship. The possibility and implications of convergence have been prevalent topics among corporate governance scholars in the past few decades – a circumstance that should not be particularly surprising, given the importance of the corporate structure as an efficient means of organising production.

However, even amidst the sporadic clamouring for increased oversight of corporations and their securities offerings and governance structures – most recently, in the wake of the global financial crisis – scholars and policy-makers have continued to regard relationships among shareholders, officers and directors as determined primarily by intra-corporate private choices and to see relationships between regulated firms and their clients as distinctly private relationships governed by private law norms.

[1] See Franklin A. Gevurtz, 'The Globalization of Corporate Law: The End of History or a Never-Ending Story?' (2011) 86 *Washington Law Review* 475, 485–94.

And, despite the revelation that the evolution of corporate law may have global implications, including implications for the efficiency of global organisation of economic production, the scholarly literature to date generally has not focused on the public law implications of corporate law convergence or re-evaluated the ongoing cabining of corporate law on the private law side of the dichotomy. Accordingly, there has been no concerted focus on how evaluating global trends in corporate governance structures, and reaching normative conclusions about them, almost unavoidably confronts tensions between, on one hand, corporate law's private law foundation and, on the other hand, policy objectives driving public law discussions.

This chapter calls into question these long-standing perceptions about corporate law, arguing that, in the corporate law context, the line between public and private has blurred as corporate governance structures have come to be shaped not only by affirmative regulation of corporations but also (and especially) by the influence of worldwide trends and developments. The chapter first discusses the basis for the prevalent assumption that corporate law is private law. Next, it delves into the scholarship regarding the prospect of global convergence of corporate law, including the assertion that convergence is all but inevitable, and the numerous counterarguments. Then the chapter evaluates how notions of public law and private law inform discussions on corporate law convergence. Towards that end, it suggests that public law conceptualisations highlight the hope of convergence – the prospect that law that shapes the global economic framework might be law that produces greater efficiency and well-being – while private law conceptualisations show the challenges of convergence – that is, the obstacles to uniformity presented by divergent economic histories and by *modus operandi* that may, however, be efficient within their own particularised spheres of norms and actors. Finally, the chapter proposes an alternative conception of the distinction between private law and public law, and, more broadly, raises the question of whether the public law/private law distinction should remain meaningful in the corporate law context or otherwise.

2 Corporate law as private law

As others have pointed out, there are a number of ways in which we might think about the public law/private law dichotomy.[2] Randy Barnett, for

[2] See, e.g., Randy E. Barnett, 'Four Senses of the Public Law–Private Law Distinction' (1986) 9 *Harvard Journal of Law & Technology* 267.

one, has compiled a four-part taxonomy. First, there is a distinction based on the harm that is perceived or, more particularly, the 'standard being applied to individual conduct'.[3] That is, whereas some conduct may be seen to cause a public harm or offend publicly shared notions of decency (possessing child pornography and releasing pollutants are examples), other conduct causes private harm by affecting particular individuals or groups (for example, negligently failing to repair a staircase on which someone is injured).[4] Regulation of the first category of harm establishes a public law cause of action; regulation of the second category establishes a private law cause of action; and, of course, conduct that causes both public and private harms (murder or theft of personal property, for example) is simultaneously criminal and tortious and thereby creates both public law and private law causes of action.[5] Second, Barnett discerns a distinction based on whether the harm caused may be redressed by public authorities (such as prosecutors or regulatory authorities) or by the private persons who suffered the harm.[6] Logically, if only public authorities may bring suit, the cause of action is public in nature; if private parties may do so, the cause of action is private in nature.

Barnett's third distinction is based on the subject of regulation. In particular, regulation that governs either the relationship between public authorities and private parties or the internal workings of public authorities may be viewed as public law, while regulation that establishes the rights and obligations of private parties vis-à-vis one another may be thought of as private law.[7] Based on this distinction, criminal procedure, administrative law and constitutional law are public law subjects, and property law, tort law, contract law, corporate law and the law of trusts and estates are private law subjects.[8] Finally, Barnett observes, there is a possible distinction relating to 'the proper institutional framework for applying and enforcing legal regulation'.[9] In this conceptualisation, public law refers to 'monopolistically or "publicly" provided legal regulation', while private law refers to non-monopolistically or privately provided legal regulation.[10] So, for example, such fields as evidence law and civil procedure may be deemed public law in that they '[govern] the administration of government institutions'.[11] However, we might be able to think of them as private law to the extent they establish the procedures of arbitration panels or other private institutions.[12] As discussed below, this framework provides a helpful point of departure for thinking about the

[3] *Ibid.*, 268. [4] *Ibid.* [5] *Ibid.* [6] *Ibid.*, 269. [7] *Ibid.*, 270–1.
[8] *Ibid.* [9] *Ibid.*, 271 [10] *Ibid.* [11] *Ibid.* [12] *Ibid.*, 272.

appropriate and evolving categorisation of corporate law, both in terms of fitting corporate law within that framework and in terms of building on the framework.

In the United States, it may seem that public law found its way into the field of corporate law early on.[13] Specifically, the US ('federal') government has, for decades, supplemented local corporate codes[14] with significant regulatory obligations, at least for those corporations that are 'public', in the sense that they are registered with the Securities and Exchange Commission (SEC) and regulated under the US Securities Exchange Act of 1934. Among these obligations are requirements that corporations comply with specific rules in connection with carrying out their management activities and oversight functions, communicating with shareholders and upholding shareholder rights. That regulation characteristically mandates customer and shareholder disclosures or specified contractual provisions, which we might otherwise expect would be left to private ordering, and specifies procedures for addressing conflicts of interest within the firm, which we might otherwise expect would be left to internal decision-making procedures. Not all of these measures may, at first blush, seem to have public law implications, to be sure. For example, requirements that corporations provide certain types of disclosures to shareholders or follow certain procedures in connection with producing and auditing their financial statements certainly are consistent with conceptions of private law, to the extent they do no more than affect the rights and obligations of private parties vis-à-vis one another.

Public law pervades US regulation of corporations not so much through the substantive requirements for ordering corporate relationships – though, to be sure, some of those requirements involve the government as well, such as requirements that public corporations file most of their shareholder disclosures with the SEC – but, rather through the mechanisms through which rules of corporate behaviour are enforced. To the extent that a public corporation fails to comply with its federally imposed obligations, whether by failing to disclose information to shareholders, to follow tender offer procedures, or to make the appropriate information available to the SEC, depending on the particular statute

[13] The tandem bodies of US regulation (consisting of more obligatory federal rules and more enabling local rules) highlighted in this section are presumably unique to the US federal system.

[14] 'Local corporate codes', as used in this chapter, refers to the corporate codes of the fifty US states. This chapter does not refer to these codes as 'state' corporate codes, however, because it uses 'state' to mean 'government' or 'governmental', whether at the local or national level.

or regulation at issue, federal regulators are typically authorised to bring enforcement measures against the offending entity. Often that authorisation is to the exclusion of actions brought by shareholders – parties to the private relationship that is the corporation – who may have been in some way harmed by the corporation's regulatory failures. In that sense, state involvement in corporate governance establishes and polices a relationship between public authorities and the corporation, a relationship that public authorities enforce in the public interest. Here we have corporate law as public law.

That observation is not particularly interesting, however, at least to the extent that the distinction between public law and private law should tell us something important about the nature of any body of law that might be characterised as falling within one camp or the other. Why have the two labels come to have lasting significance? For any particular field of law or type of regulation, as we have seen so far, the labels may tell us something about the bases for the regulation's existence (deterring and remedying either public harms or private harms), the means of its enforcement (allowing for either public causes of action or private causes of action) or its subject and substance (regulating either private parties' relationships with the state or their relationships with each other). However, the distinction's meaning arguably stems not from simply helping us label fields of law and modes of regulation but, rather, from its elucidating the role that any particular field of law or regulation plays in defining individuals' relationships with the state and, beyond that, ordering the political community. If that might seem unduly esoteric, it is perhaps useful to think more concretely about criminal law. By both defining conduct that is socially unacceptable and placing enforcement and punishment in the hands of the state, criminal statutes set forth a state-sanctioned code of conduct, an infrastructure of acceptable behaviour. By establishing what is permissible behaviour, it also makes known what is expected behaviour – both by the state and its subjects. Criminal law in that sense is constitutive and completes a task that private parties necessarily could not through their discrete relationships with one another.

The question, then, is whether we can say something similar about national regulation of corporate entities, which otherwise live and die pursuant to the local corporate codes, which, for their part, are generally thought to be enabling rather than restrictive. To be sure, local corporate codes, by virtue of their (largely default) governance rules and imposition of a (largely unwaivable) fiduciary duty of loyalty on boards of directors, go some way towards ensuring that management remains accountable to shareholders. By contrast, national regulation is premised on public policy – in particular, the judgment that regulation is necessary to promote efficiency or to counter a market failure perpetuated by power and information imbalances between corporate management and shareholders. That is, such regulation is predicated on the determination that, as to publicly traded companies, more protection is needed and gaps need to be filled. But there is nothing particularly fundamental or constitutive about this supplemental regulation, which is, indeed, primarily (and merely) gap-filling in nature. In other words, state involvement and state enforcement notwithstanding, national corporate governance rules seem not to play the role they perhaps should in order to push 'corporate law' over the line – or at least part way over the line – separating private law from public law, at least not in any particularly meaningful sense.

3 Multilateral convergence

There is a second way in which corporate law may be thought to have affinities to traditionally public law fields, which derives at least in part from the ongoing (and increasing) globalisation of corporate activities and transactions among business enterprises. Globalisation has made a deep imprint on corporate governance reform and scholarship as a result of its implications both for the relative performance of national economies in international capital markets, products markets and labour markets, and for the competitive success of business enterprises as they pursue their activities in those markets. For one thing, political decision-makers have had to contemplate the performance of local firms against the performance of firms globally and, towards that end, have been compelled to evaluate their local corporate governance regimes against alternatives, looking to whether the local regime adversely affects local firms' global competitiveness.[15] In addition, decision-makers for firms expanding into the global arena and seeking to attract capital in public markets have had to evaluate whether local corporate governance structures are conducive to attracting investors, on the premise that investors may prefer investing in firms whose governance structures they understand and are comfortable with.[16]

15 See Jeffrey N. Gordon and Mark J. Roe (eds.), *Convergence and Persistence in Corporate Governance* (Cambridge University Press, 2004), pp. 1–2.

16 *Ibid.*, p. 2.

With globalisation of economic activity becoming an increasingly important factor in corporate governance questions, comparative analysis of corporate governance structures has become a focal point of reform proposals, and an inevitable question has emerged: will global economic or political forces, or combinations of them, lead to a global convergence of corporate governance structures? Not surprisingly, then, on and off throughout the past decade, the prospect of 'convergence' of corporate norms and rules has been the subject of academic discussion, including as to whether convergence will occur, the means through which it might occur, the forces that might impede it, the norms and rules around which it likely would occur, and whether those norms and rules are the 'best' or most efficient ones.

Among the most prominent voices in this debate, Henry Hansmann and Reinier Kraakman argued in 2001 that governance practices and ideologies (if not actual laws and regulations) in some of the more advanced economies were converging on a particular model of corporate governance.[17] According to them, that model emphasises the primacy of shareholders and the notion that management's role is to promote shareholders' interests.[18] Moreover, convergence around this 'shareholder-oriented' model can be seen as the result of a number of factors, including the failure of alternative models,[19] the increasing political and corporate influence of a 'public shareholder class', and, perhaps most important, the workings of competitive forces that have laid bare the model's virtues.[20] The third factor might strike one as the most significant to the extent one also assumes that any convergence of corporate governance structures that might occur would be – or should be – efficient convergence. That assumption seems to be shared by the authors, who conclude that inefficient convergence is unsustainable: because it arises when transnational competition reinforces market failures and flawed political institutions,[21] it cannot endure either because political processes will ultimately intervene or because those affected by it will become motivated to redesign their relationships with corporations so as to make them more

[17] See Henry Hansmann and Reinier Kraakman, 'The End of History for Corporate Law' (2001) 89 *Georgetown Law Journal* 439.

[18] It also holds that creditors, suppliers, employees and other corporate stakeholders are protected not through any role in corporate governance but, rather, through contractual and regulatory rights. See *ibid.*, 440–1.

[19] Such other models include manager-oriented, labour-oriented, state-oriented and stakeholder-oriented models. See *ibid.*, 443–9.

[20] *Ibid.*, 452. [21] *Ibid.*

efficient.[22] And as much as *inefficient* convergence cannot last, neither can efficient *divergence* survive for very long, simply because of the forces of globalisation, which ultimately reveal the efficiencies of standardised rules in the global marketplace.[23]

As one might imagine, however, other scholars have questioned the existence and desirability of corporate law convergence. These scholars sound the theme of caution because, for them, myriad factors counsel that global adoption of a particular general model of corporate governance is unlikely and, indeed, that divergence is and will remain the norm.[24] For example, convergence sceptics Lucian Bebchuk and Mark Roe have argued that 'path dependence' – the notion that 'the corporate structures that an economy has at any point in time are likely to depend on those that it had at earlier times'[25] – perpetuates diversity among global corporate governance models. For Bebchuk and Roe, initial ownership structures and early corporate norms impede convergence on particular norms and rules.[26] However, they contend, this ongoing diversity of corporate governance structures is efficient, at least on a local scale.[27] That is to say, for any particular jurisdiction (for example, one that embraces block shareholding and illiquid equity markets) adopting an alternative structure (such as one based on dispersed shareholding and liquid equity markets) would entail costs sufficiently high to override any efficiency benefits arising from the new structure.[28] Beyond those costs, moreover, corporate governance structures endure as a result of the self-interested behaviour of corporate management and interest groups and possibly others who benefit from the status quo and, therefore, stand to lose under an alternative governance regime.[29]

[22] *Ibid.*, 467 ('[S]hareholders, managers, workers, and voluntary creditors either have acquired or are acquiring a powerful interest in efficient corporate law').

[23] *Ibid.*, 466.

[24] As just one example, Brian Cheffins argues that we cannot count on convergence because its occurrence, whether around the 'Anglo-American' model of dispersed share ownership and liquid markets or around other models, is contingent upon myriad political, ideological and legal factors. For example, a country's approach to bank regulation and trade policy, as well as its 'ideological orientation', may influence the structure of its corporate governance and the configuration of its system of ownership and control: Brian R. Cheffins, 'Corporate Governance Convergence: Lessons From Australia' (2002) 16 *Transnational Lawyer* 13, 13–15, 41–3.

[25] Lucian Arye Bebchuk and Mark J. Roe, 'A Theory of Path Dependence in Corporate Ownership and Governance' (1999) 52 *Stanford Law Review* 127, 129–31.

[26] *Ibid.*, 54. [27] *Ibid.*, 155–6. [28] *Ibid.*

[29] See *ibid.* For example, corporate managers of a firm owned by dispersed shareholders might seek to prevent the firm from moving to a structure with concentrated ownership,

Reinhard Schmidt and Gerald Spindler analyse convergence from a perspective reminiscent of Bebchuk and Roe's, introducing the concept of complementarity. For them, a system of corporate governance (and, for that matter, *any* system) comprises 'elements' that may or may not be complementary to one another.[30] Elements are complementary if, taken together, they augment their value and reduce their costs in terms of the system's overall operation.[31] According to Schmidt and Spindler, elements comprising a corporate governance system include the structure and function of the stock market, the nature of market regulation, board structure and composition, and 'the distribution of ownership and residual decision rights'.[32] That systems reflect complementarity means that it is difficult to reconfigure a local system or, certainly, to adopt elements of systems that may be more efficient in the abstract, since those changes may upset the balance among elements of the local system.[33] Changes, particularly more sweeping ones, are difficult also because it is costly to 'switch' from the local system to one that is more globally embraced.[34] Beyond that, complementarity exists among the elements of the legal, social and economic system surrounding the corporate governance structure.[35] Accordingly, it may be that elements of that more encompassing system would need to change as a result of changes to the local governance system; however, determining which elements are at issue presents its own challenges.[36]

John Coffee appears to agree that ideology, culture and politics may hinder convergence around any particular approach to corporate governance, noting that politics and history constrain and direct the evolution of corporate norms and rules. Accordingly, corporate norms and rules are not something that corporations can necessarily contract for, or otherwise elect at their discretion.[37] Coffee therefore rejects viewing corporate governance through the neoclassical economic lens employed by strong convergence proponents and, more to the point, also rejects the notion

out of a desire to maintain their status and independence – even if the change would be efficient. See *ibid.*, 130. Similarly, in a jurisdiction whose rules 'favor professional managers and protect diffused ownership structures', managers will use the political power arising from their favoured status to seek the continuation of those rules. See *ibid.*, 131.

[30] See *Ibid.* [31] *Ibid.* [32] *Ibid.*, p. 121. [33] *Ibid.*, 119–21.

[34] *Ibid.*, pp. 115–19. Schmidt and Spindler refer to these costs as 'switching costs'. See *ibid.*

[35] *Ibid.*, 124 [36] *Ibid.*

[37] John C. Coffee, Jr, 'The Future as History: The Prospect for Global Convergence in Corporate Governance and its Implications' (1999) 93 *Northwestern University Law Review* 641, 646.

that corporate norms and rules are determined through competition and the forces of efficiency.[38] However, in Coffee's view, national securities laws may foster convergence – at least functional convergence, if not also formal convergence.[39] Specifically, Coffee points to the dominant structures of corporate governance: 'market' systems, which are characterised by liquid trading markets and dispersed share ownership, and 'blockholder' systems, which are characterised by control by wealthy families and 'insider' groups and thin-trading of shares outside of the controlling block.[40] That market systems have taken hold in English-speaking countries, including the United Kingdom and the United States, Coffee suggests, is a result of the particular legal rules in those countries, which aim to protect small, dispersed shareholdings.[41] Moreover, convergence on market-oriented systems is likely to occur as foreign firms increasingly participate in those systems in various ways.[42]

Most recently, Franklin Gevurtz has expressed doubts about convergence, observing that global corporate norms and rules are always in transformation and flux, forming a pattern of ongoing convergence and divergence and then convergence once again, as jurisdictions respond to divergent crisis events and other stimuli, as responsive measures are imitated and transplanted, and as global governance regimes circle in around one norm and then another.[43] In addition, according to Gevurtz, although competitive processes may further efficiency, it may be the case that convergence around less efficient norms and rules can be relatively stable over time, given that convergence may also be a product of customs and 'fads' and our tendencies to mistake factors that might be correlated with efficient institutions as factors that *cause* efficient institutions (the 'endogenous variables' problem).[44] Gevurtz also notes that even where

[38] *Ibid.* (noting also that, '[f]rom this perspective, the prediction follows that the increasing globalization of the world's economy will inexorably compel at least large-scale firms to adopt a common set of structural characteristics').

[39] *Ibid.*, 705–6.

[40] *Ibid.*, 645. See William W. Bratton and Joseph A. McCahery, 'Comparative Corporate Governance and the Theory of the Firm: The Case against Global Cross Reference' (1999) 38 *Columbia Journal of Transnational Law* 213, 218.

[41] Coffee, 'The Future as History', 647. Absent those rules, 'shareholders' primary protective response to the risk of exploitation is to invest only through the protective medium of a substantial block': *ibid.* at 647. Coffee summarises his position thus: 'strong regulation permits "weak" owners, while "weak" regulation necessitates "strong" owners': *ibid.* at 648.

[42] *Ibid.*, 650.

[43] Gevurtz, 'The Globalization of Corporate Law'.

[44] *Ibid.*, 500–5.

convergence might seem to be taking place, the analysis generally has failed to employ the appropriate measurement tools. Convergence should be measured by evaluating different jurisdictions' answers to the most important questions of corporate law. These 'tough policy questions', he observes, are whether the driving principle of corporate law (even in a shareholder-oriented model) should be managerial accountability or managerial authority and whether corporate law is best structured as a system of mandatory rules or as a web of permissive, default rules that parties may modify contractually.[45] Under this critique, once the tough policy issues become the focus of convergence analysis, we can see that, in fact, very little convergence has occurred after all – and, indeed, is not likely to occur.[46]

It is difficult to glean any overarching themes or conclusions from these diverse analyses of convergence and divergence within corporate law. Indeed, the literature seems both scattered and overlapping as to each of the facets of 'convergence' noted above, which is hardly surprising given the myriad lenses – economics, politics, law, biology, psychology, or a combination thereof – through which different scholars have viewed the subject. For example, Hansmann and Kraakman's neoclassical argument regards global competition as an unavoidable force of convergence, while Bebchuk and Roe's path dependency approach emphasises the historical and localised factors that challenge those forces – and, accordingly, the analyses reach very different conclusions about the prospect of convergence. However, both approaches assume that the emergence or persistence of corporate governance structures is a product of efficiency considerations (at a local level, for Bebchuk and Roe, or at a global level, for Hansmann and Kraakman).[47] Moreover, since Bebchuk and Roe's focus on concentrated versus diversified ownership structures seems to take as a given a system 'oriented' around share ownership, both their and Hansmann and Kraakman's arguments seem to agree, if only implicitly, on the primacy of the shareholder-oriented model.[48] From that perspective, the two arguments may be more closely aligned than, say, Bebchuk and Roe's path dependency, on one hand, and Schmidt and Spindler's complementarity, on the other, as the latter entertains the pos-

[45] *Ibid.*, 511–20. [46] *Ibid.*

[47] See Gordon and Roe, *Convergence and Persistence in Corporate Governance*, p. 13.

[48] *Ibid.*

sibility of not only convergence but also (indeed, especially) *inefficient* convergence.[49]

That there are questions – as well as conflicting answers – about whether convergence is taking place, whether it is normatively desirable, and whether it produces efficient norms and rules does not detract from the importance of the conversation. If anything, that circumstance ratifies the conversation's importance – and possibly portends heightened attention to it. That result seems appropriate. Globalisation and the massive wealth that may be created or destroyed through the movement of capital across national boundaries must have some implications for the shaping of corporate governance structures. Convergence analysis provides a way of thinking about the evolution of norms and rules that arguably is taking place as corporate and political institutions adjust to a world order characterised by fewer and more porous boundaries.

4 Corporate law as public law

Although scholars have devoted time and energy to thinking about corporate law convergence and its implications for efficiency in governance structures and the capital markets, they have not stepped back to consider what the discussion might mean for the traditional characterisation of corporate law as private law (and the associated assumption that corporate law is of little relevance to public law concerns). It is no surprise, then, that the scholarship on convergence has not yet addressed the ways in which conclusions about convergence and its desirability derive from tensions between the private law grounding of corporate law, on one hand, and policy-oriented considerations that often inform discussions about public law objectives, on the other. However, that analysis is important because, as the following discussion elaborates, it suggests the fundamental role of corporate law in the global community's creation of a common framework of economic interaction and the implications of that role for policy-making processes – and, indeed, for the public law/private law distinction itself.

One way to begin thinking about how the public/private dichotomy informs convergence analysis is to consider more carefully a number of questions, suggested in section 3, that elicit considerations often associated

[49] According to Schmidt and Spindler, inefficient convergence might emerge as a result of 'myopic' and 'chaotic' decisions made in times of crisis: Schmidt and Spindler, 'Path Dependence and Complementarity', 124–6.

with public law discourse. The first question is whether convergence is normatively desirable for global economies. As the discussion above indicates, there are competing answers to that question based on, among other things, the nature of any particular incidence of convergence. For example, if the 'multilateralisation' of norms and rules through convergence reduces efficiency in the aggregate, then one might conclude that convergence is not a desirable trend, even if, in some jurisdictions, those multilateral norms and rules have replaced less efficient ones. By contrast, given the same facts, one might alternatively conclude that multilateralisation remains desirable, despite reductions in aggregate efficiency, to the extent that the prevailing norms and rules better serve the interests of constituencies such as employees and creditors or further objectives such as environmental protection or upholding international human rights norms. Or, as another example, if multilateral norms and rules generally reduce the efficiency of intra-border transactions but, on the whole, increase efficiency in cross-border transactions, then one might conclude that convergence is undesirable, to the extent that intra-border transactions play a more significant role in meeting the needs of persons in lower socioeconomic strata. Regardless of what conclusion one might reasonably reach on this question, the process of addressing it requires, in a sense, making reasonable attempts to determine what constitutes social or public goods and what types of rules and expectations help foster them. At the least, it requires thinking beyond the terms of privately negotiated relationships among managers, shareholders and other corporate constituencies.

A second question implicating public law considerations is whether converging norms and rules are necessarily efficient ones. As we have seen, there are competing ways of thinking about this question. For example, the notion, endorsed by Hansmann and Kraakman, among others, that competitive forces are the drivers towards convergence would appear to support the conclusion that any convergence that occurs is efficient convergence. An associated conclusion is that, to the extent that some convergence on inefficient rules may occur, those rules will ultimately be replaced by more efficient rules as competitive forces continue to play out. The detractors in this analysis, by contrast, observe that, in fact, convergence can occur – and maintain stability – even when not efficient, as a result of a number of seemingly plausible factors. For example, jurisdictions may find the corporate law trends of the day too alluring and important, perhaps because the trends arose in the aftermath of corporate scandals or otherwise obtained broad public support, to realise they may be wanting in efficiency.[50] Then there is the concern about endogenous variables already noted, whereby jurisdictions adopt particular rules on the basis that the rules are perceived to produce certain efficiencies that are in fact produced by unrelated factors.[51] Alongside those factors is the prospect of rent-seeking behaviour – that is, the notion that, regardless of the efficiencies or inefficiencies of a particular rule, convergence on that rule may occur simply because it is in the personal interests of those with the most influence in determining what the rule will be.[52] However, despite the competing answers to the question, the analysis required to reach one of those answers is an analysis of macroeconomic forces, microeconomic motivations and adaptive processes, which once again would seem to take us some distance from discrete default rules of local corporate statutes.

A third question that resonates in public law themes is the question of what 'efficiency' means in the convergence context, given a number of possible measuring sticks and an astounding array of competing global interests. Perhaps most obviously, 'performance' comes to mind as a measure of efficiency. For example, convergence that arises as a result of widespread adoption of the more popular (but not necessarily more effective) corporate governance practices or as a result of mistaking correlation for causation is not efficient convergence because that sort of convergence has been shown to have no impact on corporate performance. Certainly, however, the analysis needs to delve more deeply than that. As an initial matter, how is 'performance' to be measured? Basing the measurement on stock price, profits or revenues are possibilities that come to mind. Furthermore, assuming there is agreement on that point, over what period of time is that measurement most relevant or useful? Beyond those questions, and perhaps more interesting, is the question of what, exactly, it is about certain rules and modes of governance that produce better performance over the particular period of measurement. One possibility might be that certain rules create disincentives for managers to engage in self-interested activities or to focus on anything but achieving more profit and higher stock prices. Another consideration might be that certain rules lead potential shareholders to be more comfortable investing in a firm, whether because those rules appear to mitigate risk or because they seem to encourage better board decisions regarding distributions, fairness among shareholders or share transfer rights. Once again, regardless

[50] See Gevurtz, 'The Globalization of Corporate Law', 496–500.

[51] *Ibid.*, 500–505. [52] *Ibid.*, 505–507.

of what answers we may debate or settle on, the discussion centres on some of the more fundamental questions of economics, if not psychology, and takes us beyond the four corners of best practices in the boardroom.

In short, discussions about convergence (and its desirability and effects) show the relevance of public law concepts to corporate governance structures. Reaching answers to the questions of what advantages or benefits convergence can bring about, what norms and rules are most efficient and, therefore, should be dominant in the convergence process, and how we should reach conclusions as to either of those previous questions requires a process evocative of that required in evaluating formulations of norms and rules in other public law fields. When, for example, we think about the rules a polity should set forth in the name of preserving individual freedom, we think about balancing intrusions with overall individual freedom – to what extent do we limit some individuals' freedom in the name of protecting others' well-being? We also consider the meaning of 'freedom' – does it require only negative restrictions on state action or does it also require affirmative obligations for the state to maintain certain conditions or provide certain goods? Moreover, we put some thought into how best to measure freedom – might wealth or health or some measure of happiness be a reliable proxy?

There are many other examples. When we think about the circumstances under which police officers may search the boot or glove compartment of a car they have pulled over on the motorway, we think about questions of state power and upholding individuals' constitutional freedoms. When we think about how we can best assure that harms to society are redressed, we think about the economics and incentives (or lack thereof) for private parties to take the necessary actions and the need for (and possible inefficiencies from) the state's filling the void. In other words, we think about public law questions from an encompassing or, some might say, 'universalist' perspective. From that perspective, considerations of legal tradition and precedent are at best secondary to considerations of normative fairness and common objectives. Or, to put it another way, corporate law takes us into a 'public law' mode of thinking when its formulation breaks away from the sort of 'bottoms-up' evaluation that local corporate codes heretofore have countenanced, positioned as they are as an iteration of common law traditions and practices (albeit perhaps amended or updated over the years).

Of course, the questions surrounding the possible convergence of corporate norms and rules centre not only on policy-oriented considerations but also on possible obstacles to convergence, which, for their part, emanate from the pragmatic and descriptive, rather than the normative and universal. Perhaps the most important question is whether we might reasonably expect multilateral convergence of norms and rules to come about over time or whether, to the contrary, divergence is as likely as convergence or, from still another perspective, whether the indicia of convergence are not sufficiently apparent at this stage to draw conclusions on the matter. Considering these questions would seem to necessitate delving into the very aspects of corporate law that have placed it on the private law side of the line for so long. Local corporate codes emerged to provide default structures for private relationships, and their coverage has generally been relatively local, reflecting in each jurisdiction the history of the corporate legal person and commonly accepted governance practices. The traditions, cultures and practices that informed different corporate codes naturally resulted in an array of statutes that reflected divergent approaches to management–shareholder relationships. And the differences the codes embodied were likely all the more pronounced to the extent they emerged within economies on varied trajectories of development.

Also pointing to the role of private law concepts are questions as to whether the norms and rules of corporate governance can ever really 'converge' – questions that have as their unstated subtext the notion that, in fact, convergence is impossible, and hopes and expectations to the contrary are misguided. That suggestion relies on a further claim, namely that the emergence, development and evolution of corporate governance structures are driven by factors beyond efficiency or transnational policy objectives. Moreover, the circumstances cannot be otherwise because these factors, which include customs and accepted modes of interaction, create intractable tensions among different jurisdictions' approaches to corporate law. Accordingly, given the contexts in which corporate codes developed and the purposes corporate codes have served, the development of corporate norms and rules does not appear to be guided by any particular articulation of public harms to be avoided or public benefits to be achieved.

That is one implication of Gevurtz's contention that a stable convergence is unlikely to occur around the 'two fundamental questions' that arise in addressing the 'central' and 'insolvable' issue in corporate law, which is protecting shareholders from those in control.[53] As suggested in section 3, Gevurtz identifies one such tension as that regarding 'whether

[53] *Ibid.*, 512.

corporate law protections of minority shareholders should be mandatory or left for the participants to work out'.[54] He notes that the convergence regarding this tension is precluded as a result of myriad 'ideological, political and practical' factors that reflect differing assumptions about individuals' rationality, market efficiency and governments' ability to curtail rent-seeking by interest groups and government participants, as well as divergent philosophies regarding the inherent worth of individual autonomy.[55] A second such tension is that between 'the authority and accountability of those in charge of the corporation'.[56] Here, convergence (or, at least, lasting convergence) is difficult, if not impossible, because of the challenges inherent in finding a workable balance between accountability and authority and because of the differing perspectives on what that balance is.[57] Even where it might appear that convergence has emerged, such as in the near-worldwide adoption of director deference in the form of the business judgment rule, that convergence is rather illusory as a result of the disparate ways that jurists from different 'legal cultures' apply the rule in the cases before them.[58]

5 Further refinements and implications

Ultimately, then, we might discern that the prospect of global convergence of corporate governance structures and the competing viewpoints about convergence depend on answering questions that have tended to fit quite comfortably – if not exclusively – in policy debates motivating areas of law that have traditionally been seen as public law. We might also discern that, regardless of the extent to which certain norms and rules take hold globally, corporate law retains its functions of structuring private relationships and regulating both the content of those relationships and the procedures pursuant to which they are carried out. In other words, although considerations of (and hopes for) convergence may take us as deeply as we might wish into theories of the efficient, the good or the universal (depending on one's perspective), those considerations cannot easily avoid the reality of the private law functions and origins of corporate law and its associated institutions and practices.

[54] *Ibid.* [55] *Ibid.*, 513. [56] *Ibid.*, 515. [57] *Ibid.*, 515–18.

[58] *Ibid.*, 518, noting that '[s]uch differences in attitudes may both reflect and reinforce important societal differences whose significance would be masked if one only paid attention to the apparent convergence marked by [different] courts' purported decision to apply the business judgment rule'.

To be sure, it may seem that the discussions regarding corporate law convergence may not really involve questions of public law. After all, based on Barnett's schema, articulated in section 2, and its four-pronged conceptualisation of public law (and public law causes of action), as distinguished from private law (and private law causes of action), it may appear that nothing so far, including the ways in which corporate law convergence is supported or questioned, falls within any of those conceptualisations. For example, we saw that, under one notion of public law, law is deemed 'public' by virtue of its setting forth public standards of conduct and providing punishment for public harms. By establishing what members of the polity may not do, public law lays out the boundaries within which action may occur without offending the public interest. Under the corresponding notion of private law, law is 'private' to the extent it governs relationships among private parties and provides redress for private harms. Corporate law is generally considered to be private law, then, because, in the course of enabling much corporate behaviour, it establishes both minimum standards of management conduct vis-à-vis shareholders and limited rights for shareholders to participate in corporate activity. That corporate law governs private relationships and enables remedies (usually private remedies) for private harms is in no way affected by the circumstance that some discussions about corporate law, such as those concerning convergence, tend to be flavoured by themes from normative political and macroeconomic theory and other arenas that seem to fit more comfortably in public law analyses.

Perhaps, however, it is worth considering public law conceptualisations from a broader perspective, one that takes into account the relationship of the international arena to corporate law's operation and efficacy. In particular – and continuing with the conceptualisation of public law as law proscribing and providing redress for public harms – public law prohibits conduct that private law does not cover and the transgression of which private law does not remedy. By contrast, corporate codes proscribe conduct of, and require certain conduct by, private actors (for example directors and managers), against whom other private actors (for example shareholders) are fully capable of taking action in the event those proscriptions or requirements are violated or ignored. However, it is the circumstance, noted above, that discussions about corporate law convergence are wrapped in notions of economic efficiency and political and social interests that allows us to bridge the gap. That is, we can think of public law not just as law that prohibits public harm, but also as law that promotes public objectives – greater individual freedom and economic well-being, for example – that become most evident only from a birds-eye view. In the corporate law context, by similarly considering from a high perch the myriad corporate governance structures guiding global corporate activity, the observable effects of those structures almost have to be similarly public in nature. One might reasonably suppose, therefore, that the conclusions about corporate law that may emerge from the perspective of that perch should be regarded as beyond the boundaries of purely private law.

More than that, however, once we start thinking about corporate codes at a global or multilateral level, we move from the world of private law regulatory provisions to a world of theory and policy, where the only 'interests' to be considered are those of a 'public' that extends beyond national boundaries. In other words, we move from intra-jurisdictional private law to the realm of international law – *public* international law, to be precise. Public international law comprises rules and principles – deriving largely from treaties and customs – that address the conduct of states and their relationships with each other and with individuals and institutions, regarding such things as environmental matters, world trade, global communications and outer space. Public international law is also 'horizontal', in the sense that those making it are also those who are subject to it, in turn meaning that it relies on states' voluntary participation for both its formulation and its enforcement.

Certainly nothing about corporate law convergence has become anything similar to a custom or principle that could be deemed public international law. However, the discussions surrounding convergence of corporate norms and rules are reminiscent of discussions about and within fields of public international law. Moreover, to the extent that broadened conceptions of the functions and outcomes of corporate law no longer fit comfortably within notions of private law, public law is the only remaining candidate as a descriptive category. More importantly, that categorisation is apt, given the affinities between those emerging conceptions and how we tend to think of public law and its role in the universe of 'law'. This conclusion does not – or, at least, should not – end the matter, however, because there remains the question of why anyone should be concerned about it. Of what use is it to be aware of the ways in which corporate law, the private law of private business relationships, may be thought of as public law? After all, if the public/private distinction is not meaningful, there is presumably no compelling reason to explore it or, indeed, to care about it. There are at least two answers to this question, one of them focusing on corporate law and the other on the public law/private law dichotomy itself.

First, what does this analysis do for corporate law? To begin to answer that question, it may be useful to think about what the 'public law' label brings to subjects such as constitutional law or criminal law. The substance of those fields of law is informed by community norms, political customs and judicial precedent to be sure, else that substance across national boundaries would reveal many more similarities than happens to be the case. However, these fields do not depend for their emergence and evolution *solely* on norms, customs and precedent, as many areas of private law might, including tort law, property law and contract law. To the contrary, and as suggested previously, the substance of these 'public law' fields is determined through processes of political discussion and decision-making. For example, the policy-making process is critical for criminal law. Proscriptions on conduct must exist before actors in society go about their business, meaning that the substance of criminal law cannot be determined *ex post*, through a developing body of case law. The same is the case for constitutional law, which is definitional for any society. Constitutional law by definition *constitutes* and therefore must be set in place – even if only at a high level of abstraction – before political communities can go about their business.

What is important here is not so much the role of a legislature, a parliament or a constitutional congress in formulating the substance of criminal law or a constitution. Those bodies – at least the first two – are involved also in shaping and refining traditionally private law areas, including tort law and property law. Additionally, that private law, like public law, may be established in part through the legislative process (rather than by judicial precedent) does not, without more, alter its 'private law' character. The important point is that the process of creating the substance of public law, at the hands of whatever political body is charged with doing so, is a process of evaluating the public interest in the broadest possible sense, taking into account such factors as overall social welfare, efficiency, deterrence analysis, fairness, justice and freedom. To be sure, those considerations are not necessarily excluded from the process of formulating tort or bankruptcy rules, for example. However, in the process of formulating those types of rules, there arguably is less of a sense that any sort of public interest, broadly speaking, is at stake in the outcome. By contrast, 'public law' evokes public interest and the myriad interpretations of how best to further it. Based on this line of analysis, then, the placement of corporate law within public law rubric – or, at the least showing how corporate law is linked to public law – may be a call for policy-makers, in their formulation of corporate laws and regulations, to think more critically than they otherwise might about corporate law's broader social and economic effects. The associated hope might be that policy-makers will seek the perspective and pursue the critical evaluation that they otherwise might not.

Second, what does this analysis do for the public law/private law dichotomy? As an initial matter, it highlights the extent to which concepts of public law and private law may be more fluid than we may have previously thought. Fields of law are not necessarily – indeed, are not typically – all within one category or the other. Consider securities law. Like corporate law or other fields of 'business law', securities law is often assumed to be a private law field. That may not be surprising, to the extent that it is seen as part of the structural framework for private relationships, namely those between investor and issuer or between client and broker. Yet the traditional basis for securities law and regulation is the very amorphous 'protection' of 'investors', whatever meaning might be given to those terms in the policy-making process. Surely the notion that the state must step in to 'protect' those who are conducting their investing activities implies both that securities law exists to further conceptions of the public interest and that formulating securities law cannot be carried out apart from consideration of broad-scale policy goals. Among other things policy-makers presumably need to consider in that process are promoting 'investor confidence' and furthering the macroeconomic objective of 'capital formation'. Moreover, beyond those very 'public' considerations in these recent times is the mandate that securities regulation focus as well on mitigating 'systemic risk', a threat that extends beyond national borders and that, by most accounts, must be addressed at a multilateral level.

Or, consider bankruptcy law, again a field typically thought ensconced in the private law realm. That field, of course, concerns the relationship between creditors and debtors and, in particular, the procedures through which the former legally forgive the latter of their obligations. Those relationships are established within the commercial world, a world of private interaction and relationships. But, again, what is bankruptcy about? It is about the way that polity has determined to treat its debtors. One bankruptcy scholar, for example, has suggested the interplay between bankruptcy law and public policy considerations in observing that '[h]ow we choose to forgive our debtors is a moral compass that has guided humanity for centuries'.[59] Establishing the rules that govern the relationship between creditors and debtors, then, would seem to encompass more

[59] Rafael Pardo, in University of Washington School of Law brochure to introduce new faculty members, June 2010 (on file with author).

than simply procedural determinacy and also to involve notions of the public good and fairness.

With this awareness of blurring boundaries in the realm of corporate law as well as other fields, the public law/private law dichotomy would seem to be less important than we might have thought at first. Or, at least, that is one conclusion we might reach. On the other hand, maybe the opposite is the case, in fact: the more we see that public law considerations imbue even the most presumptively private of legal arenas and that viewing fields of law as public law changes our thinking about them, the more we see that the distinction is critical. In other words, 'public law' is not merely a label if, when it comes to be attached to a subject, it substantively affects both assumptions and actions as to that subject. With that insight, however, our best strategy may be to dismantle it and excise it from the realm of legal discourse. That is to say, if it is the case that our analysis of law may differ depending on whether we assume the analysis is within a private law context or a public law context, perhaps we should force ourselves to cease making any such assumption at all.

6 Conclusion

Corporate law, typically understood, sets forth the framework of internal corporate relationships and the rights and obligations of the parties to that relationship, without looking beyond the boundaries of the jurisdiction in which any particular corporation is situated. Just as corporate law governs private relationships, it is typically enforced by private parties. Not surprisingly, then, corporate law is usually considered to be a private law field. However, corporate law not only establishes and organises economic enterprises and their internal relationships but also is constitutive of the global economies in which those enterprises pursue their activities, particularly as they reach across national boundaries in doing so. As various scholars have observed, international corporate activity and competition may – or may not – be a catalyst to a convergence of global corporate norms and rules. That discussion, in turn, reveals how corporate law, with its particularistic and private origins, touches on considerations of public good and economic well-being that often inform analyses within traditionally public law fields.

10

A public role for the intentional torts

DAN PRIEL

1 Introduction

Recent years have seen wide-ranging debates on the nature of tort law. For some, tort law is firmly placed within private law: it is concerned with the rights individuals have against each other and with the legal implications of the violation of those rights. Others emphasise the extent to which broad social considerations enter into the determination of tort liability and the many ways in which tort law today serves a public role that is ill-explained by the private law model. Given the centrality of negligence in contemporary tort law, much of this debate focused on this tort, but recent litigation that culminated in the House of Lords' decision in *Ashley* v. *Chief Constable of Sussex Police*[1] and some academic commentary relating to it provide an opportunity for examining these questions in the context of the intentional torts.

Though it will be some time before I get to discuss *Ashley*, it will be useful to describe its facts right away. The police had gathered information that James Ashley was involved in illegal activities including drug-dealing. They obtained a warrant to search his house and decided to raid it in the middle of the night. When a police unit entered the house, Ashley got up from his bed and walked towards the police officers with his hands pointing towards them as though holding a gun. One of the police officers,

I thank Peter Cane, Bill O'Brian and Jane Stapleton for comments on an earlier, and quite different, version of this chapter, which is reproduced with minor editorial changes by the kind permission of Hart Publishing from (2011) 22 *King's Law Journal* 183. I also thank James Harrison, Alicia Hinarejos, Cathryn Costello and Victor Tadros for clarifications on issues relating to this chapter. Finally, thanks are due to Satvinder Juss and Jeremy Horder, and to the anonymous referees of *King's Law Journal* for their comments.

[1] *Ashley* v. *Chief Constable of Sussex Police* [2006] EWCA Civ 1085; [2007] 1 WLR 398 (*Ashley*-CA); *Ashley* v. *Chief Constable of Sussex Police* [2008] UKHL 25; [2008] 1 AC 962 (*Ashley*-HL).

PC Sherwood, fired a single shot that hit Ashley in the neck. Ashley was severely wounded, and despite the police officers' attempts at resuscitation and the prompt arrival of an ambulance, in less than an hour Ashley was pronounced dead. Ashley's dependants sued the police for negligence and trespass to the person with regard to the actions that led to his death, as well as for misfeasance in public office with regard to certain events that took place after the shooting. As the police admitted negligence, they argued that there would be no point in a trial on the trespass claim. The trial court accepted the argument, but the Court of Appeal (Auld LJ dissenting) reversed and the House of Lords, against the dissenting opinions of Lords Carswell and Neuberger, upheld the Court of Appeal's decision.

This outcome, coupled with the fact that some of the judges invoked the notion of 'vindication of rights', a shibboleth for proponents of the private conception of tort law, has led most commentary on the case to consider it an affirmation of this view of tort law.[2] One purpose of this chapter is to show that this is, at best, an incomplete account of the judges' views expressed in the case. My real concern, however, is broader. With the aid of this case I seek to challenge the private law conception of tort liability exactly in the context of those torts usually thought to be the best affirmation of this conception of tort law.[3]

My discussion therefore begins far from the intentional torts. I consider some of the important developments that have changed the face of negligence liability in the last few decades and argue that though very different, they all have in common the introduction into the decision on tort liability of considerations that look beyond the litigants. The next question is whether a similar trend can be identified with regard to the intentional torts. I argue that we can identify a role for the intentional torts within a tort regime dominated by the tort of negligence, a role that has much more to do with broad societal (or public) considerations than with those confined to the individual parties involved. More concretely, in sections 3 and 4 I distinguish between three possible interpretations of vindication of rights, two consistent with the private law view of tort law and the third one that is not. I argue that the two private law interpretations of vindication are unsuccessful, but that the third one provides a

[2] Phil Palmer and Jenny Steele, 'Police Shootings and the Role of Tort' (2008) 71 *Modern Law Review* 801, 810–11; Nicholas J. McBride, 'Trespass to the Person: The Effects of Mistakes and Alternative Remedies on Liability' (2008) 67 *Cambridge Law Journal* 461, 462; Robert Stevens, 'The Conflict of Rights', in Andrew Robertson and Tang Hang Wu (eds.), *The Goals of Private Law* (Oxford: Hart Publishing, 2009), p. 163.

[3] See, e.g., Robert Stevens, *Torts and Rights* (Oxford University Press, 2007), p. 3.

limited but potentially useful role to the intentional torts. As it happens, it is this, more public conception of vindication that was explicitly adopted by some of the judges in *Ashley*, and that, I contend, provides the best justification for the decision.

2 How tort law became public

Given the age and centrality of tort law one would be forgiven for thinking that its basic principles should be settled by now; but as many have noticed, and some have lamented, it is constantly changing. At first blush it seems that changes have mostly been in the direction of limiting liability, with the House of Lords using everything at its disposal to achieve this goal: distinguishing new cases from earlier ones on flimsy grounds,[4] making unsubstantiated claims about the effects of expanding liability,[5] limiting past decisions by declaring them 'acceptable on [their] own facts',[6] narrowly interpreting the elements of existing torts[7] and rewriting past decisions so as to effectively overrule them without saying so.[8] When all else has failed, the judges have not shied away from explicitly overruling an earlier decision in order to limit the scope of tort liability.[9]

These changes, significant though they are, appear from a broader perspective as a rear-guard battle against an ever-expanding tort law.

[4] See, for example, the way in which *Page* v. *Smith* [1996] AC 155 was distinguished in *Grieves* v. *FT Everard & Sons Ltd* [2007] UKHL 39; [2007] 3 WLR 876.

[5] This approach reached absurd levels when Lord Hoffmann speculated in *Stovin* v. *Wise* [1996] AC 923 at 958 (without a shred of evidence) that one possible outcome of *Anns* v. *Merton London Borough Council* [1978] AC 728 was that 'local council inspectors tended to insist upon stronger foundations than were necessary'.

[6] That is, for example, how *Baker* v. *Willoughby* [1970] AC 467 was treated in *Jobling* v. *Associated Dairies* [1982] AC 794 at 809. See also *Williams* v. *Natural Life Health Foods Ltd* [1998] 1 WLR 830 at 837, in which Lord Steyn circumvented *Smith* v. *Eric S Bush* [1990] 1 AC 831 by saying that it was 'decided on special facts'.

[7] *Hunter* v. *Canary Wharf* [1997] AC 655.

[8] 'Rewriting' is not my word. It is how Lord Rodger described (in his dissent in *Barker* v. *Corus UK Ltd* [2006] UKHL 20; [2006] 2 AC 572 at [71]) the majority's treatment of *McGhee* v. *National Coal Board* [1973] 1 WLR 1 and *Fairchild* v. *Glenhaven Funeral Services Ltd* [2002] UKHL 22; [2003] 1 AC 32. The rewriting of *McGhee* arguably began earlier, when Lord Bridge said that *McGhee* 'laid down no new principle': *Wilsher* v. *Essex Area Health Authority* [1988] AC 1074 at 1090. Lord Rodger rejected this statement when he said that '*McGhee* undoubtedly involved a development in the law relating to causation': *Fairchild* v. *Glenhaven Funeral Services Ltd* [2003] 1 AC 32 at [154].

[9] *Murphy* v. *Brentwood District Council* [1991] 1 AC 398; cf. *O'Rourke* v. *Camden London Borough Council* [1998] AC 188 which rejected (as *obiter*) part of *Cocks* v. *Thanet District Council* [1983] 2 AC 286.

There are various reasons for this, of which only a small number can be addressed here. One reason for the changes has to do with the substantial increase in the prevalence of accidents after the industrial revolution. That tort law now primarily deals with accidents not only explains why negligence is much more important than it used to be; it also changed the foundations of tort law. Two main features are worth highlighting: first, with industrialisation it became commonplace that momentary inadvertence could lead to serious accidents, which made it difficult to associate tort liability with moral fault. Relatedly, industrialisation also weakened the connection between the degree of fault and the amount of harm caused (and hence damages award). Although the language of 'fault' has been retained, these developments meant that tort liability (especially in negligence) no longer corresponded well to perceptions of moral fault. Ideas such as loss-spreading and general deterrence began to appear in both academic work and judicial opinions in its place, and these have led to the introduction of broader social considerations into the decision whether tort liability should be imposed or not. From this it was but a small step to the view that tort law could serve as a regulatory device and to the extent necessary should be refashioned accordingly.

The untying of fault from liability and the emergence of new bases for the imposition of tort liability also affected the legitimacy of insurance in the context of tort liability. In the nineteenth century, liability (third-party) insurance was still considered morally and legally suspect due to its potential to relieve defendants of their legal liabilities, and by implication their moral responsibilities.[10] Once the connection between liability and fault was severed, it became easier to accept insurance against liability. (Today, let us not forget, liability insurance is often *required* by law.) And once liability insurance was widely available, judges openly stated that this was a relevant factor in deciding whether tort liability should be imposed.

Other factors affected tort liability in a more indirect way. Since the eighteenth century, new mathematical tools and new technologies have been developed to gather and analyse vast amounts of information. This intellectual development, which Ian Hacking called the 'emergence of probability',[11] has transformed the way people perceive the world. If

[10] Kenneth S. Abraham, 'The Rise and Fall of Commercial Liability Insurance' (2001) 87 *Virginia Law Review* 85, 86–7 and fn. 6.

[11] Ian Hacking, *The Emergence of Probability: A Philosophical Study of Early Ideas about Probability, Induction and Statistical Inference*, 2nd edition (Cambridge University Press, 2006); see also Gerd Gigerenzer *et al.*, *The Empire of Chance: How Probability Changed*

beforehand events were considered in isolation, the result of a single causal path, the advent of statistics and probability meant that particular events were increasingly considered in terms of their place within wider trends. The effect of this has been to turn individual instances of death, disease, crime or accident into social problems, requiring some kind of comprehensive response, which many felt only the government could provide. The availability of statistics affected tort law in another indirect way: it meant that even without physical harm, statistical data could affect the value of property, a person's prospects of employability and so on. These new kinds of loss encouraged the development of new doctrines or the updating of old ones.

Alongside these scientific developments there were also political changes that affected tort law. Of the greatest importance is the advent of the modern welfare state and its enormous growth. The welfare state took it upon itself to inspect and regulate many aspects of people's lives, especially in the areas of physical and economic health and security. In New Zealand such ideas have resulted in the adoption of a social insurance scheme against accidents. In other countries their greatest impact has been on expanding the tort liability of public authorities. In other contexts the expansion of welfare provisions meant that tort rules now existed within a different normative environment. Finally, the growing prominence of human rights discourse, including the more controversial social and economic rights, has had a profound impact on the normative background against which tort law operates, which, in various contexts, has broadened the scope of considerations taken into account in determining tort liability.[12]

There are many other factors that have led to expansion in tort liability, but I focused on the ones singled out here because they not only explain the expansionary trends in tort liability, they also undermine the view that the resolution of a tort dispute can be limited only to factors that

Science and Everyday Life (Cambridge University Press, 1989), p. 260 ('statistics and probability have modified key legal concepts like negligence, liability, and intent').

[12] For example, recent defamation decisions show a growing recognition of the significance of freedom of speech and information. Discussing these matters 'would probably have astonished most of the Law Lords who considered libel appeals in the course of the preceding century. They developed the principles of defamation law, without generally much attention to the implications of their decisions for freedom of the speech and of the press'. Eric Barendt, 'Libel, Privacy, and Freedom of Expression', in Louis Blom-Cooper, Brice Dickson and Gavin Drewry (eds.), *The Judicial House of Lords: 1876–2009* (Oxford University Press, 2009), p. 653.

pertain only to the litigants: statistical information is inevitably based on a large number of events; insurance pools together many different individuals; deterrence seeks to use tort litigation to change the behaviour of others; the social costs of accidents are a public concern; human rights and the welfare state are topics that belong to public law and policy. When taken together it is not difficult to understand why tort law today is so different from what it was 150 years ago, and how misleading it is to think of it as a strictly 'private' law affair.

As already mentioned, these trends have not been uniformly welcomed, and, in recent years, several judges and academic commentators have called for a return to a more 'traditional' understanding of tort law.[13] Though many of them have couched their arguments in terms of the nature of tort law, these authors have had to concede that it is possible to have a different kind of tort law from the kind they favour. Thus, despite appearances, they have ended up defending their view by appealing to normative considerations such as separation of powers or the institutional capacity of courts. Quite often these writings have also conveyed a thinly veiled political ideology.[14] The result is that much of tort law has begun to look 'public' in at least two senses: as a matter of fact, decisions on the scope of tort liability are affected by myriad factors not confined to the parties involved in litigation, and, as a matter of normative theory, questions of the scope of liability are the subject of competing political theories.

All these developments, however, do not appear to have had much impact on the intentional torts dealing with harms to the person and to property.[15] These torts, it seems, have continued to exist as relics from a very different past, a shrinking and little loved island of private law in constant danger of being completely submerged under the rising seas of the more openly public negligence law.[16] Indeed, it may be that it is exactly

[13] See, e.g., Stevens, *Torts and Rights*; Allan Beever, *Rediscovering the Law of Negligence* (Portland: Hart Publishing, 2007); Nicholas J. McBride and Roderick Bagshaw, *Tort Law*, 3rd edition (Harlow: Pearson Education Limited, 2008). For a critique of Stevens, see Dan Priel, 'That Can't Be Rights' (2011) 2 *Jurisprudence* 227.

[14] See Dan Priel, 'Torts, Rights, and Right-Wing Ideology' (2011) 19 *Torts Law Journal* 1.

[15] Which torts actually fall under the heading 'intentional torts' is not entirely clear. See Ken Oliphant, 'The Structure of the Intentional Torts', in Jason W. Neyers, Erika Chamberlain and Stephen G. A. Pitel (eds.), *Emerging Issues in Tort Law* (Oxford: Hart Publishing, 2007), pp. 512–13 for a suggested list. Even though some of the trends I discuss can be found in many of those intentional torts, in this chapter, unless I indicate otherwise, I use 'intentional torts' as shorthand for trespass to the person (assault and battery) and trespass to land.

[16] See Peter Cane, '*Mens Rea* in Tort Law' (2000) 20 *Oxford Journal of Legal Studies* 533, 534–5, 552–3 (arguing that the intentional torts have become marginal). To see just how

because they were perceived as uniquely 'private' that these torts were thought incapable of adaptation to novel situations and were therefore left behind. Because of the sort of events they traditionally covered, they were not subject to the kind of evolutionary pressures that led to the doctrinal innovations that enabled negligence to become a versatile tool for dealing with a wide range of new types of situations. Consequently, even issues such as patients' consent to medical treatment, which might have been more 'naturally' dealt with under the heading of battery, ended up being treated as cases of negligence.[17]

3 Three unsuccessful roles for the intentional torts

All of this raises the question: what role should the intentional torts play within today's tort law regime? If, for all practical purposes, all cases of trespass can also be claimed under negligence, then despite their unquestionably separate history, we would have to conclude that the intentional torts are now redundant and should be abandoned. Some may have linguistic qualms about intentional actions being treated as cases of 'negligence',[18] but this should not be a matter of grave concern. If necessary, we could rename negligence as 'unlawful infliction of harm' and thus resolve this problem. But before we move to do so, we should examine whether there is no way of understanding the intentional torts that does not subsume them under negligence. I will consider three possible interpretations. Common to all of them is the fact that they aim to locate the unique features of the intentional torts within the narrow 'private' law relationship between claimant and defendant. I will argue that for different reasons none of them is satisfactory.

unused these torts are, consider the fact that in *Ashley*, a case decided in 2006, the Court of Appeal had to devote a lengthy discussion to the question of burden of proof in the tort of trespass to the person. See *Ashley*-CA at [19]–[33].

17 See *Sidaway* v. *Board of Governors of the Bethlem Royal Hospital* [1985] AC 871 at 894, and additional sources cited in Ian Kennedy and Andrew Grubb, *Medical Law*, 3rd edition (London: Butterworths, 2000), p. 581.

18 See e.g. Peter Cane, 'Justice and Justifications for Tort Liability' (1982) 2 *Oxford Journal of Legal Studies* 30, 38 ('There is, no doubt, a resistance to treating intentional harms generally as if they were merely negligent, if only on linguistic grounds'); W. V. H. Rogers, *Winfield and Jolowicz on Tort*, 18th edition (London: Sweet & Maxwell, 2010), p. 140 ('one can hardly describe attempted murder as "negligence"').

A *Intention as a special mental state*

According to one possible interpretation, what justifies separating the intentional torts from negligence is that intention is a unique mental state that cannot be equated with or reduced to mere prediction or indifference (let alone the lack of mental state that is often the mark of negligence) and therefore deserves special treatment by the law. In this sense what distinguishes actions done 'with intention' is that they involve a clear choice on the part of the agent.[19] John Finnis, who defended the moral significance of this distinction, has argued that the difference is the result of the

> impact of choosing and intending upon the character of the chooser … [because] *choices last*. The proposal which one adopts by choice in forming an intention, together with the reasoning which in one's deliberation made that proposal intelligently attractive, *remains*, persists, in one's will … The proposal (and thus the intention) is, so to speak, synthesized into one's will, one's practical orientation and stance in the world … Whatever consequences lie *outside* one's proposal, because neither wanted for their own sake nor needed as a means, are *not* synthesized into one's will.[20]

Though couched in somewhat mysterious terms, Finnis' point seems clear enough and corresponds with widely shared views. The intended outcomes of one's actions are what one strives for, and as such they are properly described as 'owned by' or 'belonging to' the agent. They are so much a part of the agent's identity that, as far as blame goes, we often care little whether the intended outcome materialised or not. Unintended consequences, on the other hand, do not usually reflect on one's personality in such a way. The difference between acts of intention and the outcomes of negligence is considered so fundamental that it is not surprising that even in jurisdictions where liability for (some types of) accidents is strict or absolute, there is typically an exception for the intentional infliction of harm.

[19] See Rogers, *Winfield and Jolowicz on Tort*, p. 143 ('wicked people are worse than careless people and we should not forget it').

[20] See John Finnis, 'Intention in Tort Law', in David G. Owen (ed.), *Philosophical Foundations of Tort Law* (Oxford: Clarendon, 1995), pp. 243–4. Finnis claims that this is 'a real, empirical … effect of one's adopting a proposal' (p. 244). Psychological studies, however, suggest that the ascription of intention is morally loaded. See Joshua Knobe, 'The Concept of Intentional Action: A Case Study in the Uses of Folk Psychology' (2006) 130 *Philosophical Studies* 203.

There is a straightforward argument that could support maintaining this distinction in tort law: if we accept the assumption that, other things being equal, acts done with intent to cause harm are more morally heinous or more dangerous (because they are more likely to cause harm) than those that are not, then a heightened mental element could be offset by lowered requirements in the physical elements of the tort. In this way we could capture certain undesirable behaviours that would otherwise escape tort liability. There are traces of this approach in the law. First, the concept of duty of care, which serves as a filtering mechanism for limiting liability for negligence, has no equivalent in intentional torts dealing with similar harm: compare the requirement for a 'special relationship' in the case of negligent misrepresentation with the lack of such a requirement in the tort of deceit. Second, in the case of intended outcomes there is a narrower scope for doctrines such as *novus actus interveniens*, because, as the saying goes, intended consequences can never be too remote.[21] And third, the limits on recovery for pure economic loss and pure mental injury are much narrower in the case of torts of intention;[22] in fact, certain intentional torts, such as deceit or inducing breach of contract, deal almost exclusively with pure economic losses,[23] whereas similar actions committed without intention often do not give rise to tort liability at all.

This could be a coherent and plausible basis for distinguishing between intentional torts and negligence. It received its clearest endorsement in English law in *Letang* v. *Cooper*,[24] where Lord Denning drew a distinction between negligence and trespass based on their mental element. As he put

[21] For example, *Amstrad Consumer Electronics* v. *British Phonographic Industry* [1986] FSR 159 at 198; *Quinn* v. *Leathem* [1901] AC 495 at 537 ('The intention to injure the plaintiff negatives all excuses and disposes of any question of remoteness of damage').

[22] For intentionally inflicted mental injury, see *Wilkinson* v. *Downton* [1897] 2 QB 57. More generally, see Lord Hoffmann's remark in *Hunter* v. *Canary Wharf* [1997] AC 655 at 707 that he saw 'no reason why a tort of intention should … [exclude] compensation for mere distress, inconvenience or discomfort' (although he was somewhat less committed to this view in *Wainwright* v. *Home Office* [2004] 2 AC 406 at [41]–[47]). There are also some cases that were willing to extend liability in nuisance when intention to cause harm was proven. For example, see *Christie* v. *Davey* [1893] 1 Ch 316 at 326–7; *Hollywood Silver Fox Farm Ltd* v. *Emmett* [1936] 1 KB 468 at 475. Admittedly, though, there are some well-known counter-examples.

[23] In the case of deceit, for example, the claimant needs to show an intention to bring about a certain outcome (that the victim will act on the false information). See *Langridge* v. *Levy* (1837) 2 M&W 519 at 531; 150 ER 863 at 868. If successful, she can recover for pure economic loss.

[24] *Letang* v. *Cooper* [1965] 1 QB 232.

it, a claimant must show that he has been harmed either 'intentionally or negligently. If intentional, it is the tort of assault and battery. If negligent and causing damage, it is the tort of negligence.'[25] However, as in many other instances, Lord Denning's view found few supporters. Already in *Letang* Diplock LJ favoured the view that trespass is not limited to actions committed with intention to cause harm,[26] and subsequent cases followed his view. Perhaps it is the expansion of negligence and the decline of the doctrine of privity in contract that has made the need to define the intentional torts in this way seem less pressing.

B *The intentional torts as strict liability torts*

We can identify a second way of distinguishing between negligence and the intentional torts, which, perhaps paradoxically, takes a diametrically opposed approach. Contrary to the approach that sought to locate the distinction in a heightened *mens rea* requirement for the intentional torts, the second interpretation distinguishes the intentional torts by having a *lower* mental requirement. On this view the difference between negligence and the intentional torts could be characterised in the following way: while the net of negligence is cast very wide to cover a broad range of potential kinds of interaction between individuals, the scope of liability is limited by the need to show negligence on part of the injurer; by contrast, the intentional torts are considerably narrower in the sorts of events they cover, but require a less demanding mental element.

A linguistic basis for such an interpretation of the intentional torts could be based on the distinction between acts done 'intentionally' and those done 'with intent (to bringing about a certain outcome)'. If I hit someone while driving, the actions involved in my driving that lead to the accident (turning the steering wheel, pressing on the accelerator) are

[25] *Ibid.*, at 239–40; cf. *Williams* v. *Holland* (1833) 10 Bing 112 at 117–18; 131 ER 848 at 851.

[26] *Letang* v. *Cooper* [1965] 1 QB 232 at 243–5. Ironically, Lord Denning said in *Letang* that he based his decision on an earlier decision by Diplock in *Fowler* v. *Lanning* [1959] 1 QB 426, even though it did not support his view. In *Fowler* it was held that there is no difference in the substantive law between trespass and negligence and that proof of negligence is required in both (at 434–5). Later cases emphasised the distinction between the two on the basis of the directness of the harm: *Wainwright* v. *Home Office* [2004] 2 AC 406 at [8]; *Wong* v. *Parkside Health NHS Trust* [2001] EWCA Civ 1721; [2003] All ER 932 at [7]. However, as all cases of direct harm could be claimed under negligence as well as trespass to the person, this distinction too is unhelpful for giving trespass to the person a significant role.

intentional even though I may have no intention of harming anyone. The former is, to use John Searle's terms, an example of 'intention in action' while the latter is a case of 'prior intention'.[27]

A rather strict version of this distinction may be gleaned from several seventeenth-century cases of trespass. Two cases of trespass to land maintained that a person commits the tort even when his entry onto another's land is the result of a *reasonable* mistake,[28] but that a person is not liable if his entry onto another's land was involuntary.[29] Similarly, in the context of trespass to the person one case held that one who directly harmed another could not escape liability 'except it may be adjudged utterly without his fault. As if a man by force take my hand and strike you.'[30] Though couched in the language of fault, the example suggests that only lack of voluntariness would have exempted the defendant. A more recent case that may reflect a somewhat similar view is *Wilson* v. *Pringle*, where the court said that '[i]t is the act and not the injury which must be intentional. An intention to injure is not essential to an action for trespass to the person. It is the mere trespass by itself which is the offence.'[31] On this view even an instinctive reaction may be intentional.

The difficulty with this approach, however, is maintaining a viable distinction between trespass to the person and a rather broad tort of negligence (at least where physical harm is concerned). *Ashley* provides a useful illustration. Both the Court of Appeal and the House of Lords had to consider the scope of self-defence when a person mistakenly believes he is being attacked. The Courts considered three possible rules: (1) one is entitled to defend oneself as long as one's actions are based on a genuine (even if unreasonable) belief that one is under attack; (2) the defendant is entitled to the defence as long as his mistaken belief is reasonable; (3) the defence is limited to cases of actual attack (and the defence is denied altogether in cases of mistake).

[27] See John Searle, *Intentionality: An Essay in the Philosophy of Mind* (Cambridge University Press, 1983), pp. 84–5.

[28] See *Gilbert* v. *Stone* (1647) Style 72; 82 ER 539.

[29] *Smith* v. *Stone* (1647) Style 65; 82 ER 533; also *Conway* v. *George Wimpey & Co.* [1951] 2 KB 266 at 274 (intention to trespass is not required). But see n. 51 below.

[30] (1616) Hob 134 at 134; 80 ER 284 at 284.

[31] *Wilson* v. *Pringle* [1987] QB 237 at 249.

In both Courts the unanimously adopted rule was the second one,[32] although some of the Law Lords made some *obiter* remarks that were sympathetic to the third rule.[33]

Had this alternative rule been adopted, trespass to the person could have been defended as a strict liability tort, for even in those instances in which one was in no way to blame for attacking someone else, one would sometimes commit battery.[34]

The distinction matters in those cases in which both sides are innocent but one person's actions cause harm to another. In negligence the loss in such cases remains uncompensated, whereas in strict liability torts the loss is shifted to the defendant. The rule on self-defence adopted in the Court of Appeal and left unchallenged in the House of Lords was that a reasonable mistake about being attacked would still excuse one in attacking others. This introduces into the tort those flexible elements that have made negligence such fertile ground for development and expansion, but this result is achieved by blurring the distinction between trespass and negligence.

Despite the fact that introducing a standard of reasonableness into the tort of trespass creates this possibility, there was no serious attempt to justify the choice of rule. All we are told is that the rule is justified by the different aims of criminal law and tort law: while criminal law is concerned with protecting against behaviour that is 'damaging to the good order of society', tort law is concerned with 'protecting the rights that

[32] There is some ambiguity as to the scope of the demand for reasonableness. Here is how Arden LJ explained the reasonableness requirement in the Court of Appeal: 'It would have to be shown, in addition to showing that [the person] honestly believed in the material facts, that [his] actions were reasonably necessary for his defence.' *Ashley*-CA at [206]. This is a somewhat broader formulation of the defence than the one adopted by the other judges in the Court of Appeal and the House of Lords, according to whom *both* the mistake and the response need to be reasonable. This is significant in the case of a person who genuinely but unreasonably thinks another is about to attack him and then reacts in a way that is reasonable *given the unreasonable belief*. According to the majority view, that person has no defence, but according to Arden LJ he may have one.

[33] Most explicitly Lord Scott in *Ashley*-HL at [20]. Using somewhat weaker language, Lords Rodger (at [55]) and Neuberger (at [90]) have also not ruled out the possibility of adopting such a rule in the future.

[34] See *R* v. *Governor of Brockhill Prison, ex parte Evans (No 2)* [2000] 3 WLR 843, where the House of Lords adopted a strict liability interpretation of the tort of false imprisonment, imposing liability on the state in a case in which a mistaken but reasonable calculation resulted in the claimant spending fifty-nine more days in prison than she should have.

every person is entitled to assert against … others'.[35] In a moment I will deal with the suggestion that tort law is concerned with the protection of rights, but even if one accepts this view, it is not clear that this calls for a different 'balance' in tort law and criminal law. On the one hand, criminal defendants already enjoy procedural protections not given to their civil counterparts, which may render different substantive rules undesirable. On the other hand, as already mentioned, by adding the reasonableness requirement to a defence of battery, the point of maintaining a distinct tort of trespass to the person becomes less clear. In other words, the decision maintains a particular balance between tort law and criminal law at the expense of undermining a different one *within* tort law. One may think it desirable that for the sake of maintaining a distinction between criminal law and tort law there should be tort liability, even in some cases where there would not be corresponding criminal liability; it does not follow that this liability should be in battery. Thus, one effect of *Ashley* that has not received much attention is how a decision that seemingly sought to maintain the contemporary relevance of battery did so by eroding the distinction between battery and negligence.

However, from a broader perspective that takes the whole of tort law into view, this result may have been entirely understandable and even justified: if the intentional torts had been interpreted as strict liability torts, that would have meant that when both parties are innocent, the loss would be borne by the defendant; by contrast, in negligence in such cases the claimant would normally lose. Given the ubiquity of interactions that could potentially constitute trespass to the person (and, importantly, for which individuals could not adequately insure themselves), it is understandable why the courts would seek to narrow the scope of strict liability intentional torts. In order to achieve this end, many of the traditional torts (including the intentional torts) have been undergoing a process that makes them increasingly similar to negligence. In the case of battery, for example, this was done by deciding that the tort does not cover 'all physical conduct which is generally acceptable in the ordinary conduct of daily life'.[36] The decision in *Ashley* is just another manifestation of the

[35] *Ashley*-HL at [17]–[18] (Lord Scott). Similar statements were made by the other Law Lords, e.g. at [3] (Lord Bingham), [75] (Lord Carswell).

[36] *Collins* v. *Wilcock* [1984] 1 WLR 1172, 1177 (Goff LJ); affirmed in *Re F (Mental Patient: Sterilisation); F* v. *West Berkshire Health Authority* [1990] 2 AC 1, 72. There are a few exceptions to this development but they are not difficult to explain. In the case of torts that do not pose a significant risk to the delicate balancing act of negligence, the courts were much more willing to adopt a strict liability interpretation of the tort, as the House

same trend. Once again, however, such trends force upon us the question whether there is any unique role for the intentional torts.

In sum, while the strict liability interpretation of the intentional torts could provide a plausible basis for a distinction between these torts and negligence, we see that the courts go against it exactly because of the perception that the intentional torts are a blunt tool for dealing with the many kinds of interactions that are part of everyday life. The result is that this interpretation of the intentional torts is, like the first one, ultimately not likely to succeed in maintaining a significant role for these torts.

C Intentional torts as the foundation of primary rights

Perhaps, however, considering the question as one of finding normative space for the intentional torts alongside negligence is the wrong approach to take. Perhaps the role the intentional torts play within the legal system is altogether different. Adopting an expansive view of the intentional torts (closer, that is, to the second interpretation considered above), some writers have suggested that the role of the intentional torts is to 'vindicate' people's primary rights whose content is, roughly, that one is entitled to have control over one's body and property and to be free from interference with them. This view is usually associated with the 'private law' approach to tort law.[37]

Several statements in *Ashley* indicate that the judges believe that vindication of rights is one of the main purposes of tort law,[38] and these statements may suggest that this is the true reason for maintaining the intentional torts. In fact, however, the picture is more complicated than it at first appears, because the notion of vindication is ambiguous; it can be

of Lords did in the false imprisonment case of *R* v. *Governor of Brockhill Prison, ex parte Evans (No 2)* [2000] 3 WLR 843. False imprisonment is a rather rare occurrence, and it is nowadays a tort that most commonly has the state as defendant. The severity of the impact of false imprisonment on one's liberty, the virtual impossibility of insuring against it, the very deep pockets of the state, and – in line with the thesis advanced later in this chapter – perhaps also the fear that without imposing such liability the state might be tempted to abuse its powers, all explain why it makes sense to impose liability even in cases of *reasonable* false imprisonment while narrowing the scope of battery. Indeed, *Reeves* v. *Commissioner of Police of the Metropolis* [2000] 1 AC 360 shows that in cases involving prisoners we can identify change in the opposite direction, with negligence being stretched towards strict liability.

37 See, e.g., Stevens, *Torts and Rights*, p. 325. For a case note that interprets *Ashley*-HL in this fashion, see McBride, 'Trespass to the Person'.

38 For example, *Ashley*-HL at [22] (Lord Scott), [60] (Lord Rodger).

interpreted in several different ways, not all of which support the private law view. My argument in this section is that two private law interpretations of the idea of vindication are unconvincing, and that the best interpretation of the notion of vindication, at least as found in *Ashley*, actually fits better a 'public law' conception of tort law.

The notion of vindication can be understood, first, as a 'private' power an individual has to assert the *existence of her rights* against *other individuals* (including the state). Alternatively, it may mean an individual's power to *make public* the fact that her rights (whose content is determined elsewhere) have been *infringed*. Importantly, in the former sense the idea of vindication is understood as *constitutive* of certain relations between individuals; in the latter, the vindicatory (as opposed to the compensatory) role of tort law is in providing a public forum in which claims of infringement of rights are to be both examined and, where a violation has been found, protected *by the state*. The former interpretation is the one favoured by proponents of the private law view of tort law and will be discussed in this subsection. The alternative, public law version of vindication will be considered in the next section.

The private law notion of vindication is itself ambiguous between two possible interpretations: abstract and concrete. Understood abstractly, tort law may be thought to establish such rights as freedom of speech, bodily integrity, property, autonomy and so on. Thus, for example, it has been suggested that '[t]respass vindicates the rights of property owners to exclude others from their land [and b]attery describes the obligation owed by all citizens to each other citizen not to beat, wound, or inappropriately touch another intentionally and unjustifiably'.[39] Along those lines Donal Nolan has suggested that negligence could be used to vindicate rights, such as the right to education.[40]

Do we need to use tort law for this purpose? Traditionally, the common law has not protected primary rights by means of positive declaration,[41] and so tort law has often been the only means to infer 'backwards' the

[39] John C. P. Goldberg and Benjamin C. Zipursky, 'Accidents of the Great Society' (2005) 64 *Maryland Law Review* 364, 391.

[40] See Donal Nolan, 'New Forms of Damage in Negligence' (2007) 70 *Modern Law Review* 59, 88. Nolan expresses some concern about the limits of vindication through negligence due to restrictions on the types of actionable damages, but this situation is not really different in torts that do not require proof of harm. A nominal right of action is unlikely to be of much use when there is no prospect of monetary compensation.

[41] See Michael Lobban, *The English Common Law and English Jurisprudence 1760–1850* (Oxford: Clarendon, 1991), pp. 11–13; P. S. Atiyah, *Pragmatism and Theory in English Law*

existence of certain primary rights from the existence of legal responses to their violation. The fact that the intentional torts are per se torts, and thus not subject to certain limits imposed on negligence claims, has often been offered in support of the view that one of their roles is to constitute primary rights. Even though the prospects of people bringing claims for violations of their primary rights when they have not suffered harm are small, these torts serve as the legal placeholders for the existence of those rights. They are 'placeholders' because the rights established through them (say, private property or freedom of speech in the abstract) are separate from the question of their protection in individual cases.

In this sense, English tort law has arguably not been a success story.[42] A lack of (if nothing else) the rhetorical force of a positive declaration of rights may be part of the reason why English law is a relative latecomer in respect of many issues on which other legal systems (including other common law systems) have gone much further. To be sure, opinions may differ on the matter, and no doubt looking only at the law provides only a partial explanation to what must be in part a product of the British political tradition. Be all that as it may, reliance on the intentional torts, or for that matter on tort law more generally, no longer seems necessary for the sake of vindication of rights in the abstract sense, because the existence of these rights is by now well established in English law from other sources. In fact, often these rights are so well established that it is doubtful whether anyone asked to provide proof of their legal recognition would turn to the intentional torts as evidence. Probably first among those are societal attitudes towards such matters, which, though vague, seem rather firm with regard to many of those rights the intentional torts are supposed to vindicate at the abstract level. Such societal attitudes are known to have an impact on the political underpinning or, if you will, the ideology of a legal system,[43] and it is doubtful whether without such support legal recognition of these rights would remain intact.

Even within the narrower bounds of more traditional legal materials there are ample sources for the vindication of rights in the abstract

(London: Stevens & Sons, 1987), pp. 18–19, 21–5. Dicey extolled this approach as part of English law's conception of the rule of law in his *Introduction to the Study of the Law of the Constitution*, 8th edition (Indianapolis: Liberty Fund, 1982), pp. 117–20.

42 For this view, see T. H. Bingham, 'Tort Law and Human Rights', in *The Business of Judging: Selected Essays and Speeches 1985–1999* (Oxford University Press, 2000), p. 169; cf. Atiyah, *Pragmatism and Theory in English Law*, pp.19–21.

43 I use the word 'ideology' non-pejoratively. See further Clifford Geertz, 'Ideology as a Cultural System', in *The Interpretation of Cultures: Selected Essays* (New York: Basic Books, 1973), pp. 196–200.

sense, first among them criminal law. True, criminal law gives individuals only a limited role in the proceedings and therefore only a limited power to demand the vindication of their rights, but this does not affect the abstract sense of vindication we are concerned with at the moment. So long as the criminal law system functions reasonably well, individuals can point to, say, the many crimes concerned with the protection of private property, bodily integrity, security and so on as constitutive of their rights. Furthermore, as already pointed out, since very few people would (and could afford to) sue in tort law just for the sake of vindication of their rights, the practical difference between criminal law and tort law in this respect is rather small. So long as it is the symbolic vindication of abstract rights that we care about, then criminal prohibitions seem just as capable of providing it, in some sense perhaps even better than tort law. The developed distinction within criminal law between justifications and excuses implies that in the case of a successful excuse the defendant will be exonerated from criminal responsibility even though the legal system could still acknowledge that another person's rights have been infringed. Thus, to use *Ashley* as an example, there is no problem in saying that Ashley's rights have been infringed by PC Sherwood's actions, even if the latter's actions are found to be excusable. Tort law, which lacks this distinction, fares worse in this regard.

An additional source for the vindication of rights available since 2000 is the Human Rights Act 1998. Together with the European Convention on Human Rights, it provides an additional source of positive declarations about many of the very rights the intentional torts may be supposed to vindicate (as well as some rights whose recognition in English tort law has been patchy at best).[44]

It might be countered that criminal law or the Convention cannot fulfil the role of tort law, because they deal in the relations between individuals and the state, and not with the rights and duties individuals have towards each other. But this is a mistake, which stems from confusing the abstract and concrete senses of the idea of vindication of rights: in the abstract sense it is rights like bodily integrity or freedom of speech that we seek to vindicate. And in this sense criminal law and human rights declarations are sufficient. Even if we think that murder or rape are public wrongs,

[44] See *Watkins* v. *Secretary of State for the Home Department* [2006] UKHL 17; [2006] 2 AC 395, at [64] where Lord Rodger said: 'Now that the Human Rights Act 1998 is in place, [the] heroic efforts [to find "constitutional rights" in the common law] are unnecessary: the Convention rights form part of our law and provide a rough equivalent of a written code of constitutional rights.' See also *Ashley*-HL, at [22] (Lord Scott).

when we consider what makes them public wrongs, part of the answer is that they violate individuals' rights. In the context of the Convention there is by now a familiar body of law that establishes that states' obligation to 'protect' human rights imposes on the state positive obligations to prevent violations of individuals' rights by third parties. These obligations make sense only if the Convention is a source of legal rights and duties of individuals against each other.[45]

Here is another way of making this point: suppose tort law were to be abolished completely and replaced by an extensive social insurance mechanism while leaving the rest of the law intact. Would we say that our right to bodily integrity has been abolished? In the abstract sense the answer is 'obviously not'. In fact, such a change in the law may be justified by showing that the new legal regime would better protect individuals' rights. Whether or not this is true is an empirical question, not a conceptual one.

If, despite all this, we believe that for whatever reason tort law is needed for the vindication of rights *in this abstract sense*, then negligence could provide as good a source within tort law for this purpose. Indeed, it is exactly the flexibility of negligence that allows it to be expanded to cover all sorts of rights (such as the right to education that Nolan had in mind) that would be very difficult to recognise through the intentional torts. Some have suggested, however, that it is only the intentional torts that vindicate rights such as bodily integrity or autonomy, and they can do so exactly because the claimant does not need to show harm or unreasonableness on behalf of the defendant. This, it is further argued, shows just how important those rights are.[46] Even here, however, the flexibility of negligence enables courts to take into account the bodily integrity and autonomy of individuals not only as potential victims, but also as potential injurers. Individuals' autonomy might be undermined not just by physical intrusion by other individuals, but also by overbroad legal limitations on *their actions*. Vindication of physical integrity through a

[45] Contrary to Stevens, 'The Conflict of Rights', 146. See *Campbell* v. *MGN Ltd* [2004] UKHL 22; [2004] 2 AC 457 at [132] (Baroness Hale) for the suggestion that the Convention may be applicable to private bodies.

[46] This is the sense of vindication found in T. R. Hickman, 'Tort Law, Public Authorities and the Human Rights Act 1998', in Mads Andenas, Duncan Fairgrieve and John Bell (eds.), *Tort Liability of Public Authorities in Comparative Perspective* (London: British Institute for International and Comparative Law, 2002), pp. 17, 20, 29; Tony Weir, 'The Staggering March of Negligence', in Peter Cane and Jane Stapleton (eds.), *The Law of Obligations: Essays in Celebration of John Fleming* (Oxford: Clarendon, 1998), pp. 109–10. The practical effect of this view is very similar to the view discussed in section 2 above.

broad tort of trespass to the person could undermine people's autonomy if innocuous trifles that cause no harm could constitute a tort. As we have seen, such consequences were avoided by incorporating elements of reasonableness into the intentional torts.

So in the abstract sense, the idea that tort law, or more specifically the intentional torts, are required for the vindication of the existence of rights is unnecessary. Perhaps, however, the rights vindicated should be understood differently, that is, as establishing the boundaries between activities that lead to tort liability and those that do not. In some writings by defenders of the private law model of tort law we see the view that it is not (just) broad and abstract rights such as freedom of speech or bodily integrity that tort law is concerned with. Rather, the rights in question take the form of the right not to suffer psychiatric harm by means of negligently causing harm to oneself, or the right not to suffer psychiatric harm by witnessing the immediate aftermath of physical harm suffered by one's spouse as a result of another's negligence.[47] At least in some of the instances in which the courts have spoken of vindication of rights, it appears that it is this sense they had in mind.[48]

On this view, my arguments so far have been wide of the mark, because they misunderstand the role of tort law in vindicating rights. Tort law is required in this sense in order to make concrete the boundaries of abstract rights, something that declaratory documents cannot do precisely because of their generality. On this view there is no space between the existence of a right in a concrete situation and its vindication by tort law, and so at no point in the process does tort law vindicate any rights whose existence is determined elsewhere.[49] Put differently, in the abstract sense the relationship between tort law and vindication is justificatory; the existence of a right (not itself 'established' by tort law) gives reason to

[47] The former 'right' was not vindicated in *Greatorex* v. *Greatorex* [2000] 1 WLR 1970; the latter was vindicated in *Alcock* v. *Chief Constable of South Yorkshire Police* [1992] 1 AC 310. For an actual example of a concrete 'right' tailored to fit a tort tightly, consider Stevens' claim that 'we have a right not to be told lies *we believe*': Robert Stevens, 'Torts', in Louis Blom-Cooper, Brice Dickson and Gavin Drewry (eds.), *The Judicial House of Lords: 1876–2009* (Oxford University Press, 2009), p. 635 (emphasis added).

[48] This, arguably, is also the use of vindication as understood by Lords Scott and Carswell in *Ashley*-HL, at [22] and [80] respectively; see also *Chester* v. *Afshar* [2004] UKHL 41; [2005] 1 AC 134 at [87]; cf. *M* v. *Newham London Borough Council* [1995] 2 AC 633 at 676.

[49] This is the implication of the view that it is *legal* rights, and not moral rights, that are vindicated by tort law, a view explicitly adopted in Nicholas J. McBride, 'Duties of Care – Do they Really Exist?' (2004) 24 *Oxford Journal of Legal Studies* 417, 417 n. 1.

vindicate it through tort law. In the concrete sense, the relation is conceptual. Whenever tort liability is imposed, this *means* that a right has been violated; whenever tort liability is not imposed, this *means* that a right has not been violated.

The main difficulty with vindication in the concrete sense is that to say that tort law vindicates rights is to state a tautology.[50] In this sense the view that tort law vindicates rights is thus trivially true, but in this sense it cannot carve out any distinct conception of tort law. *All* accounts of tort law, including those thought to be opposed to the private conception of tort law (such as economic interpretations of tort law), are consistent with it. Any liability whatsoever can be phrased as liability for a violated right. For example, by itself this view is consistent with the view that we have a right not to suffer loss at the hands of another, the right not to suffer loss when the costs of eliminating it are lower than the expected loss itself, the right not to be humiliated in public, or the right to be rescued by others when in danger. This is because in the concrete sense the notion of vindication is *by definition* devoid of any justificatory force.

4 A public role for the intentional torts

Had we only considered the idea of vindication of rights in these senses, we would have had good reason to doubt the point of retaining the intentional tort of trespass to the person, and, *a fortiori*, the outcome of *Ashley*.[51] This would not necessarily have meant that an injurer's state of mind had no role to play in tort law. We could still maintain the normative significance of the distinction between intentional and careless acts, and proof

[50] It is *only* in this sense that Stevens is right when he says that if tort law were to be abolished, that would mean 'the abolition of most of our legal rights' (Stevens, *Torts and Rights*, p. 325). But as in this concrete sense this is a tautological statement, this is no cause for concern. It would by no means threaten individuals' abstract legal rights or their moral rights, which (as explained already) might be better protected if tort law were abolished.

[51] See *Fowler* v. *Lanning* [1959] 1 QB 426 at 433–4, where Diplock J made it clear that it was a mistake to think that in order to escape liability in trespass to the person, one 'must comply with any higher standard of care than was needed to escape liability if the action were framed in trespass on the case', and that 'there does not appear by 1852 to have been any difference between the substantive law applicable whether the action were framed' as one or the other tort. See also David Howarth, 'Is there a Future for the Intentional Torts?', in Peter Birks (ed.), *The Classification of Obligations* (Oxford: Clarendon, 1997), pp. 266–8, 280 (his answer: not really); P. S. Atiyah, 'American Tort Law in Crisis' (1987) 7 *Oxford Journal of Legal Studies* 279, 284–5.

of intention could still play a role, for example in the determination of damages (an approach largely unrecognised in English tort law, but more common in other jurisdictions). This, however, would hardly provide a reason for retaining *separate* intentional torts. First, under no account do the cases that justify punitive damages track accurately the distinction between intentional torts and negligence: there are many instances of intentional torts that would not call for such damages; and there may be – at least on some justifications of punitive damages – good reasons to award them in some cases of negligence.[52] Second, even if we thought that proof of intention were a relevant factor in deciding whether to award punitive damages, this would not require separating intentional torts from negligence. Proof of intention to cause harm could then be treated as an aggravating factor, relevant, necessary or sufficient (as the case may be), within other torts.

Is there nonetheless a way of understanding what was decided in *Ashley*? I think there is, but it calls for a different interpretation of the decision in both the Court of Appeal and the House of Lords, one based on some elements in those judgments that have been neglected in previous commentary on the case. On this view, one of the points of contention in the case, and one that cuts across the majority-dissent lines in both courts, deals with the potential *public* role of tort law and of the intentional torts in particular. This view is consistent with something like the idea of vindication of rights appearing in the decision, although only if understood differently from the more familiar 'private law' interpretation. In this sense, vindication of a right is not synonymous with recognition of certain legal relations between individuals. Rather, vindication is understood as a particular aim of tort law (or perhaps more specifically tort *litigation*), and it is to provide *a public and impartial public forum* for declaring that a claimant's rights (the legal origin of which must be established on other grounds) have been infringed.[53]

Understood in this way, vindication may not seem at first particularly novel or exciting. Arguably, this has been the role of courts from their earliest days. Vindication through tort law in this sense is public in that it requires the existence of a public body funded by the state for its existence,

[52] See, e.g., Cento Veljanovski, *Economic Principles of Law* (Cambridge University Press, 2007), pp. 236–7.

[53] The distinction between these two senses of vindication is missed in the discussion of *Ashley* in Jenny Steele, 'Damages in Tort and under the Human Rights Act: Remedial or Functional Separation?' (2008) 67 *Cambridge Law Journal* 606, 628.

but it is one that seems true of all tort cases. Moreover, since it is *legal* rights we are concerned with, this view is, once again, consistent with any substantive theory of what the content of those rights should be.

In this sense, then, the public sense of vindication seems not much more illuminating than the private one. Even in this sense, I think it tells us something important, namely that the idea of 'private law' is in some sense incoherent so long as state institutions (be they the legislature or the courts) are involved in both the promulgation of rights and in their protection. However, it would be a mistake – indeed, a very similar mistake to the one committed by proponents of the private law view – to think that something follows from it regarding what the content of tort law should be.

If that is the case, we are again faced with a puzzle: the Courts in *Ashley* did let the claim in trespass to the person proceed to trial, and they relied on the notion of vindication in reaching this conclusion. What did they mean by that? I want to suggest that at least some of the judges involved in this case used the language of 'vindication' in a distinct sense, quite different from its interpretations considered so far. For them the decision to allow the claim in trespass to the person to proceed to trial was based on their wish that potential misconduct by public authorities be *investigated* and pronounced upon in a public forum. Thus, in this sense the vindication in question was 'public', not merely in the sense that all law is in some sense public, but in the sense that they were willing to take into account the concerns of the general public not involved in the case in the context of tort litigation. Vindication of rights by tort law is thus not the affirmation of abstract rights or the determination of the boundaries of tort liability. Rather, 'vindication' consists in a *finding* that a particular individual's rights have been violated and the recognition that on certain occasions such a finding is of general public significance. If this is correct, what is significant about *Ashley* is the willingness of the courts to use the machinery of a 'private' law trial for the sake of examining a matter of public concern.

Perhaps the clearest statement of this view is found in Arden LJ's judgment in the Court of Appeal:

> The *public* has high expectations of the police. Like everyone else, *the police are subject to the rule of law.* Those suspected of criminal activity are entitled to the protection of the law. What the claimants seek in these proceedings is an explanation and redress in a court of law in respect of the fatal wounding of James Ashley and its subsequent *disclosure to the public.*[54]

[54] *Ashley*-CA at [189] (emphases added).

In this passage Arden LJ focuses on the public interest in knowing what brought about Ashley's death and the importance of guaranteeing that the police comply with the rule of law. There are indications that this is what troubled some of the other judges hearing the case as well. First, the police admitted negligence in this case all too quickly. After all, if the facts had been as assumed by the court, the police should have stood a good chance of answering a claim not just in trespass, but in negligence as well. If PC Sherwood's mistake was reasonable in the circumstances, then it is at least arguable that he was not negligent and that the claim should have been dismissed altogether. *Exactly* the same considerations that the judges rely on to conclude that there was no trespass to the person in this case (in particular the fact that the decision was made in the spur of the moment and in highly pressing circumstances) can be found in negligence decisions explaining why the defendant did not breach his duty of care.[55] Why then were the police so quick to admit their negligence in this case? One possibility suggested by the quote above is that the judges suspected that the facts were not exactly as the police claimed them to be. In the Court of Appeal, Clarke MR mentioned forensic evidence and some conflicting accounts given by other people at the scene that suggested that the police's version of the events was inaccurate;[56] he also mentioned evidence regarding PC Sherwood's problematic disciplinary record, which at one point even led to a temporary suspension of his firearms authorisation.[57]

Alternatively, the negligence was not at the point of execution but rather at the planning stage,[58] but even in that case it may be in the public interest to know whether there were *additional* violations of police regulations by PC Sherwood. Either way, it appears that an important reason

[55] See e.g. *Marshall* v. *Osmond* [1983] QB 1034; *Wilsher* v. *Essex Area Health Authority* [1987] QB 730 at 749. *Marshall* is particularly relevant as it deals with police error during a chase after a criminal, and the Court decided that such an error does not always amount to a breach of duty of care. See *Keegan* v. *Chief Constable of Merseyside* [2003] 1 WLR 2187, where the Court of Appeal relied on policy considerations to dismiss a claim against the police when it was clearly negligent but its error was judged to have been made in good faith. This decision was overturned in *Keegan* v. *United Kingdom* (2007) 44 EHRR 33.

[56] See *Ashley*-CA at [86]–[92], [110]; *Ashley*-HL at [69] ('Frequently … a defendant cannot challenge the interest of the claimant to pursue the action without simultaneously calling into question his own real interest in defending the action').

[57] *Ashley*-CA at [117].

[58] At least three of the judges involved in this litigation located the police's negligence at the planning stage. See *Ashley*-HL at [54] (Lord Rodger), [91]–[94] (Lord Neuberger); *Ashley*-CA at [196] (Arden LJ).

for the Courts' decision to allow the trespass claim to go to trial was the need to make the police more accountable to the public for their actions. Sensing that the inquiries into the events that led to Ashley's death had not been properly conducted, but unable to order a public inquiry, some of the judges in both the House of Lords and the Court of Appeal adopted the closest possible alternative to it: they allowed the claim in trespass to go to trial and hinted that they would want to see a more vigorous investigation into what had actually happened the night Ashley died.[59]

Thus, this approach is consistent with the vague idea of vindication of rights, and yet (and seemingly paradoxically) it seems to undermine the particular view of tort law usually associated with it. In this sense vindication is quite limited because the number of cases in which it would be invoked is rather small (in contrast with the private law versions of the vindication argument, in which each tort case, implicitly at least, vindicates rights), but in those cases vindication is of real, practical significance.

This conclusion is important in several respects. Most narrowly, for the sake of understanding the outcome of the case it is worth noting that the different views on this matter were not drawn along the majority-dissent lines. In the Court of Appeal it looks as though the individualistic, private law view prevailed: it was endorsed both by Clarke MR writing for the majority[60] and by Auld LJ, who explicitly stated that '[t]he claim in battery is a private law claim, the only proper function of which is to provide a private law remedy'.[61] In the House of Lords, however, the public law view suggested here seems to have had the support of at least two (and perhaps three) members of the panel, with the views of another (Lord Bingham)

[59] In this connection it is interesting to compare *Ashley* with *Cullen* v. *Chief Constable of the Royal Ulster Constabulary* [2003] UKHL 39; [2003] 1 WLR 1763, which was not mentioned in the *Ashley* decisions. In a 3–2 decision, the House of Lords held that a person who had been wrongfully detained was not entitled to tort damages for the detention when he could not prove any harm. In explaining the majority's view, McBride and Bagshaw (*Tort Law*, p. 489 fn. 39) say that there is no point in allowing a claim 'for the *sole* purpose of having it established in a public forum whether or not the police acted lawfully in denying him access to a solicitor … [I]t is hard to see what *useful* purpose would be served in allowing him to do this.' When considered in purely private law terms, this might be true; but if we think of the public role that tort law could play, as I suggest some judges in *Ashley* did, such a claim may be useful. Indeed, I would contend that the public law reading of *Ashley* suggested here is closer in spirit to the *Cullen* dissent.

[60] *Ashley*-CA at [96] ('The role of the civil courts is not solely to provide compensation'; one reason why civil trial exists is 'to determine the parties' legal rights and liabilities').

[61] *Ibid.*, at [178].

not entirely clear on the matter.[62] (Only Lord Carswell clearly rejected this view.[63]) Lord Scott seemed to approve of the claimants' desire 'to obtain a public admission or finding that the deceased … was unlawfully killed by PC Sherwood. They want a finding of liability on their assault and battery claim in order to obtain public vindication of the deceased's right not to have been subjected to a deadly assault.'[64] Lord Rodger approved of claimants pursuing tort law claims to the end in order to 'try out another novel, and more doubtful cause of action … [or] in order to try to establish a point of law which would help others in a similar plight'.[65] And interestingly, the clearest support for this view in the House of Lords can be found in Lord Neuberger's dissent, in which he stated: 'I accept … that there is a point in seeking a declaration … because it is reasonable for Mr Ashley's estate to wish to establish that his death was unlawfully caused *and because there is a public interest element in proceeding.*'[66]

But more than head-counting, if this reading of the decisions is correct, then it may be that the most important aspect of *Ashley* is not any of the technical issues that took up most of its pages. The question of mistaken self-defence and the burden of proof in such cases are matters of relatively little practical significance because they arise very rarely (as evidenced by the paucity of cases dealing with these issues). Rather, *Ashley* is important because it shows the willingness of at least some of the judges in the Court of Appeal and the House of Lords to consciously introduce public considerations into tort law. To put matters more controversially, some of the judges may have used expressions such as 'vindication of rights', which are associated with a private law conception of tort law, to reach a 'public law' result that broadened judicial inspection of government action.

The significance of the decision lies in its particular understanding of the idea of oversight. Using tort law as a tool for guaranteeing governmental accountability is a relatively novel, but by now not unheard of, idea.[67] In this way, tort law may perhaps already be given a role that goes beyond

[62] See also Lord Bingham's vague comments on the issue in *Watkins* [2006] UKHL 17 at [8]–[10].

[63] *Ashley*-HL at [81]. [64] *Ibid.*, at [23]. [65] *Ibid.*, at [70].

[66] *Ibid.*, at [110] (emphasis added). See also *ibid.*, at [114] ('there is, at least potentially, a substantial public interest in the outcome of the battery claim').

[67] See Carol Harlow, *State Liability: Tort Law and Beyond* (Oxford University Press, 2004), pp. 49–53; A. M. Linden, 'Tort Law as Ombudsman' (1973) 51 *Canadian Bar Review* 155; Erika Chamberlain, 'Negligent Investigation: Tort Law as Police Ombudsman', in Andrew Robertson and Tang Hang Wu (eds.), *The Goals of Private Law* (Oxford: Hart Publishing, 2009), p. 283.

its traditional scope, but it is one that can be accommodated within the Diceyan conception of the rule of law. What is important about the approach of Arden LJ, Lord Rodger and Lord Neuberger is their willingness to consider the interests of the general public, that is of people who were not directly harmed in the incident and who are not represented in the litigation in the context of a tort claim.

This willingness on the part of some of the judges to blur the boundaries between private and public law and to give the intentional torts a more public role may also help in understanding the recent resurgence of the 'newly evolving tort'[68] of misfeasance in public office, also considered in *Ashley*. Originally concerned with voting rights, misfeasance in public office is an intentional tort exclusively concerned with harms resulting from abuses of power by public authorities. This tort lay dormant and little used for many decades,[69] and its new lease of life may reflect an understanding of a greater need for stronger legal means of controlling government action, and a growing awareness on the part of the judges of the potential for using tort law for this purpose.[70]

Looking to the future, *Ashley* raises three questions:[71] the first is whether it will be necessary to rely on the intentional torts for this public role in the future. Could courts in future cases not add this role to the versatile and flexible tort of negligence? Is there anything that gives the intentional torts any advantage over negligence in this context? Admittedly, the reading of *Ashley* suggested here is consistent with a broader public law role for all of tort law, and so if future courts decide to adopt a similar approach, they might not confine it only to the intentional torts. It may be that even in *Ashley* the public role given to battery was merely a pragmatic solution to the unique facts of the case. Perhaps it was battery and not negligence

68 *R Cruickshank Ltd* v. *Chief Constable of Kent County Constabulary* [2002] EWCA Civ 1840; [2002] Po LR 379 at [14].

69 The history of the tort, its long fall to obscurity and its recent re-emergence are detailed in *Three Rivers District Council* v. *Governor and Company of Bank of England (No 3)* [2003] 2 AC 1 at 29–45.

70 See *ibid.*, 190, where Lord Steyn considered the significance of the tort in maintaining the rule of law.

71 Another question I will not discuss here is to what extent ideas such as those found in *Ashley* could be used in contexts involving not the state but, for example, large corporations. There is some judicial recognition of this in *Jameel* [2006] UKHL 44 at [158] (Baroness Hale), but, despite their power, such bodies raise different considerations from those applicable to governments. It is worth noting that a recent decision that arguably was willing to extend the public rationale of *Ashley* in the context of litigation between two private parties did so when the case involved an event that was of considerable public significance. See the discussion in *Breslin* v. *McKenna* [2009] NIQB 50 at [4]–[5].

on which the 'burden' of public inquiry had been laid only because of the unusual way in which both parties decided to plead their case.

Even if that is the case, however, the decisions in *Ashley* are not insignificant: the police clearly knew that they could end the matter and avoid judicial inquiry into the events that led to Ashley's death by admitting that their actions amounted to battery, and yet they chose not to do so. In this regard the significant point is not whether other torts could have been (and in the future, might be) used for the same purpose. The point is that the Court was willing to use tort law, and specifically the intentional torts, for public purposes.

The second, related, question is how likely it is that the intentional torts would be used for a similar purpose in the future. In part the answer to this question depends on the behaviour of defendant public authorities in future cases. Having learnt their lesson, they might prefer to swallow their pride and admit to battery if only to avoid a potentially more damaging public inquiry in court. On the other hand, it may be that the otherwise unimportant linguistic point about the difference between negligence and intention would prove significant in this context, as public authorities might prefer to have a long inquiry that they might survive relatively intact to a damaging admission of the 'intentional' violation of an individual's rights.

Apart from public authorities' reaction to *Ashley*, it remains to be seen how many future courts will be willing to look behind the questions that appear on the surface of *Ashley* and read it in the way suggested here. Indeed, it may be that the matter was discussed in such vague terms exactly in order to guarantee that the decision in *Ashley* remains 'a restricted railroad ticket, good for this day and train only'.[72] Moreover, even if some of the judges do wish to expand this approach to courts' inspection of governmental bodies, it may be that Arden LJ's discussion at the end of her judgment on the effect of European law on future cases[73] indicates that there will not be much need in the future for the particular technique chosen in *Ashley* to guarantee oversight of government action, as it may be easier and more natural for the courts to rely on the European

[72] This is how Justice Jackson described in a dissent the majority's overruling of a recent earlier decision: *Smith* v. *Allwright* (1949) 321 US 649 at 669. For those who wish to find it, the escape route is already in *Ashley*-CA, which Clarke MR described as 'a very unusual case' (at [160]).

[73] *Ashley*-CA at [211]–[214].

Convention on Human Rights for this purpose.[74] On the other hand, it may be that some judges, who may be reticent about the importation of European ideas into English law,[75] will find this home-grown development more appealing. In any case, here too the issue is not so much whether future courts will follow *Ashley* as precedent. What matters more is what this case reveals about the attitude of some of the judges regarding the foundations of tort law, judges whose view is clearly different from what we are told by many commentators is the correct way of understanding (English) tort law. Only a few years before *Ashley* was decided, the House of Lords, relying on European jurisprudence, emphasised the importance of conducting a public investigation into the unlawful death of a prisoner at the hands of another prisoner in the context of a judicial review, 'public' law case.[76] In *Ashley*, ignoring the public–private divide, it allowed the use of English tort law for the same purpose. The decision thus both emphasises within tort law the deterrent role of tort law over its more private, compensatory role, but can also be seen as part of a broader attempt by the judiciary to strengthen constitutional values such as governmental transparency and accountability, rule of law, and checks and balances. Since some have questioned the capacity of monetary remedies to have an effect on government,[77] the approach adopted in *Ashley* may prove particularly fruitful.

The third question is whether the broader development that I have argued is reflected in *Ashley* is desirable and whether it is likely to be effective. Here the traditional divisions of law may lead some to the conclusion that such inspections of governmental behaviour should not be conducted as part of a tort case, because the purpose of tort law is only to deal with the compensation claims of private individuals as a result of individual wrongdoing.[78] Put this way, this objection strikes me as very weak. The scope and aims of tort law do not come to us from heaven as commandments to obey, and whatever roles tort law currently fulfils

[74] See *R (Hurst)* v. *London Northern District Coroner* [2007] UKHL 13; [2007] 2 AC 189; *Re McKerr* [2004] UKHL 12; [2004] 1 WLR 807. See also the European cases *McKerr* v. *UK* (2002) 34 EHRR 20; *Kelly* v. *UK* [2001] Inquest LR 125.

[75] See, e.g., Leonard Hoffmann, 'The Universality of Human Rights' (2009) 125 *Law Quarterly Review* 416.

[76] *R (Amin)* v. *Secretary of State for the Home Department* [2003] UKHL 51; [2004] 1 AC 653.

[77] Harlow, *State Liability*, p. 26; Law Commission, *Administrative Redress: Public Bodies and the Citizen*, Consultation Paper 187 (2008), p. 148.

[78] See, e.g., McBride and Bagshaw, *Tort Law*, pp. 30–3, 199.

should be maintained only to the extent that they serve a purpose. There may be very good reason to distinguish between the private and the public: after all, most people behave differently in private and in public and it is entirely plausible that the law should reflect this distinction in some way. But as the boundaries between private and public life have shifted in the last few decades (due to, among other things, the rise of the welfare state as well as technological changes), it is only natural that the boundaries between private and public law will shift as well. If what has traditionally been classified as public law proves insufficient for inspecting public bodies, courts should not let formal boundaries stand in the way.[79]

The objection may be put more forcefully, however. It may be argued that because *historically* tort law was conceived as concerned only with private disputes, its substantive rules, as well as the procedural rules of civil proceedings, have developed in such a way that tort law cannot adequately fulfil this new role assigned to it: the judge might not have the experience or expertise necessary to deal with such questions, adversarial proceedings might be thought inferior to a more inquisitorial process needed to deal with such questions, the judge and parties will be operating under certain time or financial constraints that will hamper careful examination of the relevant issues, the concerns of certain relevant parties may not be adequately represented, and so on. This is potentially a formidable challenge, and it is certainly possible that on certain occasions the objection could prove decisive against using tort law for the purposes envisaged here. I do not think, however, that it calls for an outright rejection of the approach presented in this chapter. First, there is a long if convoluted history of dealing with public law matters in what are formally private law disputes, so there is no a priori reason to think that judges are incapable of dealing with such matters in the context of private law disputes. Second, procedural and evidentiary rules of civil proceedings have undergone considerable change in recent years, making claims about the impossibility of adequately handling such claims within the confines of a private law dispute seem less persuasive. The more active role given to judges with the advent of case management gives them a greater ability to turn the parties to the issues and evidence they consider important for the resolution of the case.[80] Finally, while considerations based on

[79] See *Broome* v. *Cassell & Co. Ltd* [1972] AC 1027 at 1114.

[80] See Adrian A. S. Zuckerman, *Civil Procedure* (London: LexisNexis, 2003) §§ 10.66–10.67; J. A. Jolowicz, 'Civil Litigation: What is it For?' (2008) 67 *Cambridge Law Journal* 508, 512–13; and, more generally, J. A. Jolowicz, *On Civil Procedure* (Cambridge University Press, 2000), p. 396.

the path-dependent development of the law have their force, they cannot forever block a change in course, if one is needed. If one believes that these rules stand in the way of an otherwise valuable goal, they should be changed.

At the same time, it is clear that the solution found in this case is a makeshift tool, and as such it has its limitations. Not all cases can be brought within the remit of intentional torts, and as we have seen, ultimately the decision as to whether a judicial inquiry will be conducted is in the hands of the defendant. If the police had admitted to battery in Ashley's case, there would have been no trial, and thus no opportunity for judicial investigation. Anyone concerned about the adequacy of existing mechanisms for inspecting public authorities (and police activity in particular) would surely prefer to see a more comprehensive and direct treatment of this problem.

This leads to another, related, challenge, namely that there is no reason to think that such judgments are going to be an effective means of inspecting governmental action. There is a familiar view, with considerable academic support in the UK, that questions the wisdom of relying on courts to provide an effective check on the excesses of the executive.[81] Those holding this view would surely doubt that the occasional tort claim could have any noticeable impact on the behaviour of the executive. They may be right; but perhaps, especially when the powers of the executive are constantly expanding while the capacity of the legislature to adequately control it is in decline,[82] and when because of the sheer size and complexity of their operations effective control of public authorities is increasingly difficult, what is required is a willingness to consider new means of supervising public authorities.

5 Conclusion

Looked at from a narrow perspective, *Ashley* is an unusual case. Judges ordinarily try to avoid deciding on matters that have no effect on the outcome of the case. Their reasons for doing so are easy to understand and for the most part entirely justified. There is no point spending time and effort on deciding 'academic' questions when time and money are limited

[81] See, e.g., Adam Tomkins, *Our Republican Constitution* (Oxford: Hart Publishing, 2005), pp. 67–87; J. A. G. Griffith, 'The Political Constitution' (1979) 42 *Modern Law Review* 1.

[82] This was pointed out some time ago. See Richard Crossman, 'Introduction' to Walter Bagehot, *The English Constitution* (Fontana, 1963), pp. 43–47.

and there are so many other cases awaiting resolution. The case is also interesting because it goes against recent trends that have tended to be quite restrictive with regard to tort liability of public authorities. (Even though most of these decisions involved liability for negligence, many of the policy considerations relied upon against the imposition of liability are applicable to other torts as well.) Why, then, did the majorities in the Court of Appeal and House of Lords agree to let the question of whether James Ashley's person had been trespassed go to trial?

This puzzle calls for explanation. In this chapter I have considered several 'individualistic' readings of the intentional torts. Some, such as the view that the intentional torts should be limited to acts done with intention, focus mostly on individual injurers; others, such as the view that the intentional torts should be concerned with vindication of rights (in its traditional understanding), focus on individual victims. I have argued that if we try to limit the ruling in *Ashley* to these interpretations, then the decisions of both the Court of Appeal and the House of Lords are difficult to defend.

Instead I suggested that we should look beyond the parties involved in the case; then a different picture emerges. On this picture the tort of trespass to the person was allowed to go to trial for the sake of making public authorities accountable for their actions. Lord Mustill once indicated that in order to 'avoid a vacuum in which the citizen would be left without protection against a misuse of executive powers the courts have had no option but to occupy the dead ground in a manner, and in areas of public life, which could not have been foreseen 30 years ago'.[83] If my analysis is correct, *Ashley* is most convincing as reflecting a similar attitude. Over the years English courts have often been accused of tending to be overly deferential and uncritical towards public authorities and particularly the police,[84] and recent examples show that this attitude may not simply be a thing of the past.[85] This attitude might have been justified had public trust in the police been high, but revelations of police impropriety that was later covered up led one newspaper to report that '[t]he incident

[83] *R* v. *Secretary of State for the Home Department, ex parte Fire Brigades Union* [1995] 2 AC 513 at 567; to the same effect, see Lord Woolf, 'Droit Public – English Style' [1995] *Public Law* 57, 58.

[84] See Robert Stevens, *The English Judges: Their Role in the Changing Constitution*, revised edition (Oxford: Hart Publishing, 2005), p. 75.

[85] *R (Gillan and another)* v. *Commissioner of Police of the Metropolis* [2006] UKHL 12; [2006] 2 AC 307; *Van Colle* v. *Chief Constable of Hertford* [2008] UKHL 50; [2009] 1 AC 225.

undermines confidence in the accountability at the police department'.[86] Rather than concerns over an excessively defensive police force as a result of the imposition of liability, such incidents indicate that there are reasons to be concerned about an overly aggressive police force, and that part of the problem may be insufficient judicial oversight.[87] Some of the opinions in the *Ashley* decisions reflect a recognition of these problems and a willingness to develop new methods of dealing with the vacuum that has allowed such events to happen.

[86] Sarah Lyall, 'Britain's Antiterror Officer Resigns', *New York Times*, 9 April 2009; see also Suzanne Bosman, 'Police in Danger of Losing Public Trust', *Guardian*, 9 April 2009; David Howarth, 'The Police Misled Us', *Guardian*, 8 April 2009; Leader, 'Answers Please', *The Times*, 9 April 2009.

[87] English tort law may be indirectly responsible for another source of insufficient oversight of the police: an overbroad defamation law made newspapers apprehensive about publishing stories alleging excessive use of force by the police. See Eric Barendt *et al.*, *Libel and the Media: The Chilling Effect* (Oxford: Clarendon, 1997), p. 188. Changes in the law subsequent to the publication of this book may have altered that.

11

Cy-près as a class action remedy – justly maligned or just misunderstood?

JEFF BERRYMAN AND ROBYN CARROLL

1 Introduction

Class actions have an established place in the Canadian and Australian legal systems but still attract considerable debate in practice, politics and the academy. One debate concerns whether there is any legitimate justification for class actions beyond the procedural facilitation of grouped proceedings.[1] 'Access to justice' and 'judicial economy' are the goals commonly said to justify class action provisions. On one view, these goals can be achieved through civil procedures that have compensation as their sole remedial goal. At the same time, many jurisdictions that have created class action regimes also provide as another justification the promotion of behavioural modification and deterrence of wrongdoers.[2] The principal way behaviour is modified and deterrence is achieved is by ensuring that the wrongdoer is forced to internalise all the costs of any harm that may have resulted from the wrongful act, and – depending on the particular facts of the case and whether the cause of action supports recovery

A draft of this chapter was given at 'Private and Public Law – Intersections in Law and Method' (TC Beirne School of Law, Brisbane, 21–22 July 2011). Revisions were undertaken while Jeff Berryman was a Visiting Erskine Fellow, Department of Accounting and Information Systems, University of Canterbury, and Robyn Carroll was a visitor to the Faculty of Law, University of Canterbury, New Zealand.

[1] A class action can be defined simply as 'a body of procedural rules enabling one or more persons to advance an action on behalf of a group of similarly situated persons': W. Branch, *Class Actions in Canada* (Aurora, Ontario: Canada Law Book, 2008), para. 1.20. In Australia class actions are referred to in the applicable legislation as 'Grouped Proceedings'. For the sake of simplicity we refer predominantly to class actions but at times the terms class action and grouped proceedings are used interchangeably.

[2] We use the terms 'behavioural modification' and 'deterrence' interchangeably to refer to the deterrent effect of a judicial remedy on the decision-making and conduct of potential

of profits – to disgorge any profits earned from the wrongful conduct. Compensating victims may partially and concurrently achieve deterrence if all victims can be identified and the true nature of their loss quantified. However, in many claims where a class action may be the most advantageous mechanism to compensate victims, not all victims may be able to be identified or, because the amount of each class member's claim is small, the cost of administering the claim may outweigh any benefit to individual class members. In these situations, one response is to restrict the ability to bring a class action. Alternatively, many jurisdictions provide for cy-près distribution schemes, in which the class counsel and judge choose a method of distribution for the benefit of class members that involves distributing the damages paid into the class action fund by the defendant other than by direct payment to each class member.[3] In this way a cy-près scheme is a mechanism that may achieve compensation for members of the class indirectly, as well as the goal of deterrence and behavioural modification, by ensuring that undistributed damages are not returned to the defendant.

This chapter contrasts the attitudes to cy-près as a class action remedy in Australia and Canada. The origins and features of private law and civil proceedings in these jurisdictions have much in common. There is a distinct difference, however, in the views about behavioural modification as a goal of class action procedures and whether or not there is a role for cy-près. Some of the concerns expressed in the Australian debate about the nature of cy-près are based on a view of compensation that requires a defendant to pay damages only to class members who can be identified, and on the idea that to require otherwise will be in the nature of a penalty. On this view, there is said to be no justification for ensuring that a defendant pays damages assessed at the full amount of the loss they have caused. Other concerns are expressed through the references to cy-près achieving the goals of disgorgement, punishment and deterrence[4] and to

civil defendants. Although, arguably, there are distinctions that can be drawn between the terms, these are not pursued here, nor in the class action literature to which we refer.

[3] See Rachael Mulheron, *The Modern Cy-près Doctrine: Applications and Implications* (London: UCL Press 2006); Jeff Berryman, 'Class Actions (Representative Proceedings) and the Exercise of the Cy-Près Doctrine: Time for Improved Scrutiny', in Jeff Berryman and Rick Bigwood (eds.), *The Law of Remedies: New Directions in the Common Law* (Toronto: Irwin Law, 2010), p. 727.

[4] See, e.g., Ruth C. A. Higgins, 'The Equitable Doctrine of Cy-près and Consumer Protection', Australian Consumers' Association Submission to the Trade Practices Review, Annex I (2002), available at: www.tpareview.treasury.gov.au/content/subs/105_Attachment1_ACA.pdf (last accessed 29 May 2013).

the potential for class actions to result in profit-stripping of defendants in circumstances that are not supported by the existing law.[5] We suggest that these concerns might be attributable to a misunderstanding of the circumstances in which cy-près is available and of the potential remedial consequences of this remedy. We take the view that while compensation is the primary goal of civil claims and class actions, other remedial goals, including behavioural modification and deterrence, coexist as recognised and legitimate goals of private law.

The debate over cy-près distributions in class actions mirrors a wider debate concerning the appropriate function of civil litigation. Increasingly in North America, civil litigation is viewed as one component of a regulatory scheme that is not myopically focused on compensation, but that accords a heightened role to behavioural modification and deterrence. In contrast, the recent debates in Australia over the inclusion of cy-près distribution in class actions suggest a strong reservation about the legitimacy of judges going beyond what commentators in the United States have described as 'compensation hegemony'.[6] This debate occurs at a time when, within the law of remedies, there is increasing recognition that plaintiffs sometimes have a preference for remedial outcomes aimed at behavioural modification and not simply compensation. We acknowledge that it is still difficult to find empirical evidence to substantiate the claim of behavioural modification as an outcome of class action litigation and this raises obvious questions about reliance on this remedial goal. Nevertheless, we suggest that, to the extent that the law does explicitly aim to deter civil wrongdoing, courts should take plaintiff remedial preferences and the pursuit of behavioural modification seriously. Notwithstanding that the compensation goal is a strong force or 'moral compass'[7] within a jurisdiction, we argue that cy-près distribution has remedial value because it may well provide a mechanism by which compensation may be achieved more fully[8] and because it

5 See, e.g., Australian Law Reform Commission (ALRC), *Access to the Courts – II: Class Actions (Discussion Paper No. 11)* (Canberra: Australian Government Publishing Service, 1979), at [50].

6 Myriam Gilles and Gary Friedman, 'Exploding the Class Action Agency Cost Myth: The Social Utility of Entrepreneurial Lawyers' (2006) 155 *University of Pennsylvania Law Review* 103.

7 Peta Spender, 'The Class Action as Sheriff: Private Law Enforcement and Remedial Roulette', in Jeff Berryman and Rick Bigwood (eds.), *The Law of Remedies: New Directions in the Common Law* (Toronto: Irwin Law, 2010), p. 720.

8 A cy-près distribution scheme overcomes procedural impediments where the cost of distributing to individuals is grossly disproportionate to the amount distributed, or where individual class members cannot be identified or located. However, this does not detract from the fact that harm and consequent loss has been suffered that warrants compensation.

may be aligned with the plaintiffs' remedial goals. This has implications for the remedial approach in jurisdictions that allow class actions, including Canada and Australia.

This chapter is presented in two parts. The first part (section 2 below) examines the interaction between remedial goals and the goals of class action proceedings in Australia, Canada and elsewhere. In subsection 2A we provide an overview of the range of remedial goals that are currently pursued in varying degrees in civil litigation. In doing so, we illustrate that the common law fabric that courts use to embroider the remedial element of a judgment is complex and relies on more than a single compensatory thread. A single judgment may encompass multiple remedial goals, including remedies that further behavioural modification and deterrence. In subsection 2B we describe the current dominance of monetary relief in class actions and the way this influences class counsel and litigant behaviour. In subsection 2C we outline some contemporary studies that indicate that civil litigants may value a remedial response other than an award of compensatory damages. We suggest that in some circumstances where class actions are likely to be brought, awarding more than compensatory damages is likely to accord with litigants' own preferences. Subsection 2D sets out four possible ways to sharpen the focus of behavioural modification as an aim of class actions, if this is desired. By the end of this section, we hope to have sown the seed of doubt that the remedial function of class actions involving civil disputes is – or should be – exclusively confined to awarding monetary compensation. As with other areas of civil litigation, a nuanced account is required; an account that is more in keeping with a purposive interpretation of the functions of tort law, other private law obligations and statutory actions that generate class actions.

In the second part of the chapter (section 3), we set out the foundations for behavioural modification and deterrence playing a role in class actions in Canada and Australia. In subsection 3B we establish that these foundations are explicit and uncontroversial in Canada. In subsection 3C we establish that, in Australia, recognition of these goals remains highly controversial. In subsection 3D we analyse the arguments for and against cy-près and the underlying concerns about departure from a purely compensatory model of civil litigation. We conclude this part of the chapter with an exploration of the arguments that may be of benefit for the

Thus, an appropriately designed cy-près distribution scheme can more fully effect compensation where there is the possibility of indirect benefit accruing to individual class members.

ongoing debate in Australia over the role of cy-près distributions in class actions.

2 The aims of class actions and their interaction with remedial goals

A *Civil remedies – a functional overview*

Within the law of remedies, dualist and integrationist accounts (as distinct from monist accounts) are seen as providing a better fit between what courts actually do in granting relief and the substantive claim that justifies a judicial award. Dualists and integrationists see in the law of remedies a number of functions being performed by an award.[9] This mirrors their understanding of substantive law; that enforcing torts, contracts and statutes can entail the pursuit of polycentric goals, including compensation, education, deterrence and the vindication of legal rights. A functional account of the law of remedies reveals at least eight distinctive goals that may be pursued by a plaintiff.[10]

(i) Compensation

Compensation remains the dominant justification in both private and public law for granting damages. The compensation principle[11] requires the court to determine an amount in damages that will place the plaintiff in the position he or she would have been in had the injury not happened. Where the injury is to either a purely economic interest or to property, damages are normally an effective remedial response to loss or damage caused by the wrongdoing. The plaintiff is given the means to purchase substitute performance for what has been lost in a form that is relatively easy to administer. Provided there is a readily identifiable market on which to make appropriate comparisons for the purposes of valuation, a damages remedy is easily calculated. When the plaintiff suffers non-pecuniary loss as a result of personal injury, compensation remains the

[9] See Jeff Berryman, 'The Law of Remedies: A Prospectus for Teaching and Scholarship' (2010) 9 *Oxford University Commonwealth Law Journal* 123.

[10] The functional taxonomy and some of the arguments in this section on behavioural modification draw from an earlier article first published in the Supreme Court Law Review. Jeff Berryman, 'Nudge, Nudge, Wink, Wink: Behavioural Modification, Cy-près Distributions and Class Actions' (2011) 53 *Supreme Court Law Review* 2d. 133.

[11] See Jeff Berryman, 'The Compensation Principle in Private Law' (2008) 42 *Loyola of Los Angeles Law Review* 91.

dominant remedy but its quantification can be problematic. Money is a poor substitute in cases of personal injuries because money can never fully restore the physical or mental health that has been lost. Also, much of the loss is prospective, requiring speculation as to the plaintiff's future. Where the loss is of an intangible or non-pecuniary nature, such as a loss of dignity, quantification rules are in a state of flux. Non-pecuniary loss is by definition incommensurable, and yet a court is required to attempt to value it in the pursuit of compensation.

(ii) Coercion

Coercion calls into play a court's power to grant specific relief through the use of injunction, specific performance or other court order backed up with a threat of proceedings for contempt of court. Historically, these remedies derive from a court's equitable jurisdiction. Coercive orders compel a defendant's compliance on pain of more severe punishment. Specific relief is often awarded in circumstances where the claimant has experienced little or no compensable injury (for example in cases involving trespass to land and enforcement of restrictive covenants) and coerces respect for the right that has been infringed.

(iii) Deterrence

Specific relief, where it is available, has a high deterrence value in protecting against continuing or future wrongdoing by the defendant. In many instances it will be too late to prevent wrongdoing and a plaintiff will rely on damages. The Supreme Court of Canada recognises deterrence as the dominant remedial goal of damages in at least two instances in cases involving punitive damages,[12] and in awarding public law damages for the violation of constitutional rights.[13] The High Court of Australia recognises deterrence as one purpose of exemplary damages, which have punishment as their primary goal.[14] The circumstances in which exemplary damages are available in Australia are determined by the conduct and the circumstances in a particular case and are not confined by legal principle to particular causes of action.[15] That said, the High Court has made it

[12] *Whiten* v. *Pilot Insurance Co.* [2002] 1 SCR 595.

[13] *Vancouver (City)* v. *Ward* [2010] 2 SCR 28.

[14] *Lamb* v. *Cotogno* (1987) 164 CLR 1; *New South Wales* v. *Ibbett* (2006) 229 CLR 638.

[15] *Gray* v. *Motor Accident Commission* (1998) 196 CLR 1, referring to common law actions. Exemplary damages are not available in Australia for breach of fiduciary duty: *Harris* v. *Digital Pulse Pty Ltd.* (2003) 56 NSWLR 298.

clear that exemplary damages are an exceptional remedy.[16] Deterrence, as we have seen, is also arguably a function in the quantification of damages in class action suits as part of an overall scheme that seeks behavioural modification as part of its *raison d'être*.

(iv) Punishment

Punishment as a function of damages is specifically recognised in an award of punitive or exemplary damages. Punishment seeks to measure either societal condemnation or retribution for the egregious conduct.

(v) Restitution

Restitution serves the function of restoring, in the sense of giving back, to the plaintiff that which has been taken by the defendant. It is the basis of the cause of action defined as the law of autonomous unjust enrichment. It is also the function served in claims for specific recovery of property, when the law allows such a claim.

(vi) Disgorgement

Disgorgement is distinct from restoration through restitution in that it functions to award gains made by the defendant to the plaintiff. It is often sought where there has been wrongdoing to the plaintiff but where the plaintiff has suffered no or little compensable loss as a result. The defendant is stripped of the financial gain made as a result of his wrongdoing, which is paid to the plaintiff.

(vii) Self-help

By and large, the common law does not encourage acts of self-help and a plaintiff must invoke some court process before recovering or exercising distraint upon property. However, self-help relief is available in some circumstances, including: where it has been agreed to contractually, as in liquidated damages clauses; in damages-only clauses; and, to a lesser extent, in clauses that seek to influence the granting of equitable relief through, for example, admissions that damages would be inadequate (a threshold test that must be met to gain either specific performance or an injunction).[17]

[16] *Gray* v. *Motor Accident Commission* (1998) 196 CLR 1 at [22]. Exemplary damages will not ordinarily be awarded in negligence and breach of contract cases: at [13].

[17] See generally Robyn Carroll, 'Agreements to Specifically Perform Contractual Obligations' (2012) 29 *Journal of Contract Law* 1.

(viii) Vindication

Vindication operates to validate the plaintiff's understanding that a right has been violated and to mark the violation of a legally protected right.[18] Australian courts have explicitly and consistently recognised the vindicatory purpose of damages awards in tort cases, predominantly in defamation and trespass actions.[19] Recently, the Supreme Court of Canada has recognised vindication as a primary reason justifying an award of damages for violation of a constitutionally protected right.[20]

These functions are not mutually exclusive. For example, where everyone injured by a wrongdoer recovers compensation resulting in the full internalisation of the cost of wrongdoing by the tortfeasor, then compensation can also achieve a deterrence function. In fact, this is a paramount reason used to support class actions in the area of tort law, in that it creates a procedural mechanism to maximise the internalisation by the tortfeasor of the true cost of their wrongdoing. A functional classification highlights that plaintiffs may well have concerns beyond compensation and deterrence. It also illustrates the strengths and weaknesses within any particular functional goal. For example, coercive remedies may effect deterrence better than damages;[21] compensation compensates poorly for non-pecuniary losses;[22] and vindication may be better achieved through resort to innovative remedies such as ordered apology and publication than through damages,[23] to name but a few. Similarly, a plaintiff does not necessarily pursue a single goal; rather, trade-offs are made. For example,

[18] Normann Witzleb and Robyn Carroll, 'The Role of Vindication in Torts Damages' (2009) 17 *Tort Law Review* 16. More broadly, the vindicatory function of private law can be described as events occurring within judicial practice and in positive response to legal rights. See Kit Barker, 'Private and Public: The Mixed Concept of Vindication in Torts and Private Law', in Stephen G. A. Pitel, Jason W. Neyers and Erika Chamberlain (eds.), *Tort Law: Challenging Orthodoxy* (Oxford: Hart Publishing, 2013.

[19] *Uren* v. *John Fairfax & Sons* (1965–66) 117 CLR 118 at 150 (Windeyer J) (defamation); *Plenty* v. *Dillon* (1991) 171 CLR 635 at 654 (Gaudron and McHugh JJ) (vindicating the plaintiff's right to exclusive use of his or her land).

[20] *Vancouver (City)* v. *Ward* [2010] 2 SCR 28.

[21] A point made clear in the Ontario Law Reform Commission (OLRC), *Report on Class Actions* (Ontario: Ministry of the Attorney-General, 1982), vol. I, p. 140: 'The potential of civil litigation to modify wrongful behavior is most obvious in the case of injunctive relief.'

[22] Michael Tilbury, 'Coherence, Non-Pecuniary Loss, and the Construction of Privacy', in Jeff Berryman and Rick Bigwood (eds.), *The Law of Remedies: New Directions in the Common Law* (Toronto: Irwin Law, 2010), p. 139.

[23] Robyn Carroll and Normann Witzleb, 'It's Not Just About the Money: Enhancing the Vindicatory Effect of Private Law Remedies' (2011) 37 *Monash University Law Review* 216.

the effect of a public retraction or correction of a defamatory statement lessens the damages payable on the basis that the plaintiff has been vindicated and his or her reputation restored, thereby lessening the need for compensation.[24]

B *The dominance of monetary relief in class actions*

Monetary relief covers compensatory damages at law including aggravated damages, an account of profits or other monetary award as a result of an action in unjust enrichment, and punitive damages. In Canada all provincial class action legislation contains varying provisions to facilitate monetary relief as a remedy, for example provisions that enable various statistical methods and other evidentiary rules to be used to aggregate damages.[25] On the distribution side, this enables cy-près distribution even if the effect is to benefit non-parties.[26]

The remedial powers conferred on Australian courts under class action provisions are broad. Section 33Z(1) of the Federal Court Act 1976 (Cth), for example, empowers a judge, amongst other things, to make awards of damages; to grant any equitable relief; and to make such other orders as the court thinks fit. Section 33Z(1)(g) of the Supreme Court of Victoria Act 1986 (Vic) expressly provides that in making such other order as is just, it may make, but is not restricted to, an order for monetary relief other than for damages and an order for non-pecuniary damages. Notwithstanding these broad remedial powers, as in Canada, the practical purpose of the class action provisions in Australia is to facilitate the recovery of damages. Damages may be awarded in an aggregate amount without specifying amounts awarded in respect of individual group members,[27] but the court must be satisfied that a reasonably accurate assessment of the total amount of damages to which group members will be entitled can be made.[28] When an award of damages is ordered, the legislation requires a court to make provision for the payment or distribution of the money to the group members entitled.[29] In cases where the court establishes a fund for the administration of the money to be distributed, it is empowered to make orders for the payment from the fund of any residue to

[24] Raymond Brown, *Law of Defamation in Canada* (Toronto: Canada Law Book, 1987), p. 1016.

[25] For example, in Ontario see the Class Proceedings Act, S.O. 1992, c. 6, s. 23.

[26] For example, in Ontario see *ibid.*, s. 26(6)(a).

[27] *Ibid.*, s. 33cy(1)(f). [28] *Ibid.*, s. 33Z(3).

[29] Federal Court Act 1976 (Cth) s. 33Z(2).

the respondent.[30] No express provision is made for cy-près distribution. Although the view has been expressed that the power conferred upon the Supreme Court of Victoria by s. 33Z(1)(g) of the Supreme Court Act 1986 (Vic) allows that Court to 'grant cy-près type remedies',[31] we suggest it is unlikely that a court would exercise any such power if it does exist. We say this because the court is required to make provision for the distribution of damages to class members, there is no legislative indication that funds are intended to go to anyone other than to an identified class member and there is a requirement that any surplus be returned to the respondent.[32]

The United States has clearly embarked on a path that provides incentives for the private enforcement of public rights, and the class action is recognised as an important means of attaining these rights.[33] Incentives come in a variety of ways but, essentially, overcome the barriers of legal fees by awarding treble damages, liquidated or statutory minimum damages, and favourable lawyer fees rules.[34] These incentives make class actions attractive in constitutional and human rights settings, as well as in cases of securities fraud, environmental claims, product liability and consumer complaints. Often in these claims the chosen remedy will be an injunction: a remedy that arguably has greater power to achieve deterrence and immediate behavioural modification. Notably, however, the pursuit of injunctive relief may be motivated by other concerns. In the United States it will be easier to gain certification if the spectre of a court being embroiled in individual issues is reduced, which, in seeking simple injunctive relief or declaration, the class representative is able to do. The claim for injunctive relief is also often a preliminary step to shore

[30] *Ibid.*, s. 33ZA(5).

[31] This view was expressed in the Corrs Chambers Westgarth Submission ED132 to the Victorian Law Reform Commission in its Civil Justice Review: Victorian Law Reform Commission (VLRC), *Civil Justice Review, Report No 14* (Melbourne: VLRC, 2008), ch. 8, [3.7], n. 298.

[32] The VLRC describes whether the court already has the power to grant cy-près remedies as 'a vexed question': *ibid.*, at [3.7]. Doubts about whether the proper construction of s. 33Z(1)(g) is that it confers power on the court to do anything other than make orders in these terms prompted the VLRC to recommend legislative clarification to ensure that the court does have the power to do so through cy-près relief: at [3.7] and Recommendation 101.

[33] Christopher Hodges, 'Objectives, Mechanisms and Policy Choices in Collective Enforcement and Redress', in J. Steele and Willem van Boom (eds.), *Mass Justice: Challenges of Representation and Distribution* (Cheltenham: Edward Elgar, 2011), Chapter 5.

[34] See A. Conte and H. Newberg, *Newberg on Class Actions* (St Paul, MN: Thomson West, 2002), at [5.51].

up bargaining power in an eventual settlement on other terms leading to monetary relief.[35]

Canada and Australia have not embarked on the same path as the United States. In Australia costs follow the event with protection for group members from any liability to pay the respondent's costs, subject to some exceptions.[36] In Canada there has also been little change to costs rules (although some provinces have adopted a no-costs rule in which both sides bear their own costs in certification actions – British Columbia, Saskatchewan, Newfoundland, Manitoba and the Federal Court) and no statutory provisions encourage damage multipliers. In Canada some statutory damages provisions do exist, but are little used.[37] Class action claims that request an injunction as the predominant remedy simply do not exist.[38] In fact, the Supreme Court of Canada has suggested that the fact that an injunction has effect beyond the immediate litigant, and can be sought by an individual, may be a reason to deny class action certification where the constitutional validity of governmental action is in dispute.[39]

The incentives to private enforcement of public rights provided variously by court procedures, remedies, fee structures and costs rules have led to different styles of lawyering. The conventional client lawyer seeks to deploy skills to achieve what the client directs. The entrepreneurial lawyer is distant from the class client, taking little if any direction from the client but absorbing the risk to fund the class action and assuming a fee based on success. The cause or ideological lawyer is one motivated to enforce public rights in pursuit of some different vision of social justice.[40] We do not suggest that cause or ideological lawyering is not practised in Canada or Australia. In fact, the Supreme Court of Canada has altered standing rules to make it easier for an individual to challenge governmental

[35] *Ibid.*, at [5.11].

[36] Federal Court Act 1976 (Cth), s. 43(1A).

[37] For example, the Federal Copyright Act contains a right to statutory damages: Copyright Act, R.S. 1985, c.C-30, s. 38.1.

[38] A search of the Canadian Bar Association Class Action database reveals that where actions include the request for an injunction, it arises in the context of preventing the further violation of a deceptive or misleading trade practice in consumer cases; however, the primary remedy is a damages claim for past transgressions: available at: www.cba.org/ClassActions/main/gate/index/ (last accessed 29 May 2013).

[39] *Marcotte* v. *Longueuil (City)* [2009] 3 SCR 65, but, not universally so. See *Kwicksutaineuk/Ah-Kwa-Mish First Nation* v. *British Columbia (Minister of Agriculture and Lands)* (2012) 31 BCLR (5th) 215 (CA), leave to appeal denied [2012] SCCA No. 336.

[40] See Spender, 'The Class Action as Sheriff', p. 699.

action.[41] Rather, it is not presently a feature of class action litigation. The dominant lawyering model is that of the entrepreneurial lawyer.

In Canada the class action lawyer is the one funding the action through a contingency fee agreement or securing investors in the litigation. The lawyer's fee is determined on the basis of either a percentage of recovery or, more often, a base and multiplier fee (loadstar), the multiplier being determined upon hours worked, amount recovered, risk, and the factual and legal complexity of issues in dispute.[42] The monetary amount expected on recovery will condition the effort expended. In Canada chasing the money is what class actions are all about. It is fair to say that the same is true in Australia. The acceptance of 'no win no fee' agreements in Australia mirrors the use of contingency fee agreements in Canada and has become the principal way of funding class actions. However, in 2006 the High Court of Australia[43] approved the use of a commercial litigation funding agreement, setting off unprecedented growth in commercial litigation funding firms whose principal business is the financing of litigation.[44] This is in contrast to Canada, where the first commercial litigation funding firm's foray into class actions has only just gained approval.[45] The impact of this form of funding model is to transform any particular claim into a profit-making enterprise, effectively ensuring that a remedy that maximises a monetary return is the only one pursued. But does this satisfy the class representative and class member? Monetary relief in the form of damages is an obvious and rational objective when the harm caused by the defendant is tangible and can be quantified in monetary terms. But the interests that plaintiffs seek to protect by litigating may be

[41] *Finlay* v. *Minister of Finance of Canada* [1986] 2 SCR 607. It has even provided a limited discretionary jurisdiction to order an advanced interim costs award to enable a public interest litigant to pursue legal action: see *British Columbia (Minister of Forests)* v. *Okanagan Indian Band* [2003] 3 SCR 371.

[42] Branch, in a survey of class actions in Ontario between 1996 and 2006, found a median multiplier of 2.74 and a median percentage fee of 14.73 per cent: Branch, *Class Actions in Canada*. See also W. A. Bogart, J. Kalajdzic and I. Matthews, 'Class Actions in Canada: A National Procedure in a Multi-Jurisdictional Society?', paper presented to The Globalization of Class Actions Conference (Oxford University, 2007), p. 27.

[43] *Campbells Cash and Carry Pty Ltd.* v. *Fostif Pty Ltd.* (2006) 229 CLR 386.

[44] See Michael Legg, Louisa Travers, Edmond Park and Nicholas Turner, 'Litigation Funding in Australia', University of New South Wales Faculty of Law Research Series, Paper 12 (2010), available at: http://law.bepress.com/unswwps/flrps10/art12 (last accessed 29 May 2013).

[45] *Dugal* v. *Manulife Financial Corp.* (2011) 105 OR (3d) 364; *Fehr* v. *Sun Life Assurance Co. of Canada* [2012] OJ No. 2029 (Sup. Ct. J.).

non-monetary. Compensatory damages are not necessarily the only or most effective way to protect these non-monetary interests.

C *Plaintiff remedial preferences*

The argument has been made that, within the law of remedies, more attention should be accorded to a plaintiff's choice over remedial relief. This argument has been most forcefully advocated by Hammond with respect to challenging the hierarchical and discretionary relationship between equitable and common law remedies.[46] The argument also extends to other areas of choice over remedial goals. We accept that the law prescribes how a particular remedy is obtained within the functional account of remedies given above, and that, for example, coercive, deterrence and punitive remedies cannot be awarded on the basis of a whim or purely subjective preference of a plaintiff. Nevertheless, in a civil system that accords a great deal of autonomy to claimants in how to frame and prosecute their actions, we suggest that courts should give due weight to a plaintiff's remedial choice. In our view a plaintiff's preferred form of remedial relief should be favoured over the defendant's preference, unless the defendant can make countervailing arguments that demonstrate an appreciable, adverse impact incommensurate with the gain to be obtained through acceding to the plaintiff's choice of remedy.

In the usual civil action a client will set the parameters concerning the relief they are seeking and would value, although evidence suggests that they are heavily influenced by their lawyer instructing them on what they likely will receive and therefore what they should request.[47] In the class action suit there is far less scope for involvement of the 'client', even if, as might be argued, the representative plaintiff should set these parameters.[48] It is peculiar to class actions that in some jurisdictions a cy-près distribution will be favoured in which the court supposedly substitutes its decision for class members where they cannot be identified, or where the cost to administer the claim would outweigh any benefit to a class member. In these situations the court speaks for the class on remedial

[46] See Grant Hammond, 'Rethinking Remedies: The Changing Conception of the Relationship Between Legal and Equitable Remedies', in J. Berryman (ed.), *Remedies: Issues and Perspectives* (Ontario: Carswell, 1989), p. 93.

[47] Donald Harris *et al.*, *Compensation and Support for Illness and Injury* (Oxford: Clarendon Press, 1984), pp. 124, 126.

[48] See Jasminka Kalajdzic, 'Self-Interest, Public Interest and the Interests of the Absent Client: Legal Ethics and Class Action Praxis' (2011) 49 *Osgoode Hall Law Journal* 1.

selection and distribution[49] and therefore exercises a considerable discretion over shaping how a particular class action is matched to the remedial functional goal or goals. However, the court is not acting on its own volition in these cases. There are the submissions of the representative plaintiff, potentially other affected class members, both class counsel and the doctrinal constraints on the cy-près doctrine itself. These guide what a court may accept as a legitimate remedial outcome, and as according with the likely predominant remedial goal or goals of the class. If the choice is either to do nothing and effectively sterilise the class action or, to satisfy, albeit imperfectly, some of the remedial goals of class members, the better result is surely the latter. If the substantive claim is legitimate, the defendant has neither a legal, nor moral claim to hold on to the benefits that flow simply because there are procedural and costs barriers to the plaintiffs accessing the courts to make their claims. Viewed this way, cy-près distributions are consistent with advancing the aims of procedural changes brought about by class and representative action legislation, namely to enable otherwise non-viable legal actions to result in a desirable remedial outcome in furtherance of the 'access to justice' and 'judicial economy' goals behind the legislation.

What do plaintiffs want from a civil suit? Given the centrality of this question to civil law, it is surprising that there is very little empirical research available. Richard Abel has commented on the lack of empirical evidence to argue that there is little reason to award monetary relief for non-pecuniary loss ('general damages' in the United States).[50] Within his argument he cites numerous instances of anecdotal evidence that 'casts doubt on the facile assertion that victims want only money for pain and suffering'.[51] Carroll and Witzleb argue that plaintiffs often want vindication and that, in many circumstances, non-monetary relief may be a preferred way to achieve this. They document a variety of studies in the areas of medical negligence, defamation and anti-discrimination law that illustrate what many plaintiffs value in addition to, or in place of, monetary relief.[52] In a small study of plaintiffs who bring actions for medical malpractice, Tamara Relis documents that, overwhelmingly, plaintiffs

[49] Berryman, 'Class Actions', p. 727; Jasminka Kalajdzic, 'Access to a Just Result: Revisiting Settlement Standards and Cy-près Distributions' (2010) 6 *Canadian Class Action Review* 215.

[50] Richard Abel, 'General Damages are Incoherent, Incalculable, Incommensurable, and Inegalitarian (But Otherwise a Great Idea)' (2006) 55 *DePaul Law Review* 253.

[51] *Ibid.*, 266.

[52] Carroll and Witzleb, 'It's Not Just About the Money'.

are motivated by a desire to satisfy extra-legal desires rather than to seek monetary compensation. It is both plaintiff and defendant lawyers who transform the dispute into one focused on money.[53]

These studies identify that plaintiffs often crave acknowledgement of wrongdoing, accountability and education of wrongdoers and a change in future behaviour. Where members of a class action have suffered significant damage, compensation can be expected to be a significant goal of the proceedings. When they have suffered a paltry compensable injury that would lead to an award of only a few dollars compensation, it is easy to imagine the preferred relief would be of a non-monetary kind.[54] It is in these circumstances that a court may choose to exercise its power to order cy-près distribution, thereby identifying a distribution that accords with the 'next best thing' to granting compensation to the class members. Based on his study of decided cases, Berryman has previously suggested that the link between what a court has authorised in cy-près distributions and the purposes for which compensation was being assessed to compensate for injury to class members is at best tenuous.[55] In many cases other extraneous issues appear to account for the selection of cy-près distribution recipients, particularly the idiosyncrasies of legal counsel and the charities they wish to benefit.[56] Berryman suggests that, viewed strictly from a deterrence point of view, the only concern should be to ensure that the funds are not returned to the defendant; otherwise cost internalisation would not be properly achieved. Distributing the money anywhere other than to the defendant satisfies a deterrence rationale.

While compensation remains the imperative, we will argue that cy-près distribution is also consistent with this remedial goal, even though it may

[53] Tamara Relis, '"It's Not About the Money!": A Theory on Misconceptions of Plaintiffs' Litigation Aims' (2007) 68 *University of Pittsburgh Law Review* 701. The study involved is small, the data deriving from 131 in-depth interviews, questionnaires and observations of files of plaintiffs, defendants, lawyers and mediators involved in 64 mediated medical malpractice claims, an action that is often extremely difficult to prove.

[54] In the US, the problem of distributing small amounts of money to class members has been met by using alternative remedies such as ordering the defendant either to discount the price of a good or service for a period of time, or to issue redeemable coupons to class members. These types of orders are not without their own controversy for artificially distorting a marketplace; see generally, Conte and Newberg, *Newberg on Class Actions*.

[55] See Berryman, 'Class Actions', p. 757.

[56] The lack of criteria to determine cy-près distribution is also a feature of US practice. See K. Forde, 'What Can a Court Do with Leftover Class Action Funds? Almost Anything!' (1996) 35 *Judges' Journal* 1. See also *Re Lupron Marketing & Sales Practices Litigation; Rohn* v. *Tap Pharmaceutical Products Inc.* 677 F 3d 21 (1st Cir. 2012) establishing criteria to assist courts in determining how to exercise the cy-près discretion.

concurrently further behavioural modification and deterrence. In this regard, it is important to remember that cy-près is a method of distribution, not a different way of measuring or assessing the damages payable by the respondent. In most cases for which class actions are brought, there must still be a loss experienced by class members based on a substantive cause of action. Even when the cause of action supports a measure of damages other than compensation (for example, disgorgement), cy-près distribution does not determine the remedial goals being pursued. A cy-près distribution simply ensures that the defendant does not retain any of the damages assessed for loss simply on the basis that the cost of distribution, or of identifying class plaintiffs, exceeds the commensurate benefit to any one, individual plaintiff. Providing for cy-près distribution can ensure that, rather than returning compensation to the defendant, it is distributed through a scheme that is viewed by the court as providing an alternative way to effect compensation.

D Strengthening the behavioural modification goal – possible approaches

It remains controversial whether the law should explicitly embrace behavioural modification and deterrence as a legitimate goal of civil litigation by class actions or any private law actions for that matter. Historically, the common law was more about keeping the peace than redressing individual wrongdoing, and the development of common law causes of action was driven largely by the desire to remove resort to self-help relief by aggrieved parties. The strict demarcation between civil wrongdoing and criminal conduct arose later, after formal criminal processes and procedures were created. The expansion of civil wrongdoing throughout the twentieth century, a period dominated by legal formalist jurisprudence and in particular the law of negligence, has posed new challenges to provide adequate descriptive and theoretical accounts that rationally explain what courts do, or ought to do. Deterrence has long been identified as a goal of tort law, although torts scholars generally attribute a much reduced role to this purpose of tort law, largely due to the availability of third-party (liability) insurance to defendants.[57] By the 1980s, and after much of tort law with respect to actions concerning personal injury had been subsumed into a

[57] See, e.g., R. P. Balkin and J. L. R. Davis, *Law of Torts*, 4th edition (Australia: LexisNexis, 2004), p. 7. Glanville Williams, 'The Aims of Tort Law' (1951) 4 *Current Legal Problems* 137, esp. at 153.

plethora of statutory compensation schemes, we find other accounts of tort law emerging; accounts that highlight the educative, therapeutic and ombudsman functions of tort law. These debates live on today. Corrective justice theorists advance purely rectificatory accounts of tort law, economic theorists advance deterrence accounts, and civil recourse or court order theorists, arguably, can claim a foot in either camp. A mixed theory of tort law allows for recognition of corrective justice and deterrence as 'collaborators rather than competitors'.[58] In this way, deterrence as a purpose of negligence law, for example, can be understood not simply in terms of economic efficiency but also as means to achieve justice through preventing accidents. On this reasoning, Schwartz argues that the deterrent objective of tort law can appeal to those whose interests in tort law are 'humane and compassionate rather than narrowly utility-maximizing'.[59] Beyond tort law, in an age of statutes where legislatures empower courts to provide civil remedies for a variety of statutory causes of action, the same debates surface. Does the statute create only a right of civil redress for purely compensable losses, or is it part of an overall regulatory scheme in which private parties are accorded a role to ensure the attainment of the statute's purpose?[60]

Broadly speaking, all legal systems have behavioural modification as a pervasive concern; a position verified in the burgeoning literature on 'normativity'. Normativity is at the heart of work by Christopher Hodges,[61] Iain Ramsay,[62] Bill Bogart,[63] and Richard Thayler and Cass Sunstein,[64] to name but a few. Their work seeks to determine how litigation influences norms and what is the optimal mix between criminalisation, regulation, litigation and other public policy directives, and who should be empowered to bring such proceedings, whether as public or private enforcers.[65]

[58] Gary Schwartz, 'Mixed Theories of Tort Law: Affirming Both Deterrence and Corrective Justice' (1997) 75 *Texas Law Review* 1801, 1834.

[59] *Ibid*.

[60] See, e.g., the dissenting judgment of Kirby J in *Marks* v. *GIO* (1998) 196 CLR 494.

[61] Hodges, 'Objectives, Mechanisms and Policy Choices'.

[62] Iain Ramsay, 'Consumer Law, Regulatory Capitalism and "New Learning" in Regulation' (2006) 28 *Sydney Law Review* 9.

[63] W. A. Bogart, *Permit But Discourage: Regulating Excessive Consumption* (New York: Oxford University Press, 2011).

[64] Richard Thayler and Cass Sunstein, *Nudge: Improving Decisions About Health, Wealth, and Happiness* (New Haven: Yale University Press, 2008).

[65] Sanderson and Trebilcock make the interesting observation that, of all the price fixing or maintenance competition class actions brought in Canada by 2006 (sixteen in total), only two cases were truly newly discovered Competition Act violations by private parties. All the other actions were follow-on actions, resulting from prosecutions or investigations

Within the confines of civil litigation we have already set out the functional remedial goals that can be attained; goals that transcend pure compensation into areas that have normatively significant behavioural modification and deterrence aspects. Even on its own terms of confining civil litigation to purely compensatory purposes, where all claimants can be amassed and compensated, a secondary function will be deterrence if the defendant is made to internalise all the costs of its actions. In this way, the defendant is encouraged to reformulate the way it undertakes its actions to minimise future harm to others or to bear the costs of appropriate insurance to compensate for harm that is inevitable and unavoidable. In both cases the effect is behaviour modification but consistent with compensatory goals. A class action optimises this impact because it brings together all harmed claimants.

If sharpening the focus of class actions on behavioural modification is desired, a number of approaches could be taken. Although our primary focus in this chapter is cy-près distribution, we look at four possible approaches in this section. Behavioural modification as a purpose underlies each of these approaches, whether through disgorgement of gains, punitive damages, advancing causes of action that maximise deterrence over other remedial goals, or coercive remedies. They are related, but not mutually exclusive approaches. For example, disgorgement of profits can be achieved directly by using that as the measure of the monetary relief, or indirectly by awarding punitive damages in amounts that equal or exceed the profits arising from wrongdoing. What these approaches have in common is that they operate outside a purely compensatory paradigm: they embrace a behavioural modification role.

(i) Disgorgement of gains

The place for disgorgement of gains in civil remedies is a controversial subject. Traditionally, this approach to assessment was confined to violations of intellectual property rights and breaches of fiduciary duty. In the former, the approach can be justified as either constituting an appropriate licence fee or user principle, or as an accurate measure of foregone profits that the innocent party would have obtained but for the defendant's wrongful appropriation of the plaintiff's intellectual property. In the

by either Canadian or US public enforcement agencies: Margaret Sanderson and Michael Trebilcock, 'Competition Class Actions: An Evaluation of Deterrence and Corrective Justice Rationales', in Stephen Pitel (ed.), *Litigating Conspiracy: An Analysis of Competition Class Actions* (Toronto: Irwin Law, 2006), p. 33.

latter, accounting for profits has also been seen as a measure of restoring to the beneficiary a foregone opportunity following the wrongful use of trust property, or as an appropriate prophylactic remedy to deter errant fiduciaries from breaching their duty of loyalty. Disgorgement of gains is also a remedy for waiver of tort, and it is the coupling of this cause of action with its disgorgement remedy to class actions that has raised alarm. To date, waiver of tort has operated as an alternative cause of action to property and intentional torts. However, class certification actions have been brought in Canada in which waiver of tort has been brought as an alternative to actions in negligence.[66] The reason for this pleading is to overcome the difficulty that, in negligence actions, proof of loss is a necessary ingredient of the action. In a class action setting, need for individualised proof of loss will likely result in the denial of class certification because the class action will not pass the preferability criteria. However, framing the action as a waiver of tort, it is argued, avoids the issue of proof of individualised loss, and thus makes the action amenable to resolution by a class action.[67] Separating the disgorgement of gains from the need either to provide proof of loss or a property foundation disconnects the remedy from any compensatory function. However, disgorgement of gains serves an obvious deterrent function because the motivating rationale is to prevent a wrongdoer profiting from his or her wrong.

(ii) Award punitive damages, more frequently and at higher levels

Another way to enhance behavioural modification would be to award punitive damages more frequently and at higher levels. Canada is a bit of an outlier when it comes to granting punitive damages. While the Supreme Court of Canada has recognised the exceptional nature of these

[66] See, e.g., *Heward* v. *Eli Lilly & Co.* (2008) 91 OR (3d) 691; 295 DLR (4th) 175; 239 OAC 273, affirming certification of a negligence action concerning the manufacturing of an anti-psychotic drug but claiming waiver of tort. The action settled before a trial of the substantive merits: (2010) 97 CPC (6th) 382; [2010] ONSC 3403.

[67] *Serhan Estate* v. *Johnson & Johnson* (2006) 269 DLR (4th) 279; 213 OAC 298 considers whether waiver of tort is its own free-standing cause of action, or is a *sine qua non* of an analogous tort claim based on the concept that a wrongdoer should not profit from wrongdoing. In the latter, what torts support waiver of tort? At issue is whether an action in negligence and requiring individual proof of loss can be framed as one in waiver of tort where the profits to be disgorged can be readily identified. The action settled before a trial of the substantive merits: [2011] ONSC 128. The British Columbia Court of Appeal has expressed reservations on the boundaries of waiver of tort, but agrees that the law remains unsettled in Canada: *Koubi* v. *Mazda Canada Inc.* [2012] BCCA 310 at [39].

damages,[68] they are claimed and awarded relatively frequently in Canada, and in areas where they would not be awarded in other Commonwealth jurisdictions, namely contract law and negligence.[69] Within these claims, however, the amounts awarded remain modest. There are a number of class action cases where punitive damages have been certified as a common issue, including an endorsement by the Supreme Court of Canada.[70] Another line of cases has refused certification of punitive damages as a common issue on the grounds that, under the Supreme Court's guidelines, compensatory damages must be determined before punitive damages so as to ensure a rational connection between the awards.[71]

Any suggestion of increasing the utility of punitive damages invites comparisons with the United States and the perception, which is not the reality, that they are frequently awarded in that country.[72] Even where awarded in the US in apparently astronomical sums ($5 billion in the case of a jury award arising from the Exxon Valdez oil spill), they are invariably cut down on appeal or settlement.[73] However, concern over these awards has led to constitutional arguments in which the United States Supreme Court has been active in limiting the amounts awarded. Insurance problems also arise regarding punitive damages, raising the question whether they are covered by insurance when the defendant is either directly or vicariously liable for the wrong.[74] Given this chequered Canadian and US experience, class action lawyers may well believe that it would prove unwise to rely solely upon punitive damages as providing a sufficiently stable foundation with the right incentives to encourage suits.[75] There

[68] *Whiten* v. *Pilot Insurance Co.* [2002] 1 SCR 595.

[69] Bruce Feldthusen, 'Punitive Damages: Hard Choices and High Stakes' [1998] *New Zealand Law Review* 741.

[70] *Rumley* v. *British Columbia* [2001] 1 SCR 184; Michael Eizenga, Michael Peerless, Charles Wright and John Callaghan, *Class Actions Law and Practice*, loose-leaf edition (Markham: LexisNexis, 2009), at §3.93.

[71] See *Robinson* v. *Medtronic Inc.* [2010] ONSC 3777; 79 CPC (6th) 392, affirming the decision of Perell J [2009] OJ No. 4366, where the cases are analysed in depth.

[72] Theodore Eisenberg, Neil La Fountain, Brian Ostrom, David Rottman and Martin Wells, 'Juries, Judges, and Punitive Damages: An Empirical Study' (2002) 87 *Cornell Law Review* 743.

[73] See Michael Rustad, 'Unravelling Punitive Damages: Current Data and Further Inquiry' [1998] *Wisconsin Law Review* 15, 40.

[74] See Peter Braund, 'Punitive Damages: Not Covered, Eh?' (1998) 20 *Advocates' Quarterly* 442; Tom Baker, 'Reconsidering Insurance for Punitive Damages' [1998] *Wisconsin Law Review* 101.

[75] See Doug Rendleman, 'A Plea to Reject the United States Supreme Court's Due-Process Review of Punitive Damages', in Jeff Berryman and Rick Bigwood (eds.), *The Law of Remedies: New Directions in the Common Law* (Toronto: Irwin Law, 2010), p. 533;

is little likelihood of the punitive damages approach being adopted in Australia given the strong resistance there to non-compensatory damages in class actions and private law actions more generally.

(iii) Allow class actions to be pursued solely on grounds of deterrence

Under this approach, deterrence is achieved when all the compensable loss of the class members is recovered, or, more commonly, when the gains of wrongdoing are ordered to be disgorged, regardless of whether class members actually receive any part of the award. In these cases a court may be asked to make a cy-près distribution or an enhanced payment to class counsel. The important feature is that none of the award is returned to the defendant. Cassels and Jones advocate this position in the context of statutory regulatory enforcement.[76] They point to studies demonstrating that where compliance is left to regulatory enforcement, deterrence is sub-optimal. Explanations for this include the fact that regulatory agencies are often understaffed and underfunded, hampered by political interference, and lack the same incentives to vigorously pursue enforcement. Cassels and Jones suggest that resistance to private enforcement through class actions largely stems from the perceived objectionable appearance of lawyers profiting through disproportionately high legal fees. Their response is simply one based on moral equivalence. Why should the wrongdoer have greater claim to the fruits of wrongdoing than a lawyer who pursues punishing the wrongdoer and preventing the reoccurrence of the wrong?

Gilles and Friedman advocate more forcefully for a deterrence approach.[77] They argue that current US class action practices have been captured by a compensationalist hegemony.[78] Lawyers' fees in the United States, which have normally been assessed as a percentage of the damages recovered, have now become subject to a 'loadstar cross-check' linked to the hours worked and so on, so as to limit and avoid perceived windfalls being paid to lawyers. In turn, limiting lawyer fees to work that advances compensation for class members is said to lead to sub-optimal deterrence

Catherine Sharkey, 'Punitive Damages as Societal Damages' (2003) 113 *Yale Law Journal* 347, arguing that punitive damages should be reclassified as compensatory to compensate for the loss of collective societal interests.

[76] Jamie Cassels and Craig Jones, *The Law of Large-Scale Claims: Product Liability, Mass Torts, and Complex Litigation in Canada* (Toronto: Irwin Law, 2005), p. 368.

[77] Gilles and Friedman, 'Exploding the Class Action Agency Cost Myth'.

[78] See also Spender, 'The Class Action as Sheriff'.

because at a certain point in time the lawyer will not be compensated for chasing the last cent, which is the only way to ensure that the defendant is forced to internalise the full cost of wrongdoing: the central means to achieve deterrence.

There are a number of objections to the deterrence-only approach that are articulated briefly here. First, there is a questionable assumption that sufficient incentives can be created to make it cost-effective for private lawyers to engage in a form of privatised prosecution. For example, in many of the regulatory suits that form the foundation of a class action, the action has only commenced following regulatory prosecution – what is termed a 'follow-on suit'. In these cases evidence of, and from, the regulatory prosecution supplements in appreciable ways the subsequent class action.[79] This may demonstrate either lack of sufficient incentives, or lack of capacity, to engage in carrying a larger burden of evidence-gathering to prove wrongdoing.

Second, private deterrence would amount to random enforcement. There is potential for lawyers to target claims where wrongdoing can be proved according to whether litigation fees can be maximised. In contrast, regulatory prosecution is a much more nuanced and discretionary process. A regulator is often entitled to fashion the form of action and the time in which to prosecute, and choose a particular remedy suitable to the economic, political and legal climate in which they operate. All these are lost in private litigation.

Third, what would we make of class actions brought against government? Jones and Baxter have argued that deterrence arguments levelled at government are largely ineffectual. If the class action is for a past wrong, deterrence is not necessary. If the action is brought for an ongoing wrong, the deterrent effect is substantially weakened where it is the taxpayer (either directly, or as insurer of government action) who is forced to carry the costs of internalisation. Because of the size of government, apart from huge awards, there is little ripple effect on the taxpayer, such that taxpayer motivation to correct aberrant behaviour is non-existent. In the case of large awards it seems strange to order a burden on taxpayers for the very reason of preventing a governmental wrong from reoccurring to other similarly placed taxpayers. Jones and Baxter do not question the utility of class actions to achieve compensation for government wrongdoing – although even here a court should be cognisant of the effect of an

[79] See above n. 65.

intergenerational shift of the tax burden[80] – only that deterrence should not be a factor in determining preferability when considering certification of a class action against government.

Finally, any enhancement of a deterrence rationale must deal with the implications of insurance. Insurance primarily operates to enhance the compensation function by ensuring that there is a pool of money available to pay class members' awards. In turn, insurance shifts the risk away from the defendant to a broader pool of policy holders, or, in the case of a corporation, to the shareholders, up to the extent of their interest. The deterrence role of insurance is secondary; adjusting premiums according to risk assumed and, ultimately, denial of insurance. Because we all carry insurance for various risks, but the number of insurance companies is finite, at some level we therefore carry parts of the burden of insurance payouts, which then raises the issue of who actually bears the burden of cost internalisation.

(iv) Make greater use of coercive remedies

A final alternative to strengthen behavioural modification would be to have greater resort to coercive remedies, particularly injunctions as alluded to by the Ontario Law Reform Commission (OLRC).[81] Injunctions and class actions are not strange bedfellows but, as part of a court-approved settlement, they appear non-existent in Canada.[82] However, reported judgments through LexisNexis are not necessarily a reliable source for determining usage. Reported judgments do not usually pick up the terms of settlement. In contrast, a review of the Canadian Bar Association database of class actions, which catalogues statements of claim voluntarily filed, records a relatively high incidence of parties seeking injunctions as a part of orders that also call for damages. These requests are for permanent,

[80] If a court compensates one group of victims for a wrong, particularly a past wrong, it is taking money from current taxpayers to pay for the wrong. However, at the time the wrong was perpetrated, the benefit that flowed from the wrong inured for the benefit of a different group of taxpayers. These arguments have been rehearsed in the law of restitution in deciding whether to allow a defence of 'passing on' to government. See *Air Canada* v. *British Columbia* [1989] 1 SCR 1161 (defence accepted), and *Kingstreet Investments Ltd.* v. *New Brunswick* [2007] 1 SCR 3 (defence rejected).

[81] OLRC, *Report on Class Actions*, vol. I, p. 140.

[82] Plugging the search terms 'class action' and 'injunction' into LexisNexis reveals over 600 hits. After approximately one hundred of these hits failed to result in a single case that included an injunction order as part of a court-approved settlement, we discontinued this search. We also note that both Branch, *Class Actions in Canada*, and Eizenga *et al.*, *Class Actions Law and Practice*, are silent on this issue.

prohibitive injunctions requesting that the defendant discontinues the alleged wrongful action.[83] The wide remedial powers conferred on courts under the Australian class action regimes allow for injunctions.[84] While injunctive relief is sometimes sought at an interlocutory stage[85] as a final outcome of a class action,[86] and could be a term of a court-approved settlement,[87] it is evident that class action proceedings brought on behalf of class members (as distinct from regulators) are brought for the purpose of recovering damages for the class members.

Preliminary injunctions are widely used in class actions as part of a normal trial procedure, including Mareva injunctions.[88] One can also point to instances of 'cause lawyering' in Canadian class action suits where the injunction is an important remedy to support the application of some other administrative law process.[89] There are a number of potential explanations why class action plaintiffs do not pursue injunctions to deter future wrongdoing more often. Arguably, these explanations are pragmatic and strategic, rather than based on a lack of desire to achieve outcomes other than compensation. From a strategic point of view, an injunction is often sought as part of the relief at the certification stage. This argument can create something of a two-edged sword. It can be used

[83] In *Gagne* v. *Silcorp Ltd.* (1998) 41 OR (3d) 417 (CA), the class action alleged a breach of employment standards legislation. Part of the approved order contained a commitment from the employer to comply with the legislation for the future.

[84] Federal Court Act 1976 (Cth), s. 33Z(1)(a). See *Bray* v. *F Hoffman-La Roche Ltd.* [2002] FCA 1405 in which Merkel J, in light of this subsection, rejected the argument that injunctive relief was not a claim suitable for a class action proceeding. See also s. 33ZF(1), which provides that a court may make any order it thinks appropriate or necessary to ensure that justice is done in the proceeding.

[85] For example, *Courtney* v. *Medtel Pty Ltd.* (2002) 122 FCR 168 (injunction granted under Federal Court Act 1976 (Cth), s. 33ZF(1)).

[86] For example, *Australian Competition and Consumer Commission* v. *Chats House Investments Pty Ltd.* (1996) 142 ALR 177 (injunction granted under Trade Practices Act 1974 (Cth), s. 80).

[87] For example, *Bray* v. *F Hoffman-La Roche Ltd* [2002] FCA 1405. Court approval for terms of settlement is required in class action proceedings: Federal Court Act 1976 (Cth), s. 33V.

[88] See, e.g., *Tracy* v. *Instaloan Financial Solutions Centres (B.C.) Ltd.* (2007) 48 CPC (6th) 157 (BCCA).

[89] For example, in *Borisova* v. *Minister of Citizenship and Immigration* [2003] 4 FC 408, the class plaintiff (representing a class of 104,000 members) successfully sought an injunction preventing the Minister of Immigration from finally rejecting the applications of class members for permanent residence status. The plaintiff class claimed that they had filed their applications on the basis of a set of criteria that the Minister had subsequently changed. They wished their applications to be determined on the former criteria. Here, the underlying action was for judicial review.

as an argument to deny certification on the basis that a single plaintiff's application for the relief can result in an injunction, which then has ramifications beyond the immediate party, and therefore there is an alternative and preferable means to adjudicate the dispute. On the other hand, there are examples where seeking an injunction has been used to overcome a perceived threat to certification where individual damage assessment issues would be seen to overwhelm the common issues inquiry aspect of preferability.[90] This explanation is not applicable to Australia, where there is no procedure for judicial certification of a class action proceeding.

From a pragmatic viewpoint, many disputes do not call for coercive relief by way of mandatory injunction that would order defendants to play an active role in mitigating the harm done by their wrongdoing. In many cases in which a class action will be brought, the risk of further wrongdoing is low, the event causing loss having long passed, and it is not necessary to send appropriate signals to other would-be wrongdoers. Further, within class action litigation, while certification may be hotly contested, settlement is less so. Certification implies a viable substantive claim, not that it is proven. When voluntary settlement comes, it is often accompanied with a term denying any wrongdoing and thus undermines the need, justification or jurisdiction to impose deterrence. Thus we are probably left with only a small number of class action suits in which a more aggressive stance towards behavioural modification can be effected.

In this section we have discussed four alternative approaches to promote a behaviour-modifying function of class actions. In essence, the first three ways do this by making monetary awards that are equal to, or higher than, the gains derived from wrongdoing and by ensuring that, at a minimum, the full measure of all compensable losses of every victim is paid by the defendant. The fourth approach promotes behavioural modification by resort to coercive means. We premised this discussion on the assertion that all legal systems have an interest in behavioural modification, but the extent to which this is undertaken remains controversial within discrete jurisdictions. Three of the approaches discussed here, (i), (ii) and (iv), already operate outside the realm of class actions. Whether a particular jurisdiction allows disgorgement claims, or supports punitive damages, remain issues controlled by common law doctrine and statutes. Adding class actions as a procedural device magnifies whichever remedial goal is pursued as a purpose of the substantive claim. Thus, in the case of disgorgement of gains, it needs to be *all* the gains made at the

[90] *2038724 Ontario Ltd.* v. *Quizno's-Canada Restaurant Corp.* (2009) 96 OR (3d) 252 (CA).

expense of the class that form the substance of the suit. Similarly, punitive damages in a class action should be larger, because the magnitude of the contemptible behaviour is greater where it is levelled at *all* class members. Adding cy-près distribution, specifically mentioned in (iii) above, does not necessarily change the behaviour-modifying aspect of all of the above. It facilitates that goal by ensuring that there is a viable alternative to distributing an award, as opposed to simply returning undistributed funds to the wrongdoer.

Cy-près distribution can be used actively to enhance behavioural modification, with careful selection of the particular scheme approved by the court for distribution. Whereas a cy-près distribution is meant to identify with the injury to the plaintiff class, in that it should appear to benefit class members (or similarly situated people even if they are not class members)[91] and is thus supposed to mirror and ameliorate the underlying harm giving rise to the class action, a cy-près scheme could be adopted that focused the undistributed funds in such a way as to have a deterrent effect. Thus, for example, in the settlement of *Bona Foods* v. *Pfizer*[92] (a case involving price fixing over food additives) 28 per cent of the cy-près distribution went to the Faculty of Law, University of Western Ontario, to host a conference on the challenges of class actions in competition and price-fixing cases. Presumably, this was authorised on the theory that a greater understanding of class actions over price fixing would assist in encouraging this form of litigation as a deterrent.

To summarise what we have advanced in the first part of this chapter, in any civil action a claimant may be motivated by a number of reasons to pursue their claim, including reasons that go beyond recovery of compensation. In terms of the remedial goals of private law, it is difficult to isolate a purely compensatory goal to the exclusion of all other remedial goals, particularly deterrence. In class action proceedings, the reasons for the action will be multiple, reflecting the size of the class and the diversity of the class membership. Similarly, the range of remedial goals will reflect the diversity of motivational factors represented in the class. In proceedings where the amount recoverable by individuals is small, other motivational factors, including remedial goals that extend beyond compensation, are likely to be more prominent, for example goals that enhance behavioural

[91] Branch, *Class Actions in Canada*, para. 18.180.

[92] July 2002. A copy of the settlement agreement is available on the website of Siskinds, who acted for the Ontario class members: www.classaction.ca/actions/Price-Fixing/Resolved-Actions/Sodium-Erythorbate.aspx (last accessed 29 May 2013).

modification. However, as the class membership becomes larger, making it more difficult to identify members personally, or to distribute an award economically, the influence of class counsel and judge to speak for the class over remedial goals increases. In either case, cy-près distribution ensures that a wrongdoer does not receive back any of the monetary award based on procedural deficiencies concerning identification, or the cost of distributing to class members. The cy-près distribution scheme can be chosen to enhance desirable remedial goals, whether they are compensation, deterrence or some other remedial goal. In the next part of the chapter we explore this potential in light of the Canadian and Australian experience of cy-près.

3 Remedial goals, class actions and cy-près

A Introduction

At the time of their introduction, class action reforms in both Australia and Canada were described as effecting only procedural reforms of claims by private litigants. Nevertheless, in Canada, as we will describe later, provincial class action legislation that provides for some form of cy-près distribution scheme has led to behavioural modification having an explicit role for causes of action amenable to class actions. In contrast, in Australia the reforms that introduced class actions were justified solely on a compensation basis and do not allow for cy-près distributions. In recent years the issue has garnered interest in both New South Wales and Victoria, where legislation has been proposed that explicitly adopts cy-près distributions within class action legislation. In neither of these jurisdictions have the proposals been taken up by parliament, no doubt influenced by concerns expressed by corporate and lawyer groups. The issue therefore remains open for debate in Australia.

B The explicit development of cy-près distribution in Canadian class actions

Most discussions in Canada concerning the development of cy-près distribution in class actions can be traced back to the OLRC report.[93] The Commission was divided on whether to recommend the inclusion of such a distribution method. At the heart of that division was the question of

[93] See OLRC, *Report on Class Actions*.

the appropriate role of civil litigation. All commissioners agreed on the 'access to justice' and 'judicial economy' arguments to support the adoption of class action proceedings, but only a majority could agree on the 'behavioural modification' function of class action suits. Central to the majority's argument were claims that, through substantive doctrines and theory, behavioural modification had always been present as an aspect of private law. Thus the Commissioners cited developments in the awarding of punitive damages and restitution, including disgorgement,[94] and gave an exposition of law and economic theory to support their cautionary conclusion that behavioural modification was 'essentially an inevitable, albeit important, by-product of class actions'.[95] Turning directly to cy-près distribution, the majority Commissioners saw it as an important component of carrying through the compensatory and behavioural modification functions of civil law.[96]

By and large, provincial class proceedings legislation in Canada has followed the recommendations of the OLRC and all provincial statutes contain provision for cy-près distribution.[97] Some statutes also make provision for forfeiture to the Crown of unclaimed or undistributed awards, again reinforcing the idea that funds should not be returned to the defendant, and thus reinforcing the deterrent function of the class action proceeding.[98] The Supreme Court of Canada has endorsed access to justice, judicial economy and behavioural modification as lenses through which to evaluate the 'preferability inquiry', that is whether certification is to be preferred over individuals being left to bring their own distinct claims.[99] However, behavioural modification is a weak lens in comparison to the other two when considering certification. This is demonstrated through the work of Good, who has explored the ways in which Canadian courts apply access to justice, judicial economy and behavioural modification as determinative features of the preferability inquiry.[100] He concludes that access to justice is the dominant determinant, but that it is given a

[94] *Ibid.*, vol. I, p. 140.

[95] *Ibid.*, p. 145.

[96] *Ibid.*, vol. II, pp. 573, 581.

[97] Class Proceedings Act, S.O. 1992 c.6, s. 26(10). Alberta is similar to Ontario in that it allows for cy-près distribution but does not specifically require unclaimed funds to be returned to the defendant. Class Proceedings Act, S.A. 2003, c.C-16.5, s. 34.

[98] For example, B.C., Class Proceedings Act, R.S.B.C. 1996, c.50, s. 34(5)(b), and in Manitoba, the Class Proceedings Act C.C.S.M. c.C130, s. 35(5)(b).

[99] *Hollick* v. *Toronto (City of)* [2001] 3 SCR 158 at [27].

[100] Mathew Good, 'Access to Justice, Judicial Economy, and Behaviour Modification: Exploring the Goals of Canadian Class Actions' (2009) 47 *Alberta Law Review* 185.

constricted meaning largely centred on economic factors, so that certification is a process to advance what would be an economically non-viable claim for an individual to bring, either because the cost would be prohibitive commensurate to the claim, or because the amount claimed is small but the victims numerous.

Good's study is not an empirical one designed to determine whether what courts say about access to justice, when considering preferability, is, in fact, empirically verified in the practice and outcomes of these same cases. Rather, he has exhaustively gathered all class action certification actions and analysed them in terms of the meaning courts attribute to access to justice when exercising the power to certify or not. Good makes a number of points about the use of behavioural modification by courts in class action proceedings. First, courts see behavioural modification in terms of specific deterrence. The Canadian Supreme Court has referred to cost internalisation as a function of deterrence.[101] Beyond this, in lower courts 'deterrence is reduced to a fear factor of punishment by payment' and a way 'not to let the bad guys get away with their loot'.[102] Second, while deterrence is mentioned as a goal of class actions in numerous cases, as Good notes, at the preferability inquiry 'only rarely is behaviour modification determinative of anything'.[103] As Good rightly observes, deterrence presupposes a substantive outcome. At the preferability inquiry, courts are reluctant to be drawn into a merit determination on what is a preliminary procedural motion for fear of prejudicing the substantive trial, should one eventuate.[104] In this respect, behavioural modification can be distinguished from either judicial economy or access to justice. A court confronted with certification is in a position to evaluate claims of judicial economy and access to justice within the factual context presented by the applicant. The size of the class, the likelihood that individuals will make claims if certification is declined, the amount of an individual claim, and the total claim are matters about which educated guesses can be made. Whether the defendant or other similarly minded transgressors will be deterred in the future always remains a matter of faith and speculation. Good's analysis confirms the secondary role given to behavioural modification by the OLRC.[105]

[101] *Western Canadian Shopping Centres Inc.* v. *Dutton* [2001] 2 SCR 534 at [29].
[102] Good, 'Access to Justice', 219.
[103] *Ibid.* [104] *Ibid.*, at 223.
[105] See OLRC, *Report on Class Actions*.

Turning from class action certification to approved class action settlements, there is empirical evidence that demonstrates that frequent resort is made to cy-près distribution in Canada, and that undistributed funds will seldom be returned to the defendant.[106] In fact, in some approved settlements the majority of the award has been distributed on a cy-près basis, a fact which has lead Kalajdzic to express the view that courts need to undertake a more thorough scrutiny of the litigants' claims that the cost of identifying class members, or of distributing relatively small amounts to them is excessive, such that a cy-près distribution should be approved. The argument is forcefully made by Kalajdzic that courts need better guidance on how to administer the threshold test that initiates a cy-près distribution scheme.[107] In many of the approved settlements, cy-près distribution will be ordered to dispose of any unclaimed funds after individual class members have been compensated. In other settlements almost the entire fund is distributed on a cy-près basis and the chosen scheme is a complete substitution for direct compensation to individual class members.[108]

C *Cy-près as a class action remedy in Australia*

Although representative actions are available in each state and territory in Australia where numerous people have the same interest in particular proceedings, there are only three jurisdictions that have class actions provisions as discussed in this chapter. The first class action regime was created as Part IVA of the Federal Court Act 1976 (Cth), and came into effect in March 1992. Since then, two other states have enacted provisions that are essentially the same as Part IVA. Victoria introduced Part 4A of the Supreme Court Act 1986 (Vic) in January 2000, and in 2010 New South Wales introduced Part 10 of the Civil Procedure Act 2005 (NSW), which commenced on 4 March 2011. A number of Law Reform Commission reports and their recommendations concerning class actions, discussed briefly below, reveal much about the views as to the purpose of class action procedures and appropriate class action rules and devices. Despite the fact that the class action provisions are intended as procedural in nature and do not create new legal rights, they have generated considerable

[106] See Berryman, 'Class Actions'; Kalajdzic, 'Access to a Just Result', 240.

[107] Kalajdzic, 'Access to a Just Result', 238, 244.

[108] *Ibid.*, at 236 calls the former 'residual cy-près' and the latter 'fixed cy-près'.

controversy in Australia.[109] The merit of providing for cy-près distribution is one such controversy.

The Australian Law Reform Commission (ALRC) in a report in 1988 (which was significant to the class action provisions ultimately enacted as Part IVA of the Federal Court Act 1976 (Cth)) summarised the case for introducing class action proceedings as resting on two foundations: (a) to ensure access to legal remedies; and (b) to promote efficiency and consistency in dealing with multiple claims.[110] In recommending grouped procedures in the face of the concerns raised about blackmail actions, legal entrepreneurs and actions to pursue political goals, the Commission stated that class actions are 'an essential part of the legal system's response to multiple wrongdoing in an increasingly complex world'.[111] The justifications for class action proceedings being access to justice and judicial economy are reflected in the Second Reading Speech of the Bill in which Part IVA was presented to Parliament.[112] To date, no Australian legislature has embraced behavioural modification and deterrence as an express purpose of class action procedures, although the question whether to confer on courts the power to order cy-près distribution of funds paid into a class action fund has been considered on a number of occasions.

In its Report, the ALRC stated that the purpose of class action procedures is to compensate class members for loss or damage caused by a defendant liable under the substantive law, not to penalise defendants or to deter behaviour 'to any greater extent than provided for under the existing law'.[113] It recommended against cy-près, on the basis that it would be a 'significant extension of present principles of compensation' if the respondent were required to meet an assessed liability in full even though there is no person to receive the compensation and to do so would do nothing to enhance the access to justice principle.[114] A change of this nature, in the Commission's view, would go beyond procedural reform.[115]

[109] For an overview of the arguments that have been made for and against class actions in Australia, see Peter Cashman, *Class Action Law and Practice* (Annandale, NSW: Federation Press, 2007).

[110] Australian Law Reform Commission (ALRC), *Grouped Proceedings in the Federal Court (Report No. 46 Summary)* (Canberra: Australian Government Publishing Service, 1988), at [62].

[111] *Ibid.*, at [69].

[112] Second Reading Speech, Federal Court of Australia Amendment Bill 1991 (Cth), House of Representatives, 14 November 1991, 3174 (Michael Duffy, Commonwealth Attorney-General).

[113] ALRC, *Grouped Proceedings*, [239].

[114] *Ibid.*, at [239]. [115] *Ibid.*

The ALRC concluded, therefore, that 'any money ordered to be paid by the respondent should be matched, as far as possible, to an individual who has a right to receive it', and any residue should be returned to the defendant.[116] The views expressed by the ALRC have been relied upon by commentators who oppose changes to class action procedures that go beyond the compensation of identified class members.[117]

In 2008, following an extensive consultation process and a detailed report on the arguments for and against the implementation of an express power to grant cy-près relief, the Victorian Law Reform Commission (VLRC) recommended that the Supreme Court Act 1986 (Vic) be amended to allow the Supreme Court to order cy-près remedies in certain circumstances.[118] None of these recommendations has been enacted.

In October 2010, following a Consultation Draft process of the Civil Procedure Amendment (Supreme Court Representative Proceedings) Bill 2010, the then New South Wales Attorney-General introduced a Bill into the New South Wales Parliament to insert Part 10 into the Civil Procedure Act 2005 (NSW). Part 10 provides for class actions in the same terms as Part IVA of the Federal Act and Part 4A of the Victorian Act.[119] Although Part 10 was enacted (following a change of government), the Act does not include the provisions for cy-près remedies included in the Consultation Draft and original Bill. The provisions in the New South Wales draft legislation for cy-près were based on the 2008 VLRC recommendations. In summary, each of the three Australian jurisdictions that have enacted class action legislation have rejected any proposal to allow courts to make cy-près orders.

What is the explanation for rejection of cy-près distribution that would see defendants paying full damages even if the award does not go to class members? It is largely explained by adherence to compensation as the justification for class action procedures, and the view that present principles of compensation do not require a respondent to 'meet an assessed liability in full' if there is no person to receive the compensation.[120] We argue that compensation can be understood in the context of class actions to mean ensuring that a respondent meets their assessed liability in full, notwithstanding that the benefit of the damages paid is received only indirectly

116 *Ibid.*, at [62].

117 See, e.g., Stuart Clark and Christina Harris, 'The Push to Reform Class Action Procedure in Australia: Evolution or Revolution?' (2008) 32 *Melbourne University Law Review* 775.

118 VLRC, *Civil Justice Review*.

119 Civil Procedure Act 2005 (NSW), pt. 10.

120 ALRC, *Grouped Proceedings*, at [239].

by unidentified class members. Even if this view of compensation is not accepted, we maintain that recovery from the respondent of the full amount of assessed liability can be justified on deterrence grounds. The argument that compensation is the sole purpose of private litigation has been described as 'lacking cogency' in the modern litigious environment in which compensation is not the sole purpose of litigation.[121] There are circumstances within the common law, and under statute, where other remedial goals play both primary and secondary purposes, including deterrence and vindication.[122] In respect of class actions, Mulheron, for example, argues that deterrence is a legitimate element of civil litigation, 'especially where the claimants are numerous, when the defendant's culpable behaviour has harmed all of them', and when it is clear to regulators that fines are insufficient to prevent the detriment caused by unlawful conduct.[123] In this context, it is argued that it is both unfair and unjustified to deny a claim where illegal conduct has been established and has caused loss that may be quantified because it is too costly or not feasible to provide compensation to all of the victims.[124]

We maintain that deterrence plays a legitimate, albeit secondary, role in civil litigation and class action proceedings. Commentary that stresses that deterrence is not a function of the civil law by reference to the general unavailability of exemplary damages for negligence, breach of contract and misleading or deceptive conduct[125] overlooks two points. First, exemplary damages are still recoverable in Australia by private litigants in some tort actions and are available in appropriate cases in class action proceedings.[126] Second, punishment and deterrence are discrete goals of the law. The purposes of exemplary damages have been held by the High Court to extend beyond punishment to include deterrence, the assuagement of any urge for revenge felt by victims, discouragement of self-help likely to endanger the public and the denunciation of the defendant's conduct.[127] While it is fair to conclude that there is a reluctance by Australian

[121] Rachael Mulheron, 'Cy-près Damages Distributions in England: A New Era for Consumer Redress' (2009) 20 *European Business Law Review* 307, 314–15.

[122] For examples, see Witzleb and Carroll, 'The Role of Vindication'.

[123] Mulheron, 'Cy-près Damages Distributions in England', 314.

[124] *Ibid.*, 314–15.

[125] See, e.g., Clayton Utz, 'Submission in response to the Consultation Draft of the Civil Procedure Amendment (Supreme Court Representative Proceedings) Bill 2010 (NSW)', 15 November 2010, 4–5.

[126] *Nixon* v. *Philip Morris (Australia) Ltd* (1999) 95 FCR 453 at [115], affirmed on appeal: *Philip Morris (Australia) Ltd* v. *Nixon* (2000) 170 ALR 487 at [98].

[127] *Lamb* v. *Cotogno* (1987) 164 CLR 1 at 11.

courts to expand the punitive function of damages awards,[128] deterrence can be achieved to some extent at least through non-punitive remedies, for example injunctions.

Despite strong opposition to changes to class action provisions that would endorse deterrence as a justification of the procedures, it has been recognised judicially that there are multiple purposes that class actions can achieve, and in giving effect to class actions provisions it is appropriate to take into account the vindicatory and law enforcement role of private litigation. In *P Dawson Nominees Pty Ltd.* v. *Multiplex Ltd.*[129] Finkelstein J refers to these as aims of the class action. The private action being pursued in this case was brought by P Dawson Nominees Pty Ltd. (Dawson) under Pt IVA of the Federal Court Act 1976 (Cth) against Multiplex Ltd. (Multiplex) and a related company, Multiplex Funds Management Ltd. (MFM). Dawson alleged, on its own behalf and on behalf of group members, that these corporations had breached their duties of continuous disclosure under s. 674 of the Corporations Act 2001 (Cth) in relation to substantial cost over-runs and delays in the construction of the Wembley Stadium in the United Kingdom by a subsidiary of Multiplex. An order was sought by Multiplex and MFM under s. 33N(1) of the Federal Court Act 1976 (Cth) that the proceedings no longer continue as representative proceedings under Pt IVA. The principal contention of Multiplex was that His Honour ought to have been satisfied that it was in the interests of justice to make an order under s. 33N(1)(d) of the Federal Court Act 1976 (Cth) because it was 'otherwise inappropriate' that Dawson's claims be pursued by means of a representative proceeding. Finkelstein J refused to make the order, and an appeal to the Full Court against his decision was dismissed.[130] In reaching his conclusion, His Honour stated: 'the notion that it is inappropriate for this action to proceed as a representative proceeding if the true alternative is that there will be no action to vindicate the rights of any group member is equally unacceptable.'[131] Finkelstein J concluded that it would be unfair to the litigants in this case to be forced

[128] As evidenced by the absence of gain-based damages for breach of contract in Australian law. In *Hospitality Group Pty Ltd* v. *Australian Rugby Union Ltd* (2001) 110 FCR 157, Hill and Finkelstein JJ reiterate that in Australian law a party aggrieved by breach of contract is only entitled to compensation: at [159]. There is further evidence of a shift away from punishment via exemplary damages in Australia in the abolition of this form of damages in defamation by uniform legislation in Australia: Defamation Act 2005 (various), s. 37.

[129] (2007) 242 ALR 111.

[130] *Multiplex Funds Management Ltd.* v. *P Dawson Nominees Pty Ltd.* (2007) 244 ALR 600.

[131] (2007) 242 ALR 111, 124.

to give up their group claim and be left to assert their rights on their own for two reasons. First, this is because most litigants would be forced to give up for financial reasons. This reflects the 'access to justice' concern. Second, 'because it would undermine the deterrent effect of the existence of sanctions for contraventions of the law regulating securities'.[132] The latter statement endorses the class action as 'sheriff', a role that corporate law theorists regard as vital to the deterrence of breaches of the law by large and otherwise unaccountable institutions such as corporations.[133]

The rejection of cy-près in Australia has attracted criticism from commentators on a number of grounds. For example, Mulheron points out that many other law reform commissions around the world have recommended cy-près and it has been enacted in many jurisdictions where class actions presumably were introduced to deal with the same challenges facing groups of private litigants that prompted the enactment of Part IVA.[134] Morabito argues that basing a class action regime solely on the compensation principle is to impose inappropriate 'individualistic notions, as to the aims of the civil justice system, on group litigation devices'.[135] Notwithstanding the views expressed by the ALRC in 1988 as to any wider function of class action procedures, it has recognised, in other contexts, that the civil justice system more broadly plays a significant role in advancing public interests through private litigation. In its Grouped Proceedings Report[136] the ALRC refers to the availability of public actions to protect consumer interests under the Trade Practices Act 1974 (Cth), investors under Corporations legislation, and its conclusion in an earlier report that 'a significant role remains for "private attorneys-general" in public interest litigation'.[137] In support of class action procedures, the ALRC concluded in the 1988 Report that there is even less justification for making a party's individual right to claim redress dependent upon

[132] *Ibid.*

[133] See Spender, 'The Class Action as Sheriff', 701.

[134] See Mulheron, *The Modern Cy-près Doctrine*, p. 234; Vince Morabito, 'The Victorian Law Reform Commission's Class Action Reform Strategy' (2009) 32 *University of New South Wales Law Journal* 1055, 1066.

[135] Morabito, 'The VLRC's Class Action Reform Strategy', 1067. See also Spender, 'The Class Action as Sheriff'.

[136] ALRC, *Grouped Proceedings*.

[137] Australian Law Reform Commission (ALRC), *Standing in Public Interest Litigation (Report No 27)* (Canberra: Australian Government Publishing Service, 1985), at [185]. This remark is made while the public interest is to some extent protected by the Attorney-General and consumer and investor protection agencies.

a government official's decision and that 'action by public authorities cannot be regarded as an effective substitute for private action'.[138]

We suggest another possible explanation for the continued rejection of cy-près type remedies in Australia is a concern that it may involve, to use the words of the VLRC, 'a significant change in the law'[139] and the potential for cy-près remedies to create new profit-stripping remedies. As we have seen, the VLRC recommended that the Supreme Court should have the discretion to order cy-près type remedies in prescribed circumstances.[140] Recommendation 101 provides:

> The Supreme Court should have discretion to order cy-près remedies where (a) there has been a proven contravention of the law, (b) a financial or other pecuniary advantage has accrued to the person contravening the law as a result of such contravention, (c) the loss has been suffered by others, or the pecuniary gain obtained by the person contravening the law, is capable of reasonably accurate assessment and (d) it is not possible, reasonably practicable or cost effective to identify some or all of those who have suffered a loss.

The VLRC envisaged a provision in these terms would confer greater power on the courts in cases of 'unjust enrichment'.[141] The reference to unjust enrichment in this context is confusing because it does not distinguish between (on the one hand) 'unjust enrichment' in a general sense, of a defendant who recovers the residue of damages they have been assessed to have caused to a class where not all of the class members can be identified, and disgorgement damages, which are aimed at preventing 'unjust enrichment' by wrongdoers. The former 'enrichment' might equally be described as 'under-exposure' of a wrongdoer to liability to compensate. In the latter case, a wrongdoer is stripped of their profits in order to achieve the deterrence goal. There is no reference to 'unjust enrichment' in the proposed cy-près provision. Rather, paragraph (b) of Recommendation 101 refers to 'a financial or other pecuniary advantage'. Paragraphs (a) and (b) together appear to limit the circumstances in which a court would

[138] ALRC, *Grouped Proceedings*, [38].

[139] VLRC, *Civil Justice Review*, Chapter 8, [1]. A number of recommendations that accompanied Recommendation 101, for example that there be power to pay some or all of residue funds into a Justice Fund (Recommendation 102), and limiting the right of appeal against the exercise of a court's discretion (Recommendation 107), may well have fuelled concerns and political opposition to the overall proposal.

[140] *Ibid.*, Recommendation 101.

[141] *Ibid.*, at [3.7].

have the discretion to exercise the cy-près power. Paragraph (c) refers to 'the pecuniary gain', which presumably includes a 'financial or other pecuniary advantage'. The reference in paragraph (c) to the loss suffered by others *or* the pecuniary gain of the defendant allows for assessment of monetary relief both on a compensatory and a non-compensatory basis.

We question whether this proposal in Recommendation 101 does represent a significant change in substantive law. If that is intended, then it would be preferable to enact a provision that does not change the remedial goals of the substantive cause of action for which the class action is brought. We would argue that even though the result of invoking the cy-près power in the terms recommended by the VLRC may be a distribution of moneys recovered through a class action based on a claim for autonomous unjust enrichment (assuming paragraph (a) is satisfied), or on a claim for compensable loss that, if not paid over by the defendant, would remain in their hands as a gain, this should be viewed as a consequence of grouped proceedings and not a change to the law of autonomous unjust enrichment or to the circumstances in which disgorgement remedies are available.

We make two further points about the rejection of cy-près relief in Australia. First, in its 2008 Report the VLRC identified the discontinuance provisions in the current class action regimes as a 'further impediment to cy-près relief'.[142] These provisions allow a court to discontinue or partially stay a proceeding as a class action, where a plaintiff seeks an award of money for group members and it appears likely that, if the plaintiff were successful, the costs of identifying the group members and distributing the money would be excessive having regard to the likely total of those amounts. These provisions give effect to a recommendation of the ALRC, which was concerned that the aggregation of large numbers of small claims could be uneconomical.[143] They have been criticised on the basis of being inconsistent with the access to justice aim of class actions and hindering the ability of class action proceedings to enforce the law and discourage unlawful behaviour.[144] The need for the court to have the power to stay or order discontinuance of an action is a matter for debate

[142] *Ibid.*, at [3.3.1] referring to Supreme Court Act 1986 (Vic), s. 33M, which is identical to the Federal Court Act 1986 (Cth), s. 33M.

[143] ALRC, *Grouped Proceedings*, [151].

[144] V. Morabito, 'The Federal Court of Australia's Power to Terminate Properly Instituted Class Actions' (2004) 42 *Osgoode Hall Law Journal* 473, 490.

that is not pursued here. The power to discontinue a class action based on cost–benefit analysis clearly reduces the potential for these proceedings to achieve the compensatory (and deterrent) purpose. The point we note, however, is that concerns about the impact of introducing cy-près remedies in Australia need to take into account provisions like these, that already reduce the likelihood that wrongdoers will be held accountable for losses they cause to potential class members.

Second, the absence of express provision for cy-près remedies has not precluded terms of this nature being included in class action settlement agreements in Australia.[145] Morabito reports that the lack of express power in Part IVA of the Federal Court Act 1976 (Cth) to endorse cy-près remedies has not precluded the Federal Court from authorising in two Part IVA proceedings the payment of the undistributed remainder of settlement funds not to defendants,[146] but to other entities and in one case to the class representative's solicitors.[147] Further examples of instances in which cy-près type remedies have been incorporated into settlement agreements are recorded by the VLRC.[148] In recommending that an express power to grant cy-près relief be introduced, the VLRC expressed the view that the court should retain the power *not* to approve a settlement agreement between the parties as to how a cy-près distribution is to be made,[149] and we support that view. The courts have developed principles to be applied to protect the interests of class members when approving settlement of class actions[150] and there is no reason to believe that Australian courts would not similarly develop reasoned principles to identify appropriate cases for cy-près distribution and orders.

[145] Court approval is required for settlement of class actions in Australia: Federal Court Act 1976 (Cth), s. 33V; Supreme Court Act 1986 (Vic), s. 33V; Civil Procedure Act 2005 (NSW), s. 173.

[146] Morabito, 'The VLRC's Class Action Reform Strategy', 1069. Morabito refers to a case in which payments to entities such as the Australian Shareholders' Association and the Australian Institute of Management (for the purposes of training corporate officers and directors) that formed part of the settlement agreement executed by the applicant and the respondents, were approved by Moore J in Australia's first successful shareholder class action: *King* v. *AG Australia Holdings Ltd.* [2003] FCA 980.

[147] See *Guglielmin* v. *Trescowthick* [2002] FCA (Unreported, SAD 153/2002, Mansfield J., 6 March 2008); Morabito, 'The VLRC's Class Action Reform Strategy'.

[148] VLRC, *Civil Justice Review*, Chapter 8, [3.5].

[149] *Ibid.*, [3.14].

[150] *Taylor v. Telstra Corporation Ltd.* [2007] FCA 2008 at [56]–[66]. See also *P Dawson Nominees Pty Ltd.* v. *Brookfield Multiplex Limited (No 4)* [2010] FCA 1029, applied in *Jarra Creek Central Packing Shed Pty Ltd.* v. *Amcor Ltd.* [2011] FCA 671 at [68]–[77].

D *Class actions and cy-près as remedy – an analysis*

Canadian class action regimes, in sharp contrast to those in Australia, explicitly accept that behavioural modification is a legitimate goal of class action suits. In terms of any civil suit, the way deterrence is promoted is to ensure that a wrongdoer disgorges all profits from their wrongdoing, or is forced to pay the full costs of those harmed by the wrongful act. The greater availability of punitive damages in Canada parallels the sympathetic attention accorded the deterrence goal as a legitimate function in civil litigation. In class action suits, cy-près distribution, in combination with compensatory damages, can be used to promote deterrence as an additional goal, albeit secondary, to compensation.

Of course, the true test of deterrence as a feature of class actions would be to verify empirically whether either the defendant or similarly placed actors have changed their conduct post class action judgment or settlement, or have been deterred from acting in a similar way. This also raises the question as to what change in conduct has taken place. Thus, for example, take the settlement in *Cassino* v. *Toronto-Dominion Bank*,[151] a class action proceeding based on the defendant bank's failure properly to disclose to its credit card customers the exact way foreign currency charges would be calculated. The particular settlement resulted in an award of $55 million – $10 million going to individual class members, $14.5 million to the Law Foundation of Ontario, $14.5 million to Social and Enterprise Development Innovations, $4.3 million to the class proceeding fund and $11.4 million to class counsel for fees. Thus, the majority of the funds were paid on a cy-près distribution. After the settlement the bank did clarify the foreign currency charges by changes in their customers' credit card agreement. In that sense they have been further deterred. However, does this change address the fundamental nature of the offending conduct? A plausible argument could be made that the offending conduct was not only the failure to disclose the foreign interest charges (which has been corrected), but that the whole nature of the credit card agreement as a contract of adhesion written in fine print over many clauses provides an insufficient way to communicate basic information to consumers. The desirable correction is not simply to add another obscure clause to the contract, but to be more transparent concerning the charges associated with using a credit card.

[151] (2009) 98 OR (3d) 543 (Sup. Ct. J.).

Unfortunately, there is scarce empirical evidence to support the theory that damages awards in class action suits act as a significant deterrent to wrongful conduct.[152] Determining cause and effect in the sense of identifying the class action litigation as the single reason for change in a defendant's future conduct may not be possible since it may simply be too difficult to isolate the damages award from other causal factors such as regulatory prosecution, the impact of rising insurance premiums, adverse publicity and changes in managerial direction. Beyond the immediate defendant, this lack of evidence makes one pause and question the implicit assumption that behavioural modification flows from aggregating compensatory damages and cy-près distribution. Nevertheless, we are willing to accept the proposition that there is a correlation. And in any case, as we discussed earlier, studies involving individual litigants in the private law arena have identified claims where plaintiffs may well value behavioural modification ahead of compensatory damages. Realistically, this is only likely to be the case when the compensatory damages are small and/or where the plaintiff's loss is non-pecuniary. In these circumstances there is likely to be a high sense of grievance, a desire to 'put things right' (or receive some form of acknowledgement of wrongdoing by the defendant) and to discourage the same wrongdoing in the future. A cy-près distribution oriented towards assuaging these known concerns of plaintiffs can achieve both behavioural modification and meet the broader remedial needs of plaintiffs.

It is a normative question how far civil litigation should be confined to providing purely compensation, or whether it should be used in furtherance of behavioural modification. We have argued that a strict demarcation cannot be drawn between these remedial goals. In some situations, the obligation to put things right or giving an assurance and

[152] In one of the first empirical studies of the deterrence effect of class actions and enforcement brought by the United States Securities and Exchange Commission on firms that fail to report accurate financial results, the authors conclude that there is benefit in class action litigation that does deter aggressive reporting of discretionary accruals. (Discretionary accrual of earnings is used as a substitute for actual violations of Generally Accepted Accounting Principles because they are more readily available and create a larger sample size.) The authors sought to determine whether companies became more conservative in their financial reporting after a peer firm was subject to either SEC prosecution or a class action suit. However, the authors also concluded that to change behaviour required a 'sustained and repeated enforcement activity' rather than isolated and sporadic enforcement by either class action or SEC prosecution. See Jared N. Jennings, Simi Kedia and Shivaram Rajgopal, 'The Deterrent Effects of SEC Enforcement and Class Action Litigation' (December 2011), available at: http://ssrn.com/abstract=1868578 (last accessed 29 May 2013).

acknowledgement of wrongdoing simultaneously deters the defendant and satiates the claimant's compensatory demands. Making amends by undertaking not to repeat a wrong may be all that the claimant wants, particularly where money cannot be used to purchase substitute performance (cases of non-pecuniary loss), or where the sum paid is disproportionately low compared to the degree of grievance experienced by the claimant. In this sense, an assurance or acknowledgement of wrongdoing is compensation in the eyes of the claimant. It is also a distinctly normative question whether substantive law provides, or should provide, for profit disgorgement remedies, and thus clearly depart from compensatory relief in furtherance of prophylactic and largely deterrence-based relief. Enabling class actions and/or cy-près distribution does not alter the availability of remedial relief. In this sense, they are procedural changes and do not change the substantive law. It is not a valid objection, therefore, to say of both class actions and cy-près that they will create a licence for profit-stripping remedies. The remedy is parasitic on whatever the law wants in terms of substantive claims.

Nevertheless, one function of class actions is to facilitate substantive claims by overcoming the traditional access to justice barriers by aggregating claims into economically viable actions. Since those barriers are largely economic (litigation costs), it is not surprising to see class actions being framed in a way that maximises monetary damages so as to compensate class counsel and those who provide risk capital to overcome the cost barrier to the litigation. Obviously, by making non-viable actions viable there is an increase in litigation. The other rationale for class actions – judicial economy – arguably results in less litigation by finding common resolution on issues shared by a number of individually viable claims and thus hastens the settlement process. The increased prospect of litigation may be an annoyance to some, but that is a product of a step taken legislatively when enacting class proceedings.

Enabling class action cy-près distribution may, although not necessarily, have normative impact, depending upon the nature of the scheme adopted. Cy-près distribution enables a court to substitute its own remedial goals in two situations: first where the identity and/or location of claimants cannot be determined; and second, where the cost to administer distribution of a nominal sum exceeds the benefit bestowed on individual class members. In the latter case, class members can be identified and it is only a practical issue concerning distribution that results in the court turning to cy-près distribution. There is no doubt that class members are the victims of wrongdoing by the defendant. In the former, the lack of identified individual claimants also does not change the fact that someone has suffered as a result of defendant wrongdoing and that, theoretically, those individuals could be identified. Identifying a class and aggregating claims is still premised on the basis that an actual harm has been caused by the defendant to every individual class member. Even in the case of disgorgement of profits, the class is an aggregation of individuals from which the defendant has amassed profits at the expense of individual claimants, even where, practically speaking, they cannot be located or identified. In both situations, where cy-près distributions are made, the award is assessed on the basis that actual loss has been experienced by class members. It is not being assessed simply on the basis of a potential exposure to harm. Against this background, cy-près distribution should be approached as a process designed to overcome practical and procedural difficulties.

Whether cy-près distribution departs significantly from traditional compensation principles and embraces a more behaviour-modifying orientation is a product of the type of cy-près scheme that is adopted. A cy-près scheme that is drafted to have a close nexus between the cy-près recipient and the composition of the class, or one that is drafted to be 'as near as' the purpose from which the award has been derived, promises to provide compensation to the class by indirect means. For example, in *Sutherland* v. *Boots Pharmaceuticals PLC*,[153] a case involving a misrepresentation of the benefits to be derived from taking a certain drug prescribed for the treatment of hypothyroidism, the court resorted to a cy-près distribution after it determined that the cost of distributing compensation worth approximately $30–70 per class member to 520,000 class members would be disproportionate to the sum distributed. The cy-près scheme approved involved various institutions conducting specific research and undertaking educational and outreach projects for those afflicted with thyroid disease. Thus, the cy-près scheme had a close nexus to the original suit and could claim to constitute indirect benefit. Such a scheme will also be closer to furthering the 'access to justice' rationale of class actions.[154]

[153] (2002) 21 CPC (5th) 196 (Ont. S.C.J.).

[154] The United States Federal Court of Appeals (First Circuit) may have begun a tightening-up of the types of cy-près schemes that are approved in that jurisdiction in applying a 'reasonable approximation' test; one that requires the scheme to reasonably approximate the interests of the class members. See *Re Lupron Marketing & Sales Practices Litigation; Rohn* v. *Tap Pharmaceutical Products Inc.* 677 F 3d 21 (1st Cir. 2012).

Not all cy-près schemes need have a close nexus. In Canada, which has adopted a more robust notion of behavioural modification, cy-près schemes have been approved that have little or no nexus,[155] but have been adopted primarily to ensure that the defendant is required to disgorge any gains from wrongdoing.[156] Our point here is simply that the availability of cy-près distribution does not automatically carry with it a wholesale movement towards a solely deterrence function to civil law. The legislative crafting of the power to grant cy-près schemes can obviously shape the nature of its exercise.[157] Nor should cy-près doctrines be viewed as novel procedures for which courts are ill-suited. There is a long history of application within the law of trusts upon which to draw.[158]

We acknowledge the possibility that, at some stage, a cy-près scheme will either inadvertently or advertently benefit non-class members.[159] In this sense a cy-près scheme provides a substantive outcome that is inconsistent with a strictly compensatory rationale of civil litigation. This is the worst fear of those who oppose cy-près distribution in class actions. This conception of the compensation principle is extremely narrow. In reality, the compensation principle has never been drawn so narrowly. It is subject to principles of causation, remoteness and mitigation: the principal ways in which compensation is limited. Similarly, over-compensation is tolerated in such areas as insurance and benevolent exceptions to collateral benefit rules. The impact of these departures to the compensation

[155] Berryman, 'Class Actions'.

[156] This tone was set by the first approved cy-près scheme in Canada. In *Alfresh Beverages Canada Corp.* v. *Archer Daniels Midland Co.* [2001] OJ No. 6028 (S.C.J.) at [4] (a class action case dealing with price fixing), Winkler J approved a residual cy-près scheme, stating that the scheme was designed to ensure that 'no profits from wrongdoings will remain undisgorged'.

[157] Interestingly, in Ontario, the Class Proceedings Act, S.O. 1992, c. 6, s. 26(4), which empowers cy-près distributions, does state that the 'court may order that all or a part of an award under section 24, that has not been distributed within a time set by the court be applied in any manner that may *reasonably be expected to benefit class members, even though the order does not provide monetary relief to individual class members, if the court is satisfied that a reasonable number of class members who would not otherwise receive monetary relief would benefit from the order*' (emphasis added). The provision would tend to suggest that a cy-près scheme should contain some nexus so that it can be described as an indirect benefit to class members.

[158] D. Chalmers and G. Dal Pont, *Equity and Trusts in Australia*, 4th edition (Rozelle, NSW: Law Book, 2007), [29.280]; D. Waters, M. Gillen and L. Smith, *Water's Law of Trusts in Canada*, 3rd edition (Toronto: Thomson/Carswell, 2005), p. 762.

[159] In fact, in Ontario the Class Proceedings Act, S.O. 1992, c. 6, s. 26(6)(a) specifically authorises this effect, stating that a court can make an order even if it would benefit persons who are not class members.

principle is in furtherance of distributive goals, principally through insurance. Thus, there is already a lot of remedial creep in the idealised relationship between wrongdoer and victim, although these are largely principles that lessen the burden on the wrongdoer. A notion of the compensation principle more widely drawn admits of a variety of facilitative functions performed by the doctrine, namely to provide victim compensation, allocate risk and require wrongdoers to internalise the costs of wrongdoing.

Even within the concept of compensation there is a great deal of fluidity. For example, the law does not diminish compensation where a plaintiff uses his or her award for a purpose totally unrelated to that for which it was designed to compensate. Similarly, if plaintiff autonomy is to be valued, what constitutes compensation carries with it a subjective connotation. If a plaintiff values an apology more than a monetary award, how is that anything less than compensation in the eyes of the particular plaintiff? It is also difficult to justify why compensation should have elevated status over other remedial goals where it is admittedly a poor exemplar of what it purports to do. For example, it has been recognised that in the case of non-pecuniary losses, particularly where dignity has been infringed, compensation does a poor job. A plaintiff's claim to vindicatory damages makes a more perfect fit in such settings. It is for these reasons, as explored in the first part of this chapter, that we suggest that disaggregating and isolating any single remedial goal is extremely problematic. It is particularly difficult to separate compensation from deterrence. And deterrence will be most effective where all the costs of harm have been shifted to the wrongdoer. In this sense, deterrence can be distinguished from punishment and is not antithetical to compensation. Rather, the deterrent effect is simply maximised where all possible compensatory claims have been met.

It must be emphasised that, from the point of view of defendants, they are not being required to pay anything more than the compensable losses that it has been calculated they have caused. Cy-près overcomes procedural difficulties in administering compensation, not in fundamentally altering its quantification. The action ultimately requires a definable class. This distinguishes compensation and deterrence from pure punishment, which would be indifferent to the losses caused, other than to ensure that the punishment extracted has some proportionality with the harm caused. Thus, in the context of a class action, before a court gets to a cy-près distribution, it must be satisfied that individual awards to class members are not administratively viable, it must then consider a cy-près scheme that has a close nexus to the class such that it amounts to an indirect benefit, and only then does it risk a scheme in which a non-class member may benefit. Even where this happens, we have argued that it still preserves a legitimate remedial goal – deterrence – which is perfected when all compensatory claims are internalised by the wrongdoer. Rather than simply raising the objection of a non-class member receiving from a pool of money assessed to compensate class members as a reason to remove cy-près distribution from class actions, opponents to cy-près distribution should be asked – what goals are being advanced in returning undistributed funds to a wrongdoer? Surely it is better to advance compensation, albeit indirectly, in furtherance of the access to justice claim associated with class actions, and to realise the potential for better deterrence (not punishment, we hasten to add), than to remain solicitous of defendant interests.

4 Conclusion

Class actions were introduced to improve access to justice for civil litigants whose losses are otherwise not likely to be recovered from the defendant. The ability for multiple parties to group together to pursue what would, individually, be uneconomic claims is also justified on the basis of efficiency and judicial economy. In each jurisdiction in which class action proceedings exist there is a point at which access to justice is outweighed by factors of economy and efficiency. In Canada and other jurisdictions that have expressly adopted behavioural modification as justification for class actions in addition to compensation, cy-près schemes are available for this purpose. In those jurisdictions, debate concerning cy-près centres mainly on how the remedy can be used to achieve these goals. There is scope for improvement in the way cy-près remedies are fashioned to ensure that the compensation goal is achieved as fully as possible.

By contrast, in Australia the introduction of the class action procedure was accompanied by provisions aimed at ensuring that class actions would not be brought for uneconomic amounts or where there would be difficulties identifying the class members. This was motivated in part by the desire to prevent class actions being launched in circumstances where the only benefit of the action was to the plaintiff lawyers, rather than to class members because of the costs and other difficulties associated with distribution of the class action fund. A further concern was to avoid burdening the courts through proliferation of class action suits that would in practical terms yield little in the way of compensation for class members.

These concerns have continued to contribute to the rejection of cy-près as a class action remedy in Australia. The view has been maintained that cy-près is punitive and not compensatory and it therefore goes beyond the aims of class action reform.

In this chapter we suggest that this characterisation is based in part on a misattribution of a penal character to deterrence and a misunderstanding of the operation of cy-près in the class action context. The explicit alignment of deterrence with punishment overlooks the role, albeit secondary, that civil litigation plays in deterring wrongdoing. Deterrence and behavioural modification underlies and supports private law rights in which compensation is available as a primary remedy once the specific enforcement of rights is no longer available. Justifying class actions on compensatory grounds alone does not reflect accurately the potential for civil litigation and class actions to achieve a more complete form of compensation and behavioural modification and deterrence.

INDEX